The Victorian Countryside

Edited by

G. E. Mingay

Professor of Agrarian History,
University of Kent at Canterbury

Routledge & Kegan Paul   London, Boston and Henley

Victorian Countryside

Volume One

First published in 1981
by Routledge & Kegan Paul Ltd
39 Store Street, London WC1E 7DD,
9 Park Street, Boston Mass. 02108, USA, and
Broadway House, Newtown Road,
Henley-on-Thames, Oxon RG9 1EN
Set in Monophoto Century Schoolbook
and printed in Great Britain by
BAS Printers Limited, Over Wallop, Hampshire
© G. E. Mingay 1981

British Library Cataloguing in Publication Data

Mingay, Gordon E.

The Victorian countryside.
1. Country life—Great Britain—1837–1901
2. Natural history—Great Britain—1837–1901
I. Title
941.08′100973′4   DA667   80-42190

ISBN 0-7100-0734-5 (Vol. 1)
ISBN 0-7100-0735-3 (Vol. 2)
ISBN 0-7100-0736-1 (The set)

Contents

Contents

II Agriculture in the Victorian Countryside

III Country Towns and Country Industries

Volume Two

Contents

Illustrations

Volume One

II   *Between pages 208 and 209*

Illustrations

Volume Two

xii

The Contributors

W. A. Armstrong   Reader in Social and Demographic History, University of Kent at Canterbury

Philip S. Bagwell   late Professor of Economic History, Polytechnic of Central London

T. W. Beastall   Deputy Headmaster, Maltby Comprehensive School, Rotherham

John Burnett   Professor of Social History, Brunel University

Raymond Carr   Warden, St. Antony's College, Oxford

C. W. Chalklin   Reader in History, University of Reading

J. A. Chartres   Senior Lecturer in Economic History, University of Leeds

E. J. T. Collins   Director, Institute of Agricultural History, University of Reading

L. M. Cullen   Professor of Modern History, Trinity College, Dublin

Anne Digby   Research Fellow, Institute of Social & Economic Research, University of York

Jill Franklin   Lecturer in History of Art and Architecture, University of London Extra-Mural Department

Enid Gauldie   School of Architecture, Dundee

Alan D. Gilbert   Senior Lecturer in History, University of New South Wales

Nicholas Goddard   Lecturer in Geography, Cambridgeshire College of Arts & Technology, Cambridge

The Contributors

Malcolm Gray	Reader in Economic History, University of Aberdeen
Michael Havinden	Senior Lecturer in Economic History, University of Exeter
David Hey	Lecturer, Division of Continuing Education, University of Sheffield
B. A. Holderness	Senior Lecturer, Department of Social Studies, University of East Anglia
Pamela Horn	Lecturer in Economic & Social History, Oxford Polytechnic
David W. Howell	Lecturer in History, University College, Swansea
Alun Howkins	Lecturer in History, University of Sussex
Louis James	Reader in Victorian and Modern Literature, University of Kent at Canterbury
David Jones	Senior Lecturer in History, University College, Swansea
W. J. Keith	Professor of English, University of Toronto
Barbara Kerr	rural historian, Dorset
Stuart Macdonald	Lecturer in Economics, University of Queensland
Robert W. Malcolmson	Associate Professor of History, Queen's University, Kingston, Ontario
G. E. Mingay	Professor of Agrarian History, University of Kent at Canterbury
D. C. Moore	Professor of History, University of California, Los Angeles
R. J. Olney	historian of Lincolnshire
Charles Phythian-Adams	Senior Lecturer in English Local History, University of Leicester
Hugh Prince	Reader in Geography, University College, London
Eric Richards	Professor of History, Flinders University of South Australia, Adelaide
Roger Sellman	formerly County Inspector of Schools, Devon
J. D. Sykes	Estates Bursar, Wye College, University of London
Jennifer Tann	Reader in Economic History, University of Aston
F. M. L. Thompson	Director, Institute of Historical Research, University of London
Rosemary Treble	specialist in the History of Victorian Art
G. L. Turnbull	Senior Lecturer in Economic History, University of Leeds
Michael J. Winstanley	Lecturer in History, University of Lancaster

I   The Land

1 Introduction: Rural England in the Industrial Age

G. E. Mingay

I

The sixty-four years of Victoria's reign saw industrial growth, imperial expansion, and domestic reform. It saw, too, a far-reaching change in the way of life of the English people. They became an urban rather than a rural people. The towns grew and the countryside shrank. The very face of the country was changed as fields and pastures succumbed to invasion by bricks and mortar. Great ports and centres of industry now dominated the land. Liverpool, for instance, saw its inhabitants swell in number from under 300,000 to nearly 700,000 in the period in which Victoria occupied the throne. The population of Birmingham, too, nearly trebled to reach over half a million at the first census of the twentieth century; Glasgow, with 762,000 in 1901, had more than trebled, while Nottingham's townsfolk increased by nearly five-fold. The new Teesside port of Middlesbrough dwarfed all this: its numbers rose by more than fifteen-fold, from under 6,000 to 91,000. To cap all, London, the greatest of the 'wens', proliferated from an already enormous 2 millions to a monstrous $4\frac{1}{2}$ millions. Fortunate, perhaps, that Cobbett was in his grave.

The effects on the countryside were profound. Its very appearance was permanently changed, and as a major element in the country's life it declined both economically and socially. Already by 1851 the typical Englishman had ceased to be a countryman. Within another thirty years the towns could boast twice as many people as the countryside. Agriculture, mainstay of the nation from time immemorial, lost its pre-eminence. In the Britain of 1851, it is true, the agricultural labour force was at

3

its absolute peak. Farming, together with horticulture and forestry, supported over 2 million men and women, well over a fifth of the total, and was still by far the largest single source of employment. But at Victoria's death the figure had shrunk to under $1\frac{1}{2}$ millions, representing only one in every eleven of the employed population.

The physical changes were most in evidence in the Midlands and the north, where the countryside became sometimes a mere appendage of industrialism, a dwindling strip of green steadily squeezed between the encroaching fingers of the towns. Within the countryside itself the expansion of the old mining communities—another way of life, but one that was old-established and accepted by the farming population—was accompanied by the sudden eruption of factories and the dwellings of their 'hands', raw new settlements plonked down incongruously in the midst of the trees and meadows. Old villages and country towns were seen to sprout belching chimneys and noisy workshops. Even sleepy Dorchester, Hardy's home, was not immune, and the piercing whistle of Francis Eddison's steam plough works impinged upon the author's slumbers at the inconveniently early hour of 5.45 a.m. The same ugly lines of plain, square houses, with red-brick walls and black slate roofs, disfigured the countryside as they stretched in dismal serried ranks and formed swelling towns. Amongst the streams and leaves they seemed even uglier, because more alien, more out of place. The new mansions, too, looked foreign and brash, their gothic pinnacles new and artificial, their bricks and stone still too fresh, unmellowed by time. By 1837 the lines of railway had already begun to scar the land, sweeping across wide valleys on rows of solid brick arches, now driving on obtrusively through fields and orchards on raised embankments, then mercifully dipping out of sight into the cuttings. And by mid-century the telegraph poles and their wires already marched unpicturesquely over hill and dale, a forerunner of their giant relations, the brutal pylons of the electricity age.

II

More than ever before, agriculture had to adapt to the needs of the towns. The growing numbers of the townsmen, many of them with more to spend, were demanding more meat, milk and cheese, more poultry, potatoes, and the produce of market gardens, as well as hay for their horses. King Wheat was in the course of being dethroned. In the manufacturing districts, wrote Sir James Caird in 1851, 'the use of butcher's meat and cheese is enormously on the increase'. His researches showed that grass had become much more profitable than arable. In the pastoral north and west farm rents were higher by an average 7s. 9d. per acre than in the arable south and east. 'Every intelligent farmer', he said, 'ought to keep this steadily in view.' The intelligent farmer, indeed, had to shift with the market. He had to concentrate on increasing the output of his most profitable products. 'In this country the agricultural improver cannot stand still. If he tries to do so he will soon fall into the list of obsolete men, being passed by eager competitors, willing to seize the current of events and turn them to their advantage.'[1]

In another quarter-century there were indeed many farmers (and many landlords too) who found themselves among Caird's obsolete men. Free trade had unlocked the floodgates, railways and the steamship pushed them wide open. The swelling produce of the freshly tapped soils of the Americas and Australasia poured through. Prices fell, and farmers unable to adapt, reduced by a series of disastrous seasons to living on their capital, collapsed and eventually disappeared. Caird was still there to see the *débâcle*. Writing on the occasion of the Queen's golden jubilee, he lamented that free trade had set at naught the progress of half a century. Since 1840 the yield of wheat had gone up by 2 bushels per acre, but the value of the 28 bushels per acre of 1886 was only £6. 6s., while that of the 26 bushels of 1840 had been £10. 14s. 6d. The twenty-five years of prosperity which were just beginning when he published his *English Agriculture in 1850–51* had come to an end. Since that time, he wrote, much of the increase in the capital value of land had been lost:

> first by a series of bad years unprecedented in their continuance, causing
> not only diminished crops but also heavy loss in the live stock through the
> wet and unhealthy character of the seasons. The subsequent collapse of
> prices, which took place in 1885, falling as it did upon agricultural class
> already impoverished, has completely disheartened both landlords and
> tenants, and has severely crippled their power to give employment to their
> labourers.

The reaction was the time-honoured one: 'down corn, up horn'. The area of grass and of specialist crops expanded; the arable contracted. 'In the last twenty years', Caird continued, 'three million acres, nearly one-seventh of land under rotation, have been added to the permanent pastures.'[2]

Thus the late Victorian landscape: wider expanses of unbroken pastures, new vistas of freshly planted orchards, multiplied acres of hop grounds and extended market gardens. The cornlands diminished, as did the numbers of the work-people employed on them. There were more machines in the fields and barns, and more deserted cottages in the lanes. There were village schools with many fewer pupils than at any time since they had opened their doors. The reality of the rural scene was explored by Rider Haggard, novelist and squire of East Anglia. The situation, he found, was very mixed. Some favoured areas showed little evidence of depression, with the farmers quietly prosperous and complaining only of the universal decline in the numbers and quality of the labour force. But others were badly hit, with marginal land reverting to waste, and arable allowed to tumble down to some apology for a pasture. There were landlords and farmers who saw a return to protection as their only salvation. Failing that, as one farmer said graphically enough, they were 'up the spout'. Even in the heavily depressed districts, however, newcomers had worked the miracle. Thrifty Scots fleeing from high Scottish rents, and hard-working men from the West Country, were much in evidence. They had taken on bankrupt farms at knockdown rents, and by severe economy in labour and cultivation had made the land pay once more. Mostly they thrived by turning to milk or some other produce strongly in demand in the towns.[3]

In general, Haggard's picture of rural England was a gloomy one, and the prospect at best uncertain. The agriculture of 1901 was indeed very different from that which Caird had seen in 1850–1, in some ways more advanced, in others much less prosperous. It was an agriculture in transition, in the course of being reshaped and restructured by the twin forces of free trade and urban demand, though when Haggard completed his journeys the worst was, in fact, just about over.

III

In that transition one class—that of the farm labourers—had come out rather well. That is, if one can describe an average cash wage of under 15*s*. a week as 'doing well'. Wages had been much lower—less than 10*s*. on average at mid-century, though there were wide regional variations. The wage, it was true, was usually supplemented by a cheap or free cottage, by free fuel and drink, and some other perquisites. Wages rose substantially after 1850, and in the last thirty years of the nineteenth century the falling prices of food, clothing, drink, and tobacco produced an advance in the labourers' purchasing power of some 25 or 30 per cent. Before this, in the low-wage districts of southern England, the labourer's situation was often pitiful. In the 1860s, an American visitor, Elihu Burritt, saw a good deal of what life was like for the country worker. On a walking tour from London to Land's End, Burritt got into conversation with a man on the road near Swindon. The man, his head bent down by the burden of an empty chest he was carrying, told the American of his daily life:

His ordinary wages were eight shillings a week, and an additional shilling in haying time. By milking cows as an extra job, he was earning about eleven shillings, working from sun to sun. His wife received eightpence per day, making up fifteen shillings per week. He paid 1s 6d. weekly for house-rent; had a garden-patch on which he had grown from twenty to twenty-five bushels of potatoes. His food was entirely bread and cheese on week-days for breakfast, dinner and supper. On Sunday he had a piece of bacon for dinner. He never spent anything for beer at the public-house, and drank only what his master allowed him, which was three half-pints a day. He could not lay by any of his wages for old age or sickness, do the best he might. When he came to be too old to work, he should depend upon the parish for out-door relief. . . . His head was bent towards the ground under his load as he thus spoke of his earthly lot and expectations. He had fought all the forenoon battles of life, and spoke of the last tug of the war with want and poverty with a cheerful voice, uttering no complaint nor a word against landlord or parish authorities. Indeed, he seemed to have realised all the enjoyment he expected when he looked forward from the threshold of the life to which he was born. And who could have the heart to break the even spell or darken the dreams of this content in such a man's heart![4]

Burritt believed that the farmers made a sad mistake in paying their labourers so miserably. Experience in the slave states of America, he argued, showed that this was false economy. Piece-work at an adequate reward brought forth additional effort. 'I am persuaded', he wrote, 'that every able-bodied field-hand in England is able to perform a daily amount of labour for which his employer could afford to pay him four shillings, or ninety-six cents. What he does now is no measure of what he could perform under the stimulus of a compensation proportioned to his work.'[5] Traditional rates of wages produced traditional rates of work. Plough teams in Gloucestershire, consisting of cumbrous oxen and labourers of lethargic gait, took seven hours to plough less than three-quarters of an acre. Indeed, as one observer remarked, the pace was so slow that 'many times have I been compelled to look at some tree at a distance to ascertain whether or not the plough-teams were moving'.[6]

In time, labour shortage began to force the wages up. The new village schools, so farmers complained, made country children discontented and footloose. Rural by-employments, such as straw-plaiting, lace-making and gloving, declined and were not replaced. Railways made it possible to do the Saturday shopping in a nearby town. Philanthropists preached the wisdom of moving poor families away from the underemployment of the country, and the agents of railway and steamship companies offered more positive inducements to emigration. Whatever the influences, men and women moved off the land. The towns, with their more varied employment, their newer houses, their shops and pubs, were an obvious magnet, though country works and factories could also attract the venturesome. Some men were drawn away by the secure jobs and pensions offered by the railways, the police, or the army. Some were driven into the towns by their womenfolk, who never ceased to complain of tumbledown two-room cottages where mud was tramped in endlessly and every drop of water had to be carried from the pump. By the end of the century the old abundance of cheap labour was largely gone. Good men were now hard to find, so Rider Haggard was told, and skills had declined. The hands still available were much more choosy, and refused the more arduous and unpleasant tasks. In some places, for instance, it was impossible to get milking done, and farmers were obliged to give up their dairies.

IV

There were other portents of change. The windmills stopped turning when steam-powered mills appeared, and especially after 1879 when the roller milling process began to replace the ancient millstones. The increased imports of American 'hard' wheat, better suited to roller milling than the English 'soft' wheat, encouraged a shift of the industry to large centres near ports and railways. The old country windmills declined, were turned to other uses, or were abandoned. Silent mills, their sails rotting in decay, became a common feature of the late Victorian countryside. Accompanying them were disused country breweries, victims of the trend to amalgamation as the brewing industry concentrated in larger plants situated in the greater towns. The country inns, too, once a centre of village business, were hit by the advent of railways and easier access to market towns. In the villages the inns no longer had the same attraction for farmers and dealers, carters and tradesmen, while the drovers, who once made their regular calls to collect the beasts to be taken to distant markets, had all but disappeared. Commercial travellers, pedlars, cheap-jacks and the bagmen drapers were now less frequently seen. The old independence of the countryside and its near self-sufficiency was whittled away by the growth of town-based dealers who brought round their factory-made bread and clothing, their branded groceries and railway-carried fish. Town emporiums drove the village craftsmen out of business, unless they could survive by turning to some new specialization, like the wheelwrights and blacksmiths who made agricultural implements and still throve on the continued importance of the horse and cart and pony and trap. The larger villages, however, saw their once large array of crafts and trades decline to a mere handful. Villages in general tended either to shrink and become more purely agricultural, or to grow and become more thoroughly industrial. The displaced tradesmen and craftsmen moved into towns and factories, or emigrated; a few, as Rider Haggard noted, took up some land and combined a country business with some highly economical form of farming. The professional men, too, who had once been quite numerous in the larger villages, were not replaced as they moved out or retired. Increasingly the doctors, lawyers, veterinary surgeons and chemists practised in the towns and travelled out to the villages. Soon only the clergyman and the teacher were left in residence.

While the bigger villages were gradually losing many of their tradesmen, craftsmen and professional people, the more important country towns—their importance enhanced by the arrival of a railway line—became more business-oriented and less residential. By the 1880s, Richard Jefferies tells us, the larger rural centres were pretty much given over to offices, shops, markets and workshops. The wealthy people had moved out to villas where they could have more extensive gardens and find room for tennis courts, croquet lawns, and paddocks for the ponies. The growth of middle-class villas was matched by the spread of suburbs around the major cities. Inner suburbs were largely the creation of private carriages, short-stage coaches, and horse-drawn buses. Later, the introduction of suburban railway services made it easy to combine the pleasures of a rural retreat further out with regular attendance at one's place of business. In London the railways at an early date began to compete with coaches, omnibuses and river boats for the short-distance traffic. The London and North Western Company, for instance, offered a free rail pass for eleven years to anyone taking a house in Harrow at a rental of not less than £50 a year—though few people were tempted by the bargain. At mid-century, the stations most convenient for the City, London Bridge, Fenchurch Street, and Waterloo saw a small but growing stream of daily commuters. In the last quarter of the century the central London lines began to fan out to catch the suburban traffic. The District Railway, for example, began to serve Richmond in 1877, and Hounslow six years later; and soon it was combing a wide arc of territory to the west and south-west of the metropolis. The Metropolitan Railway, too, ventured out beyond Swiss Cottage, Willesden and Harrow to reach Pinner in 1885 and Aylesbury in 1892. With this the old mail coach which left the Old Bell inn, Holborn, for Wendover at 3 p.m. finally came to an end.

How many acres of fields and woods disappeared under the trampling encroachment of suburbia we can only guess, but between 1871 and 1901 the resident population of the City fell by 48,000, as much as 64 per cent; that of Holborn declined by 34,000 or 36 per cent; while that of Westminster fell by 65,000 or just over a quarter. By no means all the suburban growth was a middle-class phenomenon, of course; clerks, craftsmen, and shop-workers moved out too, attracted by new housing in more pleasant surroundings and encouraged by cheap workmen's fares. In 1855 it was remarked:

> The passion for country residence is increasing to an extent that it would be impossible for persons who do not mix much with the poor to know. You cannot find a place where they do not get a broken teapot in which to stuff, as soon as spring comes, some flower or something to give them an idea of green fields and the country.

As witness to this 'passion for country residence' the four places in England and Wales which had the fastest rate of population growth in the 1880s were all London suburbs: Leyton, Willesden, Tottenham and West Ham. And in the following decade eight London suburbs were again among the fastest-growing places.[7]

A similar story could be told of other areas within the ambit of major centres of expanding employment. Within ten years of the opening of the line from Manchester to Chester in 1849, a superior suburb had been created fifteen miles out at Alderley, where 'the greater part of the edge is covered by gardens and villas', while impressive avenues of detached houses had come to grace Altrincham and Bowden. And later, in the 1870s and 1880s, other lines radiating from Manchester had a powerful expansionary influence on suburbs like Urmston, Flixton, Heaton Park, Cheadle Heath, Chorlton, Withington, and Didsbury. Before this the wealthier inhabitants of Liverpool had taken advantage of steamboat and horse-bus services (as well as their own carriages) to take up residence by the seashore 'from Southport to Hoylake', or in 'pleasant villages from Bootle to Aigburth'. Again, in Birmingham the railway suburbs, like Acock's Green and Olton, followed on those developed nearer in by private carriage and omnibus, such as New Hall, Edgbaston, and Islington, or the less select Small Heath, Sparkbrook, Aston, and Ashstead.[8]

In addition to commuting, the horse-buses, steamboats, and railways had other notable influences on the country population. They helped spread the fashions and ideas of the towns, and they began to widen the horizons of country people—such as those who, we are reliably told, lived within a dozen miles of the sea and had never

9

seen it. They brought newspapers to the cottage, though for the most part newspapers whose function it was to amuse rather than inform. In the 1890s a London paper called the *Weekly Budget*, full of 'hotly-spiced divorce cases, sensational stories by authors one has not heard of, and answers to correspondents', was the one most widely favoured by country work-people, though in the north provincial journals led the field—in Northumberland, for example, the higher-toned *Newcastle Weekly Chronicle*.[9] Little by little Hodge was ceasing to be the traditional rustic dullard, the ignorant butt of the stock country-yokel jokes in *Punch*.

The railways, too, brought the resident townspeople into the country. Long before the age of the locomotive, private carriages, coaches, and steamboats had fostered the growth of inland spas and coastal resorts. The railways created many new seaside towns and speeded the expansion of old ones. Brighton, reached by railway in 1840, was already the most popular of resorts: in 1835 the coaches plying there had carried as many as 117,000 passengers. But within four years of the railway's arrival the trains had dwarfed this figure, carrying 360,000 in 1844. The town's permanent population also grew, nearly doubling in the sixty years after the beginning of the railway era to reach 123,000 in 1901.[10] Cheap excursions at holiday times to the seaside, exhibitions, beauty spots, and places of interest were a feature of almost the earliest years of the railway era. The seashore and the countryside became the lungs of the cities, allowing people to breathe and relax, enabling them to return refreshed to the dull round of urban life, the dreary streets, the grime and smoke. Even before the railways, townspeople escaped to the country, on horseback or in carriages, or walking on their own two legs. Thus Howitt, writing in 1844, says:

> It is curious to observe from the earliest hour of a Sunday morning, in fine weather, what groups are pouring into the country. There are mechanics who, in their shops and factories,—while they have been caged up by their imperious necessities during the week, and have only obtained thence sights of the clear blue sky above, of the green fields laughing far away, or have only caught the wafting of a refreshing gale on their fevered cheek as they hurried homeward to a hasty meal, or back again to the incarceration of Mammon,—have had their souls inflamed with desires for breaking away into the free country. These have been planning, day after day, whither they shall go on Sunday. To what distant village; to what object of attraction. There have come visions of a neat country alehouse to them.... Others have seen clear hurrying trout-streams.... They will take angle and net; they will strip off clothes, and take the trout with their hands....
>
> Then again you see another Sunday class; tradesmen, shopkeepers and their assistant and apprentices—all those who have friends in the country— on horseback or in gigs, driving off to spend the day with those that come occasionally and pay them a visit at market and fairs. The faces of these are set for farm and other country-houses within twenty miles round. There is not a horse or gig to be had for love or money at any of the livery-stables on a Sunday.[11]

V

Yet despite the invasions by townsfolk, the breakdown of rural isolation, all the modernizing influences of railways and cities, there was still a curiously unchanging character about much of the countryside. Great areas, after all, were hardly affected by industrialization or railways or urban sprawl. There were districts still wild and untouched, like the high moorlands of northern England and of Wales; or less remote and more cultivated, but still quietly somnolent, like the Midland wolds and vales, the southern hills and downs, the plains of Lincoln, Norfolk, and Wiltshire, the deep wooded countryside of much of Kent, Sussex, Dorset, and the West Country. Very often the old-style husbandry still held sway. At mid-century the threshing machine, after more than sixty years, had still not driven out the flail from farms on Salisbury Plain and other places, and everywhere the horse-drawn mechanical reaper was as yet very much a novelty. In parts of Wiltshire, Caird noted, the dairy cows were still being kept in winter

> in open yards, wading often to the knees in filth, there being no straw to
> spare for litter. Here they stand shivering at the old-fashioned racks where
> their scanty provender is supplied. The young cattle, having no sheds
> provided for them, are wintered in the fields. Manure is looked upon as a
> troublesome nuisance. . . .[12]

This was in 1850, but even eighty years later one might see on the downs of Sussex wooden ploughs drawn by ponderous teams of oxen. And the amount of labour employed on the land was often regulated, at the end of Victoria's reign as in ancient times, by the prescription of one man for every 25 or 30 acres of arable and another for every 50 or 60 of pasture. The really big farms of the Lincolnshire wolds, Norfolk sands, and Wiltshire downs continue to deploy small armies of forty, fifty, even seventy hands.

Nor did the appearance of many of the villages change very much. Though horse-drawn traffic might multiply, the deep lanes still wound tortuously and muddily from farm to hamlet and from village to market town. True, there might be now a gaunt red-brick chapel to compete for souls with the greyed-stone church, and brash rows of squat red-brick cottages obtruded here and there. But the old stone and pantile, mud and thatch, were still in evidence. Indeed, in the early Victorian period even many of the newer cottages had been constructed with the traditional mud walls and thatched roofs, because these were cheaper and more resistant to heat and cold. Burritt, descending into the Vale of Pewsey, passed through

> several queer little villages and hamlets which looked as if the cottages
> were built by the immediate followers of Hengis or Horsa. Indeed, they were
> of the same pattern as those you will find in Jutland and Shleswig-Holstein,
> whence our Saxon progenitors brought their models for houses and barns.
> The gables were all 'dubbed' off in the same way at both ends. Here were the

longest haired cottages I ever saw. The windows all looked like a glass face in a great straw hood, of the old gipsy order, tied closely under the chin. The doors wore cowls of straw, and the thatching of many houses must have been a century old at the bottom. I was told by one occupant that it was *six feet* thick on his tenement. Everything new or old was thatched, not only dwellings, barns and out-houses great and small, but barn-yard and garden walls. I saw a new two-storey inn of red brick with a roof of straw which had not yet been rusted by a single rain, but was as fresh as if just from the flail.[13]

The inhabitants might well be as traditional as their buildings. Howitt wrote about the old-style farmer who rose at three and rang the bell to wake the girls for milking, then roused the horsekeeper and went on to feed the horses while he was getting up. Next he

called the boy to suckle the calves and clean out the cow-house; lighted the pipe, walked round the garden to see what was wanted there; went up to the paddock to see if the weaning calves were well; went down to the ferry to see if the boy had scooped and cleaned the boat; returned to the farm, examined the shoulders, heels, traces, chaff and corn of eight horses going to plough, mended the acre-staff, cut some thongs, whipcorded the ploughboys' whips, pumped the troughs full, saw the hogs fed, examined the swill-tubs, and then the cellar; ordered a quarter of malt, for the hogs want grains, and the men want beer; filled the pipe again, returned to the river, and bought a lighter of turf for dairy fires, and another of sedge for ovens; hunted out the wheelbarrows, and set them a trundling; returned to the farm, called the men to breakfast, and cut the boys' bread and cheese, and saw the wooden bottles filled; sent one plough to the three roods, and other to the three half-acres, and so on; shut the gates, and the clock struck five; breakfasted. . . .[14]

Cobbett deplored the rise of the new gentlemen-farmers who adopted the manners of polite society, and to make their farmhouse more fashionable turned the labourers out to live in cottages. These were the farmers, he complained, with 'a painted lady for a wife; sons aping the young squires and lords; a house crammed up with sofas, pianos, and all sorts of fooleries'. They destroyed the old fellowship which once connected master and men, as they had replaced the old farmhouse kitchen with its plain oak furniture by—of all things—a *parlour*, complete with mahogany table, fine china, fine glass and decanters: 'Aye, and a *carpet* and *bell-pull* too!'[15] But Cobbett's revolution in manners was only a partial one. In northern districts, especially, there still survived the old wide chimney and settle, with the farmer and his wife on one side, the wenches nearby, and the men on the other side of the hearth with their shoes off.[16] The men were of a piece with the farm and the farmer. A labourer began his service in the fields at perhaps six or seven, scaring birds or picking stones; he

12

graduated to plough-boy or carter's lad, and so arrived at his maturity. The old kind of farm servant was slow, conservative, unlettered:

> there he is, as simple, as ignorant, and as laborious a creature as one of the wagon-horses that he drives. The mechanic sees his weekly newspaper over his pipe and pot; but the clodhopper, the chopstick, the hawbuck, the hind, the Johnny-raw, or by whatever name, in whatever district, he may be called, is everywhere the same; he sees no newspaper, and if he did, he could not read it; and if he hears his master reading it, ten to one but he drops asleep over it. In fact, he has no interest in it. He knows there is such a place as the next town, for he goes there to statutes and to the fair; and he has heard of Lunnon, and the French, and Buonaparte, and of late years of America, and he has some dreamy notion that he should like to go there if he could raise the wind, and thought he could find the way—and that is all that he knows of the globe and its concerns, beyond his own fields.[17]

Again, it was only in the later decades of the century that old rural crafts sank into decline, though by the accession of King Edward some were indeed far gone. By then bone-lace had largely disappeared from the countryside of Buckinghamshire, Northamptonshire, Bedfordshire, and Devon where it had once employed some thousands of women and girls. Straw-plaiting, too, had become unusual, while in the West Country and Oxfordshire glove-making had pretty much moved from the cottages into factories. To some extent, new trades took the place of old. Certain of the stages in the making of shoes became well established in the cottages of Northamptonshire and in neighbouring villages of Bedfordshire, as the making of clogs was in Lancashire and Wales. Iron foundries were widely introduced for the local manufacture of farming implements. Here and there some branches of the textile and clothing trades continued and prospered, as did for example, the making of braces, belts, and garters round Banbury, and silk, satin, and velvet manufacture at Croscombe and Shepton Mallet in Somerset. Many villages had always been partially industrial, and when country factories appeared they continued, in a manner, the old tradition in a different way. Little country factories produced chairs in parts of Berkshire and Oxfordshire, collars at Bideford and Yeovil, and gloves at Charlbury, to mention but a few examples. In addition, sawmills and joinery works, paper mills and potteries were widely found, together with the new and more occasional canning and jam and pickle factories. Brick works had sometimes come to be of great importance, as in south Bedfordshire, and cement works, too, as in the Medway valley in Kent. Boat-building, inshore fishing, cockling, and shrimping were old-established and still thriving activities in many river estuaries and coastal areas. Some of the factory work merely represented the transfer of an old trade from small-scale cottage production to larger-scale manufacturing. But the factory, even when small and rural, was not the same thing as the cottage workshop or kitchen. The knitting mill, for instance, was a far cry from the 'going-a-sitting' which once engaged the spare time of both men and women in the dales of Yorkshire and Lancashire.

There, in Howitt's day, when work was over and the children put to bed, the cottagers took their cloaks and lanterns

> and set out with their knitting to the house of the neighbour where the sitting falls in rotation, for it is a regularly circulating assembly from house to house through the particular neighbourhood. The whole troop of neighbours being collected, they sit and knit, sing knitting-songs, and tell knitting-stories. Here all the old stories and traditions of the dale come up, and they often get so excited that they say, 'Neighbours, we'll not part tonight,' that is, till after twelve o'clock.[18]

VI

The life of the country houses also seemed to go on much as ever. The duke in his mansion and the squire in his hall still exerted a traditional influence over the community of the land. Until fairly late in the century the old relationship between landlord and tenant seemed to endure through all the vicissitudes of the age. And the significance of the relationship may be appreciated when it is remembered that landed estates and their tenants occupied some 85 or 90 per cent of the farmland, leaving only between an eighth and a tenth in the hands of independent owner-occupiers. Under the landlords, both private and institutional, the tenant-farmers provided the working capital of the farms and took the risks and profits of working them. The landlords were primarily *rentiers*, supplying the land and the buildings, and where necessary such protection as river embankments and sea-walls. Their return in rent was generally a modest 3 per cent on the capital value of the land, as compared with a tenant's profit on his capital generally believed to be about 10 per cent, but possibly higher. The provision of costly improvements to the farm such as subsoil drainage with pipes or tiles, much in vogue in the middle decades of the century, was usually a joint enterprise, with the landlord perhaps supplying the tiles, and the tenant the labour for putting them in the earth.

Though basically a business connection, governed by the laws applying to property and tenures, there was a strongly customary, even feudal, air about the landlord–tenant relationship. Landlords expected their tenants to farm to the customary standard of the district (which might not be very high), to pay their rents with a reasonable regularity, and to conduct themselves with the due propriety expected of the dependant of a more or less distinguished family. Some landlords expected to have their tenants' votes at election time, and many assumed the right to hunt over the tenants' fields and keep game reserves in close proximity. The tenant, for his part, generally enjoyed a 'good bargain', that is to say, a rent kept at a modest level, perhaps as implicit compensation for political deference and the depredations caused by game and hunt. Even where there was no lease, which was commonly the case with the smaller farms, the tenant expected to enjoy *de facto* security of tenure.

14

Eviction was rare, and when times were bad the tenant might look for an abatement of rent and perhaps some help with repairs and improvements, and might not look in vain.

Although this sums up the usual nature of the relationship existing over much of the countryside, there was a tendency, particularly marked in the last quarter of the century, for tenants to show a growing independence of landlords. In particular, they sought a greater security in respect of 'tenant right', compensation for investment in improvements which still remained effective when a tenant left a farm, a compensation which varied from one area to another according to local interpretations of the matter. More fundamental than this, and than farmers' other concerns over game and the malt tax, was the tenants' gradually aroused conviction that the landlords' leadership was failing them. The political balance had swung conclusively in favour of the urban electorate, and the problems of agriculture were becoming increasingly irrelevant to a Parliament that governed a primarily urban and industrial people. In the 1840s the conflict over the Corn Laws had split the landowners and aroused the active opposition of the farmers. And again when, after thirty years, free trade brought in its flood of cheap grain, its frozen meat, and its foreign dairy produce, it became yet more evident that the landlords were unable to put back the clock. In the depression years the landlords of the badly hit arable districts could not even do very much to help their failing tenants. Old farmers who had farmed on the estate for generations made way for new men, men with new and economical ideas about how the land should be farmed, and new attitudes towards both landlords and labourers. Thus the old landlord–tenant relationship weakened and broke down, until eventually the independence of the farmers was signalled by the formation in the early years of the new century of their own entirely separate organization, a National Farmers' Union, a body from which the landlords and their agents were excluded.

While estates and their tenants drifted apart, the landlords found themselves in an increasingly alien environment. Industrial and commercial wealth could now match and overshadow the resources of even the greatest aristocrats. It was true that those landowners with command of varied revenues might still compete; and their social distinction enabled them to absorb new wealth through marriage, as had always been the case. The great country houses remained powerful centres of influence, and the aura of rank coupled with the cachet of ancient lineage still enabled their owners to wield extraordinary sway over men and affairs. The lesser landowners, with more restricted incomes, were those more commonly affected by the agricultural decline which set in about 1875. In the worst hit areas they might have to struggle merely to keep their farms occupied at any rent at all. Some found the upkeep of estate and house beyond them, and eventually they sold or let their family home and retired to some agreeable watering place or continental spa. Those who remained on their estates found themselves held to blame for 'the land problem'; they found, too, a diminishing local influence as the countryside became more industrialized and the functions of magistrates were taken over by Whitehall and county council.

At the end of Victoria's reign the old cohesion of the countryside was breaking up. Non-residence severed completely the ancient ties which linked landed families with country communities, ties which, however, had long been growing frail and tenuous. The ultimate effects of the new influences in the countryside were not apparent, of course, at Victoria's death: indeed they are still working themselves out in the last quarter of the twentieth century. But already at that century's beginning the various manifestations of change were clearly evident: in the converted country houses and those standing empty; in the expanded industrialized villages, and in the decaying farming communities where employers sought in vain for men with the old skills; in the newly grassed ploughlands and their new occupiers, and in the old farmers, broken in spirit as much as money, the men who told Rider Haggard they should have gone long before.

The Victorian countryside was thus very far from quiet, peaceful, unaltering. The casual visitor, it is true, might have found many a rustic hamlet with its ancient hall and cluster of cottages looking much as it always had done. But behind this tranquil façade, powerful forces were at work. The march of industrialism, the expansion of towns, the infectious influence of railways and the press, the consequences—good and bad—of unbarred ports—these were only some of the more obvious which touched the land and the people who belonged to it. If one word could be said to sum up the essence of the studies which follow, then it must be 'transformation'. It was much more than the lapse of a mere six and a half decades which separated the countryside of the young queen from that of her successor.

Notes

1 Caird, 1968, 484–5, 503.
2 Ward, 1887, 143, 151–2.
3 Haggard, 1906, *passim*.
4 Burritt, 1865, 118–9.
5 Burritt, 1865, 123.
6 *Journal of the Royal Agricultural Society of England*, XI, 1850, 164.
7 Barker and Robbins, 1963, 52–5, 199–200, 209–10.
8 Perkin, 1970, 242–5.
9 Graham, 1892, 90–1.
10 Perkin, 1970, 213–4.
11 Howitt, 1971, 560–2.
12 Caird, 1968, 77.
13 Burritt, 1865, 133–4.
14 Howitt, 1971, 110.
15 Cobbett, 1912, I, 265–6.
16 Howitt, 1971, 111.
17 Howitt, 1971, 113.
18 Howitt, 1971, 238.

2 Victorian Rural Landscapes

Hugh Prince

I

In 1838, a year after Queen Victoria ascended the throne, William Howitt observed rural England throbbing with life. He depicted landscapes bustling and humming with the sights and sounds of multifarious activities. 'Villas amid shrubberies and gardens; villages environed with old-fashioned crofts; farm-houses and cottages, singly or in groups—a continuous chain of cultivation and rustic residences stretches from end to end and side to side of the island.'[1] At that time one person in every two in England and Wales lived in a rural area. When the queen died in 1901, scarcely one in four was a countryman. While the total population quadrupled, the increase was confined to towns and cities. Over England and Wales as a whole the rural population barely maintained its numbers and in each succeeding decade areas of decline grew more extensive. The population of many small parishes decreased before 1841, but Wiltshire was the first English county to record an overall decrease in population; this was between 1841 and 1851. In the following decade, decreases occurred in upland Wales as well as in southern and in eastern England. After 1861, no part of the country was exempt from rural depopulation. Young men and girls descended from the moorland edge, and people of all ages, particularly the young, drifted away from lowland villages.[2] Some moved to newly built farmsteads and cottages at a distance from village centres, but more left the country to settle in neighbouring towns. Village schools were drained of children and churches of worshippers. Rural craftsmen departed and their mills and smithies were closed. Village life stagnated.

17

In 1851, in the 'counties of maximum rusticity' as Clapham termed east Yorkshire, the southern counties and Devon, over 60 per cent of the adult male population were engaged in agriculture.[3] In 1901, no county recorded more than 45 per cent of its men so occupied.[4] The reduction of the agricultural work-force was hastened by the coming of labour-saving machinery. In the 1840s threshing machines were widely used in corn-growing districts in southern and eastern England. In the late 1860s some 200,000 acres were ploughed with steam ploughs. At the same time, most large farms mowed their hay with mowing machines and harvested their corn with mechanical reapers. By the 1880s hedgerows in the West Country were being replaced with wire and barbed-wire fences.[5] By 1900 English farms were more highly mechanized than those in any other European country and the farming landscape looked much emptier than it had looked at the beginning of Queen Victoria's reign. Many thousands of labourers still worked in the fields, but they were widely scattered, mostly hidden from view. Looking at rural Staffordshire at this time, Arnold Bennett remarked: 'The cuckoo was much more perceptible than man, dominating whole square miles with his resounding call.' Because the teeming population of the Potteries perceived the countryside as empty, it was 'surely well justified in treating the county as its back garden once a week, and in blindly ignoring it the rest of the time'.[6]

II

Decade after decade from 1841 onwards, the population censuses record movements of people to the towns. Before 1866, when farms in England and Wales began to make annual returns of crop acreages and livestock numbers, land use changes cannot be traced from year to year.[7] The field-by-field surveys carried out by assistant commissioners appointed under the Tithe Commutation Act, 1836, contain an accurate record of much of the agrarian landscape in the 1840s. The amount of detailed information that awaits abstraction about land use, land tenure and field systems is unequalled by that available from any other source.[8] But until a tithe atlas has been compiled, the most reliable evidence on early nineteenth-century land use is provided by various estimates reported to the Board of Agriculture or calculated by agricultural writers. These indicate that the area of arable land increased until 1870, and decreased by about the same amount from 1870 to 1901. At the beginning of Queen Victoria's reign, the arable area of England and Wales covered about 12 million acres.[9] By 1870 it reached some 15 million acres, and in 1900 it had fallen back to about 12 million acres.[10]

Before 1870 farmers in all parts of the country faced every crisis with the same remedy. 'Grow more wheat' was the answer to low prices following a glut; 'grow more wheat' was the natural response to high prices following a harvest failure; growing more wheat was prescribed as a means of paying arrears of rent, taxes and tithes. Heavy dressings of manure and artificial fertilizers were applied to raising wheat yields, and strenuous efforts were devoted to enlarging the area sown with wheat, either by substituting wheat for other crops in a rotation or by bringing new land into cultivation. High among the aims of the Royal Agricultural Society, founded in 1838, stood the increase of wheat production. The society's scientists tested and assessed the benefits to be derived from dressing crops with Peruvian guano, nitrate of soda and superphosphate of lime. In 1840 agricultural chemistry gained publicity among English-speaking readers through Lyon Playfair's edition of Justus von Liebig's *Chemistry in its Application to Agriculture and Physiology*. For observant farmers, the field experiments conducted by John Lawes and J. H. Gilbert at Rothamsted demonstrated the practical utility of different techniques.[11]

In the first half of the nineteenth century the acreage under wheat was continuously enlarged. Extensive tracts of common arable fields in the lowlands between Oxford and Cambridge, in low-lying parts of Lincolnshire and elsewhere in the East Midlands were newly enclosed and bare fallows abolished.[12] Before 1850 on the Yorkshire Wolds, in the Cotswolds, in the Chilterns and on the chalklands of southern England, wheat gained ground at the expense of other cereals.

But on some soils improvers worked to no avail. The heavy clay lands, once regarded as 'the true wheat soils of the country', not only failed to keep pace with the progress of the light soils, but became problem areas, burdened with high rents, heavy tithes and high labour costs.[13] Without adequate drainage roots were difficult to cultivate and the surface was poached by folded sheep and cattle. On Weald clay lowlands, in the Vale of Aylesbury, in Durham and Cleveland, sales of wheat brought only meagre returns, and when prices fell in the 1830s and 1840s many farmers went bankrupt. A few patches of the lightest and driest sands also went out of cultivation. Sandy tracts in Staffordshire, Nottinghamshire, Norfolk, Suffolk and Berkshire, ploughed during the Napoleonic wars, reverted to sheepwalks in the post-war depression. Farmers on different types of poor soils responded differently to falling wheat prices, but on hungry sands as well as on stiff clays livestock husbandry became more profitable than crop production. On soils of intermediate quality few farmers contemplated changing the objectives of their enterprises until a succession of bad harvests in the late 1870s was followed by a flood of cheap grain from North America.

III

After 1880, fundamental adjustments had to be made. Over much of the country, beef cattle and dairy cows displaced wheat as the mainstays of farming systems. A multiplicity of agricultural regions, based on soil characteristics, was reduced to a simple duality: grazing in the west and corn growing in the east. Throughout the west of England and over much of Wales a change to pastoral farming was accomplished with little difficulty. Farmers abandoned their ploughs and laid arable fields down to permanent grass. The western lowlands emerged as continuous stretches of greensward. In parts of northern England, accessible by rail to growing cities where local markets were flourishing, as in the colliery districts of Durham and Lancashire, most farmers, even largely arable farmers, suffered no hardship from the fall in wheat prices.[14] In the north and west most farms became greener and many benefited from the cheapness of imported feeding stuffs.

Farmers in the eastern counties, while supplementing their earnings from fattening and dairying, clung desperately to corn growing. In all parts of eastern and southern England, the polish went out of cultivation. Rents were remitted, imports of fertilizers reduced and hedges and ditches neglected, water meadows fell into decay, and only the most urgent repairs to farm buildings and cottages were carried out. On the poorest soils in eastern England, in the Breckland and in the Suffolk Sandlings, arable fields tumbled down to grass and were overrun by bracken and heather. In Cambridgeshire and Essex land out of cultivation soon became choked with brambles, briars and thorns, and Pringle's 'terrible map dotted thick with black patches' showed that from 1880 to 1894 one-eighth of the surface of south-east Essex reverted to 'coarse, weedy pasture'.[15]

While between 2 and 3 million acres of arable land went out of cultivation during the second half of Victoria's reign, the area of improved meadow and pasture did not increase by an equivalent amount. The enlarged area under permanent grass included an increasing proportion of rough grazing. In Essex clay soils, which in the 1870s raised fine crops of wheat, beans and clover, were in 1894 'lying in wretched pasture, next to useless'.[16] As suburbs spread some arable land was built over and some taken for other non-agricultural uses. At the beginning of the twentieth century fewer fields of golden wheat were harvested than at the time of Victoria's accession, but cattle were more numerous.

As the area growing wheat, barley and turnips contracted, sheep folding declined. Flocks were reduced to a greater extent in arable districts than in grazing districts, but the overall decrease was not spectacular. From 1870 to 1900 numbers of sheep kept in England and Wales fell from a little under 22 million to just over 19 million. During the same period the numbers of cattle increased from 4,361,000 to 5,606,000. The origins of 'down corn, up horn' may be traced back to 1850, but after 1870 the ascendancy of beef and milk over corn and sheep farming was evident throughout the country. In every district herds were enlarged, but the greatest gains were achieved where cattle were fattened for expanding urban markets. When railways reached upland Britain, store cattle were moved rapidly from hill farms to the most profitable fattening pastures, thence, without loss of weight, to town butchers. In 1870 shorthorns, fattened on arable farms on a diet of roots, oats, straw and oilcake, were absolutely dominant over all other breeds of cattle. In 1908 two-thirds of Britain's cattle were still shorthorns, but a majority were grass-fed. They were also the most numerous breed of dairy cows. Devons, Ayrshires and Herefords, bred for rich grasslands, together accounted for less than one-fifth of the nation's herd.[17] At the end of the period livestock selection still had not adjusted fully to grass feeding.

IV

In the 1830s, grassland management was backward throughout the kingdom. Few farms were equipped with spacious yards or warm cowsheds, and dairy hygiene was scarcely known. Some landlords believed that grazing by dairy cattle impoverished the soil, whilst others stipulated that tenants were not to plough up permanent pastures. Tenants were given little help or encouragement. Many were uneducated men without capital. In most grassland districts they occupied small farms divided into small fields. Deep hedges covered a large proportion of the surface. In south Devonshire in 1844, an area of 36,976 acres was divided into no fewer than 7,997 fields. Over 7 per cent of the area was taken up by 1,651 miles of hedges.[18] Similar proportions were estimated in the Weald, in different localities in the Midlands and in eastern England. The smallest, most irregularly shaped fields suffered the greatest damage from hedges. 'The luxuriant foliage of summer', Caird explained, 'must overshadow the surface, and draw from the soil that nutriment which fields would otherwise yield to the farmer's stock.'[19] At that time the Vale of Gloucester was one of the few districts where hedges and pollard trees were being removed.[20] Many landowners refused to pull up hedges because they provided shelter for game and trees in hedgerows produced valuable crooked timber for shipbuilding. A few observers valued hedges because they enhanced the beauty of the landscape; but many others saw them as disfigurements—unkempt, crawling with vermin, casting dark shadows across productive grassland.

In the early nineteenth century pastures were not only encumbered with hedges, they were also ill-drained. Before James Smith of Deanston published *Remarks on Thorough Draining and Deep Ploughing* in 1831, very little land was effectively underdrained. In 1836 tiling was reported to have progressed in Huntingdonshire.[21] The advance accelerated in the following decade when machines began to mass-produce pipe tiles, but in 1850 it was plain to an observant traveller that 'if there be any land which requires improvement it is our real heavy clays'.[22] In the 1850s, government grants came to the assistance of drainers, and millions of tiles were laid, notably on large estates in Surrey, Berkshire, Bedfordshire and other parts of southern England. Progress was slow on the stiffest clays in Durham, in north Yorkshire and elsewhere in northern England. In 1873 a Lords' Committee on the Improvement of Land heard James Caird submit his opinion that probably 2 million acres of land had been drained, while another witness put the total as high as 3 millions.[23] Uncertain as these estimates are, the vast scale of the improvement is not in doubt.[24] Many quagmires, fouled with reeds, rushes and buttercups, were transformed into dry, sweet pastures.

V

Dairying expanded in response to growing demands from towns for butter, cheese and, above all, fresh milk. As railways intersected the country, milk could be transported rapidly over long distances. In 1851 Caird wrote of Essex that 'there is nothing in the distance to prevent daily supplies being sent to London, and milk is a commodity in which we are not likely to have much foreign competition'.[25] While urban cow-keepers continued to supply Birmingham and the Black Country, dairy farms up to thirty miles distant were sending milk to Liverpool and Manchester. In 1865 an outbreak of cattle plague reduced the number of beasts kept in London's cow houses from 24,000 to 14,000.[26] To maintain supplies farmers in many parts of southern England diverted milk from butter and cheese making to dispatch it by fast trains to the metropolis. In 1866 London received 7 million gallons of milk by rail; in 1880 the figure had risen to 20 million, and some of that milk was brought from farms in Somerset, over a hundred miles away.[27] At stations from north-west Wiltshire, through Berkshire to Paddington, the sight of milk churns had become so familiar by the end of the century that the Great Western Railway's main line was called 'the Milky Way'. A similar traffic was to be seen along the lines into Dorset, Hampshire and Sussex. Ayrshire farmers introduced dairy herds to vacant arable farms close to railways in Essex and Suffolk.[28] In the east Midlands milk producers served not only London but also northern manufacturing centres, while dairy farmers in coastal areas and in the Lake District catered for a seasonal influx of holiday visitors. While liquid milk production rose, butter and cheese making declined and was increasingly transferred from farmhouses to creameries and factories.

Fruit and vegetables, like milk, are perishable, and until the present century British growers were insulated from foreign competition. The coming of the railways extended the reach of urban markets and brought, in return, train loads of town manure to the countryside. Chat Moss, crossed by the Liverpool and Manchester railway, was drained, fertilized and planted with potatoes. In the 1850s a tract of Lower Greensand soils between Biggleswade and Sandy in Bedfordshire was opened for market gardening by the Great Northern Railway.[29] Later in the nineteenth century railways served new market gardening districts on sandy soils on the north coast of the Wirral peninsula, in the Vale of Evesham, around Bromham in Wiltshire and on the shores of Mount's Bay in Cornwall.[30] Glasshouses and tomato growing advanced up the Lea valley ahead of suburban developments and London's smoke. At the end of the century new areas of glass were erected around Swanley in north Kent and between Worthing and Littlehampton in Sussex.[31]

Rail links performed a vital role in extending the range of fruit growing. In England and Wales the total area occupied by orchards rose from 141,000 acres in 1873 to 230,000 acres in 1900, and in seven years from 1888 to 1895 the area under small fruit more than doubled, from 33,000 to 69,000 acres.[32] The hop acreage fluctuated from year to year, reaching a maximum in 1878 of 71,000 acres.[33] All these activities shifted away from the cities. London's nurseries migrated up the Thames away from Hammersmith and Chiswick in the direction of Kingston, Staines, Slough and Reading. Orchards spread eastwards along the North Kent railway line towards Sittingbourne and Faversham. New orchards and small fruit farms were planted around jam factories at Histon in Cambridgeshire and at Tiptree in Essex. But much new planting agglomerated close to centres already specializing in fruit or hop growing, where growers benefited from established services and economies of scale.[34] The Maidstone district in Kent and the Vale of Evesham attracted a large proportion of new plantations and produced increasing quantities of home grown fruit and hops. At the beginning of the twentieth century the monopoly enjoyed by British growers was disappearing as barriers of distance and transport costs were lowered.[35] Large quantities of apples, potatoes and onions were shipped cheaply not only across the Channel but from beyond the Atlantic.

VI

In the nineteenth century the enclosure of wastes slowed down and stopped. By 1860 only a few small patches of marsh remained undrained. On the other hand, large areas of heath had not been ploughed up, and after 1870 the reclaiming of new land ceased to be profitable. The upward advance of the moorland edge came to a halt and in places improved land reverted to rough grazing.

A new era in fen draining was inaugurated in 1819, when a steam pump was installed at Littleport in Cambridgeshire.[36] Steam engines pumped while windmills stood becalmed, and steam engines alone had the power to lift water from the depths to which the peat shrank. New channels were cut to straighten and shorten the courses of the Great Ouse and the Nene, and silt was scoured from the tidal reaches. Secured from seasonal flooding by steam pumps and deep outfall channels, the fens around Ely appeared 'a wonderfully fine district and one in which more improvement had taken place within a few years than any other'.[37] In 1851 Whittlesey Mere, the largest remaining expanse of inland water in the fens, was completely drained. Two years later it was raising crops.[38] Across the drained land spread 'an immense plain of dark arable fields' producing an 'abundance and luxuriance' of grain crops, potatoes and vegetables.[39]

The draining of the Lancashire mosses was completed with the aid of steam engines and liberal applications of marl and lime. Martin Mere was pumped dry in 1850, and draining in the Fylde continued until 1880.[40] As a result of these exertions some of the most productive oats and potato growing soils were brought into cultivation. On the Somerset Levels steam pumps helped to improve the quality of pastures, but on Humberside and in the Hull valley ancient ditches and windmills persisted.[41]

From the beginning of the reign no technical innovation gave heathland reclamation a fresh impetus, and as the profitability of cash crop farming declined, investment dwindled. The show-places of eighteenth-century improvements, such as the good sand region in Norfolk, continued to be 'tilled with garden-like precision and cleanliness'.[42] In the early years of the nineteenth century improvers followed the well-tried methods of their predecessors. Large areas of chalkland in southern England and also on the Yorkshire and Lincolnshire Wolds were pared, burned, marled, limed, enclosed and subjected to a system of alternate husbandry. On Lincoln

Heath sheep walks and rabbit warrens disappeared. In 1843 'every stubble field was clean and bright; all the hedges kept low, and neatly trimmed; every farmhouse well built', and the harvest was stacked in 'rows of high, long saddle-backed ricks'.[43] In western Nottinghamshire heather and ling were stripped from tracts of light sands. Folded sheep took the place of wild rabbits and closely cut thorn hedges enclosed large fields. No district in England had 'undergone a greater change for the better'.[44]

Elsewhere, landowners paused to count the costs and abandoned the struggle. The soils of the Breckland, driven by the wind, were condemned to 'ever remain poor and comparatively barren'.[45] The Suffolk Sandlings, the Bagshot Sands and the Lower Greensand escarpment in south-east England resisted repeated attempts to improve them. The Tertiary sands in the Hampshire basin were similarly obdurate. To the end of the nineteenth century the Dorset heaths, in Thomas Hardy's phrase, still wore 'the same antique brown dress, the natural and invariable garment of the particular formation'. Here and there attempts to tame the wastes left visible relics. Such was Wildeve's Patch, 'redeemed from the heath and after long and laborious years brought into cultivation. The man who had discovered that it could be tilled died of the labour; the man who succeeded him in possession ruined himself in fertilising it.'[46] The rage for agricultural improvement spent itself on the sands of southern England.

When agriculturalists despaired, aesthetes rejoiced. Wild scenery appealed to a new generation of writers. Viewing the Dorset heaths from the crest of the Purbeck Hills in 1910, E. M. Forster embraced 'all the wild lands that come tossing down from Dorchester, black and gold, to mirror their gorse in the expanse of Poole'. Turning aside, he remarked: 'Nor is Suburbia absent. Bournemouth's ignoble coast cowers to the right, heralding the pine trees that mean, for all their beauty, red houses, and the Stock Exchange, and extend to the gates of London itself.'[47] Where William Cobbett had fulminated against 'those miserable tracts of heath and fern and bushes and sand called Ashdown Forest and St Leonard's Forest', Lord Eversley in 1894 found refreshment in 'an exceedingly beautiful and valuable open space', a place 'where the bracken and willow-herb is higher in summer than a man, and the day-long solitude is broken only by the play of wild things'.[48] In 1895 Matthew Arnold described Leith Hill as 'a noble, wild scene of heath and scattered pines and whortleberries, with an immense view', whilst George Borrow sang the praises of the wind over Breckland heaths.[49] By the end of the century, untamed sand country had won many devotees.

In the first half of the nineteenth century agricultural writers complained that vast areas of mountains and moorlands lay idle, a reproach to the skill and enterprise of their owners. In northern England schemes to enclose upland commons and wastes proposed during the Napoleonic wars were implemented in the post-war period. Between 1815 and 1850 about 38,000 acres of commons in Cumberland were enclosed, approximately 30,000 in neighbouring Westmorland, 13,000 in Northumberland, 23,000 in upland Durham, possibly over 50,000 in the West Riding of Yorkshire and about 50,000 in the North Riding.[50] Squatters, part-time miners and small independent farmers, as well as large landowners, nibbled at the edges of northern fells, at the heads of Pennine dales, around Cornish moors and the Welsh uplands.[51] The cultivation of small patches of oats was carried to a height of a thousand feet above sea level and improved grasses were sown at higher elevations. Reclamation was most extensive in the north of England, but an act of 1815 authorized the enclosure of 20,000 acres of Exmoor Forest. The Knight family's work in reclaiming part of these uplands was one of the largest individual contributions to nineteenth-century improvement.[52] Not all efforts were equally successful. In the West Riding many intakes were shortlived, and Westmorland farmers were discouraged in the 1860s by the sight of land cultivated during the Napoleonic wars having become 'permanently depreciated'.[53]

In the second half of the nineteenth century arable fields on steep slopes went out of cultivation, stone walls fell down, drains became blocked, bracken was left uncut and herds of cattle were reduced. Landowners paid more attention to deer and grouse than to farming. The preservation of game went hand in hand with absentee ownership and the abandonment of farms. In the Pennines valleys were drowned to supply water to the manufacturing centres of the West Riding and Lancashire. Manchester drew water also from the Lake District, while Liverpool and Birmingham built reservoirs in Wales. By 1904 over 90,000 acres in England and Wales had been acquired as water gathering grounds, and from a large part of this area farmers, together with their sheep and cattle, were evacuated.[54] As farmers left, increasing numbers of tourists came to the Lake District and Peak District to ramble on the moors and enjoy mountain scenery. Some stayed to build homes for retirement or for holiday retreats. Among newcomers to the Lake District were 'merchant princes of the manufacturing districts, who eagerly buy up any nook where they may escape from their own smoke and enjoy pure air and bracing breezes, with shooting and fishing'.[55] Outdoor recreation and the preservation of landscape beauty had taken priority over agricultural improvement. In 1865 the Commons Preservation Society was founded to safeguard open spaces around London and to prevent encroachments upon commons accessible to townspeople. Eleven years later the Commons Act brought enclosure of mountains and moorlands to a standstill. The Malvern Hills, Burnham Beeches and other areas of great beauty were protected by Acts of Parliament. The National Trust, formed in 1895, received private benefactions and marshalled public concern in preserving landscape amenity.

VII

At the end of the Napoleonic wars England and Wales were among the least-wooded countries in the world. Shipbuilding had denuded maritime counties of free-standing oaks, whilst mature woodlands in interior counties were exploited from the banks of inland waterways. Oaks planted during the wars had not reached maturity when the era of wooden ships ended in 1862.[56] Many oak trees destined for naval shipyards survived to adorn the landscape in the Forest of Dean, the New Forest and other royal forests in southern England. In the early nineteenth century firewood had ceased to be the principal fuel for heating homes or charging furnaces, yet woods around London and other places distant from coalfields had not recovered from the ravages of commoners and woodcutters. In the Weald, the Forest of Dean and other centres where charcoal had been used for iron smelting, natural regeneration and coppice plantations were restoring woodland cover. A forge at Ashburnham in Sussex burned charcoal for the last time in 1828, after which Wealden lime-kilns, oast-houses, gunpowder mills and dyeworks consumed only small quantities of wood.[57]

In lowland England clearings for agriculture continued until 1870. During the 1850s the Commissioners of Woods and Forests actively promoted the enclosure and sale of royal forests. Hainault Forest in Essex was disafforested in 1881 and within a few weeks 4,000 acres were grubbed up and converted into farmland. In the following decade tracts of Delamere Forest in Cheshire and Cannock Chase in Staffordshire were enclosed, and in 1856–8 in Wychwood Forest in Oxfordshire. 1,970 acres were cleared and divided among seven new farms.[58] As the area of forest wastes shrank, resistance to further enclosures stiffened. A Parliamentary Committee recommended in 1863 that the Crown should stop selling rights in the royal forests of Essex, and urged that the remaining forests be preserved as open spaces for the health and recreation of Londoners.[59] For fifteen years protests against encroachments grew more clamorous, fences were pulled down, and disputes filled the courts and newspapers. In 1878 the Epping Forest Act appointed the Corporation of the City of London conservators of 6,000 acres of forest. The 'natural aspect' of the landscape was to be preserved. Ancient monuments and standing timber were to be protected. The forest was to be managed as public open space.[60] Similar measures were taken to preserve the amenities of Ashdown Forest and Burnham Beeches. Among the objects of the New Forest Act of 1877 were provisions 'to maintain the picturesque character of the ground'.[61] While Crown lands and commons were safeguarded for outdoor recreation and the enjoyment of natural beauty, private woodlands continued to be acquired by speculative builders. London's suburbs cut deeply into woods between Highgate and Finchley and between Bromley and Norwood. Wherever railways passed, houses sprang up like mushrooms in the woods.

After 1870 the area replanted exceeded the area cleared. Between 1870 and 1905 the extent of woodland increased from 1,314,000 acres to 1,683,000 acres. In lowland England much cut-over land was planted with coppice. Coppiced ash, hazel, sweet chestnut, hornbeam and oak yielded crops at intervals of seven to twenty years, producing materials for making hurdles, gates, fence-posts and hop-poles. By 1905 coppices covered 538,000 acres, or 30 per cent of the total area of woodland.[62] In the uplands and on poor soils conifers were planted extensively. They mantled the lower slopes of the Pennines and the mountains of Cumbria. Pines were planted as windbreaks in the Breckland, to anchor drifting sands in Sherwood Forest, to cover bare soils where agricultural improvement failed on the heathlands of Dorset and in Surrey. British producers could not compete with lumbermen cutting down virgin forests in northern Europe and North America, and softwoods could be sold more readily than hardwoods. The demand for softwoods for building timber, pit props and pulp was expanding rapidly. Deciduous trees continued to be planted as cover for game birds and for ornament.

The area of parkland increased during Victorian times although contemporary taste favoured small, intimate gardens rather than the vast sweeps of lawns and lakes admired by eighteenth-century landowners.[63] John Claudius Loudon addressed his *Suburban Gardener and Villa Companion* of 1838 to possessors of villa residences. The Gardenesque, as he called his style, displayed the beauties of individual trees and flowers. Plants were placed in sunken gardens, ferneries, rockeries and herbaceous borders, to be inspected at close quarters. Exotics introduced from the Himalayas, China, Japan, South America and Australia were segregated into collectors' gardens. Palms, rhododendrons, monkey puzzle trees and camellias were appreciated because of their strange shapes, their brilliant colours, their varied textures and their fragrance. At the end of the century William Robinson renounced the studious artificiality of Italianate gardens: he banished terraces and fountains and paved walks, but delighted in colour and textural diversity. His gardens flourished on sandy soils.

The second edition one-inch Ordnance Survey maps, published in the 1880s, show that the area of parkland was greater than it had ever been. Some parks had been enlarged to provide settings for country houses newly reached by railways. Places beyond the Chilterns, previously remote from London, became the seats of the Astors, the Rothschilds and the Roseberys. Some parks were enlarged by the addition of coverts and spinneys for raising game birds. Some reintroduced or increased their stock of deer. Joseph Whitaker's *Descriptive List of the Deer-Parks and Paddocks of England* mentions 400 places possessing deer in 1892. But, in addition, old parks were extending their plantations year by year, following the designs of earlier generations of landscape gardeners.

An early nineteenth-century traveller would have recognized a few parks, woods, commons and open moors in the rural landscape of 1900, but little else would have been familiar to him. A returning William Cobbett might have measured the exodus of villagers and lamented the decay of arable husbandry. But the most striking changes were those associated with the coming of the railway and the spread of houses and gardens into the depths of the country. An adventitious population had arrived to take over rural England and Wales.

Notes

1 Howitt, 1838, I, 29.
2 Saville, 1957; Eversley, 1907, 275; Haggard, 1902, I, 251, 295; II, 539.
3 Clapham, 1926, I, 252; Census of 1851: Population Tables.
4 Census of 1901: Summary Tables, 224–9.
5 Clapham, 1932, II, 267, 268, 503; Coppock, 1973, 606.

6   Bennett, 1935, 4, 5.
7   Coppock, 1956, 4–21, 66–79.
8   Prince, 1959, 25; Kain, 1975, 39–48.
9   McCulloch, 1839, I, 531.
10 BPP, Agricultural Returns, 1870, 24; 1900, 4.
11 Orwin and Whetham, 1964, 28–34; Lawes and Gilbert, 1851, 33; Lawes and Gilbert, 1868, 368.
12 Yelling, 1977, 16; Harris, 1973, 475–7.
13 Caird, 1852, 476.
14 Fletcher, 1961b, 17–42; Coppock, 1973, 615.
15 BPP 1894 XVI: Report by Mr R. Hunter Pringle on the Ongar . . . Districts of Essex, 48, 129; Clapham, 1938, III, 79.
16 BPP 1894 XVI 42.
17 Orwin and Whetham, 1964, 131–7, 360.
18 Grant, 1844, 420–9.
19 Caird, 1852, 40; Harley, 1973, 546.
20 Bravendar, 1850, 128–9; Grigor, 1845, 194–228; Cambridge, 1845, 333–43; Turner, 1845, 479–88.
21 BPP, S.C. on Agriculture, 1836: First Report and Minutes of Evidence, 60, 168; Second Report, 73, 173.
22 Pusey, 1850, 406.
23 BPP, S.C. on Improvement of Land, Minutes: Evidence of Caird, Q. 4125–6; Evidence of Denton, Q. 830.
24 Darby, 1964, 190–201; Sturgess, 1966, 104–21; Collins and Jones, 1967, 65–81; Sturgess, 1967, 82–7; Phillips, 1969, 44–55.
25 Caird, 1852, 142.
26 Barnes, 1958, 179–80.
27 Whetham, 1964–5, 372; Taylor, 1971, 33–8.
28 McConnell, 1891, 311–25; Rew, 1892, 265.
29 Beavington, 1963, 89–100; Evershed, 1871, 432.
30 Palin, 1844, 59–62; Udale, 1908, 95; Tariff Commission, 1906, vol. III: Report of Agricultural Committee, paras 938–9, 956; Pratt, 1906, 104, 117, 121.
31 Bear, 1898, 528; 1899, 268, 283; Whitehead, 1899, 431.
32 Orwin and Whetham, 1964, 272–4; Whitehead, 1883, 368–87; Whitehead, 1889, 156–73; Departmental Committee upon the Fruit Industry of Great Britain, 1905: Report, 2.
33 Pocock, 1959, 14.
34 Harvey, 1963, 123–44.
35 Bear, 1897, 212–15, 226–7; Haggard, 1902, II, 536; Hall, 1973, 694.
36 Darby, 1940, 222; Boucher, 1963, 136.
37 Jonas, 1846, 62; Darby, 1940, 237–46.
38 Wells, 1860, 141.
39 Clarke, 1847, 132.
40 White, 1853, 165; Garnett, 1849, 24–8.
41 Williams, 1970, 144, 160–1; Creyke, 1844, 398; Edwards, 1850, 180–3; Sheppard, 1958, 15–18; Henderson, 1853, 136, 140.
42 Caird, 1852, 163.

43 Pusey, 1843, 287.
44 Corringham, 1845, 2–3.
45 Read, 1858, 265–6.
46 Hardy, 1974, 35, 64.
47 Forster, 1974, 170.
48 Eversley, 1894, 170.
49 Russell, 1895, II, 14, 201; Borrow, 1903.
50 Harris, 1973, 478; Tate, 1978.
51 Watson, 1845, 95; Redding, 1842, 143; Macrae, 1868, 321; Hunt, 1970, 152–9; Osborne, 1978, 233, 243.
52 Orwin, 1929, 20–1.
53 Charnock, 1848, 299; Webster, 1868, 7.
54 BPP Cd 8881, 1917–18: Forestry Subcommittee, 93; Walters, 1936, 99.
55 Webster, 1868, 8.
56 Albion, 1926, 137–8, 399.
57 Straker, 1931, 369.
58 Eversley, 1894, 119; Grantham, 1864, 369–80; Caird, 1852, 243; Belcher, 1863, 274.
59 Fisher, 1887, 352–5.
60 41 & 42 Vict. cap. ccxiii.
61 40 & 41 Vict. cap. cxxi.
62 Census of Woodland, 1924: Report, 6; Edlin, 1956, 100.
63 Prince, 1967, 10.

3   The Decline of Rural Isolation

Philip S. Bagwell

I

The census returns for 1841 reveal that all sixty-three men listed as labourers in the Dorset village of Stinsford, the model for Thomas Hardy's *Under the Greenwood Tree*, were born in Dorsetshire. By 1851 the number had increased to eighty and forty-nine of them were born in the village itself and only seven came from outside the county.[1] Twenty years later, 756 of the 1,417 inhabitants of Ringmer, Sussex, were born in the parish and 93 per cent of the remainder were born elsewhere in the same county.[2] If the limited mobility of the inhabitants is one measure of isolation, then these villages were isolated. It could be argued that Stinsford and Ringmer were exceptional in their degree of immunity from the forces of change. They represented the 'very old' in that 'curious mixture of the modern and the very old'[3] which was the Victorian countryside. It is the purpose of this chapter to show how rapid innovation in the modes of transport undermined the age-long isolation of the villages and hamlets of Britain.

II

If attention were confined to coach and railway timetables it would be easy to draw the conclusion that barriers of distance were rapidly declining in the last seven decades of the nineteenth century. At the beginning of the queen's reign it took two whole days to reach Edinburgh from London by the fastest mail coach, a full day, by the same means, to arrive at York, and twelve hours to get to Leicester. By train, in 1900, the Scottish capital was only eight and a half hours' travelling time from London, while York could be reached in five hours and Leicester in three. These dramatic improvements in accessibility were much discussed and keenly appreciated by the small number of property owners and professional people of the countryside but they did very little to change most villagers' concept of distance. Whereas Robert Kilvert in Radnorshire,[4] and the Rev. D. N. Yonge, vicar of Broxted in Essex,[5] acquired new perspectives of distance in the 1870s by their utilization of railways, the height of ambition for the families of agricultural labourers in the hamlet of Lark Rise in Oxfordshire in the 1880s was to make the journey by foot or spring cart 'over to Candleford'.[6] The life of the typical Ringmer family of the 1870s was

> strongly based upon the immediate locality into which they had all been born. They would rarely travel away from the village and would never have seen the sea, just a few miles down the Ouse valley. Their movement pattern would be almost entirely confined to the parish itself, with occasional journeys on foot to Lewes, three miles away.[7]

Edwin Grey, who had been Field Superintendent of the Rothamsted Experimental Station, recalled in the late 1860s and 1870s that the labourers of the vicinity did not venture 'very far afield', the limit of their travels being a walk of six or seven miles to visit relatives on a Sunday or Christmas Day.[8] In the Wensleydale village of Askrigg until the late 1870s children grew up without stirring further than a few miles from their homes.[9]

For the better-off the last quarter of the nineteenth century was a time of widening horizons. Visits to distant relatives, hitherto regarded as unattainable except in extreme emergency, were now more frequently realizable, thanks largely to the railway. For wage-earners a journey beyond walking distance was no longer seen as an impossible dream. Nevertheless, for Leonard Thompson and Fred Mitchell, farm workers of Akenfield, it took the emergency of the First World War to carry them beyond the horizons of Suffolk.[10] Their experience was by no means exceptional.

III

In early Victorian times the stage coach was the traditional means of public transport for the wealthier members of the village community. The network of services was about at its peak at the time of the queen's coronation, but even so it linked only the main towns and those villages which had the good fortune to be situated astride the routes. For the large majority of villages there was no direct access to the network, and private transport or the carrier's cart had to be used to reach the staging post. Travelling by coach was not cheap. The basic charge for an inside seat was not less than 4*d*. a mile, while those who travelled 'outside' paid a minimum of 2*d*. If the journey were a long one incidental charges, including the cost of overnight accommodation at inns and the tipping of the drivers and guards, could double the overall cost. Travelling by Royal Mail coach or by stage coach was, however, the fastest means of land transport before the days of the railway, eight or nine miles an hour being regarded as good average speeds and the ten and a half miles per hour of the Liverpool–Preston coach exceptionally fast.

The inconveniences of travelling by public stage coach sometimes provoked the wealthier of country residents to 'travel post', using their own carriages and hiring horses at post-houses along the route. This was an even more expensive mode of travel—at 1s. a mile—but probably more comfortable, and certainly more private, than the stage coach. Members of landed families were driven in the family coach with their arms boldly displayed on the door. The passage of such a vehicle through a remote hamlet would be an occasion of note. At Lark Rise 'people rushed to their cottage doors' to see a 'carriage with gentry' pass by.[11]

In late Victorian times, when the railway train had replaced the stage coach for longer journeys, the well-to-do made their shorter expeditions by brougham, open landau or gig. The more prosperous farmers went about their business in handsome new gigs, as did Mr Shiner, the wealthiest farmer of Mellstock (Stinsford and Lower and Upper Brockhampton) in *Under the Greenwood Tree*. Farmers of more modest means travelled in the spring carts which were manufactured in wheelwrights' shops and larger specialist establishments throughout the country. Oxley's, the coach builders of Beverley, Yorkshire, offered an improved version of spring cart, with an adjustable seat to allow for the carriage of up to four persons, for the sum of £21.[12] Wheeled horse-drawn transport took an infinite variety of forms, each county's vehicles having their own individuality. In Cheshire, for example, there was the chandry, a high open cart used to carry people to market in Whitchurch or Chester.[13]

It is easy to overlook the fact that the most frequently used form of transport was what the Victorians called Shanks's pony. Cottagers thought nothing of walking six or seven miles with their children to visit relatives in another village and walking back home at the end of the day, using such footpaths and short cuts as were available.[14] Necessity obliged many men to walk even longer distances to and from their places of work. In the 1880s a carpenter living at Chalford Hill regularly walked twenty-eight miles a day, six days a week, to and from his work in Gloucester. Another Chalford man who worked at Cirencester had a less daunting total of eighteen daily miles to cover on foot. Although the large majority of villagers found employment much nearer home the two examples cited were by no means freakish exceptions.[15] The one concession these great walkers might make to 'luxury' was to travel by carrier's cart to take their produce to the nearest market town. That this means of transport was inexpensive was a more important consideration than that it was often painfully slow.

As the branch lines of the railway companies filled in more of the gaps in the 1870s and after, the better-off villagers used increasingly varied means of transport. Within the space of just over one year (1870–1) Robert Kilvert used a brougham, an open carriage, a mail phaeton, a dog cart, a fly, the railway and—when the road was too icy for his horse to be employed—Shanks's pony, to carry him to his various engagements in Radnorshire and further afield.[16] The Rev. Yonge, in his Essex parish of Broxted, was almost equally versatile. At different times in 1877 he had occasion to use a horse-drawn bus, the carrier's cart, a fly, a dog cart, a brougham and the railway.[17]

IV

At the beginning of Victoria's reign the inland waterways of Britain were at their maximum extent with some 4,000 route miles open to traffic. For nearly two generations they had played an increasing part in breaking down rural isolation. Until the late 1850s the canals in some parts of Britain offered a convenient and inexpensive means of passenger transport. This was particularly true of Scotland. In 1837 some three-quarters of a million passengers were carried on the Scottish canals, principally in the Central Lowlands where village life was given new vitality through commercial and social links with Glasgow, Edinburgh, Paisley, Perth and many other towns.[18] South of the Border, on the Lancaster Canal 'swift', i.e. five-miles-per-hour, passenger boats carried customers from villages along the route between Kendal and Lancaster.[19] The fares charged were at the remarkably low rate of a halfpenny per two miles.[20]

On most of the English and Welsh canals where local topography necessitated the construction of numerous locks, passenger traffic died out early in the Victorian era; thus the principal contribution of the canals to the decline of rural isolation was through the spread of commerce. Village carriers had close links with the canals of their district. On the Birmingham canal network, which covered rural as well as urban areas, the canal boatmen were recruited from the class of local carriers and worked equally happily on land or on water.[21] They were also one of the principal means for the conveyance of news and of ideas from the city to the surrounding countryside.

The canals helped to make villagers less completely dependent on their own resources, and particularly so in respect of fuel. Before canals opened Britain's hinterland, supplies of coal were rarely available beyond twenty miles from the limit of navigation because of the prohibitive cost of land transport, sometimes as high as sixpence a ton-mile. When in 1821 the final stretches of the Montgomeryshire canals were completed from Welshpool to Newtown, the cost of coal and lime in Newtown was lowered by a third, to the substantial benefit of householders, local flannel manufacture and farmers.[22] Agricultural practice, hitherto backward in the less accessible districts, was increasingly brought closer to the standard of the most advanced farming: guano and other fertilizers, and coal, for the manufacture of lime, were made available, and were paid for through the revenue gained from back carriage of agricultural produce to the wider market the canal network made possible. For this reason farmers in Cheshire, by the 1840s, were applying an average of four tons of lime per acre, whereas previously, in consequence of the high costs of carriage, only half that amount had been used.[23]

In sum, it was through their contribution to the widening of the national market, rather than through any major influence on personal mobility, that the canals diminished rural isolation. Thus, the greater part of Wiltshire before the canal age was very difficult of access for bulky goods; but the opening of the Kennet and Avon and the Wiltshire and Berkshire canals brought Somersetshire coal into those parts of the country where hitherto coal was rarely seen.[24] Thanks to an extensive canal network the economic isolation of former years was much reduced; and with the decline in economic isolation went the breaking down of social and cultural barriers between regions and between town and countryside.

V

For thousands of villages and hamlets in Britain the most important links with the outside world were made by the country carriers. These oft-forgotten characters were 'never more numerous' than at the end of the Victorian era. When it is recalled that only a very small minority of villages were located by canals, and that even when the railway network was at its fullest extent no more than one in six of them had a railway station, it is no cause for surprise that the number of carrier services grew throughout the century. At a conservative estimate there were at least 20,000 carriers in business in the 1880s.[25] The canals and railways must be seen as providing increased opportunities for local carriers' activities rather than as destroying their livelihood. It is true that there were important changes in the structure of the carrying trade, particularly in the years 1840–60. During these two decades many long-distance carriers, who had linked important towns and industrial centres, deserted the roads for the railways. But during this same period the network of local carrier services increased. Thus in Hampshire the opening of the railway between London and Southampton in 1840 and London and Gosport (for Portsmouth) in 1842 led to the quick demise of long-distance carrier services over these routes but simultaneously provided the basis for an extension of local carrier activities.[26] In the neighbouring county of Sussex the existence of railway services linking the principal towns did not preclude even small towns, such as Horsham, from serving as the hub of a whole network of local carrier services. On 31 December 1881, for example, the *Horsham Advertiser* listed nine carriers who, between them, collected and delivered from eighteen nearby villages.

Since one of the most important functions of the local carrier was to link a group of villages to the nearest markets there were probably more of their carts on the road on Wednesdays and Saturdays than on other days of the week. Zachary Cripps, R. D. Blackmore's fictional carrier, made his visits to Oxford on these days and was 'in and out with the places and the people, as busy as the best of them'. At the market he had 'a great host of commissions' to execute for his numerous contacts in the outlying villages. He had dealings with 'farmers, butchers, poulterers, hucksters, chandlers and grocers', and the villagers for whom he traded knew that he would 'spend their money quite as gingerly as his own'.[27]

Cripps's task was to carry out an immense variety of small assignments; other carriers traded on a larger scale. In Cumbria some took coal or farm produce into Carlisle, to return with loads of city manure for the farmers.[28]

Like the celebrated Barkis, Dickens's Suffolk carrier, most carriers provided a somewhat primitive country bus service with 'many deviations up and down lanes', their carts drawn by horses which were not generally the noblest specimens of their kind. Nevertheless, the carrier's cart was often the only form of public transport available to those of limited means. In the 1870s 'in every Dorset village eager girls with small corded trunks awaited the carrier's cart to take them on the first stage of their townward journey' and a life of domestic service.[29]

The fact that very many carriers combined their carrying business with other part-time occupations in their village base serves to underline their influence in breaking down rural isolation. Thus among the carriers of Wiltshire in 1865 Richard Dyke of Lavington described himself also as a 'hairdresser and newsagent'; thirty years later Samuel Bristow of Great Cheverell was a blacksmith, and Isaac Whiting a 'cow keeper and coal dealer'.[30] Though seemingly omnipresent, carriers did not penetrate all inhabited parts of the countryside. The remoter hamlets, farmhouses and cottages were reached by pedlars or specialist salesmen or saleswomen who travelled on foot or with the aid of a pony or donkey cart. The hilly district behind Stroud in Gloucestershire was known locally as 'Neddyshire' in recognition of the large number of donkeys employed there in the distribution of newspapers, farm produce, haberdashery and other goods.[31] Flora Thompson's grandfather pursued the occupation of 'eggler', 'buying up eggs from farms and cottages and selling them at markets and to shopkeepers'.[32] Only the appearance of the motorized delivery van led to the gradual disappearance of these important means of contact with the remoter parts of the countryside.

VI

For many coastal and island villages the steamboat, rather than the railway, was the principal agency for breaking down rural isolation. A leading historian of the Scottish economy had no doubt that 'the real transport revolution—if there was such a thing in the Highlands—... was the use of steam at sea'.[33] The improvement in communications in the county of Argyll, with a coastline deeply serrated by the sea, presented enormous difficulties. With the coming of the steamship the very barrier which had denied previous generations communication with the outside world became the region's principal highway. Contemporary observers found the effect of this innovation 'incalculable', and declared that steamboats were 'at once the herald and the cause of every kind of improvement in Argyllshire'.[34] The regular passage of steamboats to and from the Orkney and Shetland Islands from the mid-1830s brought the inhabitants of these northernmost territories more within the mainstream of British culture. The nearest approach to a department store experienced by these islanders was the regular appearance from April 1886 onwards of Robert Garden's purpose-built 'shop' steamship, *Summer Cloud*. The ship's arrival was such a big event that it was frequently announced by the schoolmaster.[35] Long before the railway reached the district the villagers of the Furness peninsula had the opportunity of quick and inexpensive access to Liverpool through the swift steam-packet *Windermere*. Other steam-packet services connected Ulverston with Fleetwood and the coach services going north and south.[36] The long-established maritime links between the ports of South Wales, Chepstow and Bristol on the one hand, and the numerous village harbours of the coasts of North Somerset and Devon on the other, were greatly strengthened as steam propulsion replaced sail, since the steamships were far more dependable. In 1862, for example, there were regular steam-packets plying between Watchet and Cardiff, giving accommodation in the fore cabin for a fare of as little as 2*s*.[37] Looking still further south, it is not difficult to demonstrate that the isolation of villages in the Isle of Wight was shattered at least as much by regular steamship communications with the mainland, which began as early as 1820, as by the railway, which did not arrive on the island until forty-two years later.[38]

VII

Those who travelled on the first, crowded train of the West Somerset Railway to reach Williton on the opening day, 31 March 1862, saw across the main street a banner bearing the words 'Hail, Steam the Civilizer!' Even the workhouse inmates had prepared a banner which read: 'Accept our Best Wishes'. Though on that day the citizens of nearby Watchet marred the idealistic image with their banner inscribed 'May prosperity attend the WSR with a good percentage to the shareholders',[39] there can be no doubt that on this line and everywhere else in the kingdom the arrival of the railway was regarded as an immense boon. The first train to arrive at Llanidloes in Central Wales in September 1859 was made up of forty-eight carriages or wagons and carried, 'at a moderate estimate', 3,000 people. Business in the town was entirely suspended for the occasion and the day was 'ushered in by cannon-firing, bell ringing and the hearty congratulations of the people of the town with their country friends who flocked in to take part in the proceedings'.[40] The first train to reach Askrigg in Wensleydale on 1 February 1877 had been 'besieged by delighted crowds at every station' along the way.[41] Everywhere the railway's arrival was celebrated by gargantuan feasts in which even the navvies were allowed to participate. Twenty-four toasts were proposed at the 'sumptuous feast' at Watchet. They included, besides the 'Queen' and the 'Prince of Wales', the 'Wooden Walls of old England', the 'Harbour Commissioners', the 'Navigators', the 'Clergy of the Western Division of Somerset' and the leader of the band, 'Capt. Bridges'.

Why such great enthusiasm? Partly it sprang from the belief that the railway was synonymous with progress; no part of the country liked to be regarded as a backwater, lacking the most modern means of communication. But also substantial material gains were anticipated in the form of cheaper coal, a greater variety of domestic goods, wider markets for farmers, fishermen and manufacturers, and more job opportunities. Many of these expectations were realized. When the East and West Junction Railway came to Eydon in Northamptonshire in May 1868, coal, which had been carried to the village partly by canal and partly by wagon, was immediately reduced in price.[42] The inhabitants of Askrigg had the same experience. Although those who were employed on the new railways were obliged to work long hours, this was no novelty to farm labourers, many of whom were attracted by the slightly higher wages, more regular employment and brighter prospects of promotion. For many a farm worker the railway opened up new horizons. William E. Bear reported to the Royal Commission on Labour in 1893 that 'those who obtain employment as railway porters getting comparatively high wages and many tips, better themselves there cannot be any doubt'.[43] D. Llenfer Thomas, reporting to the same commission on the agricultural labourers of central Anglesey, noted:

> I do not know of any district which, while remaining purely agricultural, has been so greatly influenced by the introduction of railways as this portion of Anglesey. It has enabled the poorer classes to make large sums of money out of commodities which, in other districts, are generally neglected, and it has also enabled them to spend such money freely upon excursions and other forms of pleasure previously unknown to them.[44]

The spread of the railways helped to make farmers more conscious of the potentialities of more distant markets. Inevitably their knowledge of urban conditions increased. The milk not needed by the people of the village was taken to the nearest railway station to be dispatched to the big cities. In Wiltshire Richard Jefferies

> heard the ringing noises . . . caused by the careless handling of milk tins dragged hither and thither by the men who are getting the afternoon milk ready for transit to the station miles away. Each tin bears a brazen badge engraved with the name of the milkman who will retail its contents in distant London. It may be delivered to the Countess in Belgravia and reach her dainty lips in the morning chocolate or it may be eagerly swallowed up by the half-starved children of some black court in the purlieus of Seven Dials. The tins . . . are swung up into a waggon specially built for the purpose. It is the very antithesis of the jolting and cumbrous waggon used for generations in the hay fields and among the corn.[45]

Likewise in Wensleydale the coming of the railway in 1877 meant the sale in Leeds, Newcastle and Liverpool of milk which would previously have been made into cheese and butter.[46] In the Bledington district of Gloucestershire milk from the larger farms was sent by train to London and Oxford, 'leaving the local milk and butter market to the hard working wives of the smaller farmers'.[47] In Dorset, where the railway provided a 'lifeline' for dairy farmers, the problem was how to get the milk to the station, rather than that of finding markets. To meet this difficulty in the Sherborne district members of the Moore family instituted a twice-daily service of spring wagons to collect the churns from the surrounding villages, thus, incidentally, providing an important new medium for the dissemination of the latest news.[48] In sum, there is much evidence that the arrival of the railway shook farmers out of a complacent acceptance of age-long practices and greatly reduced their isolation from developments in the urban areas of the country. A Mr John Davies, speaking to a large gathering consisting mainly of members of the farming community on the occasion of the opening of the railway to Llanidloes, declared, 'It could no longer be said of us (as it had been said) that darkness covered their land and gross darkness their people.'[49]

There was no more influential person in connecting villagers with the outside world than the village stationmaster. Ernest J. Summons, who was stationmaster at Aynho in Northamptonshire in 1863, was undoubtedly a key figure in the local community, though this importance was hardly reflected by his meagre salary of £80 a year. Local tradesmen depended upon him to expedite their claims for delay and damage; the vicar needed information about fare concessions for Sunday school outings; an old lady gratefully sent him a basket of plums once a year because he allowed her to take her dog in the passenger compartment rather than in that 'dreadful dungeon of a dog box'; the stockbroker handed him his cigar case. 'In fact all but magistrates and the shareholders paid homage to the stationmaster.'[50]

The coming of the railway widened the horizons of those concerned with school excursions. On 15 July 1880 the members of the Langley Marish School Board in Buckinghamshire decided to take advantage of the special train booked by the members of the Royal Benefit Society to send the school children on a day excursion to Portsmouth. The decision was taken despite the opposition of one member of the School Board who considered such outings for children undesirable since 'they encouraged habits of extravagance and restlessness and unfitted them for the position in life in which they were placed'.[51]

Within the counties, especially in the closing years of the queen's reign, the railway brought an enhanced mobility to the labouring population. The Cambrian Railway timetable in the early 1900s included four pages of 'market ticket arrangements' giving details of departure times and fares from over 150 local stations to the twenty-two market towns served by the company. Special market return tickets were sold, in many cases at less than 1s. and in some at only 3d.[52]

The die hard member of the Langley Marish School Board was right. Market trips and school outings engendered a restlessness, particularly in the younger generation, which was frequently the subject of comment by older members of the village community. Mr Rowe, a farmer of Dartmoor, told Rider Haggard of the policeman or London porter who returned home by train on his holiday 'wearing rings and an Albert chain, to fill the ears of listeners with fine stories which so stir their imaginations that they are never content until they have also set out to seek their fortunes in the towns'. The novelist, Thomas Hardy, in a letter to Rider Haggard, saw the main cause of this restlessness of country folk as insecurity of tenure, but recognized that the coming of the railways had been the main agency for the much greater mobility of village populations. In consequence he found 'village traditions—a vast amount of unwritten folk lore, local chronicles, local topography and nomenclature . . . absolutely sinking . . . into eternal oblivion'.[53] According to Mr Bear, reporting on Bedfordshire, it was the females who were responsible for increased mobility of labour in the 1890s. The young girls who travelled by train to service in London 'acted as a magnet to the men they left behind them'.[54]

The younger generation, reaching maturity as the nineteenth century drew to its close, had far less attachment to local institutions than their elders. Young men were reluctant to join local benefit clubs, encumbrances 'which would render their removal more difficult'. National friendly societies, with branches all over the kingdom, had more appeal to 'young men of migratory tendencies'.[55]

It is all too easy to conclude that the railways spelt the doom of horse-drawn transport. Nothing could be further from the truth. The arrival of the railway was often the necessary spur for the introduction of road improvements so that traffic could be sped to the stations. By the end of the 1850s the arrival of the railway at Chirk in Denbighshire prompted the local gentry and farmers to finance a turnpike road eleven miles long from Chirk railway station to Llanarmon, up the Vale of Glyn-Cieriog.[56] The greatly increased volume of both passenger and goods traffic which the railways carried created 'new and expanding demands for horse labour'. The 3,276,000 horses in use in 1901 were more than double the number employed at the time of Queen Victoria's accession.[57] It was the longer-distance horse-drawn traffic which suffered some decline; but this was more than offset by the increase in local traffic. Horse-drawn bus services multiplied to fill the outstanding gaps in the railway network.

It is arguable that the railways' greatest contributions to the decline of rural isolation were indirect: tremendous improvements in the postal service and the introduction of the electric telegraph. The decision to introduce the national penny post for letters in 1840 would scarcely have been possible but for the appearance then of a basic railway network.[58] Before the introduction of the penny post postage charges on letters and newspapers varied with distance as well as weight. The charges for the conveyance of newspapers were particularly severe. The *Ames Correspondence* reveals that the cost of sending a newspaper from Shrewsbury to Lakenham in Norfolk—£1. 2s. 6d.—was so steep that Charles Ames refused to accept it although he was anxious for news. In 1836 a government decision that newspapers which had paid the newspaper stamp duty (then 1d.) would be carried free with the mail greatly encouraged their circulation. The abolition of the stamp duty in 1855 and the paper duty in 1861, together with the decision of the Superintendents' Conference of the Railway Clearing House in 1866 to carry newspapers at half the normal parcels rate, still further enhanced circulation. Finally the nationalization of the telegraph system in 1870, the trebling of the number of telegraph offices by 1873, and the introduction in 1870 of a specially cheap night-time rate of 100 words for 1s., with 2d. extra per 100 words for duplicated copies of telegrams, encouraged the growth of local newspapers which relayed a large amount of national news. The need to transmit messages about the movement of trains had occasioned the introduction of the telegraph, and the further spread of the railway network was the *sine qua non* for the further dissemination of news and information.

It was not only newspapers whose circulation increased through the agencies of the railway, the cheaper posts and the telegraph. Jefferies's 'Mademoiselle the Governess', the London-trained daughter of a Wiltshire farmer, brought home some of the 'many cheap illustrated papers giving the latest details of fashionable costumes' which she sought to emulate.[59] And village sports fixtures could now be more widely publicized—thanks to the local newspapers—and be more widely attended—thanks to the railway branch lines. In the last quarter of the nineteenth century All England cricket teams used the railway to tour the country districts at the close of the season. In Wiltshire 'a broad-shouldered cricketing farmer, from a gigantic on drive downhill, ran his partner out attempting the eleventh run'. By the end of the century the spread of knowledge of M.C.C. rules rendered such outrageously irregular practices far less likely to occur.[60]

VIII

No single influence was responsible for reducing rural isolation in Queen Victoria's reign. At the time of her accession the process of breaking down the barriers of communication between country and town was well under way. Each year some 10 million coach journeys were being undertaken. As many as 2 million additional journeys may have been made in estuarial and coastal vessels, and nearly a million more in canal boats. There is no means of telling how many trips were made in carriers' carts. The spread of railways greatly quickened the pace of change—over 922 million passenger journeys were made by rail in 1899—and virtually killed passenger travel by canal. The fact that railways directly served only a small fraction of the villages helps to explain why the number of horses doubled in Victorian times. Each of these two forms of transport fed on the other, while together they made possible an enormous growth in the three other principal means of communication, the post, the telegraph and the newspaper.

After the queen's death, early in 1901, the decline in rural isolation continued. It is significant that her successor to the throne, Edward VII, was a keen motorist. During his reign many blacksmiths followed the example of the one at Candleford who had decided to make 'Motor Repairs a Speciality'.[61] It was the motor vehicle which completed that undermining of rural isolation which the stage coach, steamboat, and railway had begun.

Notes

1   Howard, 1977, 187.
2   Ambrose, 1974, 26.
3   Clark, 1962, 132.
4   Plomer, 1964, 101, 119, 123.
5   Brown, 1972, 107.
6   Flora Thompson, 1973, 249.
7   Ambrose, 1974, 23.
8   Grey, 1935, 191.
9   Hartley and Ingilby, 1953, 173.
10 Blythe, 1972, 21, 53.
11 Flora Thompson, 1973, 18.
12 Dorset RO: JO 1452.
13 Cheshire Federation of Women's Institutes, 1961, 35.
14 Grey, 1935, 191.
15 Gloucestershire Community Council, 1950, 14.
16 Plomer, 1964, 19, 101, 107, 119.
17 Brown, 1972, 107.
18 Lindsay, 1968, 42–8.
19 Hadfield, 1970, 170.
20 Gladwyn, 1976, 104.
21 Hanson, 1975, 8.
22 Roberts and Owen, 1924, 61.
23 Davies, 1960, 114.
24 Hadfield, 1970, 158.
25 Everitt, 1976, 179.
26 Freeman, 1977, 66.
27 Blackmore, 1876, I, 182.
28 Williams, 1975, 97–9.
29 Kerr, 1968, 117.
30 Greening, 1971, 170–1.
31 Gloucestershire Community Council, 1950, 13.
32 Flora Thompson, 1973, 91.
33 Gray, 1957, 148–9.
34 *Topographical, Statistical and Historical Gazetteer of Scotland*, 1842, I, 59–60.
35 Cormack and Cormack, 1971, 148–9.
36 Melville and Hobbs, 1947, 97.
37 *West Somerset Free Press*, 9 August 1862.
38 O'Brien, 1969, 393. *Isle of Wight Observer*, 19 July 1862.
39 *West Somerset Free Press*, 9 August 1862.
40 *Oswestry Advertiser and Montgomeryshire Mercury*, 7 September 1859.
41 Hartley and Ingilby, 1953, 180.
42 Tyrrell, 1973, 106.
43 BPP 1893–4 XXXV 19.
44 BPP 1893–4 XXXVI 128.

45   Jefferies 1966, 78.
46   Hartley and Ingilby, 1953, 181.
47   Ashby, 1974, 381.
48   Kerr, 1968, 163.
49   *Oswestry Advertiser and Montgomeryshire Mercury*, 7 September 1859.
50   Simmons, 1974, 83.
51   Delgado, 1977, 108.
52   Cambrian Railways, 1904 (reprinted 1977), 40–2.
53   Haggard, 1906b, I, 185; II, 283–4.
54   BPP 1893–4 XXXV 19.
55   BPP 1893–4 XXXVI 118.
56   *Oswestry Advertiser and Montgomeryshire Mercury*, 25 April 1860.
57   F. M. L. Thompson, 1976, 64.
58   Norfolk Record Society, vol. 31, 1962, 23.
59   Jefferies, 1966, 115.
60   Bradley, 1907, 81.
61   Horn, 1976b, 91.

4   The Land and the Church

Alan D. Gilbert

I

The history of English and Welsh society has been shaped to a considerable extent by changes over time in relationships between the people and the land, and nowhere is this more evident than in the history of the Church of England. Indeed, in an almost literal sense Anglicanism has been able to take root much more firmly in some soils than in others. Grass was the natural product of rural Durham and the North Riding of Yorkshire, William Cobbett noted in September 1832, knowing it to be a fact of immense social as well as agricultural significance. Land tenure arrangements, social structures, the attitudes and values of the local population, their historical experience and their religious habits—all these things were linked in an interlocking relationship with the nature of the land itself. Or as Cobbett put it 'The size and shape of the fields, the sort of fences, the absence of all homesteads and labourers' cottages, the thinness of the country churches, everything shows that this was always a country purely of pasturage.'[1]

The scarcity of country churches greatly impressed Cobbett on this rare foray into northern England, for village churches, picturesque and prominent, dotted the landscape of the southern counties which he knew so well. Untravelled northerners would be amazed, he knew,

> if they could go down the vale of the Avon in Wiltshire, from Marlborough
> Forest to the city of Salisbury, and there see thirty parish churches in a

43

distance of thirty miles; if they could go up from that city of Salisbury up
the valley of Wylly to Warminster, and there see one-and-thirty churches in
the space of twenty-seven miles; if they could go upon the top of the down,
as I did, not far (I think it was) from St Mary Cotford, and there have under
the eye, in the valley below, ten parish churches within the distance of eight
miles. . . .[2]

Cobbett himself was impressed but unastonished by the contrast. Knowing as well as
any social geographer that religious allegiances varied from one type of community
to another, and that community structure mirrored patterns of land ownership and
land use, he would have been capable of an acute analysis of the strengths and
weaknesses with which the Church of England entered the Victorian era.

II

The unique Census of Religious Worship, carried out in March 1851, shocked many
churchmen by revealing that only about half of those who attended religious services
in England and Wales did so as Anglicans, and by indicating also that well over half
the population attended no religious services whatever.[3] The figures might come as
more of a surprise because religious habits varied considerably from area to area. The
census, for example, not only confirmed the failure of the Church of England to obtain
the allegiance of people in the kinds of urban and semi-urban settlements which had
multiplied with industrialization, but also highlighted marked variations in the hold
of the Church over the rural population. Even at a county level these variations
formed a significant pattern of Anglican strengths and weaknesses. The geographical
perspective of Map 4.1, based on county figures, clearly reveals a heavy Anglican bias
towards the south, the south-east, the south Midlands and East Anglia, and a relative
weakness of early-Victorian Anglicanism in Cornwall, Wales, the north Midlands,
the west Midlands and the north of England.

It was no accident that this broad pattern of Anglican religiosity coincided with
the distinctive geographical and socio-geographical zones identified by the well-
known 'lowland–highland' distinction.[4] Historically the typically 'lowland' areas of
southern and eastern England had been the most densely populated parts of rural
Britain, and by the beginning of the Victorian era the Church had spent centuries
concentrating its greatest efforts and resources there. Parishes were smaller, more
workable. In 1811, for example, the average size of a parish in the south-eastern zone
was below 3,000 acres, while in Yorkshire it was over 6,000 acres, and in the counties
of the north and the north-west almost 12,000 acres.[5] In the traditional Anglican
strongholds parishes were also better endowed, and the relative inadequacy of
clerical benefices in much of the West Country, in Wales and in the north, meant that
the enfeebling effects of pluralism and absenteeism had long been most prevalent
there.[6]

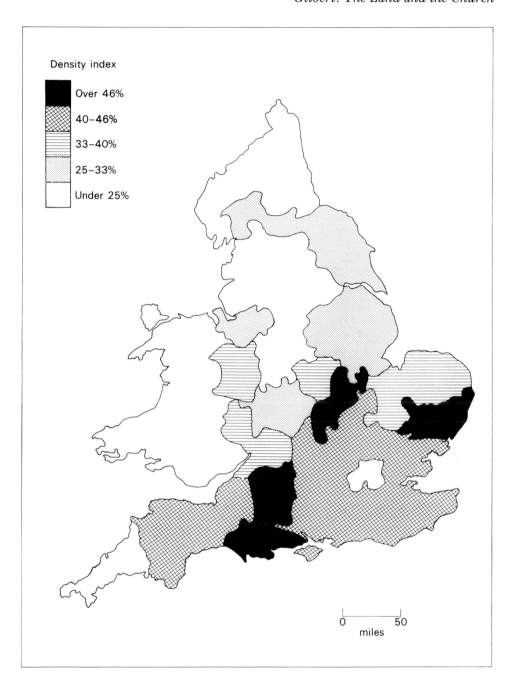

Map 4.1 The geography of Anglicanism in 1851: church attendance by county as a percentage of county population

Source: based on 'Census of Religious Worship, 1851', BPP 1852–3 LXXXIX.

But Anglicanism was not just better organized in 'lowland' areas of the countryside. In its monopolistic, prescriptive religious culture, and in the primary social roles which it discharged, the Church of England had adapted itself over the centuries to the kinds of social, economic and political situations typical of the nucleated agricultural communities which had evolved in the arable farmlands of England. Obversely, however, Anglicanism fitted rather uneasily into the social forms and settlement patterns of regions where moorland and mountain, and soil types encouraging pastoral rather than arable agriculture, had shaped a distinctive rural culture. Scattered communities mixing pastoral agriculture with domestic industry, or engaged in mining or quarrying, had proved less reachable and less amenable to paternalistic constraints than had their 'lowland' counterparts.

Obviously, neither the 'lowland–highland' pattern nor the social geography of Anglicanism fitted snugly into broad regional divisions of the kind indicated by Map 4.1. Essentially local factors remained, at the beginning of the Victorian era, the major determinants of social behaviour in the English and Welsh countryside. There were many pockets of typically 'lowland' agriculture and settlement within the general 'highland' zone of the north and west, just as in the Weald of Kent, the Chilterns, the Berkshire Downs, or the residual forests of the Midlands and the south, social and economic circumstances had produced communities lacking the nuclear structures, the highly integrated social order, or the strongly conformist religious habits of the surrounding countryside. Yet a study of such atypical local communities serves only to confirm the importance of land use and land tenure as vital factors in the social history of English and Welsh religion.

III

'The landlords have absolute power in the country,' Richard Cobden told the House of Commons in 1845, asserting something which his own formidable power as a leader of the Anti-Corn Law League effectively disproved.[7] By the beginning of the Victorian era the traditional hegemony of landed wealth and power was under fundamental attack. Yet Cobden was correct in anticipating no swift or dramatic abdication by the landed elite in face of the challenge. 'I tell you', he continued in the same speech, 'that the people of this country look to their aristocracy with a deep-rooted prejudice—an hereditary prejudice, I may call it—in their favour. . . .'[8] The prejudice may have been fading. The traditional assumptions of paternalism and deference which supported it certainly had weakened in the previous half-century with an emergence of rudimentary class consciousness and a sharpening of vertical social antagonisms in rural communities. But the waning of the landed interest was to be a long, slow process. Even at the end of Victoria's reign the power of the great landlords in national politics would remain immense, and away from the cities and larger towns the primary realities of social structure, status, authority and influence would be derived still from the relationship of an individual or a family to the ownership or control of landed property.

Partly by an historic attachment to the landed interest, partly through the familial associations, outlook, expectations and social affiliations of most of its clergy, the Church of England was involved inescapably in the slowly changing fortunes of Victorian landed society. But the relationship between landowners and clergy was itself neither uniform nor unchanging. Indeed, to understand the history of Anglicanism in the Victorian countryside, it is vital to examine relations between the clerical profession and the landed classes both in historical perspective and in terms of the options open to each party after 1837.

The ideal parish, most early Victorians continued to believe, was one in which squire and parson presided jointly over a close-knit and deferential local community. The gradual abandonment of this eighteenth-century paradigm was to be an important aspect of Victorian Church history, but equally important was the fact that Anglicans generally abandoned it with great reluctance, and often long after fundamental social changes had turned it into an ecclesiastical liability. 'I entirely agree with you', Matthew Arnold wrote to a working-class essayist whose work had attracted attention in 1872, 'that its Tory and squirearchical connexion has been and is of the greatest disservice to the Church of England.'[9] But on the eve of the agricultural depression this was still a radical judgment of the squire–parson alliance. So deep had been the Church's historic commitment to the influence of the great landed families—so strong was the nostalgia for an idealized past in which social mores had been prescribed under the paternalism of the 'big house' and the parsonage—that the Church adjusted very slowly to the less prescriptive, more pluralistic type of society which was emerging.

Almost within living memory of Arnold's generation, the society had virtually been ruled by its landed gentry. Through the economic power and social status which landed property had conferred, as Justices of the Peace, as clergymen or as the patrons of the clergy, and through those elitist associations which had dominated county affairs generally, the gentry had played a major role in all but the most specifically national processes of government. Matters of social control and public administration in pre-industrial society had been highly localized and, *ipso facto*, highly personalized. A local community had depended on a network of primary relationships linking dominant and subordinate social groups, and as a social system it had functioned well only when paternalism on one side and deference on the other side had softened the obligations and responsibilities governing community life at all levels.

The parson had been an important figure in such a community. Sometimes he had been a major landowner in his own right: a 'squarson', to adopt the not quite flattering contemporary nomenclature. In many cases he had been given a seat on the county bench. Indeed, on the eve of the Victorian era somewhere between a quarter and two-fifths of all justices had been clergymen.[10] And less formally, but no less importantly, the parson had been in a position to exploit thoroughly all the 'influence' that went with landed status. This had been true even when he was not himself a substantial property owner, so close had been the squire–parson alliance; but it is noteworthy that the rapid spate of Parliamentary enclosures in the period 1760–1830 had actually increased very substantially the extent of clerical landholding. By commuting tithes for land some parsons had even become 'squarsons', and many more had cemented their alliance with the squirearchy by raising themselves more securely into the ranks of the independent landed gentry.[11]

Ironically, however, these very processes which had strengthened the association between clergy and gentry had helped to undermine the cultural system through which the landed classes had exercised their traditional social and political hegemony. Enclosure and tithe commutation had been aspects of a profound rationalization of the agrarian economy, and by the beginning of the Victorian era rural England had advanced far along the road to complete agrarian capitalism. One social cost of this process had been the virtual elimination of the so-called 'dependency system'.[12] Capitalism, with its functional and legal separation of capital and labour, with its impersonal economic rationalism and emphasis on profit-making, had slowly destroyed the customary usages, paternalistic concessions and archaic economic values of older relationships between a local community and its landed gentry. Its effect had been to produce instead a class society in the English and Welsh countryside.

By 1837 the Church of England had become alienated from growing sections of the rural population. In place of the more or less respected image of the gentleman-squire, the parson's ally had assumed the role of capitalist landlord; and the parson, for his part, seemed often to have been a more than willing accomplice. In the contentious matter of enclosures, for example, whereas the seventeenth-century Church had opposed them as 'an offence to God and man', the early nineteenth-century clergy had been the beneficiaries of large-scale enclosure.[13] Nor had their involvement simply been that of beneficiaries, for as magistrates many clergy had been seen to take part in the legal enforcement of agrarian capitalism's unpopular aspects. Not surprisingly, anti-clericalism had been an ominous feature of much of the popular protest associated with the 'Swing' rioting of 1830–1,[14] and by the beginning of the Victorian era 'Church landlordism' had already become a useful slogan in a growing Nonconformist campaign against the Anglican establishment.

An alliance between squire and parson could still be thoroughly effective. The problem was that as deference and respect for status diminished, 'influence' became an increasingly coercive phenomenon. This was obvious particularly during periods of crisis in relations between the landed classes and the wider society of the Victorian age. The dramatic confrontation with the Anti-Corn Law League in the 1840s, the protracted wrangling over church rates which spanned the first half of the reign, fiercely contested electoral battles in 1857, 1859, 1874, 1880 and 1885, and the challenge of agricultural unionism in the 1870s—all tended to place the 'landed interest' in the invidious position of defending seemingly intolerant attitudes and petty privileges. Moreover, where deferential compliance was forthcoming no longer, the acquiescence of social subordinates often was extorted by economic or other sanctions. An example of religious conformity maintained in this way appeared in the *Carmarthen Journal* of 7 September 1860, which quoted the following letter from a local landowner to his tenants:

> Having been placed by Divine Providence here as a landowner, I feel the responsibility of my situation, and have come to the conclusion of making that use of the property entrusted to my care which I deem consistent with the religion of our blessed Saviour, by conscientiously choosing those persons to be my tenants who can and will support our Church from principle and conscience. Deeply impressed with these considerations, I feel myself morally bound to set before you two alternatives, and you are at liberty to choose for yourself, namely, either to attend our church services with your family, and thus support its principles or . . . quit the farm which you hold of me.[15]

This letter provided a typical example of what its victims sometimes called 'the screw': the use of economic power derived from landed wealth to impose the social, religious or political wishes of a landowner on his tenants and labourers. Widely used in Wales in the late 1850s and 1860s, it remained an instrument of social coercion in many areas of the country throughout the Victorian era.

Coercion, however, was effective only in 'closed parishes' (sometimes called 'squire's parishes'), where the land was concentrated entirely or almost entirely in the hands of a single individual, and where the whole community was dependent on the agrarian economy which the landowner dominated. For wherever the existence of freehold tenure or non-agrarian enterprises released sections of a local community from direct economic coercion, neither squire nor parson could extort compliance once deference had disappeared. The problem for the Church as a whole, of course, was that resort to 'the screw' in some parishes, where it continued to be feasible, left clergymen elsewhere open to insinuations of intolerance. And as the Victorian era went on the typical parson was obliged to struggle against mounting secular distractions for the voluntary support of parishioners whose religious behaviour could no longer be prescribed.

In the Victorian period the squire–parson alliance thus came to epitomize the dilemma of a Church unsure whether its monopolistic past had left it with a unique advantage or a grave handicap in the modern world. Could religiosity be prescribed, or had it become a voluntary aspect of social behaviour and human consciousness? By the middle of the nineteenth century this question had been more or less settled in the towns. Religious prescription was dead. But for the society as a whole, the legitimacy of squire and parson to exercise social leadership raised the entire question of the nature and prerogatives of national Church and territorial aristocracy alike. For the Church of England, in short, relations between clergy and landowners mirrored variations in time and place in the nature of its peculiar status as an Established Church.

Generalizations about conflict and change inevitably do injustice to the realities of particular communities, clergymen and landowners. Examples of benevolent squires working closely with diligent, respected clergymen in villages more or less untroubled by class antagonisms survived in considerable number throughout the Victorian era.[16] But the Church never really solved the problem of being bound to the landed interest, by structure and history, during a period when the landowners were locked into a protracted and often bitter struggle with other classes. Indeed, what the Rev. Llewelyn Davies, a Christian Socialist, told the Church Congress in 1873, 'that the Church of England greatly needs the help of divine grace to preserve it from an undue reverence for station and property', might serve as an epitaph for the Victorian history of relations between clergymen and landowners.[17] Yet the temptation to revere 'station and property' was strong not simply because the squire–parson alliance had worked so well in the past, but because as the nineteenth century advanced the status of the clerical profession was itself undergoing marked decline.

IV

The Victorian Church was a church reformed through wide-ranging ecclesiastical disciplines and economies imposed in the 1830s and 1840s by Parliamentary legislation, by the Ecclesiastical Commissioners, and by the enterprise and dedication of individual churchmen alarmed by evidence of Anglican decline. This reform movement made the beginning of the Victorian era a watershed in the social status of the clerical profession. Around 1830 holy orders could reasonably have been considered the most promising career open to the son of a lord or a gentleman. There might have been declining popular support for church services and mounting public criticism of the unreformed religious establishment, but the social prestige, wealth and political influence of the clergy had not been higher since before the Civil War. The proportion of Anglican bishops drawn from the peerage, for example, had reached a peak between 1810 and 1830, only to decline rapidly in the early Victorian era.[18] Likewise, the proportion of magistrates drawn from the clergy, a good measure of the social position of the clerical profession in local society, had peaked around 1830 after increasing rapidly during the previous century, and thereafter fell away to almost insignificant levels by the final quarter of the century.[19] Unlike their counterparts in Ireland and Scotland, the early Victorian clergy of the Church of England had inherited an assured and eminent position among the ruling classes in the countryside.

But the Victorian era witnessed a slow decline from this apogee of social status and influence. Fewer clerical magistrates and fewer aristocratic bishops were not the only symptoms of the change. Another was the piecemeal but effective decline of the vestry meeting as an instrument in the ordering of local communities, a process which began with sporadic defiance against vestry-levied church rates in the 1830s and ended in 1894 with the passage of the Local Government Act. Loss of clerical influence and prestige was mirrored also in patterns of clerical recruitment. For while the total number of Anglican ordinands increased during the first twenty years of the reign, the number of Oxbridge graduates fell steeply—a sure indication that a new, less privileged element was being accepted into the ministry.[20] In the generation after 1830, Owen Chadwick has pointed out, the 'social incentives' which had made the clerical profession perhaps 'the most attractive of all professions' declined noticeably.[21]

What had set in was a process of status decline which would continue throughout the Victorian era and beyond. Its causes were partly economic, and partly a reflection of the broad movement of secularization which played a major role in the evolution of Victorian society. Secularization did not depend essentially on anti-religious motives or ideas, or induce widespread loss of faith in the society; but it did gradually reduce the significance of religious ideas, functionaries and institutions in the life of the nation, and by so doing it threw religious organizations and church leaders on to the defensive. By 1901 the man in holy orders could no longer take for granted the kind of social esteem and public importance which had been normal sixty years earlier. The society had become too secular, too pluralistic; and with the undermining of a social position once secured by important magisterial, administrative and other leadership functions in a local community, the village clergyman was in danger of becoming a slightly archaic, somewhat marginal figure.

If secularization caused social and cultural problems for the Victorian Church, the day-to-day anxieties of the typical country parson probably centred more, by the end of the century, on grave economic difficulties associated with the agricultural depression. By the final quarter of the nineteenth century the income of the Church of England, still derived largely from landed wealth, was being devalued (relatively) by the increasing predominance of non-agrarian sectors in the national economy, and devalued (absolutely) by the protracted decline of British agriculture. The traditional rural community in England and Wales was threatened with de-moralization and disintegration by the twin processes of depression and de-population, and the resulting air of decay was as evident in the parsonage as in the labourer's cottage.

The Church shared directly and indirectly in the late-Victorian crisis of landed society. Pew rents fell. In one typical instance a rural deanery which had received £800 from pew rents in 1880 received only a little over £100 in 1901.[22] Depression also reduced the value of rents from glebes, and tightened the purse strings of many of the clergy's once beneficent private patrons. And worst of all in some parishes were the financial difficulties arising from decline in tithe-rent charges once the provisions of the 1836 Tithe Commutation Act began to operate in the depressed agricultural climate of the late 1870s onwards. For forty years the Act had succeeded in removing much of the acrimony and disharmony which tithing in kind had imposed on clerical relations with rural communities before 1836, but as the depression deepened the Church faced what has been called 'its worst financial crisis since the middle of the sixteenth century'.[23]

A tithe-rent charge valued at £100 in 1835 retained its value in the period up to 1877, except for a few short-term fluctuations, but in 1878 a prolonged downward movement began which by 1901 had reduced its value to less than £67.[24] All in all, clerical incomes fell drastically during the reign, although the trend was very pronounced only in its final quarter. The average clerical income in 1837 had been about £500. By 1901 it was only £246, and while the structure of the profession had changed in the intervening period with the increasing employment of curates, the distortion of the figures so produced alters the overall picture only marginally. The fall in clerical incomes represented, in real terms, a decline of at least a third.[25] It can scarcely be wondered that by the end of the Victorian era the medical profession, the civil service, and the world of business had all surpassed the clerical life in appeal to the well-educated, well-connected young men leaving the public schools.[26] Schoolboys are fairly realistic creatures and, as the Bishop of Lincoln put it to Convocation in 1901, 'the hero of the modern schoolboy is not connected with the ministerial life as it was formerly'.[27]

There may have been something heroic, but nothing particularly glamorous in the life of the country clergyman engaged in the later Victorian period in an often distressing and ultimately hopeless struggle to maintain old economic and social standards. Before the end of the century, for example, the Ecclesiastical Commissioners were beginning to worry about the problems created for later incumbents by clergy of independent means who set standards of affluence which were no longer realistic for a country parson and his family. According to Chadwick, now that his relative economic position had deteriorated, the parson seemed 'somehow less easy in society, less like ordinary gentlemen, more likely to go to a tennis party than to walk across the stubble with the farmer's shooting party'.[28] At the beginning of the reign it had been a common sight to see a country clergyman rounding his parish in the style of a gentleman, in carriage and pair: by 1901 the sight would have been a curiosity. The frock-coated ally of the squire had been replaced by a more narrowly professional, less pretentious figure, whose short black coat was practical for pedalling a bicycle along country lanes.

V

Reduced social status was not the only thing which distinguished the clergyman of 1837 from his successor of 1901; the effects of partly deliberate, partly unavoidable changes in the kinds of roles expected of him in a rural community were also important. The reformist climate of the 1830s and 1840s had initiated many criticisms of traditional clerical behaviour. In particular, as the concept of squirearchic paternalism became increasingly odious to middle- and working-class opinion, radical churchmen discovered what they called the 'gentleman heresy'. They attacked excessive clerical involvements in genteel society, and were suspicious particularly of clerical participation in the amusements of the ballroom, the card table or the hunt.[29] The objections were both vocational and social. Frivolous or boisterous amusements, it was felt, tended to vitiate the effectiveness of a clergyman as a spiritual leader; and even if the pleasures of the hunt might not adversely affect the vocational commitment of the clergyman himself, the social consequences for his relations with ordinary villagers could be unfortunate. For what was for the wealthy a sport was poaching when done by the poor!

But it was not just the traditional recreational habits of the clergy which could emphasize social distance in a now divided local community. As paternalism lost credibility, rural labourers, tradesmen and artisans demanded social justice, not charity; and the kind of 'influence' to which they responded emanated less and less from their social superiors and more and more from their peers. Their relations with the parsonage inevitably changed. Symbolizing the traditional social roles of the country parson had been the soup and blankets dispensed from the vicarage, the medical advice and assistance visited by the parson's wife, and the genteel oversight by squire and parson alike over manners and morals. New symbols, new roles, were called for by the middle of the century. It was a 'mockery', Charles Kingsley told a group of clergymen's wives in 1855, 'to visit the fever-stricken cottage while your husband leaves it in a state which breeds that fever'.[30] But it was also bad clerical business, for the mood of the rural population was often frankly hostile to any ideal of clerical behaviour based on charity or paternalism. In place of the gentleman-clergyman, the radicals argued, rural parishes needed men of 'rough exterior' who might 'show a constant sympathy with the common life'.[31]

The Victorian Church did not of course change so radically. True to its history, Anglicanism compromised between the past and the present. The ideal of the clerical gentleman remained normative, and the tendency for clergymen to see their social obligations in paternalistic terms certainly outlived Queen Victoria. But within this continuity there was profound change. An important aspect of the social transformation of Victorian society as a whole saw the 'Old Gentry'—those amateur guardians of the traditional landed interest, whose position as landowners had given them ubiquitous influence and immense authority—gradually forced to share social status and leadership with a 'New Gentry' comprised of doctors, barristers, civil servants, literary men and others, for whom education and professional competence, not landed wealth, were the guarantees of social acceptance.[32] It was the fate of the Victorian clergy to move from alliance with the 'Old Gentry' into the ranks of the 'New'. This was a slow, uneven and often largely unconscious transformation. In many cases traditional clerical roles survived in uneasy relationship with newer, more strictly professional ones. But in the long run even the country parson more or less succeeded in making the painful adjustment from the associations of the squirearchy to those of the newer professional gentry.

Less closely identified with the landed ruling classes, many clergymen tried conscientiously to behave as neutrals in the sharpening class conflicts of the age, and a significant number took leading roles in organized movements for social justice. Allotments schemes of one kind or another continued to attract clerical reformers throughout the century, mainly because they promised a reversal of the trends which were eliminating smallholdings in England and Wales, and creating instead an alienated rural proletariat. But the idea of providing allotments for the poor, as D. C. Barnett has pointed out, smacked less of 'social progress' than of 'a backward-looking appeal to a golden age of a landholding peasantry'.[33] The emergence of an essentially landless rural working class could not be halted; and although arcadian schemes for the countryside were never short of clerical supporters, by mid-century the more advanced social thinkers in the Church were coming to terms with the existence of a rural class society, and grappling with various methods of serving its divided social strata.

In 1868 the evangelical incumbent of Olveston in Gloucestershire, Edward Girdlestone, became an advocate of agricultural unionism, and after his death in 1884 he was remembered by the Agricultural Labourers' Association as 'the first man of any position' to take up their cause.[34] Girdlestone was merely the best-known of a growing number of Victorian clergymen who felt that the national Church might best serve the society by changing it. Radical enough in abstraction, their ideas generally became in practice the epitome of moderation. Where the early nineteenth-century parsons had administered parochial justice and championed the *status quo* in alliance with the great landowners, their successors initiated rural migration schemes, farm-machinery co-operatives, education projects, and community health and insurance organizations.

But Anglicanism remained the established religion of England and Wales. The Church as a whole never completely solved the problem of role conflict between its continued (if somewhat residual) privileges and responsibilities as an official body, and its efforts to serve all sections of the society. It had appeared to side 'as a body' with the landowning opponents of the Anti-Corn Law League,[35] and thirty years later it generally echoed the view of the Bishop of Gloucester, announced to a meeting of the Gloucestershire Agricultural Society, that the National Agricultural Labourers' Union was an 'iniquitous' organization.[36] The inevitable response of the rural poor was a virulent anti-clericalism which touched even those clergy who sympathized with the union, including Girdlestone. And in the period 1889–90, when under the pressures of agrarian hardship hostility to tithe rents turned into civil disobedience and violence, the role of the clergy as tithe owners and tithe recipients made them once more the targets of bitter rural protest, especially in Wales.[37]

The 'tithe war' was more or less resolved in 1891, when Parliament made landowners rather than tenants responsible for the payment of tithe-rent charges. But the legacy of such confrontations lingered long in the countryside. Even at the beginning of the twentieth century it took very little to revive the spectre of clerical oppression, or to confirm lingering suspicions that the Church of England was a subtle enemy of social justice. The role of the Anglican parson in rural society, in short, never ceased to be an ambivalent one; and at times of social crisis, especially, Nonconformity and irreligion were able to advance against a Church inescapably identified with the established social order.

VI

By the very early years of the Victorian era the growth of Nonconformity was slackening in England, and during the remainder of the century none of the Nonconformist denominations, including Methodism, escaped the grave problems which secularization, urbanization and the decline of the rural community were creating for the Church of England. In Wales the Nonconformist cause continued to gather momentum into the 1880s, by which time Welsh Nonconformists outnumbered Welsh Anglicans by three to one.[38] Not until after the great revivals of 1904–5 did Nonconformity begin to decline in Wales, and by then its position was so dominant that a reluctant Parliament was forced, a few years later, to disestablish the Anglican Church in the Principality. When Disestablishment actually took effect in 1920 it created in Wales the kind of religious situation to which English Nonconformists had aspired for almost a century: one of religious equality, in which Anglicans, state-supported no longer, would be obliged to compete or co-operate with other religious bodies without any special advantages.

The struggle between Church and Chapel became one of the great political issues of Victorian history. Over compulsory church rates, education, the access of Nonconformists to parochial graveyards, and over Disestablishment itself, Anglicanism and Dissent formed battle lines which acquired profound social and political symbolism by running precisely along the deepest divisions opened in the society by industrialization, urbanization and the associated development of liberal democracy. The Nonconformists became, in Gladstone's words, 'the backbone of British Liberalism', and despite recurrent disappointments with the slow and niggardly progress which the Liberal Party made towards the goal of religious equality, they continued to supply votes, organized support and moral fervour to the Liberal cause throughout the century. Meanwhile, the activities and attitudes of Victorian bishops, clergymen, Church Defence Associations and other Anglican bodies gave credence to the famous aphorism that the Church of England was 'the Tory Party on its knees'.

In the English and Welsh countryside these major conflicts were shaped and modified by local circumstances. In some rural parishes they were virtually non-existent. Dissenters who attended Church as well as Chapel, a parson who co-operated with the local Nonconformist minister, a landlord who was indifferent towards religion or tolerant of religious pluralism, or some combination of these factors, could effectively insulate a rural community from most of the divisive influences of the wider society. But more often, wherever rural Nonconformity existed Church–Chapel relations mirrored the social tensions of the local society. For Nonconformity was an ideal vehicle of social protest, especially because of the historic connection between the landed classes and the Church.

Examples of coercion by squire and parson certainly diminished greatly as the century progressed, but even in 1905 the *Liberator*, an organ of militant Nonconformity, was able to find contemporary examples of Nonconformist tenants harassed by Anglican landlords.[39] The legacy of bitterness could survive long after actual persecution had ceased. Joseph Arch never lost childhood memories of his parents being obliged to wait for Holy Communion until their social superiors had received it. In his autobiography the leading agricultural unionist recalled vividly an occasion when his mother's independent and assertive manner had prompted the local clergyman to reduce the family's allowance of soup and coal.[40] There were also memories of battles uniting an entire chapel community. In many rural parishes before 1868 the local Nonconformists had either used their numbers to swamp vestry meetings and defeat attempts to levy compulsory church rates, or had failed to do so and suffered distraint of goods rather than pay.[41] And until as late as 1881 bitter divisions continued to arise over clerical control of parish graveyards.

It was a measure of the depth of the divisions which had appeared in rural society after the breakdown of the dependency system that class and religious animosity was often the last element to be affected by depopulation and declining morale. The parish church and the village chapel, with emptying seats and ageing worshippers, struggled separately into the twentieth century, symbols of both the vitality and the antagonisms of an era which scarcely survived beyond the Victorian period.

VII

If this chapter has dwelt on the problems and difficulties which the Victorian Church faced in the countryside, it has done so because decline was without doubt the basic trend in the social history of rural religion after 1837. No religious group avoided it, although common problems took somewhat different forms from one denomination to another. In the case of the Church of England, oversized and ill-maintained churches and manses provided physical evidence of decline, and the reduced living standards and less assured social status of the clergy confirmed it. Indifference and overt hostility grew at the expense of the deference which once had assured the Church a major role in rural life. There were of course exceptional situations where remarkable clerical leadership and a tenacious sense of community combined to defy the processes of decline; more commonly, however, the rural parish shared in the decay of the traditional local community. It would take the motor vehicle and the commuter rail to reverse the demographic trend away from the countryside, but the new communities which such post-Victorian developments would create would be 'rural' only in a limited sense, and for the Church they would prove almost as intractable as the urban centres of which they were satellites.

Notes

1 Cobbett, 1967, 506.
2 *Ibid.*, 511.
3 BPP 1852–3 LXXXIX clxxxii.
4 See Thirsk, 1967, 2–14.
5 Gilbert, 1976, 100–1.
6 *Ibid.*, 102–3.
7 Cobden, 1878, 144.
8 *Ibid.*, 145.
9 Arnold, 1895, 84.
10 *Church Reformers' Magazine for England and Ireland*, 1832, I, 63, 249–50.
11 Ward, 1965, 72, 74.
12 See Perkin, 1969, *passim*.
13 Tate, 1967, 145.
14 Hobsbawm and Rudé, 1969, 112–3, 219–20, 229–33, 289–91.
15 Quoted in the *Freeman*, 3 October 1860, 639.
16 The fullest elaboration of this point is in Chadwick, 1970, II, 151–217.
17 *Church Congress Report*, 1873, 33.
18 Soloway, 1969, 11.
19 McClatchey, 1960, 190–1; Mingay, 1976a, 127.
20 Gilbert, 1976, 133.
21 Chadwick, 1966, I, 522.
22 *Chronicle of Convocation*, 1901, 114.
23 Best, 1964, 471.
24 *Ibid.*, 470–1.
25 Chadwick, 1970, II, 168.
26 *Chronicle of Convocation*, 1901, 146.
27 *Ibid.*, 150.
28 Chadwick, 1970, II, 170.
29 For an elaboration of this point see Heeney, 1973, 209–15.
30 Kingsley, 1855, 59.
31 *Chronicle of Convocation*, 1862, 947.
32 The distinction was drawn by Kitson Clark, 1962, 206–74.
33 Barnett, 1967, 172.
34 Perry, 1977, 301.
35 Cobden, 1878, 183.
36 Chadwick, 1970, II, 155.
37 BPP 1887 XXXVIII 250–5, 261–8.
38 On the growth of Nonconformity see Currie, Gilbert and Horsley, 1978, 140–52.
39 *Liberator*, April 1905, 55. Cf. *Liberator*, July 1905, 97; *Nonconformist*, 8 December 1875, 1223.
40 Arch, 1898, 20–4, 53–5.
41 BPP 1856 LXVIII, *passim*.

5 The Politics of Land*

R. J. Olney

I

The Victorian and early Edwardian period was the last in which the possession of vast acres was a passport to political power. The cabinets of Victoria's reign were not confined to the great landed families, but representatives of those families took their place almost effortlessly at the head of affairs. Russell, Stanley, Fitzmaurice, Cecil, Manners, Cavendish, Spencer—no government was formed between 1830 and 1900 that could not boast at least one of those names. By the 1890s the House of Lords, though diluted with landless peers, had been neither ended nor mended, and indeed could still provide a prime minister, the third Marquess of Salisbury. Many sons of peers continued to sit in the House of Commons, and the elected Commons leader of the victorious Liberal Party in 1880 was Lord Hartington, heir to the magnificent dukedom of Devonshire. The great town and country houses of the aristocracy maintained some of their importance into the age of political clubs and party organizations. Noblemen were sent to rule Ireland and India, and their younger sons continued to find berths in the civil, military and diplomatic services.

The local bases of aristocratic power appeared to be equally well preserved. It was held in 1865 that the landed aristocracy could 'still without doubt, so completely control provincial opinion, as, with the aid of the classes who habitually follow them, to select a majority of the Legislature'.[1] The claim was exaggerated. But it has been

*For permission to quote from manuscripts in private hands I am indebted to the Most Hon. the Marquess of Salisbury, His Grace the Duke of Wellington, and the National Trust.

estimated that after 1832 there were still between forty and fifty boroughs where a patron could return one of the members, if not both.[2] In the counties large landowners could muster battalions of voters, and one recent historian has written (again, with what degree of exaggeration we shall shortly see) that 'the political character of a county was decided almost entirely by its landlords, the recognized leaders of social, administrative and judicial life'.[3] This political power was based on a widespread acceptance of the social system. In 1866 John Stuart Mill deplored the 'axiom that human society exists for the sake of property in land—a grovelling superstition which is still in full force among the higher classes'.[4] Even working men could evince 'a sneaking kindness for a lord'.[5]

Such deferential views did not, however, command universal acceptance, and in a period of rapidly growing commercial and industrial wealth the existence of a politically privileged landed class was bound to provide a focus for discontents. Landed interests were involved in many political battles of the period, and added bitterness to many controversies. The great reform campaign of 1830–2 was in one of its aspects an attack on aristocratic privilege. The prolonged agitation in favour of free trade in corn threatened landlords' rents as well as farmers' profits. Religious controversy put at risk the endowments of the established Church, and the status of its bishops as spiritual peers. Legislation on Irish land tenure involved interference with the 'ordinary rules of property',[6] and home rule threatened the final destruction of the Irish landlord class.

The landed interest was most exposed to attack in Ireland, that country of impoverished small tenants and large absentee proprietors. But English landlords, too, were denounced as feudal survivals. Some reformers recommended the abolition of strict settlements and primogeniture, others, more radically, advocated the nationalization of land. Yet others wished to see the taxation of the 'unearned increment', the wealth accruing to the ground landlord from the enterprise of the capitalist and the effort of the labourer.[7] During the nineteenth century, however, the heavy artillery of the land reformers fell wide of the mark, and their grapeshot did comparatively little damage. The great estates were not nationalized, nor were their owners taxed out of existence. Despite the fears of the twelfth Duke of Somerset, the pinnacles of Burghley and the oriels of Longleat were not pulled down for the purpose of planting cabbage gardens.[8] There were many reasons why the Victorian land campaigns were only modestly successful, but among them must be counted an urban failure to understand the countryside. To examine more closely the realities of rural politics may therefore help to explain why, despite its vulnerability, the landed interest managed to survive into the twentieth century.

II

In the county constituencies the first Reform Act, passed in 1832, provided a framework that lasted substantially unchanged until 1885. In England and Wales the forty-shilling freeholders survived as the majority element in the electorate, but they were joined by voters on new qualifications, principally respectable tenant-farmers with holdings rented at £50 a year upwards. With this enlargement of the electorate went an increase in the county representation. Hitherto, apart from Yorkshire, the English counties had been single constituencies returning two members each. Now some of the larger counties were divided into two double-member constituencies, and some medium-sized counties were given a third member. Matters had to be somewhat differently arranged in Ireland, which had lost its forty-shilling freeholders in 1829, and in Scotland, which had never had any. In Ireland the enfranchisement of ten-pound leaseholders in 1832 resulted in a moderate enlargement of the electorate, and enabled county politics to be conducted in two-member constituencies similar to those in England and Wales. In Scotland, however, the ten-pound ownership and fifty-pound tenancy qualifications resulted in small single-member constituencies, lacking the characteristic traditions of county politics south of the border.[9]

The second Reform Act, passed in 1867, involved a further downward revision of property qualifications, and a further re-drawing of constituency boundaries. However, for the partial democratization of the electorate, achieved in the boroughs by the introduction of the householder franchise in 1867, the counties had to wait until 1884. Throughout the period 1832–85 the counties were distinguishable in general from the boroughs by their more aristocratic representation, their comparative weakness of party organization, their less frequent contests and (an obviously related factor) the greater expense of contests when they did take place. Although the 1832 Reform Act preserved the over-representation of the boroughs in terms of population,[10] it gave rural interests the chance to consolidate themselves in the counties. The rights of borough residents to vote in counties were restricted, and borough politicians began to leave the counties to their own devices, thus widening the gulf between town and country. By 1841 the Whigs regretted what they had done.[11] 'I always thought', wrote Lord Spencer to Lord John Russell, 'that in our Reform measure we gave rather too great a preponderance to the Landed interest.'[12]

When it came to the promotion of candidates for county seats, it is undeniable that the nobility and gentry were able to maintain a virtual hegemony down to 1885. In Worcestershire the choice of candidates was 'in the hands of two or three magnates of no particular note'.[13] When Walter Long was adopted for North Wiltshire in 1880, he was summoned to a meeting at Chippenham that consisted of 'about half-a-dozen country gentlemen', who deliberated for no more than a quarter of an hour before offering him the candidacy.[14] The county families were a small and partially in-bred class, and it is not surprising that they preferred private arrangements to public strife. They entered into compacts with their opponents to avoid contests and preserve the 'peace of the county', and they looked askance at partisan agitations. Constituency associations were formed to assist paid agents to get voters on to the register, but were not encouraged to express their views on the selection of candidates until late in the century. Dorset, a particularly Boeotian county, was found in 1880 to have no Conservative organization at all.[15]

But although the landed proprietors were generally successful in getting themselves returned to Parliament, they were not always successful in avoiding the expense and ill-feeling of a contested election. A county might enjoy peace for several years, only to be disrupted at last by an outbreak of political animosity. Banners were then unfurled, bills posted and squibs distributed. Music played and drink flowed. Canvassers poached on hostile manors, and bands of roughs were encouraged to make sallies into enemy territory. Neighbours quarrelled, and old scores were settled. It was as if the tensions in an apparently peaceful society required a periodic outlet. Two rival interests might be at war, as in the Flintshire election of 1841, when Glynne fought Grosvenor. In a new division, such as North Devon in 1868, the relative strengths of the parties had to be tested. But in other cases contests were precipitated when a sitting member offended his agricultural constituents.

Difference in outlook between the nobility and the gentry could also spoil the harmony of rural politics. In the English counties magnates could not behave as though they were dealing with a proprietary borough. The dukes of Rutland could not exercise in North Leicestershire the kind of control to which the dukes of Sutherland were accustomed in the county of their title. The grander a peer, the more likely he was to spend much of his time outside his own county. The consequence was a certain remoteness from local affairs, and a certain contempt for the average rural elector. 'The agricultural animal', observed Lord Henry Bentinck, 'certainly feeds on very coarse fodder.'[16] The gentry, on the other hand, knew their localities well, and moreover valued the social distinction of representing their county in Parliament. 'Kings might make peers', said Coke of Norfolk in 1820, 'but they could not make a County Member.'[17] When a peer, from partisan or family motives, attempted to bring forward his own nominee, there could be resentment in the county from political friends and opponents alike. In national politics, however, it was the gentry who revealed their political weakness. Their natural role was that of a country party of back-benchers, and they lacked the skills of the parliamentary orator and tactician. Even when putting forth their full strength during the battle to save the corn laws in 1846, they were difficult to manage. 'The squires cannot in the least comprehend our schemes of voting,' wrote Stafford O'Brien to Disraeli.[18]

Whig or Tory, peer or squire, the landowner who chose to exercise political influence could normally rely on the support and co-operation of his tenants and dependants. The almost complete unanimity of voting on many estates was attributed by some to coercion, by others to the unthinking deference of the lower orders to their superiors' wishes. In reality the apparently simple phenomenon was the product of a variety of factors, the relative importance of which varied from voter to voter, from estate to estate, and from period to period. In politics, as in other things, the Victorian age was one of transition in the countryside, as new motives informed old patterns of behaviour. The landlord continued to regard the possession of property as entitling him to influence the actions and even the thoughts of those who lived under him. But the 'legitimate' or allowable extent of this influence was shrinking. To evict a tenant for voting the wrong way was already unacceptable, in England if not in the

Celtic fringe, and even threats of eviction, however veiled, were widely condemned by the middle of the century. Whig landlords were accustomed to state publicly that they respected the conscientious scruples of their tenants, though their agents might drop heavy hints in private.

Tenants had a range of motives for wishing to oblige their landlords. Most English farmers grew up in the tradition that at least one of their two votes was due to their landlord almost as a matter of course, and the tradition seems to have survived, albeit much weakened, to the end of the century and beyond. But they also believed that something was due to them in return—a farm rented at slightly less than its full commercial value, fixtures kept in good repair, and consideration if rent day fell at a time of temporary financial embarrassment. A parliamentary committee stated in 1869 that inducements to vote in the desired way proceeded 'rather from the hope of future advantages to be conferred than from the fear of injury to be inflicted'.[19] So willing were tenants to oblige that they sometimes withheld their promises until their landlord had given an indication of his views.

Landlord–tenant relations varied from region to region, the main factor being the wealth and status of the tenant–farmer class. In Ireland evictions were not unknown, though they were much less common than milder forms of retaliation, such as distraints for arrears of rent or loss of abatements.[20] In Scotland the small tenants were susceptible to direct instruction from landlords or agents, but the large leaseholders, investing their capital in permanent improvements, could take the view that politics formed no part of their bargain with their landlords. In the famous case of the East Lothian farmer, George Hope of Fenton Barns, his politics were publicly at variance with those of his landlord. In the end his lease was not renewed, but by then he could afford to retire to his own estate.[21] In England, too, there was a wide range within the farming class, from the small tenants of Cheshire, said to be worse educated than their labourers, to the prosperous agriculturalists of Norfolk, Lincolnshire or Northumberland. In 1852 twenty or so Northumberland tenant farmers, paying between them £32,000 a year in rent, urged the adoption of two Conservative candidates, and both seats were in fact carried in the ensuing contest.[22]

Promising one's vote, and going to the poll to record it, were all part of the open and public style of politics so characteristic of rural society. Both landlord and tenant took pride in making a public demonstration of their harmony of feeling. The idea that one's vote was a matter of private conscience, to be given secretly and soberly, was slow to gain ground, and even the introduction of the ballot does not appear to have had a profound effect on the political mores of the countryside. It is also important to remember (though the fact is less easily detectable from the poll books) that a strong interest reached beyond the estate on which it centred. A landowner with a direct interest in the representation of his county would work hard to maintain a network of connection and obligation that involved tradesmen and professional men as well as farmers. Money spread around the district was essential to success, and subscriptions to the county hospital and investment in a local railway line were alike productive of political capital. Beyond this was the realm of popularity, fostered above all by the generous support of a pack of fox-hounds. The county member who depended on the narrower and more direct forms of influence was always more vulnerable than the 'popular' type of member, and what he saved in subscriptions might well be mulcted from him in the form of huge election bills.

In England these landed interests, even in their wider and less concentrated form, could never cover a whole county. Counties like Cambridgeshire or Lincolnshire had whole districts where landed influence was weak, if not altogether non-existent. These were the regions of large parishes and small proprietors, where no country seat, park, plantation or fox covert gave variety to the landscape. Even where the countryside bore the usual signs of estate management, there were parishes, often owned by corporations but sometimes by individuals, where no regular influence existed. Estate or 'close' parishes were interspersed with open parishes whose freeholders liked to show their independence of the neighbouring great houses. 'Think of the beauty of the forty-shilling freeholder!' exclaimed Cobden.[23] Alas, the average rural freeholder, returning home drunk in a wagon after having performed his constitutional duty, was not a particularly beautiful sight.

In many counties the urban and industrial freeholders were more politically important than the rural. Indeed, no English county could claim to be purely rural or agricultural. In the most rural between a quarter and a half of the population was concentrated in the towns, and no more than a third of the adult male population was directly employed in agriculture. In several counties miners or fishermen, both prone to dissent and radicalism, constituted pockets of independence, although comparatively few of them possessed the vote. In Berkshire, a mainly agricultural county, the non-corporate towns of Maidenhead, Newbury and Hungerford provided support for the Liberal cause.[24] In North Durham the large (but by no means exclusively rural) interests of Lords Durham and Londonderry were counterbalanced by an exceptionally high proportion of urban freeholders.[25] Moreover, despite the fact that urban politicians neglected the early and mid-Victorian countryside, borough voters carried weight in some rural county divisions. Some 1,500 Leicester freeholders were reckoned to have votes for South Leicestershire in 1867.[26] The great cities and industrial towns were bound to make their proximity felt in neighbouring counties— London in Buckinghamshire, Surrey and Essex, Birmingham in Warwickshire, and Manchester in Cheshire.

How far did the agricultural boroughs make up for the industrial counties? Despite the extinction of fifty-six small boroughs in 1832, a number of very moderate-sized market towns retained the privilege of returning at least one member. Lymington, Thetford and Wenlock, to name three towns of under 4,000 inhabitants in 1841, retained both their representatives. Such places were dependent for their trade on the surrounding countryside, and their leading men—brewers, bankers, solicitors, corn merchants—had close ties with the farming class. It is not surprising, therefore, that at times of agricultural depression and discontent borough voters showed a strong sympathy with their county neighbours. Almost all the Berkshire borough members opposed Peel in 1846, and in Lincolnshire a medal was struck in 1852 to commemorate the return of protectionists for all thirteen county and borough seats. Following earlier precedents, a number of boroughs had been greatly enlarged in 1832, and extensive tracts of countryside had swelled the rural element in their electorates.

Before the passage of the first Reform Act the Duke of Wellington had described the close boroughs as the 'true protectors of the landed interest'.[27] Although in this sense the Act was a blow to the great proprietors, they did not all lose their patronage, and after 1832 Bruces continued to sit for Marlborough, Fitzmaurices for Calne, Churchills for Woodstock, and Foresters for Wenlock. Boundary extension brought in many cases an accession of landed influence. In boroughs such as Horsham, where no single interest was dominant, party politics were closely related to the allegiances and activities of neighbouring landowners.[28] Occasionally two landed families struggled for supremacy over many years, as did the Erle-Draxes and Calcrafts at Wareham.[29]

Despite these rural connections, the small boroughs developed their own style of politics. Deference counted for less than in the counties, money, party management and personalities for more. Indeed, in some English and more Irish boroughs, money counted for everything. Between parliamentary elections partisan feelings were kept alive by municipal politics, and by religious issues such as the payment of church rates or the establishment of burial boards. Factions festered in the smoking rooms of back-street public houses, and the urban middle class of tradesmen and shopkeepers set the prevailing tone. As Wellington wrote to a friend in 1832, 'I don't know of anything so disgusting as the details of the little intrigues and oppression of little Authority in a small town.'[30]

Clergymen, doctors and butchers might vote Conservative, but they were outvoted by dissenting shoemakers and radical grocers. Farmers were not infrequently borough voters, even in such places as Leeds and Oldham, but they could not make themselves felt as a class.[31] In 1867 a number of agricultural labourers came on to the register in the large rural boroughs, though they were not as yet politically aroused. George Howell, the trade unionist, made little rural impact at Aylesbury, and George Brodrick, the future author of *English Land and English Landlords*, had only moderate success among the poor men at the gates of Blenheim.[32]

III

Hitherto in this chapter the farming class has been considered mainly in the context of landlord–tenant relations. An account of the mechanics of rural politics—the selection of candidates and the exercise of influence—is bound to centre on the activities of the great landowners. But the historian intent on eavesdropping in aristocratic drawing rooms may fail to notice the equally important activities of the market place. The 1832 Reform Act gave new stature to the market town by making it a polling place for county elections. Market-day dinners or ordinaries were a natural place for farmers and their friends to discuss political questions, and for M.P.s to meet their constituents. A new county member, having braced himself to make a tour of duty and condescension through his division, would soon discover that farmers, though generally quiescent, could hold strong views on questions that directly affected their livelihood. Moreover, though a scattered class, and disinclined to formal organization, they could on occasion transform their after-dinner grumblings into an effective agitation.

The political consciousness of the farmers has been under-rated, partly because they were normally content to leave the county representation in aristocratic hands. A prosperous agriculturalist might achieve the income of a small squire, but he continued to respect the cultural distance between his own class and the class above him. This distance was perhaps most clearly marked in the early Victorian period, but it did not lessen greatly in the more prosperous mid-century years of high farming. Standing for a rural constituency was a very expensive matter, and few small squires, let alone farmers, could call on two or three thousand pounds of ready cash for electioneering purposes. Of course it was possible to be returned free of expense, as was the tenant-farmer Edward Ball for Cambridgeshire in 1852.[33] A few farmer-politicians were carried into Parliament on the crest of a particular agitation, as was the Norfolk farmer, Clare Sewell Read, by the anti-malt tax movement in 1865. But generally speaking the average working farmer would no more think of standing for Parliament than of putting up for a London club or renting a grouse moor.

The farmers' acceptance of their social position was perhaps the central element in their political conservatism. They wished to preserve the stable society in which they found themselves, and to defend rural culture against the onslaughts of the large manufacturing towns. The march of mind had no appeal to the agriculturalist: the philosophical radicals could not influence the weather, unless perhaps to make it worse. In these views many farmers found themselves in accord with their equally conservative landlords. As a prominent Whig complained,

> The evil of the fifty-pound tenants is that they agree in opinion with their landlords, and their landlords are against us mainly on Corn Laws and such things. There is little or no need of coercion, for they vote according to their own prejudices.[34]

The retention of the corn laws was the ideal platform on which to display the unanimity of landlord and tenant. When the farmers led the way, as they did in 1843–4 they were nevertheless concerned to carry the landowners with them. When in 1846 the landed interest in Parliament had to fight with their backs to the wall, they needed to show that the agricultural constituencies were fighting with them.[35] The essentially conservative nature of the protectionist programme was a large part of its appeal, an appeal that extended to districts dependent much more on dairying or livestock production than on the wheat crop. The fluctuations of the corn market, especially in the weeks after harvest, were a convenient indicator of agricultural prosperity in general, and when farmers met on market days the price of corn was bound to be uppermost in their minds. Even after the defeat of 1846 the farmers did not give up, and some of the bitterest constituency battles to reverse the decision of the country were fought in 1852, when the issue was rapidly passing out of the realm of practical politics.

Thenceforward the issue went underground. Few farmers became convinced free traders, but in public they turned to questions such as the repeal of the malt tax, which had a particular attraction in the sheep and barley regions, and the reform of the rating system to alleviate the 'burdens on land'. This did not satisfy the radicals, who wished to follow up their triumph and complete the destruction of the landed interest. To this end they urged tenant-farmers to agitate about matters on which their interests were at variance with those of their landlords, such as the repeal of the Game Laws and the establishment of compulsory tenant-right. Farmers were also encouraged to demand the end of the magistrates' monopoly in county government. The response of the farmers to these promptings in the late 1840s was disappointing from the radical point of view. Even in the 1880s, when substantial progress was achieved on all these issues, it was neither preceded nor accompanied by a class war (at least in England) of tenants against their landlords. In the 1870s an attempt to get the farmers to side with the labourers against the landlord system had met with even less success. 'Farmer and labourer had improved the land together', wrote Joseph Arch, 'but the landlord took the increase thereof.'[36] It would have been nearer the truth to say that landowner and farmer had evolved a system of reciprocal advantage, based on the exploitation of the labourer.

Where the economic discontents of the small farmers were most inflammable was where they were fuelled by political dissent, as in the Welsh timber war of the 1880s.[37] A few English counties had significant numbers of Baptists and Independents, but the predominant religious sect among the farmers was that of the Wesleyan Methodists, a much less militant, and for the Liberals less reliable, brand of nonconformity. At times of political excitement, such as the early 1830s, the mid-1860s, or the late 1870s, the Wesleyans counted among the reformers in rural politics. But in bad times they might be found voting for a Conservative agricultural candidate, and when the Scarlet Woman reared her head they would rush to the defence of their creed. Below a vein of anti-clericalism in the countryside lay a deeper vein of Protestant prejudice. The outbursts of feeling at the time of Catholic emancipation[38] were repeated, though less vociferously, when the Roman Catholic hierarchy was established in England in 1850. As late as the 1890s the idea of granting home rule to Catholic Ireland was a stumbling block to otherwise loyal rural Gladstonians, and ritualism in the Church of England became a popular target for attack.

Before 1832 reforming sentiments in the counties had been fed as much by the tradition of independence as by religious dissent. County members were fond of proclaiming their independence of ministers, and more radical politicians encouraged the small freeholders to vote independently of the large landowners. Demands for retrenchment and reform were aimed not only at political corruption but also at economic mismanagement, and could therefore appeal to farmers in times

66

of depression. The survival of this feeling helps to explain the real, if moderate, reforming enthusiasm of the rural districts in the period 1830–2. But thenceforward independence lost its relevance in county politics, and the cry of retrenchment was lost in that of protection. The excitements of the next big reform agitation in the mid 1860s found only muted echoes in the agricultural constituencies.

IV

The third Reform Act and subsequent redistribution of seats (1884–5) effected the transformation of rural politics that the second Reform Act had postponed. Towns with fewer than 15,000 inhabitants ceased to be parliamentary boroughs, and in the counties the extension of the franchise to (male) householders greatly increased the electorate. The old two- and three-member county divisions disappeared, to be replaced by smaller single-member constituencies with very little county character. The number of polling districts was increased, and the focus of rural politics shifted from the town to the village. County members found the burden of constituency work, already growing in the early 1880s, even heavier. Although the rural electorate was enlarged, the farming element was proportionately diminished, and it was no longer sufficient for M.P.s to confine their attentions to a few agricultural meetings. As J. W. Lowther wrote to Sir Stafford Northcote, 'every petty hamlet expects its member or members to pay annual visits in person as well as contribute to its local charities etc etc'.[39] The period 1885–1900, after the third Reform Act and before the appearance of the motor car, was the most strenuous in English rural politics.

As the mode of politics changed, so did its content. The farmers were suffering from a severe depression in wheat prices, but protection, however disguised, was no longer a popular cause. The newly enfranchised labourers were as attached to the maintenance of cheap bread as any section of the urban electorate, and the older men amongst them could recall the starvation days before 1846. In the early 1890s an attempt was made to associate the political interests of landowner, farmer and labourer in a National Agricultural Union, whose programme involved the movement of rents and wages with the price of corn, but the labourers received it with little favour. Nor, despite the claims of politicians, were they passionately interested in obtaining the three acres that were needed to graze a cow. What they did want was allotments in convenient positions and at reasonable rents.[40] The loss of common rights was in some places a fresh wound, and the red vans of the Land Restoration League, advocating the reassertion of popular rights in the soil, were welcomed in many villages in the 1890s.[41] The labourers (and especially the Primitive Methodists amongst them) also wished to see free, unsectarian elementary education and the reform of the licensing laws. They were often described as innocent and gullible, and as having 'extremely crude ideas of representative government'.[42] Yet they could draw on many years' experience of parish politics, in struggles over charities, allotments and schools. They had learned organization in the Methodist class meeting, the friendly society and, latterly, the trade union branch. In their local battles it was the clergy and above all the farmers, rather than the landowners, by whom they had most frequently been confronted. The strikes and lock-outs of 1872–4 showed the true lines of division in the countryside, and their legacy of class bitterness was far from spent by 1885.

The farmers resented the emancipation of the labourers all the more because it had been achieved with the aid of urban politicians. The original impetus of Primitive Methodism, that leaven of the village mind, had come from the industrial towns. In the 1870s Arch's National Agricultural Labourers' Union was moulded and directed by Birmingham politicians. In other ways, too, rural politics were being partially urbanized several years before 1885. In the late 1870s a wave of dissenting enthusiasm swept the market towns, and local party associations were formed on the Birmingham model. The Liberal Party had notable successes in the counties at the general election of 1880, but they were due not so much to a Whig revival, or to militancy among the farmers, as to the fact that the towns were at last exerting a strong influence on rural politics.[43] The third Reform Act and consequent redistribution of seats further strengthened the urban element in the counties, and encouraged the emergence of new middle-class politicians soon to take a greater part in local affairs as county councillors and aldermen.

Despite the activity of the townsmen, and the favourable predisposition of many labourers, the Liberals failed to establish a secure hold on the English counties after 1885. In some divisions, such as North-West Norfolk or South-East Suffolk, they benefited from a strongly nonconformist and well-unionized labouring vote, and from a certain weakness in upper-class influence.[44] But everywhere they had to contend with the solid unionism of landowners, the growing Conservatism of the small towns as the depression deepened, and the relentless Toryism of the farmers. Liberal associations found it hard to obtain local candidates, and they could not match their opponents when it came to subscriptions. At elections, conveyances to take voters to the poll were virtually a Conservative monopoly, and in some constituencies non-resident voters could decide a contest in the Conservatives' favour. The wives of the gentry came out in splendour as Primrose Dames, eclipsing the female Liberals. And doubts continued about the real secrecy of the ballot.[45] The alleged coercion of tenants by their landlords was nothing to the way in which some farmers put pressure on their work-people.

Enough has been said to indicate that the landed interest had not been entirely extinguished. Territorial considerations had lost their importance in rural politics, and the landowning monopoly of the county representation came to an end in 1885. A few country gentlemen continued to hold their seats, but they did so more precariously. Walter Long was defeated in the Devizes division of Wiltshire in 1892, Henry Chaplin in the Sleaford division of Lincolnshire in 1906. Others, their incomes in rapid decline, left the field to carpet-baggers or local upstarts. What the landowners lost in real power, however, they gained in other ways. They exchanged an exposed position for a much more easily defensible one. The Whigs, alarmed by

Gladstone's plans for Ireland, almost unanimously left the Liberal Party, and the landed interest closed its ranks. It did not do so in isolation, however, but as part of a wider propertied interest that included brewers, bankers, industrialists and railway directors. At the same time the depression took some of the steam out of the land reform campaign. Agricultural landlords were now receiving precious little unearned increment from their property, and the rural problem came to be seen as something wider than the landlord system. There was now more political capital in creating small estates than in destroying big ones, and greater national advantage in keeping labourers on the land than in driving the aristocracy from it.

Moreover, viewed from the countryside itself, the political changes had not been accompanied by equally sweeping social ones. The great estates were not yet breaking up, and traditional ties, though perhaps weaker, had not yet dissolved. As late as 1904, when Lord Wimborne changed his politics, the tenants on his Dorset estate were expected to do the same.[46] Lord Wimborne's money came from South Wales steel, and there were others like him who used urban wealth for the maintenance of rural style and influence. The towns may have become more vocal, the open villages more politically conscious, but landed influence shrank rather than crumbled. Tenants in bad times needed tolerant landlords, although once an old tenant had sold up and gone the new one might not be so deferential. And the emancipation of the labouring class was not accomplished quickly: deference lingered there too. The landed interest, benefiting perhaps from a certain agility gained in the hunting field, had not yet been forced into the last ditch.

Notes

1 Sanford and Townsend, 1865, 3.
2 Gash, 1953, 438–9.
3 Hanham, 1959, 6.
4 British Library of Political and Economic Science: Mill-Taylor collection, vol. 3, f.42, Mill to Fawcett, 1 January 1866.
5 A phrase doubtfully attributed by G. M. Young to Gladstone (*Victorian England, Portrait of an Age*, 2nd edn., 1953, 84).
6 BM Add. MS 44104, f. 181, Gladstone to an agitated Duke of Argyll, 15 June 1880.
7 F.M.L. Thompson, 1965, *passim*.
8 Saint Maur, 1880, 151.
9 Gash, 1953, 34–64.
10 *Ibid.*, 90.
11 Moore, 1976, 256 ff.
12 PRO 30/22/4A//263, 2 May 1841.
13 Bridges, 1906, 48.
14 Long, 1923, 71.
15 Cornford, 1963, 47.
16 Disraeli (Hughenden) Papers, B/XXI/B/356, Bentinck to Disraeli, 15 January 1850.

17 Quoted by B. D. Hayes, 'Politics in Norfolk 1750–1832', unpublished Cambridge Ph.D. thesis, 1957, 20.
18 Stewart, 1971, 63.
19 BPP 1868–9 VIII 17.
20 Hoppen, 1977, 88.
21 Hope, 1881, 314–22.
22 McCord and Carrick, 1966, 96.
23 Bright and Rogers, 1870, 334.
24 Gash, 1953, 300.
25 Nossiter, 1975, 58–60.
26 Mackay, 1908, 203.
27 Gash, 1953, 6.
28 Albery, 1927, 272 *et passim*.
29 Hanham, 1959, 52.
30 Wellington (Apsley House) Papers, portfolio 218, Wellington to the Rev. G. R. Gleig, 10 January 1832.
31 Vincent, 1967, 14 *et passim*.
32 Davis, 1972, 207; Brodrick, 1900, 148–53.
33 Moore, 1976, 304.
34 PRO 30/22/4A/224, Sir Charles Wood to Lord John Russell, 15 April 1841.
35 Mosse, 1947, 134; Lawson-Tancred, 1960, 162 ff.
36 Arch, 1898, 129.
37 Dunbabin, 1974, 211–31.
38 Julia H. Andrews, 'Political Issues in the County of Kent', Unpublished London M. Phil. thesis, 1967, 144–52.
39 Salisbury (Hatfield) Papers, Lowther to Northcote, 20 November 1884.
40 Ashby, 1961, 114.
41 Springall, 1936, 112.
42 Bourne, 1955, 173.
43 Olney, 1973, 247.
44 Pelling, 1967, 97, 101.
45 Pelling, 1967, 12–13.
46 BPP 1910 LXVIII 453.

6 The Regions and Their Issues: Wales

David W. Howell

I

Welsh agriculture and the Welsh rural community differed in many ways from their counterparts in England. One vital respect was that the farming of Wales formed a part of the 'highland zone' of pastoral farming which lay roughly north-west of a line drawn from the mouth of the river Tees to the mouth of the river Exe. Within this area as a whole agriculture was characterized by family farms, lack of capital, and backward methods, and by a class of peasant tenants who were stubbornly attached to the old ways and mentally orientated towards a semi-subsistence farming.

The problems facing the farmers of Wales were of a different kind from those experienced in the sunnier, cereal-producing 'lowland zone' to the south-east. The mixed farming, with a livestock and dairying emphasis, shielded the farmers of the highland zone from the acute depressions in corn production which periodically smote the occupants of the heavy clay areas. In addition, the farmers in the highland zone lived frugally at the best of times, merely expecting their land to pay the rent rather than make them a fortune, and so they were psychologically better equipped to withstand adversity than were the cereal producers.[1]

The pressure of poverty, over-population, and rising demand for holdings remorselessly ground down the peasantry of the highland zone. The Welsh situation, however, was additionally affected by the separate socio-cultural factors of the Principality. The deeply felt ties of the nonconformist chapels and the Welsh language, which made people reluctant to leave the locality, together with the fact

71

that the status deriving from possession of a farm was enhanced in a society where the gentry had abandoned their 'natural' role as leaders, certainly intensified the raging land hunger of the Welsh peasantry.[2] Again, the limited prospect that men of capital would settle in the region, and the dearth of information about new farming ideas, were acute local problems.[3] Finally, many contemporary Radicals believed that the low level of farming was essentially the harmful consequence of the widening of the gap between the anglicized, Anglican, and Tory landowners and their Welsh-speaking, Nonconformist, and Liberal tenants. Such a rift, they emphasized, was significantly absent in English landed society: whereas in England there was a 'community of feeling and of interest' between landlords and their tenants, 'there did not exist that community of feeling between landlords and tenants in Wales which alone could make agriculture successful'.[4] It was this absence of good relations which accounted for the tenants' debilitating feelings of insecurity and their consequent servile, fawning behaviour towards their landlords. The latter were accused of cynically manipulating land hunger and permitting secret bidding in order to charge high rents, of failing to recognize the seriousness of agricultural depression in the 1880s and 1890s, of raising rents upon tenants' improvements, of neglecting to improve their estates, of administering harshly the game laws, of favouring churchmen before Nonconformists in the selection of tenants, and of capriciously evicting occupants from their holding for political and religious reasons.[5] This picture of Welsh tenants living in terror thus matched some of the worst features of the land system in Ireland. Such a vexed situation, it was urged by the Nonconformist Radicals in the last quarter of the century, made it imperative that separate legislation be granted to Wales along the same lines as that achieved for Ireland—the implementation of a land court to secure 'fair rents', fixity of tenure, and free sale.[6]

II

There is no doubting the crucial role of dissent and Liberalism in imbuing the Welsh peasantry with a new set of values that were ultimately to topple the political and social ascendancy of the landlords and thereby hasten the drive to modernization within the Principality. Already by the years of the Rebecca Riots, 1839–43, peasant resentment was apparent towards what they deemed to be injustices and abuses within the old society, and much of the animus was provided by religious dissent.[7] One informed observer wrote to Sir James Graham in 1843: 'I find the tithes excite the greatest dislike, then poor rates (church rates they hardly know anything about) and the high amount of the rents.'[8] Although tithe commutation in south Wales (and in this area alone) was aggravated in some localities by an increase in net tithe payments after commutation of between 20 and 50 per cent,[9] dislike of tithes stemmed as much, if not more, from religious principle as from financial hardship.[10] Nonconformity also accounted for some of the hostility harboured towards the New

Poor Law.[11] The influence of the Nonconformist preachers in shaping the discontent felt within the rural community was emphasized by the poor law assistant commissioner, William Day, in 1843:

> The landlords are most of them of the old Church and King school—the tenantry are almost all Dissenters, with a spice of the fanaticism of the Covenanters about them. Still there is—or rather has been—a sort of feudal deference existing between the parties—but I suspect it to be the result of habit, rather than of feeling resulting from conviction, and which may readily be put aside on a change of circumstances. There is moreover another class more powerful perhaps than even the landlord—and this is the Preachers—and the great bulk of the population are as much in their hands as the Papists of Ireland in the hands of their priests.[12]

At this time of acute economic crisis for the peasantry there was, indeed, no mistaking the antipathy felt towards the squires as a class for their high rents and their frequently arrogant, unsympathetic conduct as magistrates, particularly in administration of the poor laws. Yet the riots were not an ideologically inspired anti-landlord movement.[13]

With the work of the Welsh Nonconformist press, and in particular of the Liberation Society in the 1850s and 1860s, traditional Nonconformist grievances were channelled into a radical and distinctly Welsh political programme.[14] The imminence of the conflict between tenants and landlords was clearly sensed, a clash the squires foresaw with annoyance and indignation. Thus in 1852 E. C. L. Fitzwilliams of Cilgwyn, Cardiganshire, wrote to Lord Emlyn of Golden Grove, Carmarthenshire, concerning the parliamentary election for the Cardigan boroughs:

> Mr Richard Jenkins writes me that the preaching influence was exerted to the utmost at every place. If all Landlords do not unite as one man to repel the invasion in these Counties, by making their displeasure felt in the unmistakable way of putting a termination to the connexion of landlord and tenant..., and dealing only with [ie, supporting] those tradesmen who will support the landlords and their interest, they will be acting with great folly from a present feeling as to what is the natural course of proceeding for self preservation.[15]

Landlords were on the offensive, and the story of the petulant, vicious political evictions of 1859 and 1868 is well known. Recrimination flowed fast: the charges of the Nonconformist Radical leaders that tenants regarded 'with dread' the consequences of voting according to their consciences were met by the landlords' insistence that their coercive measures and threats were merely a legitimate counter to the 'chapel screw'.[16] Lord Cawdor's agent wrote with indignation to his lordship on 21 May 1869:

> It ought to be represented to the World that at the last election there was not more interference by the Conservative than by the Radical Landlords—

> with the freedom of voting by their tenants—and certainly nothing to be compared with the systematic intimidation by the Dissenting Preachers.[17]

By this time it was manifest that the 'chapel screw' was a power which the landed gentry could not hope to meet: in fact, spiritual pressure replaced economic sanctions as a subtle form of coercion.

Dr. K. O. Morgan has stressed the crucial significance of the evictions in furnishing the Welsh Liberal cause with its first martyrs. 'For half a century', he writes, 'the memory of the homeless victims of 1868 powerfully stimulated the radical cause on the platform and in the press.'[18] The attack on the landlords did not reach its bitterest intensity until the mid-1880s when to the old charges of political tyranny and religious discrimination was added the new one of economic oppression.[19] Clearly, the fact that the depression in Welsh livestock and dairy farming really began only in the mid-1880s had much to do with the emergence of a Welsh Land Question at this particular time. With the Irish and the Scottish crofters' land agitation providing a powerful stimulus, local 'land leagues' were instituted in Caernarvonshire and Flintshire at the beginning of 1886, and in February Michael Davitt addressed meetings at Flint and Blaenau Ffestiniog (Merioneth).[20] (Likewise, in the impoverished years of Rebecca her 'children' called for security of tenure, as was then advocated in Ireland.)[21]

Significantly, it was the landowners' championing from 1886 of the Church's cause over tithes which did most to fuel the powerful campaign against landlords in the Nonconformist vernacular press. The *Baner* newspaper announced with venomous satisfaction in August 1887:

> If the Church and Tory landlords were to leave their tenants alone, they would make short and unceremonious work of the tithe. The landlords are fools enough to shield the clergy. The effect of this will be to change, or rather to extend, the battlefield.[22]

Hatred of tithes, we have seen, reached back into the early part of the century. Opposition to the system mounted with the greater politicization of the community in the later decades. The 'Tithe Wars' of the late 1880s and early 1890s were sparked off by the acute fall—by at least a third—in the price of livestock in 1885 and 1886. Farmers complained that although the tithe-rent charge had fallen, it had not dropped sufficiently because of the operation of the seven years' average.[23] The first agitation towards gaining a reduction occurred in Denbighshire in January 1886, and when the farmers' requests were refused and distraints were made on their goods, there came into being the Anti-Tithe League of early September, ostensibly to support the farmers in their efforts towards gaining rebates.[24] The farmers' plight was genuine enough, but upon reflection it is perhaps surprising that far more trouble should have occurred in Wales than in south-eastern England where the community was more heavily tithed and agricultural depression more keenly felt.[25] Once again, the power of Nonconformity and the brilliant propaganda of its leaders explain

74

the Tithe Wars of the Principality. John Lloyd, member of the London County Council and chairman of the Tithe Question Association, wrote to Stuart Rendel: 'The Welsh have their grievance, and the English corn-growing counties have theirs, the one religious and the other pecuniary.'[26] The Nonconformist leadership of the league grasped the troubled economic situation as an opportunity for advancing sectarian and political ends. Farmers who strongly resented tithes on political grounds were now particularly malleable: they were ready to follow the advice of their leaders to oppose tithes on principle, as a step towards the achievement of disestablishment and disendowment.

The attack on Welsh landlords by the Nonconformist Radical leaders from the mid-1880s was unmerciful: the *Baner* pronounced in November 1887: 'The landowners of our country are, in general, cruel, unreasonable, unfeeling, and unpitying men.' It certainly weakened the old ties of loyalty and respect which had hitherto existed between many owners and their tenants despite their wide differences in politics and religion. Tenants now became far more critical of their landlords. Besides continuing their traditional and legitimate hostility towards issues like the game laws, consolidation of holdings, and (from the 1870s) sales of property without compensation to tenants, they came to question conditions which they had formerly accepted as the natural order of things. Pinched by depression, they gave support to land reform as a means of gaining immediate rent reductions, though not to free sales of land which, by capitalizing the effects of land hunger, would have led to rack-renting of the tenants to come.[27]

III

If the campaign of the preachers, editors, and politicians led many farmers to support measures directed towards land reform it would nevertheless be unwise to overstress the degree of the breakdown of the old relations. No spontaneous mass tenant movement for land reform occurred as in Ireland and the Western Highlands of Scotland despite the efforts of the vernacular press to establish a Welsh land league.[28] The direct action taken to prevent the levying of tithes contrasted strongly with the absence of any such direct action as a boycott of payment of rent. The poor response of the Welsh farmers to both Michael Davitt and his Welsh friend, the land nationalizer, Dr Pan Jones, needs to be emphasized.[29] Similarly, it is not so much that tenants were afraid to testify before the Welsh Land Commission of the early 1890s (as the party of agitation argued) as that the land reformers had overestimated the degree to which the old landlord–tenant relationships had crumbled.[30]

The influence of Nonconformity was paramount, and its dedicated leaders often exaggerated the evils of Welsh 'landlordism' as a means of achieving the goals of political democracy and national fulfilment. Certainly the land question was a figment of the political imagination in so far as it applied to the large estates, for tenants on such properties were treated fairly and often liberally. Despite the intense land hunger, tenants felt reasonably secure—virtual hereditary succession prevailed; and they were charged fair, not to say lenient, rents—competition for holdings not being the decisive factor in determining rent levels. Landlords carried out substantial improvements for only small returns and cushioned the tenants in times of adversity. Political and religious considerations in determining the choice of tenants were never so important as they were made out to be, and the impetuous eviction of tenants in the 1850s and 1860s by a few large owners was not repeated. Besides the protection afforded by the secret ballot, the public outcry following 1868 meant that thenceforth landlords came under intense public scrutiny and simply did not dare to act despotically. Local arrangements for providing compensation for unexhausted improvements do not seem to have been widely advocated in the years before the granting of statutory compensation by the Agricultural Holdings Acts of 1875 and 1883. Perhaps this was simply because occupiers with capital whose families had held farms over many generations on the large estates—where the big holdings were located—were seldom faced with the problem of compensation. It was precisely when this feeling of security weakened with the sales of outlying properties from the 1870s (Welsh capital values were kept up in the depression years by the pressure for land) that lack of compensation became a meaningful factor in retarding improvements. Tenants might well have their improvements confiscated in higher rents upon a change in the ownership of their farms. No remedy was provided in the Agricultural Holdings Act of 1883 for they were not given the right to have their interest in unexhausted improvements valued and the amount charged to the new tenant. Despite this genuine grievance and the injustice felt by the tenants over the game laws, large owners could justifiably complain of the groundless nature of many charges levelled against them.[31] Thus Lord Dynevor of Dynevor Castle, Carmarthenshire, wrote feelingly: 'The landlords have done their part, but the worst of it is, the Radicals and Revolutionary Party are trying to make capital out of the Farmers' losses and the depression of trade.'[32] The favourable conditions on the large estates meant that, despite the assertions of the party of agitation, personal relations between tenants and owners were harmonious.[33]

Conditions on the smaller estates of under 3,000 acres or so (which in the 1870s comprised just over half of the cultivated area of the Principality) were far less favourable. Both owners and tenants lacked capital, and their interests inevitably clashed. Although lesser landlords often allowed families to stay for lengthy periods on the same farms it is likely that many felt insecure, realistically fearing that pressure for farms would push up their rents. Even so, small hereditary Welsh landowners were seldom rapacious, and the difficulties arose usually from lack of capital rather than from deliberate oppressiveness. Their poverty inclined them to take what rents they were offered by land-hungry applicants, but it is doubtful if they squeezed the last penny; indeed, the long stay of many families suggests otherwise. The most unsatisfactory conditions were to be found on those properties of under a thousand acres belonging to the new 'commercial' landlords, who felt no ties of responsibility and personal obligation towards their tenantry but rather looked upon landownership as a business enterprise and an avenue to sport and amusement.[34]

Circumstances on the large estates were such that the notion of a land court was irrelevant and, in view of the landlords' continuing willingness to improve, positively harmful. Indeed, with regard to Welsh landed estates as a whole, the reformers were unrealistic in claiming likenesses between the Welsh and the Irish situations. What in Ireland justified the legislation implementing dual ownership and the practice of tenant-right was the belief that almost all improvements on Irish estates were the work of the tenant, and the ensuing benefits were appropriated in rising rents by the landlords. While this was in fact a simplified view, the concern did not arise in Wales, because Welsh tenants usually contributed towards improvements by providing the haulage and unskilled labour. Thus while Welsh tenants played a part in making improvements, it could not justly be claimed that agricultural improvements were the fruit of the tenants' labour and expenditure, nor that landlords as a body confiscated these fruits. Furthermore, absenteeism was less common than in Ireland and Welsh landlords were not of an alien stock. Finally, control by the landlords in Wales prevented that sub-division of holdings which would lead to the congestion of a rural population upon holdings too fragmented to support them, a situation familiar in the poorer regions of pre-famine Ireland, and in Scotland prior to the clearances in the crofter districts.

IV

In Wales, therefore, agricultural backwardness was only partly a result of imperfect tenurial relations. Other more crucial factors of constraint were the existing poor communications with the great centres of industry, the language barrier obstructing the easy flow of new ideas, the wide tracts of unenclosed moorland rendering useless any attempts at improved livestock breeding, the shortage of capital of most farmers and, most important, the attitudes of the tenants. The Welsh peasant mentality, equating 'successful' farming with low expenditure, regarded any rise in rents, the consequence of permanent improvements, as a veritable calamity. Rent was an item in farm costs which always had to remain stationary. Not only did this mentality govern the relationship between tenant and landowner, it also influenced the occupier's own activity. If there was the remotest possibility of a rise in rents, the farmer must avoid manifesting any sign of prosperity. There was consequently a total reluctance to improve. It is contended that the fear of revaluation was the crucial obstacle standing in the way of improvement, and though on small estates this fear stemmed partly from the landlords' behaviour, it derived fundamentally from the tenants' belief that their advantage consisted in their rent remaining unchanged from one generation to another.[35]

Furthermore, the peasant mentality shrank from innovation and change, believing old, tried methods to be the best. Land was not looked upon as a commercial speculation but simply as a source of livelihood. The local peasant community indeed had fixed ideas about the precise number of livestock a particular farm should carry, and should a farmer exceed that number he was looked upon with question, even disfavour, as overambitious and perhaps even tempting fate.[36] Thus improvement was discouraged within the peasant community at large. Conservative attitudes were also held towards new machinery. The whole concept of time-saving involved an entire reorganization of the old routine, and many were just not equal to it.[37]

V

The important division in Welsh rural society was between the landlords on one hand and on the other the peasantry, who comprised both the tenant-farmers and the cottagers or 'people of the little houses'. This last group was made up of farm labourers, non-farming cottagers such as road-menders and quarrymen, and craftsmen like blacksmiths and carpenters. On family farms there was a relatively low ratio of hired agricultural labourers to farmers: whereas in England in 1891 the ratio of labourers, farmers and their relatives was 73.0:20.5:6.5, the corresponding figures for Wales were 48.4:38.9:12.7. Tenancy of a farm was not expected to bring handsome profits. The English farmer when intending to take a certain holding asked himself, 'Can I make a living here?'; the Welshman simply considered, 'Can I pay the rent?' Nevertheless, a farm bestowed independence and status, and farmers were sensitive about their social standing. While Welsh farmers, therefore, shared a strong feeling of corporate identity and regarded themselves as superior to the labourers (they discouraged intermarriage, for instance), the difference was one of rank and status and not of class.[38] For once again the smallness of family holdings meant that the distinction between farmers and labourers was less marked than was generally the case in England (outside areas like Cumberland and Westmorland). There was little evidence of conflicting economic interests between the two categories: farmers worked alongside their labourers, many servants were farm children either on the parental holding or on neighbouring farms, and labourers could realistically aim at becoming tenant-farmers themselves.[39] The fact that until the end of the century over half of the Welsh labour force comprised indoor servants, and that even outdoor labourers received their food at the farms as part of their wages, established close personal contact; and these ties were strengthened by common worship at the Nonconformist chapels, albeit as social unequals. There was thus a greater community of feeling between farmers and labourers in Wales than was generally to be found in England, and this was reflected in the social composition of the political movements of the period. Labourers and farmers made common cause against the landlords and the Church. In England the larger farmers adhered to the Anglican Church and tended to remain Conservative in politics.[40]

Down to 1914 the continuing close ties between farmers and labourers formed the single most important factor in accounting for the lack of agricultural labourers' disturbances. Most of Wales was quiet in 1830–1, and trade unionism was absent in the 1870s.[41] Although in certain years of severe hardship, especially 1841–3, tension between the labourers and their employers understandably crept in, feelings of a separate identity as a class simply did not develop. On the other hand, the old quasi-patriarchal relationship between farmer and labourer was fragmenting from mid-century onwards. Greatly facilitated by the railways, a large-scale migration of labourers, mainly to the industrial valleys of south-east Wales, occurred towards the end of the century, so that between 1851 and 1911 there was a drop of 45.7 per cent in the number of hired male agricultural labourers on Welsh holdings. This rural exodus strengthened the bargaining position of those who remained on the land and made them more independent and less easy to manage. Symbolizing the growing rift between farmers and their indoor servants was the substitution around mid-century of the formal 'Master' and 'Mistress' for the intimate old terms, 'Uncle' and 'Aunt'.[42] The crucial change in relations, however, came only during the war years of 1914–18. At this time increases in the labourers' wages fell behind the rising cost of living, and wage earners blamed their employers for not passing on to them a share in the big war-time profits.[43]

Notes

1 Perry, 1973, xxxvii–xxxix; Hobsbawm, 1968, 254. Small tenant-farmers were to be found, of course, in the 'lowland zone': Chambers and Mingay, 1966, 172–3.
2 BPP 1896 XXXIV 313; Parry-Jones, 1972, 50.
3 BPP 1882 XV 8.
4 House of Commons Debates, Tenure of Land (Wales) Bill, 16 March 1892.
5 As in Hughes (Adfyfr), 1887, 3–4, and in the *Baner*, 24 November 1886 and 2 November 1887.
6 BPP 1896 XXXIV 924–5.
7 Williams, 1955, 124–6.
8 PRO HO 45/454: E. C. Lloyd Hall to Sir James Graham, 23 July 1843.
9 Evans, 1976, 157.
10 For this view see PRO HO 45/454: W. D. Jones to Sir James Graham, 19 September 1843.
11 Williams, 1955, 138.
12 PRO HO 45/1611: Day to G. C. Lewis, 9 July 1843.
13 PRO HO 45/454: E. C. Lloyd Hall to Sir James Graham, 23 July 1843; for the strong feeling against landowners' charging high rents in the face of rock-bottom prices see the threatening letter of 19 June 1843 of 'Rebecka' to William Peel of Taliaris, Carmarthenshire, in PRO HO 45/454, and also National Library of Wales, MS 21209C: T. H. Cooke to his mother, 24 August 1843; J. H. Davies, 'The Social Structure of South-West Wales in the Late Nineteenth Century', unpublished M.A. thesis, University of Wales, 1967, 82–3.
14 Morgan, 1970, 8–9, 17–18; I. G. Jones, 1961, 193–224.
15 National Library of Wales, Cilgwyn MS 34.

16 For evidence concerning the evictions of 1868 see BPP 1868–9 VIII, Qs 5047–227, 6541–616, 8455–94.

17 Carmarthen RO Cawdor MSS, box 141.

18 Morgan, 1970, 26–7.

19 *Ibid.*, 58.

20 Douglas, 1976, 98–9.

21 PRO HO 45/454: George Rice Trevor to the Home Office, 11 July 1843.

22 *Baner*, 13 August 1887, quoted in Vincent, 1896, 18.

23 BPP 1887 XXXVIII, Qs 1955–6: evidence of W. Jones.

24 *Ibid.*, Qs 2628 and 2640: evidence of Owen Williams, secretary of the Tithe Defence Fund. A recent study of the Tithe Wars is available in the Welsh language in Menna Cunningham, 'Y Gymdeithas Amaethyddol yn Nyffryn Clwyd, 1880–1900' (unpublished M.A. thesis, University of Wales, 1977).

25 Dunbabin, 1974, 286.

26 Lloyd to Rendel, 5 April 1891, in National Library of Wales, Rendel MS 19453C, fo. 411, quoted in Douglas, 1976, 101.

27 Howell, 1978, 152; BPP 1896 XXXIV 937.

28 The *Baner* in 1886 repeatedly urged Welsh tenants to form a land league on the Irish model.

29 Douglas, 1976, 99. For Evan Pan Jones see Jones-Evans, 1968, 143–59.

30 This point is strongly made for south-west Wales in Davies,89. *op. cit.* The allegation of fear is discussed from the landlords' point of view in Vincent, 1896, 84–8.

31 Howell, 1978, 87–90.

32 National Library of Wales, Picton Castle MS 3905.

33 BPP 1895 XL, Q. 38970: evidence of Gwilym Evans.

34 Howell, 1978, 150.

35 *Ibid.*, 91.

36 Mr Emrys Williams of the Manuscript Department of the National Library of Wales kindly provided me with this information.

37 Parry-Jones, 1972, 69–70.

38 BPP 1870 XIII N 30; Parry-Jones, 1972, 51; Jenkins, 1971, 100–1. I am grateful to my colleague, Mr Peter Stead, for offering helpful insight into the differences between rank and class.

39 Gibson, 1879, 47; BPP 1896 XXXIV 598; BPP 1893–4 XXXVI 6.

40 F. M. L. Thompson, 1963, 200–4; Olney, 1973, 249; Douglas, 1976, 97.

41 The best treatment of 1830–1 in Wales is in David Jones, 1973, 58–9; for trade unionism towards the end of the century see BPP 1893–4 XXXVI 29–30.

42 Evans, 1948, 31.

43 BPP 1919 IX 24.

7   The Regions and Their Issues: Scotland

Malcolm Gray

I

Except in a few areas—such as parts of the counties of Ayr, Fife, Stirling, Renfrew, Dumfries and Lanark[1]—most of the land of Scotland was owned until very recently by people who took no direct part in practical farming, and who, at least in part, depended upon their rents to maintain a social position distinct from that of the main farming population. Nevertheless, by the middle of the nineteenth century, owners of land (feuars being considered as owners) formed a group of miscellaneous origin and standing. The older families—whether of peers or of lairds of a middling or lesser sort—had long been losing land, particularly around the main towns, to merchants, industrialists, lawyers, and retired officers of the army and the navy seeking to own land for the social prestige it conferred.[2] Some of the older estates crumbled and were dissipated; others again held their position; and some old families accumulated more and more.[3] Yet, on the whole, at least among the greater estates, the old landed families remained dominant. In 1873, of seventy-two estates which accounted for a rent of £10,000 or more in at least one county, forty-five were owned by holders of Scottish titles originally created in the eighteenth century or earlier.[4]

Even the parvenu owners appear to have been mainly of Scottish origin and there is little dilution of the Scottish names to be seen in the roll of landowners of 1873.[5] At least for the higher aristocracy, however, this apparent integrity might be misleading; among the greatest landowners partial family fusion with the English aristocracy blurred any concept of a landowning class wholly Scottish in family origin and confining its interest and power to Scotland. In fact, marriage through the upper levels of the aristocracy had created links of ownership between English and Scottish estates or sections of estates, and increasingly the higher aristocracy was becoming anglicized by specific family connections, as well as in manners and education.[6] Great landowners like the Dukes of Gordon and Sutherland and the Marquess of Bute had substantial lands in England and intermarriage aligned them in many respects with the English aristocracy. A more complete form of alienation into English hands seems to have gained strength in the last quarter of the century with the selling of sporting estates (although most of the rich who came to Scotland to shoot did so as tenants). In 1921 well over half of the 151 owners of deer forests had acquired the land since 1873, and a substantial proportion of the newcomers appear not to have been Scottish.[7]

Even in some parts of the industrial Scotland of the 1870s giant estates and landed wealth made a blatant show; some estates, indeed, stretched into four or five counties and had rentals totalling over £100,000. But Scotland was also a country of many small lairds, with pride of position but little wealth. Thus every part of the country had its own intricate balance between great and small. In the north, through a region extending as far south as the hill country whose rivers drained towards the southern shore of the Moray Firth, the large estate was in every sense dominant, with well over half the land in big units. Southwards over the densely populated lowland counties the middling and even the small landowners had a stronger hold. In most of these counties between a quarter and a half of the total rent of agricultural land went to large owners (that is, holders with a rental of more than £5,000). Generally, too, middling lairds were more important than lesser ones (with less than £1,000).[8] The belt lying athwart the country from Fife to Lanark was an exception in that the high proportion of rents went to the small landowner (who might, in fact, be an owner-occupier), and the relatively small share went to the largest.

II

The agricultural constitution of these estates was determined largely by the underlying physique of the country. The superficial geographical impression is of dark, rough, and uncultivated mountain and peat moss. Yet the position of these mountainous areas leaves a relatively open surface of manageable land which is sufficiently extensive to support a solidly-based system of arable agriculture and which was to become as productive, man for man and acre for acre, as any in Europe. It is with this area—the lowlands, containing by 1870 by far the greater part of Scotland's rural population—that we deal first. The areas suitable for spacious cultivation are firmly outlined and limited, on the one hand by the coasts, on the other by the slopes of the mountain masses to levels, generally around the 1,000-foot contour, above which the local climate makes effective cultivation impossible. The greater of these solid mountain masses lies over most of the northern part of the country; but it is so set as to place the country's watershed close to the west coast, and the eastern slopes, falling gradually, give way to a cultivable plain which, though of varying width and intersected by isolated ranges of higher ground, runs the entire length of the coast from Caithness in the north to the lower reaches of the Forth. There the arable edge turns westwards to create a corridor of arable land extending across the country. To the south another, lesser, mountain mass serves as a limit to arable areas along both its eastern and western sides, with also, along the spur of the Solway coast, a southern edge; the south-flowing rivers also channel fairly wide arable flats.

Across most of these lowland areas agriculture was conducted on principles which were to hold good, with only minor adjustments, throughout the century, and which were, in many ways, particular to Scotland. Thus, the practice of agriculture in Victorian Scotland had a distinctiveness which was partly a matter of crops, partly of the shape and sweep of the land, partly of the materials used for construction, partly of the colourings inherent in climate, partly of the nature of the society which inhabited the buildings and managed the land.

The middle decades of the century saw the last stages of the conquest by the plough of the land below the arable edge, accomplished by the stern efforts of poor smallholders on the inclement, high-lying stretches of the north-east.[9] Then, apart from small plantations and occasional impossibly rough sections, the cultivated fields stretched without interruption over the modest undulations and the flat plains of lowland Scotland. The situation on the Haddo estate in the last decade of the century illustrates how thorough had been the conquest. Haddo lies in the heart of Aberdeenshire, a county which a century before had been cultivated only in patches; but by the 1890s, 43,000 of 53,000 acres were under the plough.[10]

Almost all the farm land was under rotation crops; the only permanent pasture lay beyond the farm boundaries among the rough surfaces of the hills, much of it being above the arable limit, and most lowland farms had no share in this hill pasture. Rotations varied regionally, and sometimes within districts, but there were common underlying characteristics which after the period of experiment had become almost permanent features of the scene. Except close to the bigger towns, which offered a supply of manure and a tempting market for hay and turnips, the endeavour of the advanced farmer was to recuperate his soil through the self-sufficient management of the farm; abundant crops of oats, straw, turnips, and grass were converted not only to bone, flesh, and wool for sale but also to the manure that went back into the soil. The system was particularly successful owing to the suitability of the climate for the production of grass and turnips,[11] and it was given permanence very often by the terms of the leases which ruled the tenant-farmers. By 1870, such principles were beginning to be resented, but on the whole the established systems and rotations persisted.[12]

The main key to the recuperative cycle was the turnip break; it was the occasion of heavy dunging of the land and of careful cultivation and weeding which prepared the soil for the rotation that was to follow. Some soils were too heavy for turnip cultivation—particularly in the carses of flat alluvial lands—and the cropping regime of the dairy districts of Ayrshire utilized a simple rotation of oats and grass, with grass predominant and unbroken for years at a stretch.[13] However, on the whole the soils and climate of Scotland tended to keep the turnip crop at the centre of the various local systems.[14] In some way they nearly all combined grain, whether wheat, oats, or barley, with grass and green crops in the form of turnips or potatoes. Much of the colourful display of the Scottish lowland countryside lay, and lies, in the colour gradations and contrasts of these crops changing from season to season and sitting every year in a different pattern over the intricate surfaces and contours of an undulating landscape.

The cash products of the farms varied considerably from one farming region to another. In eastern areas where the soil is strong and the climate favourable to the growth of wheat—on, for example, the arable lands south of the Forth, on the carses bordering the Forth and the Tay, and on the stronger coastal soils as far north as Kincardine—grains, notably wheat and barley, were the main cash crops. Even in these areas, however, grain tended to lose something of its importance in face of the rather fluctuating increase in potato growing.[15] Since, except on the heavy clays, turnips played a big part, forming the second green crop in a six-shift rotation or the only one in a four-shift rotation, the feeding of animals was the essential complement, indeed the basis, of heavy grain cropping. The big grain farms might keep a breeding stock of sheep, or might take in cattle or sheep for winter fattening. After 1870 the dependence on animal production was to increase.

However, the rearing and feeding of cattle and sheep, usually on the basis of a five-shift rotation (with two years of grass), provided the main income over probably the greater part of lowland Scotland.[16] The production of fat cattle was based partly on the breeding stocks kept on the fatteners' own farms but also on a widespread and increasing supply of beasts from farms, usually on upland sites, which confined themselves to rearing for sale as stores, and from external sources such as England, Ireland and, for a period, Canada.[17] The flow increased after 1850 with the rise in the feeding capacity of the farms both of the cattle-producing and of the grain-producing areas. There were also many breeding stocks of sheep scattered over the lowland farms, particularly where grain was the main cash product. But here again there was a regional interlocking, with some of the stock of the hill farms being sent to the lowlands for wintering or providing a supply of lambs, wethers, and cast ewes for fattening.

Finally, each main centre of population had its narrow surrounding belt of milk producers. In the western part of the central belt and to the south through Ayrshire the urban dairying area widened and extended. North Ayrshire on its inland clays had a long tradition of cheese production and its own particular form of rotation—a long sequence with several years of grass—to maintain its cows. In the second half of the century the edge of the cheese-making area tended to move southwards as districts previously given over to livestock production turned to dairying, but in so doing they tended to stick to the typical Scottish rotation of five shifts.[18]

III

The farms of lowland Scotland were of varying size—from 'crofts' of less than thirty acres, on which the holder could scarcely hope for an independent livelihood, to great arable farms of 600 acres. However, each of these units was quite separate from its neighbours in the position of the lands that it used, in the housing of its labour force, and in providing for all the material needs of farming.

This completeness, with each farm containing within itself a society of some complexity, was most evident in the large units—the farms, say, of more than 300 arable acres. The occupier of such a farm would normally be a tenant whose landlord might be little removed from himself in society. For, in the lowlands at least, tenancy carried no implications of weak or lowly status. There were tenants who paid rents of over £2,000 and made commensurate profits. And many a tenant would proudly assume the name of 'his' farm as a form of address; it carried the suggestion of property and of enduring right.[19] Invariably he would have a lease, usually of nineteen years, to confirm his position. Yet even the large farmers did not form a completely secure hierarchy. While estate practice varied, reputedly it was quite common for farms to be re-let by competitive bidding, in response, it might be, to open advertisement. In 1873 in East Lothian—the county above all others of wealthy and apparently powerful farmers—the majority of tenants were found to be of a different name from those of only twenty-five years before.[20]

The farm itself would give little sign of the possible vulnerability of its occupier. It would comprise a substantial group of buildings, suggestive of the concentrated management of the countryside and of the compact, if limited, social units in which so many rural inhabitants lived. The most notable symbol of the nature of this society was the farm-house. This would stand a little apart from the steading, turning its back on the noise and smells of work-a-day farming, a social distancing that might well be emphasized by a sheltering and dividing group of trees. The view from the house would be over a garden, walled and perhaps with an elaborate gateway, in whatever direction the aspect was most pleasant. On a farm of any size it would be a building of at least two storeys. Some were of eighteenth-century construction but many were more recent or were still in the course of building in the third quarter of the nineteenth. The architectural style was usually dignified, even imposing, but disdaining ornament. Generally it seems to have been defined by the estate owner's taste rather than by any distinctive regional idioms. Such buildings were bold but not obtrusive, partly because the surrounding trees, growing to age and size, reduced human pretension, partly because they were so often built of a local stone, which might be anything from warm red to sombre grey, and which mellowed to blend with the landscape. The scale of the buildings and the variety of the accommodation was strictly related to the size of the farm.

The farm group was completed by the steading and the cottages. The steading usually took the form of three sides of a square, and was given a more distinctive architectural stamp by the placing and design of the arches of the cart-houses; or sometimes, when the square was completed along its fourth side, by an imposing entrance; or by the form of the circular or polygonal horse-engine house for the threshing machine. Some, however, showed their importance by the tall chimney which betokened a steam-driven threshing machine. Always the use of local stone or the overall wash of lime sustained local idiom, appropriate to the look of the country and the character of its inhabitants. Roofing material had become more standardized when transport improved, allowing a wider use of grey slate, but residues of thatch and red pantiles continued to give a distinctive touch of colour in some districts.

Finally there was the housing for the workers, and here again the buildings tended to reveal something of the social world of their occupiers. Each farm contained much of the housing for its work-force, situated close to, although not always within, the steading, the central place of work. Farming depended, in fact, to a high degree upon full-time staff, labourers—or more correctly 'servants'—who were hired for periods of six months or a year at a time, and were housed on the farm, in buildings that were part of its essential accommodation (and as such were hired by the farmer from the landlord as part of the farm let).[21] Given that, roughly speaking, one full-time hand—or equivalent in part-time labour—could work twenty acres of land in rotation crop, a large arable farm might collect, as permanent dependants, up to a hundred individuals.[22] Such was the human substance of the great arable farms which depended mainly upon married men for servants. Solidly through the south-eastern arable sector and in diminishing proportion as far north as the Tay, large farms would have such a married work-force, living in one or two rows of cottages, making perhaps ten units all told.[23] Sometimes, however, the servants were unmarried. A large farm thus staffed would have a 'bothy', a sparsely furnished apartment inconspicuously set among the other buildings. Such bothies were, sometimes, the main means of housing farm staff in the larger farms between the Forth and the Dee.[24]

The farm, under the Scottish system of manning, formed almost the whole social world of its staff. Only to attend kirk and school did the workers, or their dependants, go beyond the bounds of their own farm. This apparently narrow social world was in fact broadened by the notorious restlessness of the Scottish farm servants; even a married man might well move periodically from farm to farm and from employer to employer, and at each move would find himself in a new association. The mixing and re-mixing of the farm groups and the absorbing combination of economic interest and sociability at the feeing markets must have induced a wider sense of community among the farm workers.[25] It is doubtful, on the other hand, whether the arrival of seasonal workers on the farm—the Irish or Highland folk, the women from the fishing villages or industrial towns—brought more than help with the tasks of the moment.

Farm society was not only limited, it was also almost rigidly hierarchical, and not only in the obvious division between the farmer and his workers. Predominant in numbers and importance in this staff would be the ploughmen or horsemen. According to the conditions of soil and crop, one ploughman could handle anything between forty and a hundred acres of ground in rotation.[26] Thus a large arable farm might have as many as ten, and only the smallest farms would have as few as one (though sometimes the need would be met by the farmer's sons). Each would have his own pair of horses—a plough-team—for which he was responsible as if it were his own and from which he would take much of the pride and incentive of his job. Servants were graded according to experience, and a strict order of precedence prevailed not only in pay but also in the daily routine of house and field. There would be others on the staff, according to the degree of specialization; cattlemen ranked rather lower in status and were sometimes former ploughmen who had not now their full strength; 'orramen', who were not specialized or skilled in any particular task, ranked lower still, but shepherds, something of a class apart, had high standing. A farm of any size would have a grieve who had the powers and duties of day-to-day control.

The large farms of 300 or more acres were completely dominant in a few areas, and most of all in East Lothian. There the countryside had an almost empty appearance, with the population concentrated in 'farm villages'—great farm-houses with their substantial steadings and rows of workers' cottages—standing each amid its wide fields. Over most of the lowlands, however, farms of smaller size were much more in evidence and sometimes they would entirely dominate large areas, as in northern Kincardineshire, Aberdeenshire, and Banffshire, where they lay across the great arable stretch of the north-east knuckle.[27] Many of the units of this area were family farms, each of which would be worked by a single plough-team, and it was not uncommon to find men struggling along as independent farmers on as little as thirty acres. Even these small units required more full-time labour than the farmer himself could give, and unless he was fortunate enough to have the help of a son or sons, one or two servants would be employed. In addition to the mass of smallish but independent farms there were also even greater numbers of lesser holdings, below the thirty-acre level, too small for any hope of independence but cropped on rotational principles so as to give some subsistence and support to the raising of stock—usually calves—for sale.[28] The livelihood of the occupants came partly from the work they could find nearby, in particular by making up the seasonal labour requirement of the larger farms, Altogether these small farms and crofts gave the countryside a much more crowded appearance; the fields were smaller, and the clusters of farm buildings, modest and low in outline, were dotted more frequently over the countryside.

The west of Scotland, too, had its area where the family farm was typical. The dairying of Ayrshire, Lanarkshire, and Renfrewshire was pursued mostly in units of between fifty and a hundred acres, with stocks of fifteen to twenty cows.[29] Often the family labour sufficed, with the women deeply involved in the dairy work. Even where servants were employed, there was reputedly a comparatively easy relationship between master and servant, with the habit of sharing the same table persisting more than in other parts of the country.[30]

IV

North and west of the lowland areas with their many spacious farms rise the mountain masses which stretch ridge upon ridge, mile after mile, to the west coast. In many of the western and northern isles the mountains again rise steeply, and where they do not, the land, often enough, is locked in impenetrable moor. In such conditions the land had to be used very differently from that of the lowlands and the way of life of the inhabitants was equally at variance. Most of the land is too high or too rough for cultivation, with the arable lying in pockets and discontinuous stretches mainly round the coastal margins. But a more genial environment exists alongside the rivers flowing north, in Orkney, and in some of the western isles. The southern uplands also have their high uncultivable tracts but here the ground falls into broader valleys, in which the life of the farmers was akin to that seen in the lowlands.

Within these restricted bounds, in the western Highlands and the Islands, lived a numerous population of small cultivators whose condition was by 1870 beginning to trouble the conscience of the nation. Unlike the farmers of the lowlands, they held their small pieces of land at the will of the landlord who was very often a remote figure of vast possessions, although this condition of helplessness was to end in 1886 when legislation accorded some protection to crofters. The holdings were small—indeed usually too small to provide a full livelihood.[31] Partly the difficulty lay in intractable natural conditions; large numbers of people, all eager for a bit of land of their own, had to live within a restricted area of arable cultivation. But holdings were also small because arable land had been cleared to make way for incoming sheep farmers, men of a very different social stamp. By 1860 the clearances were over but the crofters and cottars still suffered from their consequences.[32] Nearly all the arable land, as well as the rough pasture, of the interior was taken for sheep. This had hit hard in Sutherland with its wide valleys; and in the Islands, to which clearances had come in the last desperate phase, the sheep men were occupying considerable tracts of good land. Even where arable land remained in the hands of the small cultivators, clearance had exacerbated the overcrowding. Some of the dispossessed had left the country, but just as many clung to what they could sustain of an old way of life on newly created holdings, usually small rocky pieces of inferior land, or moved into older settlements already overcrowded by the century-long increase of population.[33] It is true that, except in the Outer Isles, the tide of population increase had by 1851 turned to a decrease, continuing decade by decade as the migrants trickled to the lowlands or overseas; but the pressure on land was still great and the land lay in the tiny sections of the original crofts, sometimes subdivided, each supporting its family.

A croft consisted of a small, compact stretch of cultivable land, seldom amounting to more than five acres, and frequently less, together with the right of turning a restricted number of animals on to the common grazing, a rough pasture usable only in summer. Usually crofts were grouped in townships and were laid side by side to give a frontage on the shore, running back in elongated shapes to meet the rough edge of the moor. Until the cheapening of groceries in the 1870s the arable ground was intensively cultivated, sometimes by labour with the spade, to provide a supply of potatoes and oats, the main forms of subsistence. The cash products of the land were the animals, cattle and, increasingly, sheep, pastured on the hills in summer but free to roam over the cultivated land from harvest to sowing (for the individual plots were not usually fenced). Cheap food from the grocer led to falling subsistence cultivation after 1870 but not to any concerted effort to develop grassland or the means of supporting the limited seasonal resource of hill pasture.[34]

These crowded lands were but the broken fringe of the vaster area of mountain and rough moorland; a little part of this was given over to the stock of the crofters, but mostly it was the sheep of a very different group—the specialized and large-scale sheep farmers—which grazed on the hills. By 1860 every district of the Highlands and Islands had its big sheep farms. The grassy slopes of the western ranges carried the heavier stocks but even the drier east, with its heather slopes, had a considerable sheep population. The conversion of so much of the higher ground to specialized and large-scale sheep-farming implied a world of endeavour and human relationships dramatically different from that of the crowded townships. The sheep farmers were mostly incomers—tenants who, unlike the crofters, were protected by lease—and they ruled over great tracts, usually with at least 2,000 sheep to the farm, pasturing areas of at least 10,000 acres.[35] Attached to the upland tracts would be some low-lying sections for wintering, either under cultivation or in fine grass. Sheep, with perhaps a handful of cows, would represent the entire stock of the farm. The human population was sparse and scattered, for one shepherd could handle a hirsel that would occupy at least 4,000 acres. Yet most of the landlord's rent came from these arrangements and not from crofting with its close-packed population.[36]

In the early 1870s sheep-farming was at a peak of power and prosperity, still profitable and apparently unchallengeable; yet its very basis was being slowly eroded and had been for years. The carrying capacity of the pastures was falling because of the very practice of sheep-farming itself.[37] Before the coming of the large flocks, when the valleys still contained some remnants of forest covering and when stocks of cattle, the main grazing animals, only occupied small areas, pastures were yearly regenerated in a natural equilibrium.[38] But the close nibbling of the sheep, the stripping from many areas of the last vestiges of forest covering, and the careless burning of heather produced deterioration in the herbage, erosion, and a spread of destructive bracken. It was a decline that could not quickly be reversed and it was already to be seen in the 1870s. With the land carrying less, by the end of that decade, and even more in the 1880s, falling prices were adding to the sheep farmers' troubles; no longer could they pay rents at the old levels.[39] In addition, landlords now found themselves able to refuse the enfeebled offers of the sheep tenants; a new and profitable use for their high ground had emerged—letting to sportsmen for the shooting of deer.

Of old, some high tracts, particularly on the eastern side of the high central core of the Highlands, had been used for shooting, uncommercially, by chieftains and their guests, but since the limited stock of cattle that grazed the hills did not encroach on the feeding areas of the deer, there was no need for rigid preservation. After 1760 letting to sheep farmers became so profitable that deer were left undisturbed only in small sanctuaries.[40] By 1840, however, there were signs that profit could also be made by the letting of shooting rights, and the idea of devoting some ground exclusively to deer took hold even while the area under sheep was still growing. Shooting was, in fact, pursued adventurously in the small and very high-lying deer sanctuaries, and also over ground occupied by sheep; landlords, however, were able to negotiate on the letting of shooting rights through a London agency. By 1870, then, a letting organization was in being and a fashion was beginning to spread; in conjunction they were to turn the trickle of adventurous bachelors into a flood of rich men now intent on comfort and entertainment for their families as well as good sport on the hills. Many factors contributed. Rail communication from London to Perth and Inverness and, in particular, the provision of sleepers made for the easy transportation of entire households complete with servants; the dispatch of food boxes from London stores blunted the discomforts of going native in Highland glens; the construction in due course of massive shooting lodges created foci of entertainment and social life; the high-velocity percussion-cap rifle made the prospects of a kill somewhat better, although deer-stalking never ceased to be arduous; and landowners, with sheep rents falling, were looking for means of reviving their incomes. Now began the clearance of sheep to make protected sanctuaries for the deer.[41] For about forty years ever wider tracts were given over to deer and animals purely of the wild (including those, such as foxes and hooded crows, regarded as destructive under other forms of land use). By 1872, nearly 2.5 million acres, estimated as capable of maintaining 400,000 sheep, were designated as deer forest.[42] Most of this ground lay over 1,500 feet, but the belt at intermediate level, between 1,000 and 1,500 feet, was also invaded. The economic effect was considerable. Much shooting, of course, was based on the renting of forests and moors by local owners to the seasonal incomers, but commercial and industrial wealth from the south also moved in to buy shooting estates outright. Possibly for the first time a substantial portion of Scotland's land surface came under outside ownership. Many of the older landlords now depended heavily on shooting rents, and even the lesser folk found some employment. Yet for the majority of the people the switch from sheep to deer probably made little change in the impact of age-old problems. It was merely the last stage in the division of the land between the high, thinly used, and almost uninhabited ground, and the congested lower areas with numerous smallholders clinging to the spots of arable they had sustained through the commercial manoeuvring of 150 years.

We have seen many of the high-lying tracts of the Highland area switched to a new form of use, accompanied by considerable changes of ownership. The lowland agricultural areas had a different experience, for only in isolated parts was there major transformation. Of course, it was a time of agricultural stress, but Scottish lowland agriculture, with its great dependence on rotations in which grass and turnips played a large part, was well suited to meet by small adjustments the problems posed by a changing price structure. There were subtle alterations of balance but no broad rifts in a system, social and agricultural, that had, in broad terms, stood firm for half a century. Rather more resources were put into animal production, rather less into grain. Rotation grasses and root crops expanded their hold while grain acreage

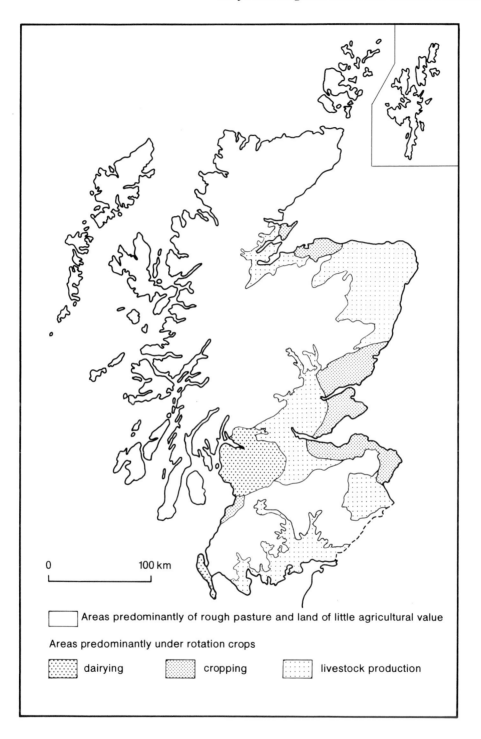

Map 7.1 Land use in Scotland, *c.* 1870

slightly declined. Altogether the total cultivated acreage showed little change and permanent pasture took over only a tiny fraction of the arable surface. In a few small areas, it is true, there was a marked retreat of cultivation and disastrous decline; parts of Kinross were so affected, and even in the resistant north-east a few sections, nearly always characterized by heavy clay soils, were in great difficulties. But the retreats were more than compensated for by advances elsewhere. The visible focal points of farming—the steadings, farm-houses, and cottages which we have seen always in some form of close grouping—were the result of accretions through successive phases of planning and building. In 1875 some were already a century old, but many, perhaps most, had been added in the great burst of investment of the previous quarter-century. These, the buildings of 1875, were to comprise the bulk of the stock of 1900, their rawness by then somewhat mellowed by weather; further investment, on a very reduced scale after 1875, made only minimal additions. Few of the buildings fell vacant, for the core of the farming population—the tenants and the full-time servants—was little diminished in size. Surprisingly perhaps in the time of depression, there were always plenty of applicants eager for the vacant farms. Thus the composition of the independent farming classes, the balance between the large farm and the small, remained steady, small units, if anything, being more resistant during depression than large, although their occupants were scarcely likely to take in more land. Economies in the use of the labour force enforced by rising wage-costs or aided by the adoption of harvesting machinery did not cut deeply into the solid core of skilled servants; rather it was the seasonal and casual workers who were thinning in numbers. The permanent resident population of the farms remained in full possession of the cottages and houses, though probably fewer would be seen at work on the land at the end of the century than twenty-five years earlier. It was still a thickly populated countryside, carefully cultivated and utilized to its geographical limits.

Notes

1 Aiton, 1811, 64; Naismith, 1813, 49; Robertson, 1829, 534–5; Thomson, 1800, 47; Wilson, 1812, 39–41, 53.

2 Naismith, 1813, 47; Somerville, 1805, 28; Trotter, 1811, 15.

3 Somerville, 1805, 28–30; Wilson, 1812, 39–41, 53.

4 BPP 1874 LXXII Pt III; Foster, 1883, *passim*; Thomson, 1800, 48.

5 BPP 1874 LXXII Pt III.

6 Foster, 1883, *passim*.

7 BPP 1874 LXXII Pt III; 1922 VII 60–81.

8 BPP 1874 LXXII Pt III.

9 Carter, 1976a, 159–60; Gray, 1973, 137.

10 BPP 1895 XVII Q 30357.

11 Wilson, 1878, 57.

12 Caird, Alex M'Neel, 1878, 128; Stephens, 1891, III, 193–8.

13   Drennan, 1878, 79–80.

14   Wilson, 1878, 24, 35.

15   Dickson, 1867, 78–9; Macdonald, 1876, 45; Macdonald, 1881, 141.

16   Drennan, 1878, 64; Wilson, 1878, 28–9.

17   Macdonald, 1876, 31–2.

18   Drennan, 1878, 79–80.

19   Gilbert, 1973, 178.

20   Skirving, 1873, 47.

21   BPP 1870 XIII App. Pt I, 46.

22   BPP 1870 XIII App. Pt II, 64–5, 179–88.

23   Macdonald, 1876, 56; Macdonald, 1881, 170; Skirving, 1878, 142.

24   Caird, 1878, 138; Macdonald, 1881, 170.

25   Carter, 1976b, 110–3.

26   BPP 1870 XIII App. Pt I, 32; Pt II.

27   Wilson, 1878, 30–1; 'Agricultural Statistics of Scotland', 1875, 303.

28   BPP 1870 XIII App. Pt II, 12, 14.

29   Drennan, 1878, 88–9; BPP 1870 XIII App. Pt I; Sturrock, 1867, 87–8.

30   BPP 1870 XIII App. Pt I, 105–6.

31   Gray, 1957, 197–9; Hunter, 1976, 30–51.

32   Hunter, 1976, 107.

33   Hunter, 1976, 26–31, 45–9.

34   Darling, 1955, 219–22.

35   Gray, 1957, 73–4, 89.

36   Gray, 1957, 195.

37   Hunter, 1973, 203–5.

38   Darling, 1955, 167–76.

39   Hunter, 1973, 206–9.

40   BPP 1922 VII 2–5.

41   Hunter, 1973, 217–18.

42   BPP 1922 VII, 5–6.

8   The Regions and Their Issues: Ireland

L. M. Cullen

I

Irish agriculture is best viewed, as a first step, from the concrete perspective of its physical characteristics rather than in a more analytical framework. The 1,500-odd sheets of the Ordnance Survey of the 1830s and 1840s give a more remarkable and more precise picture of the character and variety of the country than a literary description, contemporary or retrospective, can provide. The modern field system existed, the seats of the gentry had with few exceptions been long there, and the farmhouses already stood where they still stand in the middle of the fields. The maps highlight the misbelief inherent in seeing rural Ireland as engulfed on the eve of the Famine in a pattern of subdivision and tiny fields, or in seeing a new rural field and settlement pattern emerging phoenix-like from the holocaust of the Famine years and attendant emigration. Even the Great Famine itself contrasted with the preceding famine of 1740–1. In the earlier famine the rural population at large was at risk, mortality being equally evident (as in the Scottish famine of the late 1690s) in the comparatively prosperous grain-growing and grain-eating districts of the east as in the poorer regions farther afield. In the 1840s, on the other hand, famine did not threaten the farming population at all; even among the labourers in the better-off regions the number at risk was reduced by some degree of regularity of employment; famine was more menacing in pastoral districts, with their sharp cleavage between farmers and underemployed labourers, and especially among the smallholders of the extensive western fringe of Ireland, where in areas such as Schull, Skibbereen or

Kilrush, famine was a community disaster of terrifying proportions. In north County Dublin, it was the news from County Cork that caused indignation, not the comparatively mild local suffering.[1]

A process of social differentiation had proceeded far since the 1730s. The growth in migratory labour and in the flow of living-in servants, male and female, between labour-abundant and labour-short regions is one measure of it.[2] Another is the fact that by the early nineteenth century conflict between farmers and labourers, either about the rent of potato plots or about wages, increasingly predominated in agrarian unrest.[3] The relative absence of social differentiation below the level of the large cattle-owning tenant aptly illustrates the comparative poverty of rural Ireland as compared with more developed regions of Europe around 1730. The comparatively large number of living-in servants, and the fact that they were often recruited even by quite small farmers, both illustrate the enduring poverty at the social base which, as in Latin America today, made for a very large domestic class. In fact, as Irish *per capita* incomes relative to English incomes may have changed very little between 1600 and modern times,[4] the low levels of Irish incomes at the end of the Victorian era seem a consequence, not of an absence of growth rates comparable with those in western Europe, but of the initial low level of living standards three centuries previously.

II

These considerations remove Victorian Ireland from the realm of the tenure question and unremitting poverty that filled the blue books and preoccupied journalists and politicians who made the acquaintance of Ireland in the nineteenth century. Poverty was not universal, despite reports like that of the Commission on the Poor in the mid-1830s which by definition dealt with poverty and found it in abundance. Land tenure, too, was complex, with long tenures and beneficial leasing based on English legal precedents, producing in a country where the land market had been subject to periodic upheaval and subsequent massive re-leasing a bewildering variety of problems unforeseen at the time. The tenurial problem was not, however, one of insecurity. It lay in the difficulties posed by perpetuity leases and intervening interests, and derived its immediate relevance from the fact that landowners with their lands out of their control through beneficial leasing on long tenures faced bankruptcy to a greater degree than in England; and that such landowners were not in a position, legally or economically, to support the investment which English observers and their Irish followers wrongly believed would resolve the social problems of Irish agriculture. Tenure in fact implied security; the tenants and the intervening middlemen, whom landlords were increasingly anxious to get rid of, were both difficult to dislodge; and the social as opposed to the legal problems lay in the growing substratum who lived outside the formal tenurial system altogether.

A careful reading of the Poor Law Commission evidence, or of the great Devon report of 1845 on the occupation of land, points to the social complexity of rural Ireland.[5] But Irish issues were already beginning to acquire their controversial character which, happily or unhappily, simplified them for the protagonists on both sides of the Irish Sea. The controversial character became ever more evident after the 1840s. The sharpening hostility (itself to some extent imported from England, where the anti-landlord wind blew more bitterly) was partly political, in a politically divided society where literacy was undermining the rural paternalism of the past; partly legalistic, as in the influential writings of the Protestant lawyer, Isaac Butt, in the 1860s, who argued that even if landlords did not abuse their powers, the very existence of unexercised powers constituted a tyranny; and partly social, reinforced by the belief that if post-Famine emigration was depopulating rural Ireland, somehow the landlords, not yet altogether divested of their paternalistic responsibilities, were responsible. In the case of emigration, 'clearances' of broken tenants coloured the issue. The contrast between the evidence in landlord sources of well-intentioned and expensive measures to subsidize the emigration of broken tenants from poor regions where social cohesion was undermined by the Famine, and the grim view of landlord actions taken in local popular tradition, illustrates how elusive was the prospect of finding common ground in facing the social problems of post-Famine Ireland.

Low incomes, in association with a relatively undifferentiated social structure in seventeenth- and early eighteenth-century Ireland, were almost certainly the basis for a sustained population growth through both centuries, a growth unparalleled in Britain or lowland Scotland. Populations of 'villagers' or 'common labourers', village communities of small farmers, owing labour services to their landlords, had little stake in the countryside; they readily abandoned their holdings in years of low prices or cattle mortality; and rural Ireland was characterized by a degree of mobility rarely found elsewhere in western Europe at this time. Such a population, marrying earlier than more settled farmers whose decisions on marriage were determined by expectation of a farm or the negotiation of a dowry, is likely to have had a relatively high birth rate. It is significant, for instance, that lowland Scotland, in contrast to Ireland, may have experienced little population growth in the eighteenth century.[6] In Ireland itself a better-off farming population existed in the east, relatively well-housed and owning livestock. In the country at large this category increased over time, a trend illustrated in the comparatively backward dairying districts of Munster by the shift from cow-hiring to cow-owning occupiers.[7] The very obvious demographic contrast in post-Famine Ireland between better-off counties with a small natural increase and poorer regions with a higher natural increase[8] points to the more elusive but comparatively long-established social patterns lying behind them.

The tenant-farmer's position strengthened in pre-Famine Ireland. The rents paid by occupiers, which perhaps had risen six-fold between 1720 and 1812, may have been only 1 or 2 million short of £12 million in 1815, and probably had not exceeded that figure in 1845.[9] The employment of labourers had increased, and labourers' potato plots were allocated by the farmer not to suit the convenience of the labourer but the requirements of the farmer's crop rotations. It is hardly surprising that the cultivation of the potato, the sole significant root crop in Irish rotations, increased rapidly in the course of the sustained rise in cereal cultivation from 1800 to 1840. A dire necessity for the cottier, it was increasingly relied on by the farmer, who probably had serious difficulty in maintaining his income in years when grain prices were low. This implies, paradoxically but realistically, that the farmer increased his consumption of potatoes in years when grain harvests were good but grain prices low.

III

The rural system of Ireland was therefore very different from that of lowland Scotland or England, where incomes were higher, a cereal diet was entrenched, and a long-standing tradition of mixed farming existed. English observers, confident in the pronouncements of the new political economy, misread the Irish situation, believing that capital investment would solve Irish problems and that agriculture reorganized in the hands of large tenant-farmers would provide remunerative wages for Irish labourers. In fact, capital was not a problem. Of the £26.4 million spent up to 1862 on land purchases under the Incumbered Estates Courts (set up in 1849 to sell indebted Irish estates), only 12 per cent came from outside Ireland.[10] Returns on investment by landlords in England were lower than in non-agricultural outlets, and it is not surprising, therefore, that investment was even less attractive in Ireland, where the more pastoral orientation of the economy also provided less scope for initiative in investment by landlords. The proportion of the landlords' rental invested may have been only of the order of 3–4 per cent.[11] Nevertheless, investment by landlords and by large intermediate tenants had a demonstration effect which should not be underestimated. Improvement by tenants in a relatively primitive society was necessarily imitative of the patterns of investment in housing, outhouses, draining, planting and orchards on demesnes and larger holdings. Investment by tenants predominated in dwellings and outhouses, being prominent also in subsoiling and tiling. The sharp switch from ridge cultivation, which provided a degree of drainage on badly drained land, to drill cultivation necessitated investment,[12] and interest in undertaking it was accounted for in part by the tenants' initiative in the switch to drill cultivation. Kickham's novel, *Knocknagow*, a perceptive commentary on farmer mores and attitudes in the third quarter of the century, illustrates the tenants' involvement in drainage.[13] It illustrates, too, the tenants' investment in building, as on Tom Hogan's farm where there were the 'snug thatched dwelling-house, and the new slated barn, of which he was particularly proud'.[14] To quantify the order of investment, a real-life instance of a dairy farmer of fifty acres laying out £500 on a barn, stable and byre in the late 1870s may be cited, with a new dwelling house also proposed in place of the existing thatched one.[15] The parliamentary inquiries had addressed themselves to the wrong problem in seizing on the tenurial aspects—on the English analogy that investment was a landlord activity—rather than on the economic aspects of investment; although, of course, rising investment by tenants was closely related to the advance of rural social differentiation.

The contrast in investment attitudes between farmers in Ireland and those elsewhere in the United Kingdom is exaggerated. If, as suggested, extensive investment was undertaken by tenants, the contrast in security of tenure seems exaggerated also. Security of tenure was the norm rather than the exception, eviction notices constituting a routine step in the collection of rent rather than evidence of a drastic policy of clearance.[16] The most abiding contrast in agriculture in the three kingdoms was in the size of the home market, which with relatively low incomes and, before the late eighteenth century, few towns, was smaller in Ireland than in lowland Scotland or in England. The only pre-1800 exceptions were the compact region in the hinterland of Dublin and Drogheda and the more southerly region centred on Waterford. Both regions afforded in 1841 the best instance of comfortable indigenous farm-houses. They also had most of the counties with a high ratio of horses to farms. Significantly, too, only in the case of four counties all within this region—Dublin, Louth, Meath and Wexford—did the number of horses exceed the number of farms of from five to fifteen acres, suggesting even at the level of the small farmer a competence unattained in any other counties. Densely populated and economically advanced for Ireland, the counties in these two regions experienced little immigration in the sixteenth and seventeenth centuries. In settlement patterns and modes of agricultural production, they display the most remarkable continuity in Irish history.[17] Immigration was more evident in the river valleys of Munster, the midlands or Ulster. The distribution of orchards is an interesting barometer of the relative distribution of English and indigenous cultural values. Relatively absent among farmers in the prosperous tillage areas of Leinster, orchards were numerous in the English-settled areas around the Fermanagh lakes, on the east side of Lough Neagh, in north Wexford and in the Munster river valleys, where they produced in Limerick and Cork strong local traditions of cider making.

IV

The Great Famine was a catalyst of many changes. But its immediate impact on agriculture was limited. Major change came only in the late 1860s or early 1870s. Up to then output rose sharply, there was a dynamic shift from subsistence to commercial farming, tillage remained substantial, and the fall in the labouring population was fairly limited. Comparison of output across the divide of the Famine is misleading because of the contracting potato acreage. Gross output, including potatoes, was probably stable between 1840–5 and 1852–4;[18] excluding potatoes, farm output rose by 36 per cent between 1854 and 1874.[19] With a decline in population the increase *per capita* was even sharper: including potatoes, it was of the order of 50 per cent between 1847 and 1861.[20] With tillage remaining extensive, the post-Famine rise in livestock numbers at first represented an expansion of the mixed base of Irish agriculture, given the sharp increase in cereal output in the thirty years before 1845 and the heavy dependence of the major tillage districts on wheat. The acreage of land under crops and pasture was extended until the 1870s, the direction of reclamation corresponding to movements in cattle prices.[21] Some shift to livestock was not in itself socially harmful in view of the excessive dependence on cereals on many tillage farms. Moreover, the rise in livestock farming increased the price of calves and young stock, some of the benefits being redistributed through the complex inter-regional livestock trade to Munster dairy farmers and to smallholders on marginal land with a few young cattle to sell. The labouring population fell relatively little: after the steep post-Famine drop between 1841 and 1861, the numbers fell only slightly in the 1860s,[22] while wages rose sharply between 1853 and 1870.[23] Change came abruptly in the early 1870s, the tilled acreage falling sharply between 1872 and 1874, and the number of labourers falling by no less than 42 per cent in a single decade—1871–81—slightly more than in the two decades 1841–61 when less comparable data probably overstated the effective decline in employment.[24] Between 1868 and 1908 output virtually stagnated: in fixed prices gross output rose by only 10 per cent between 1868 and 1908.[25] The shift to livestock was marked, and within livestock the proportion of dairy cattle fell from 43.4 per cent in 1854 to 31.6 per cent in 1900.[26]

The real weaknesses of Irish agriculture lay in the comparatively limited extent and depth of mixed farming. The pastoral regions were not intensively farmed, being dependent in dairying areas on selling calves, and in the fattening regions on buying in stock for fattening. Only in the tillage regions is there some evidence of a more intensive pattern, with cereal output on the farms combined with some raising of livestock from the calf stage to the fat bullock. But even there they were rarely stall-fed. A more balanced agriculture may have helped lowland Scotland and Denmark to better survive agricultural depression. It is striking that as Ireland swung more decisively to pastoral farming, she became more dependent on Scottish rather than English farmers as the outlet for store cattle: in 1900, 41 per cent of Irish stores were sent to Scotland, a fact accounted for by the continuing high proportion of lowland Scotland under the plough.[27]

Ireland's export orientation as a primary producer was uniquely high for a long-settled country. One half of agricultural output was exported. The steep rise in exports, the sustained growth in output between 1854 and 1874, and a continuing decline in population suggest a sharp rise in *per capita* incomes. This is all the more certain as by 1880 rents did not greatly exceed the 1845 level.[28] A decline in the relative share of rents in national income also served to defuse the grievance of absentee rents, which had doubled in absolute size between 1804 and 1835. A buoyant export trade, allied to the absence after 1826 of trade statistics thus removing the basis for any informed concern about the balance of trade, effectively pushed the absentee landlords from the central place they had previously enjoyed in economic controversy. In fact, the decline in rents relative to output and exports was linked in a dynamic fashion to soaring imports. Tea and tobacco consumption rose sharply between 1850 and 1870, and while the data are treacherous, consumption of wheat—in other words of white bread—probably doubled between the 1860s and 1900. The traditional excess of exports over imports had probably disappeared by the 1870s and, when export figures became available from 1904, it was seen that the excess of exports had been replaced by one of imports.[29] The trade orientation of the economy was reflected in many directions, as for instance in imports of bacon as large as bacon exports. Farmers had ceased to consume their own bacon, now sold for export; instead they relied on cheap, fat, imported bacon. Rural shops multiplied; the growth of shops in rural post offices illustrates the two-fold dimension of communication and rising living standards; and the bar-cum-grocery store points to one of the sources from which came the capital for the expansion of retail trade. In a busy rural community, despite relatively strict Sabbatarianism, the sale of groceries took place to a large extent on Sundays after mass.[30] Town observers overlooked the significance of these changes, bewailing the increase in the number of unproductive dealers in the countryside. The number of females occupied in rural shops fell by 5,000 between 1901 and 1911,[31] a reflection of the strengthening of retail trade. As a precarious sideline it had frequently been the preserve of the wife of a farmer or of a rural professional man; on a sounder basis, it acquired an enhanced attraction for rural males. There is much evidence of enormous vitality in rural Ireland between 1880 and 1914, in culture, sport, pastimes and life styles—quite the reverse in fact of the demoralized rural community, lacking in initiative, suggested retrospectively in many accounts written in the twentieth century.

Irish agriculture was highly responsive to price changes. In fact, Irish agricultural output *per capita* rose slightly more rapidly between 1861 and 1909 than did the Danish figure.[32] The creamery movement, it has been recently argued, spread almost as impressively as in Denmark.[33] If the performance of Irish agriculture was deficient in raising incomes it was in part because the gap had been wide to start with. As one would expect in a region recently underpopulated and underdeveloped, output was geared to export demand, the regional emphasis on cattle or tillage becoming accentuated as export demand warranted. Dependence on tillage in the main arable regions during the grain export boom of pre-Famine Ireland itself predisposed farmers to a sharp swing to pastoral farming when exports failed after mid-century and there was little countervailing demand from home. The fact that in the middle of the century pigs were potato-fed, not grain-fed, was an added factor in offering the farmer little cushioning from the adverse effect of American grain on home and British markets alike. Plentiful potatoes and the most abundant supply of summer grass in Europe meant that little grain was fed to livestock. In pre-Famine times a very high proportion even of the huge horse population was fed almost exclusively on grass and hay. It is very significant that the barley-growing regions—Wexford and the south midlands—which catered for the home market in the form of the burgeoning brewing and distilling industries, continued to have a high proportion of land under the plough. The dairy industry was stagnant from the 1870s. But what is striking is not that Ireland competed less effectively after the 1870s, but that Irish butter was already at a disadvantage at an earlier date, and that lagging adjustment in quality to meet changing market requirements was greatest in the Munster region, the main dairying area, where the relatively late change in industry's social structure illustrated its primitive condition.

As late as 1880 about two-thirds of Irish farms were below thirty acres. The 1879 crisis bode ill, particularly for the smallholders of the west: the loss of potatoes, turf and hay in the wet summer undermined their local economy, and migrant earnings were down because of short employment on British farms. What was simply an economic crisis for eastern farmers was a more fundamental social crisis in the west. The economy of these western regions was already of doubtful viability, sustained in part by migrant earnings which rose rather than fell in the 1850s and 1860s.[34] Emigration itself may be understated in the official statistics.[35] The character of emigration, moreover, whatever its real scale, was different from that in the east, fluctuating between good and bad years, with whole families constituting a significant proportion of emigrants in contrast to the outward movement of young adults in the rest of the country.[36] The west was also remarkably backward, still in part Irish-speaking and illiterate. In the parish of Tullaghobegley, County Donegal, for instance, 72 per cent of the population over five was illiterate in 1881.[37] The west's population was also relatively undifferentiated in social structure, in sharp contrast to the complex structure, both before and after the Famine, in the rest of the country. The region's demographic transformation occurred largely after 1870, and with very low incomes literacy and the modest economic improvement of later decades whetted the appetite for emigration rather than restrained it.

The advent of statutorily fixed rents in the 1880s introduced in effect dual ownership of land, a fact inevitably translated in time into the transfer of ownership into the hands of the tenant-occupiers. The transfer is post-Victorian—even in 1917 the process of transfer was only half completed. Reduced rents contributed to improved incomes for farmers, but more important was the rise in prices of agricultural goods relative to other goods; for a sustained fall in prices, in fact, would have quickly made the annuities as onerous as the rents they replaced.

V

The outstanding features of Victorian Ireland were the somewhat contradictory combination of explosive development of literacy and national consciousness in a framework of inherited racial and colonial resentments, and a rapid growth in *per capita* incomes, a growth not sufficiently rapid, however, to reduce the disparity in income relative to other countries. The Victorian era in Ireland has fallen victim to polemics about the origins of the 'land war' and about the reasons for the failure of the 'emancipated' tenant to raise output. The land system was never oppressive in the crude way usually asserted. On the other hand, the failure of the tenant to advance more rapidly in economic condition has to be sited in a background of initial relative backwardness and low incomes. With such inherited factors, to require or to have

101

expected a more rapid growth of *per capita* output in Ireland than in lowland Scotland or in Denmark, in a period moreover of growing international competition and falling prices, would have been to ask the impossible.

Notes

1 Kettle, 1958, 8.
2 Cullen, *A New History of Ireland*, Vol. iv, Clarendon P., Oxford.
3 Lee, 1973.
4 Cullen, 1975.
5 BPP 1835 XXXII; 1836 XXX–XXXIV; 1837 XXXI, XXXVIII, LI; 1845, XIX–XXII.
6 Cullen and Smout, 1977, 10.
7 Dickson, 1977, 353–4, 356–7.
8 Cousens, 1961; Cousens, 1964.
9 Cullen, 1975; O'Gráda, 1974.
10 MacDonnell, 1862, 274.
11 O'Gráda, 1975, 153.
12 Kettle, 1958, 10–11.
13 Kickham, 1879, 267, 295.
14 *Ibid.*, 273.
15 O'Brien, 1878, 163.
16 The fullest published discussions are in Solow, 1971, and Donnelly, 1975.
17 Cullen *The Emergence of Modern Ireland, 1600–1900*, Batsford, London.
18 O'Gráda, 1974, 390.
19 Vaughan, 1977. The figure of £40 million in Cullen, 1972, 138, includes potatoes and is for net income (with estimated cash wages and certain other expenses deducted). See also Cullen and Smout, 1977, 17, note 10, on the effects of further adjustments.
20 Staehle, 1950–1, 460.
21 Grimshaw, 1884, 523–4.
22 Cullen, 1972, 137.
23 MacDonnell, 1862, 276.
24 Cullen, 1972, 137.
25 O'Súilleabháin, 1970.
26 BPP 1901 LXXXVIII.
27 *Ibid.*
28 O'Gráda, 1974; Lee, 1969; Solow, 1971, 69.
29 Cullen, 1972, 170.
30 Brady, 1958, 178.
31 Finlay, 1913, 24.
32 Staehle, 1950–1, 460–1.
33 O'Gráda, 1977a.
34 O'Gráda, 1973.
35 O'Gráda, 1977b, 68–71.
36 Cousens, 1961; Cousens, 1964.
37 Cullen, 1968, 158.

9   Free Trade and the Land

F. M. L. Thompson

The English countryside has probably never looked more prosperous than it did in the 1860s. The farming landscape was neat and trim, businesslike and well cared for, and bore the marks of careful, even lavish, management: hedges were neatly laid by skilled hands, fences and gates were in good order, ploughland in a high state of tilth showed barely a weed, crops marched in tidy, straight lines across the fields, roots were hoed to garden levels of cleanliness; everywhere were to be seen new or renovated farmhouses and farm buildings, and well-dressed farmers bowling along the country lanes in their smartly painted gigs or traps. The countryside has seldom looked more dejected than at the turn of the present century: neglected and overgrown hedges, weed-infested meadows and pastures, decaying thatch, dilapidated buildings, untidy farmyards; everywhere examples of lack of attention, misfortune, or despair could be seen. Appearances do not altogether deceive: the contrast between the landscape of prosperity and the landscape of depression was the visual evidence of the depression which struck agriculture in the 1870s, and which in the view of some did not fully clear until the 1940s.[1] On the other hand, appearances do not tell the whole truth. It is no object of this chapter to conjure away the Great Depression; but it would be a mistake to suppose that the signs of economizing on labour meant that everyone in the farming community was impoverished, any more than the visible evidence of the lavish use of labour implied that everyone was prosperous.

I

There is no particular mystery about the agricultural prosperity of the twenty years from the early 1850s to the early 1870s. In this period rents increased by about one-fifth,[2] farmers' net incomes doubled,[3] and the earnings of agricultural labourers rose by around 40 per cent, with particularly rapid wage increases in the 1860s.[4] In the same period retail prices, although they cannot be measured with great accuracy, probably rose by about a quarter; and the general level of agricultural prices, on which all agricultural incomes rested, increased by much the same amount.[5] In aggregate terms farmers and labourers were becoming better off, although landowners may as a group have suffered a slight fall in real rents; overall, this is the stuff that prosperity is made of. This good fortune confounded the protectionist politicians who had been so shrilly convinced in the 1840s that repeal of the Corn Laws would ruin British agriculture, and had silenced those farmers who had believed that their livelihoods depended on wheat and on selling wheat at prices that would be drastically undermined by free trade. The simple view is that the prophets of disaster were fundamentally right, but got their timing wrong. The prosperity was due, in other words, to a fortunate interlude during which the effects of free trade were held in abeyance, partly by fortuitous interruptions to international trade and the growth of overseas grain-exporting capacity caused by the Crimean War and the American Civil War, but mainly by the time necessarily taken in opening up new areas of cereal production in Russia and North America, in developing their internal transport systems, and above all in developing low-cost long-distance steam shipping. In this interval import competition was held at arm's length; then, as the steppes and prairies came on stream and the transport developments came to fruition in the 1870s, the full force of import competition was unleashed on free trade Britain, and swamped its agriculture. Continental Europe put up its tariff shutters against cheap American and Russian grain, and preserved its peasant farmers; industrial Britain, a nation of consumers, contentedly fed itself from the cheapest sources the world could offer, and allowed its agriculture to go to the wall. For those who fancy their history simple, dramatic, and memorable, it is an enticing view. The truth was more complicated.

The good fortune was not evenly spread over the entire country and all farming regions, nor was it simply the effortless result of enjoying a prolongation of the effective protection of distance for a period of twenty years' grace. A farmer reminiscing in the 1930s about these golden years of the 1850s might comment, 'They did not have to make money, it was brought home and shot down on their doors', but nostalgic hearsay and gossip misled him.[6] Profits were made in farming in the middle of the century, certainly; but they had to be worked for. They were made by studying the markets, and by adapting farming practices and the mixture of products to trends in demand. The food market was growing in size, through population growth, but changing in composition as a result of the general rise in real incomes. Cereal consumption per head remained constant, imports, which had provided about 10 per cent of the annual consumption of bread grains in the 1840s, grew to 50 per cent of the supply by the early 1870s, and the price of wheat remained broadly unchanged. The average consumption of animal food, on the other hand, as Caird had foretold in 1849 and confirmed in 1878, rose as more and more people could afford to satisfy their preference for more varied and tasty foods, and by the 1870s had more than doubled; the prices of meat and dairy produce rose by 40–50 per cent, and the major part of the increase in supply was produced by British farmers.[7]

This pattern of demand and prices did not mean in any simple or straightforward fashion, however, that easy money was earned by farmers who went in for raising or fattening livestock while cereal growers had a lean time. The relationship between costs and farming techniques was such that the livestock could most profitably be raised within mixed farming systems, where the farm grew fodder crops and produced both grains and animals for sale. Farmers increased output in two complementary ways. On the one hand, advanced mixed farming practices were extended into light soil and free-draining areas that had previously been limited to raising store stock through limitations on their fodder supply, chiefly by adopting higher standards of cultivation for their root crops through heavier manuring and the introduction of horsepower for seed drilling and hoeing. On the other hand, mixed farming practices were themselves intensified by the increased inputs of feed and fertilizer which were the essence of high farming.[8] The result was more wheat or barley, and more meat, per acre, joint products of the feed–stock–manure–grain cycle. In the predominantly grazing areas, by contrast, stocking ratios were much less flexible and for both technical and economic reasons it was difficult to raise livestock output so rapidly. The yield of the grass itself was not much increased, and in many of these areas root crops did not answer well; and while it was possible for these farmers to purchase feedstuffs and thus increase stocking capacities, their farming systems tended to lack sufficient outlets for the efficient use of the resulting augmented supplies of enriched manure, so that the returns on purchased feed grains or oilcake were more limited than in the mixed farming areas. It is true that much effort and capital were devoted to field draining in this period, predominantly in the midland counties where lay most of the heavy, wet, clay lands. While this effort improved the soil conditions, and hence the growing conditions, on the 2–3 million acres which were drained, on the whole it did not render them well suited to the adoption of the classic mixed farming systems; the telling sign is that root acreages tended if anything to decline in these districts, which indeed raised their output through purchasing feeds and fertilizers, and through growing such other fodder crops as vetches and pulses, without however coming on level terms in costs and productivity with their light-land competitors.[9]

The best and most rapidly rising incomes, therefore, were enjoyed by the most efficient, and most favourably located, mixed farmers who succeeded in operating their finely balanced and integrated grain and livestock enterprises at high levels of inputs and outputs and with commercially shrewd adjustments in the proportions of grain and stock in their marketed produce. When grain prices were particularly poor the mixed farmer could feed part of the crop to his stock instead of selling it, and look

105

to good stock prices to maintain his total income; while in response to longer-term market trends he switched between cash-crop grains and feed grains, and met generally less attractive grain prices by increasing his emphasis on stock raising, all within the mixed farm structure and without any radical alteration in the pattern of land use.[10] The conditions of farming prosperity were indeed continually shifting throughout the 1850s and 1860s, and success involved the ability to read the shifts correctly, and the effort, technical skill, and experience to make appropriate responses. It also required the backing of sound estate management which did not suffer from hidebound insistence on adherence to once fashionable but obsolete crop rotations, and of adequate investment by landlords in fixed equipment suited to the productive capacity of the farm, especially in covered yards for stall feeding and in facilities for conserving manure.

Such conditions were far from universally met. But apart from differing fortunes of neighbouring farms within the same farming region, which might be accounted for by their lying on different estates with different investment and management records, or by the varying abilities of individual farmers, the most obvious contrasts were between the areas that were suited by soil and climate to mixed farming, and those which were not. If the behaviour of rents can be taken as an indicator of the fortunes of the farmers who paid them and of the kind of farming that they practised, as they generally have been, then the regional contrasts were indeed marked. In England as a whole agricultural rents, as recorded in the income tax assessments, increased by 25 per cent between 1852/3 and 1879/80; in individual counties the increases ranged from over 70 per cent above the average in Surrey, with a rise of 43 per cent, to nearly 50 per cent below the average in Leicestershire, with a rise of 14 per cent.[11] While the county figures do not show an entirely clear-cut distribution the general picture is reasonably plain. All the midland counties[12] had below-average rent increases, as also did East Anglia and the Shropshire–Cheshire–Lancashire region; these can be taken as the main regions in which there was an actual fall in real rents, and in which farm incomes and output did not expand with any vigour. In the Midlands extensive drainage and other farm improvements presumably did not succeed in producing any great improvements in incomes; in East Anglia the largest advances in high farming had already been achieved before 1852, so that further increases in this period in output and net returns were below average; while in the immediate farming region of the industrial north-west the scope for further expansion of predominantly pastoral systems to supply the large urban market must similarly have been limited by the effectiveness of pre-1852 development. It is not so simple to explain the pattern of counties which, on the evidence of above-average rent increases, were the most prosperous. It included the home counties,[13] which benefited from their proximity to the metropolitan market; most of south-eastern and southern England[14] as well as Lincolnshire,[15] which had been later starters than East Anglia in adopting high-output mixed farming systems, and where these spread rapidly during these years, but not Hertfordshire, Berkshire, or Wiltshire where the same developments were taking place; Devon and Cornwall in the south-west, grazing and dairying counties, but not Somerset; and the three northern counties, Westmorland, Cumberland, and Northumberland, which are generally thought of as mainly grazing areas. Sizeable areas of Northumberland, however, in the Till valley, and of Cumberland, in the Eden valley, which contributed large proportions of the total county rentals, were notable for their vigorous development of the turnip–barley husbandry to a high standard, so that as a broad generalization it can be said that the highest rent increases were concentrated in the arable counties where the conditions were most suitable for the expansion of high farming.

To a large extent these differential rent movements can be viewed in terms of the previously lower-rented counties closing the gap with the pastoral western counties which traditionally had higher rents per acre. But while in terms of incomes per acre both owners and farmers in many of the pastoral western counties may have remained better off than owners and farmers in eastern counties throughout this period, this is not a measure of individual incomes or welfare since it takes no account of the size of holdings. If it is the rate of growth of real incomes which makes people prosperous, then the clear implication is that agricultural prosperity in the third quarter of the century was concentrated in eastern and southern England, and that in about one third of the country, the Midlands and north-west, where rents rose by at least 5 per cent less than prices, it is doubtful whether owners or farmers saw much at all in the way of prosperity. Agricultural labourers, on the other hand, although the wide regional differences in their wage rates and earnings, already long-established by 1850, did not narrow appreciably in this period, seem to have obtained increases in earnings which more than matched the rise in retail prices, in low-paid and high-paid regions alike.[16] They were the one group in the farming community that enjoyed a measure of prosperity wherever they worked, even if in many low-wage regions this had scarcely lifted their living standards as far as the poverty line by the early 1870s. This is a reminder that prosperity is an ambiguous term. If it is used to mean something entirely different, affluence and the enjoyment of real incomes ample enough to support comfortable or extravagant life styles, then landowners were generally a great deal more affluent than farmers, and farmers than labourers, who were not prosperous at all. In particular, many landowners were becoming more affluent because they drew rising incomes from outside agriculture, even if their agricultural incomes may have been falling, both because their estates were in regions where real rents declined, and because estate expenditure on management, repairs, and improvements was generally a rising proportion of gross rents.

II

The farming business as an industry, however, was far from uniformly prosperous in the third quarter of the century, and those sectors and regions which did prosper enjoyed their good fortune by dint of the constant changes and adaptations needed to keep on the right side of movements in costs and prices. Costs were imperfectly known and impossible to allocate with any accuracy, then or now, to the variety of products of a single mixed farming enterprise; while profitable changes were generally in the direction of increasing inputs and raising output, which gave an expansive and optimistic air to the process. Nevertheless, the picture puts the 'golden age' into a perspective which suggests that it was a great deal more golden in retrospect than at the time, and that what followed was not a complete break with the past, since there were few farmers who can have been accustomed to making easy money by following an unchanging routine, and to whom change was unfamiliar and unpleasant. Contemporaries experienced what followed as a deluge which washed away the harvests of 1878–82, and posterity saw it as a deluge of cheap imports which in the next twenty years washed the heart out of English agriculture. Mesmerized by the statistics of a precipitous fall in wheat acreages and a general contraction of arable, confronted by pictures and stories of abandoned farms and derelict land, mortified by the casualty lists of personal misfortunes and individual disasters, and thoroughly bewildered by the commercial downfall of the farming systems that had been regarded as the essence of perfection and progress, it was natural for even a knowledgeable observer to conclude, at the end of Victoria's reign, that English agriculture was in permanent decline, undergoing a lingering death from which it had thus far only been, barely, spared through the magnificent obstinacy of those landowners and farmers who insisted on continuing to keep the land under cultivation even if it did not pay. For the industry as a whole, however, these were years which saw the merest check to the growth of real output, in the 1880s, followed by a resumption of growth, accompanied by a continuous dwindling of the numbers of people employed to produce it, which lasted until 1914.[17] This is the paradox of the Great Depression: personal tragedy and hardship, impersonal expansion.

The seasons of 1878–82 were so atrocious, with the wet spring and delayed sowing of 1878, the three notoriously wet summers of 1879, 1880, and 1882, and the late and difficult ploughing conditions associated with such weather, that for a while farmers thought they were the hapless victims of a cruelly unlucky run of bad weather rather than anything more permanent. It could not escape notice, of course, that the poor harvests were not balanced by any compensating rise in prices, indeed that cereal prices continued the fall which had started in 1874; but with the growth of imports it was already accepted that the British price was a world price no longer determined by the state of the domestic harvest. It was part of the price of living in a free trade world that bad harvests and bad prices might go together, something which made farming much more precarious than it had been but which did not necessarily threaten to undermine its foundations unless by pure mischance there were too many disastrous harvests in a row. The argument, frequently made by farming witnesses to the Royal Commission on the Depressed State of the Agricultural Interest, sitting from 1879 to 1882, was that given a normal harvest and an adequate volume of good quality wheat and barley to sell, farmers could still find the lower grain prices profitable, or at any rate would only suffer such marginal losses on their grain production that the overall viability of their sheep-and-corn farming would not be called in question. Falling prices, although not welcome, were not by themselves seen as the cause of their misfortunes.[18] For some years, therefore, the signs of agricultural distress were met by the cry that all would be well if only the rain would stop. When the sun did shine again in the 1880s, however, the clouds did not lift from agriculture; prices continued to fall, to levels where British farmers could not compete; farmers lived on their capital until it was all gone, and then quitted; arrears of rent mounted; farms were given up, land was left to tumble down to grass or went out of cultivation altogether; and when the sun shone with untypical persistence it produced the droughts of 1892–5, more harvest failures, and the lowest prices of all. By then everyone was convinced that the weather was no more than a fortuitous aggravation of the farmers' troubles, which were caused by foreign competition and falling prices; a more sophisticated view was that they were caused by over-expansion and over-production in the great primary producing countries of the world, which unloaded their surpluses on the open British market, often at a loss to themselves and to the distress of their own farmers.

What lay in ruins by the mid-1890s was the edifice of high farming, the economics of its doctrine of maximum production through high input levels being undermined by the collapse of prices and rising labour costs. Wheat prices fell by 50 per cent between the early 1870s and the mid-1890s, while those of barley and oats fell less steeply, by a third or less. Price falls of this size inevitably caused acute distress as farmers with fixed outgoings, particularly where they had interest payments to make on borrowed capital, were faced with falling incomes, and demands for rent remissions and reductions were widely made, and granted, as one way of reducing costs. The differential movement of grain and livestock product prices, continuing within a generally falling trend the divergence manifested in the 1850s and 1860s, was also bound to produce shifts in production patterns. Import competition certainly became stiff in meat and dairy products with the development of refrigeration techniques from the 1880s, and prices fell by 15–20 per cent. The imported frozen or chilled meat, however, was generally of poorer quality than the home product, and English beef and mutton maintained their prices considerably better than did the imported varieties.[19] Wool prices fell precipitously as over-production in Australia flooded the market; this was the one livestock product with a price behaviour resembling that of wheat, but it was of generally minor significance, although locally it could be of importance, since already by the early 1870s wool provided only 4 per cent of the total receipts of English farmers.[20] Butter and cheese prices slumped sharply in 1879, the year when American Cheddar first arrived in quantity and saturated the market, but then recovered, and over the whole period fell by no more than 15 per cent; of much greater importance to English dairy farmers, the price of liquid milk scarcely altered at all. The selling prices of produce were one element determining the fortunes of farming; the other was the cost of production. To the farmer rent was a cost, and one which was reduced, by widely varying amounts in different parts of the country, by perhaps a quarter on average. The prices of purchased inputs fell much more markedly than this: oilcakes and maize, the most important of the purchased feeds, were 40 per cent cheaper in the mid-1890s than they had been in the early 1870s, while purchased fertilizers went down in price by 55 per cent.[21] The fall in the price of feeding stuffs helped to reduce the cost of horse labour; but human labour was by far the largest single element in farming costs, and it did not become any cheaper. Agricultural wages had been rising quite rapidly in the early 1870s, both before and after Joseph Arch's unionizing activities; they fell back a little in the 1880s, but by much less than retail prices, and by the mid-1890s had recovered their earlier level in money terms, increasing their real value by 20 per cent or more.

Such rapid and large changes in the relative prices of the different major farm products, and in the relative prices of the different factor costs, produced a severe challenge to English farming and imposed heavy stresses on the system. Contemporaries, and an earlier generation of historians, believed that the stresses were so heavy that they broke the back of English agriculture, and that the challenge could not be met without universal suffering, hardship, and distress. Even those who have drawn attention to the differing fortunes of cereal and livestock farmers have tended to present their picture in a frame of general depression in which some regions merely suffered less than others.[22] It was left to Fletcher to argue that depression was confined to the corn-growing regions, and that the livestock farmers did not suffer at all.[23] The idea that there might have been considerable areas of prosperity, in terms of rising real output and real incomes, within a period that is firmly rooted in the historical subconscious as the Great Depression, has not found ready acceptance. The difficulty is that farmers failed and went bankrupt in pastoral and livestock districts as well as in the corn-growing regions, not in as large numbers but still much more frequently than they had done in the 'normal' years of the early 1870s, and more frequent failure is an indicator of depression in the industry.[24] The solution to the problem is to distinguish between the fortunes of individuals and the fortunes of the farming business; some managers may be forced out of business, unable to make a go of it in difficult trading conditions, without this meaning that the whole industry is in decline.

There will never be any doubt about the steep decline in wheat growing, with the acreage under wheat falling from over 3 million to 1.75 million in twenty years, and there is a temptation to regard the whole depression as a crisis and contraction of wheat. Certainly the wheat-growing districts of eastern and southern England were hard hit, and the heavy clay areas were hardest hit of all; in Essex rents fell by over 50 per cent, in some cases by two-thirds, there was a massive exodus of ruined farmers, large numbers of untenanted and unlettable farms, and a concentration of derelict land which was displayed in a truly depressing official map in 1894 of 'coarse, weedy pasture'.[25] But there was more than a depression in wheat, and on heavy clays, even if these stood out. Everywhere that mixed farming was practised the pressures of costs and prices produced a decline in the intensity of cultivation, a decline in output, and a decline in incomes. Some few individuals made a success out of going against the grain, and increased their profits by raising their output through a further turn of the high-farming screw, but this could only succeed because the majority did not have the resources to follow suit; some extended their operations by adding holding to holding, and maintained their incomes by spreading a thinner profit over a larger area; but most ended up with the reduced incomes which spell depression. On all but the heaviest soils it was relatively easy to switch from wheat to barley, or even oats; and since the demand for horsefeed from the town stables continued to increase vigorously throughout the period, those who could supply oats and hay—which retained its effective protection from foreign competition since it was too bulky in relation to value for any considerable import to develop—were assured of a good market.[26] The situation, however, called for larger adjustments than these, since it was more a question of reducing costs until a profitable level of output was attained than simply of switching from loss-making to profit-making crops. Labour was the chief cost which had to be reduced by managerial action, since other costs were reduced by market forces. This could be achieved through increased productivity, either as a result of better nutrition raising the physical capacity for work, or by mechanization, and both did occur. But the major economies in the labour bill came from employing fewer labourers to do fewer tasks on the farm.

The most labour-intensive operations in the classic sheep-and-corn mixed farming systems were those devoted to the root crop, whose proper cultivation to yield maximum fodder weights required between two and three times as many man-hours per acre annually as did grain crops, and in addition required proportionately more horse labour. When the labour needs of folding sheep on the roots, with frequent moving of the hurdles, are added to the labour required for root growing itself, the high labour demand of the cycle is apparent. With the fall in the cost of feeding stuffs, particularly of imported maize and oilcakes but also of home-grown feed grains, and of fertilizers, it became cheaper to purchase feed and fertilizer and reduce the amount of roots which were grown and the number of sheep which were kept on the farm. In itself this substitution of purchased inputs for labour need not have affected the volume of saleable output. In practice, however, it ceased to be worthwhile to cultivate the very lightest soils: the margin of cultivation retreated from the tops of the downs and wolds as these reverted to poor grass, arable acreages declined, and the amount of labour saved more than balanced the amount of output forgone, but at the price of lower incomes for the farmers. The agricultural statistics permit a rough measure of the net effects of these processes: in the arable districts of the official classification the total arable acreage declined by 12 per cent between 1875 and 1895, while the acreages under corn crops and roots, and the number of sheep, all declined by 20 per cent.[27] Although the number of cattle kept in these districts increased by 12 per cent in the same period, there is no doubt that the volume of saleable output fell, and farm incomes with it. In the most dramatic situations, as in Essex, a whole generation of farmers was virtually wiped out and in part replaced by new tenants moving in from Scotland, who largely abandoned corn growing, laid land down to grass in a somewhat slovenly way, stocked it with cattle, dispensed with hired labour and worked the farms with their own family labour, eking out a living on a much lower level than their more gentlemanly predecessors had enjoyed. Elsewhere, out of the limelight, there was more genteel contraction and poverty without sharp changes, as in upland Lincolnshire where there was no wholesale turnover of tenantry, but a contraction of tillage, a switch from wheat to barley, a relaxation of cultivation standards, and a slide in real incomes.[28] Decline might be a steep road to ruin or a gentle slope to reduced circumstances; either way, it was a symptom of depression.

Other farmers and farming regions experienced no decline at all, in output, incomes, or living standards. They were the farmers who were well placed to satisfy the growing demand for milk and meat, had no extensive corn-growing enterprises to liquidate, and employed only a small amount of hired labour to supplement that of their families. Total milk consumption grew more than three-fold between the 1860s and 1900, with the main period of growth in the 1870s and again in the 1890s; total milk output increased by about 50 per cent in the same period, the difference being explained by the shift out of butter and cheese production into the sale of liquid milk.[29] Total meat consumption doubled in the same period, but imports provided an increasing proportion of the supply so that domestic output grew by only 35 per cent; in the shorter period from the early 1870s to the mid-1890s domestic meat output grew by about 10 per cent.[30] Such was the demand facing dairy and fatstock farmers, and many were able to profit from it. They did so in Lancashire, but in many other counties as well.[31] Which others can be roughly identified from an examination of rent movements, bearing in mind that the income tax assessments lagged behind actual rent decreases since they did not take rent remissions and abatements into account as these were supposed to be purely temporary. Thus the income tax assessments show a decline of 17 per cent in agricultural rent for England as a whole between 1872/3 and 1892/3, whereas the real decline was in the order of 25 per cent. The spread between counties, however, remains a good indicator of their fortunes, ranging from a decline of 33 per cent in Essex to a rise of 5 per cent in Westmorland. Cornwall, Cheshire, and Cumberland also recorded increases in rent, and Lancashire and Devon were very little behind with decreases of under 3 per cent. These, if farmers' incomes kept in tune with rents as they had usually done, were six prosperous counties; and bearing in mind that the general price level of manufactured goods and non-competing foodstuffs, such as tea, sugar, and coffee, fell by about 30 per cent, there is little doubt that the next half-dozen counties, whose rents fell by 11 per cent or less, were also reasonably prosperous: Derby, Shropshire, Surrey, Sussex, Durham, and Somerset. This group included all the western counties, with the rather surprising exception of Hereford, and suggest that about one third of the country enjoyed moderate to quite unmistakable prosperity. By the same token at least another third of the country suffered from depression, with rents falling by more than the price level; this group included East Anglia and much of the Midlands,[32] which had also fared comparatively poorly in the 1850s and 1860s, and much of eastern and southern England which fell heavily from its high-farming days.[33] On the middle third, comprising parts of the Midlands and southern England, as well as Yorkshire and Northumberland, the rent evidence is neutral, suggesting neither depression nor prosperity.[34]

III

The broad conclusion, that farmers for whom milk and meat formed a fairly high proportion of total output—to which potatoes, hay, poultry, eggs, and fresh vegetables should be added— and whose relatively small arable area was devoted to growing grains and green crops for fodder, were likely to have been reasonably prosperous right through the years of the Great Depression, is not particularly startling. It is subject to the qualification that the prosperity attached to farming regions is a function of the general climate of costs, demand, and prices within which they operated, and does not mean that every individual farmer in those regions at the beginning of the period was still there at the end, purring with satisfaction at the size of his bank balance. There were undoubtedly many individual casualties in these areas as farmers here and there plunged to disaster because of the short, sharp crisis of a single-year price drop, or an outbreak of sheep rot. It also rests on the assumption that farmers' incomes moved in sympathy with rents. For England as a whole the evidence is that total agricultural rents remained a fairly stable proportion of gross agricultural output, with a slight tendency to decline from around 35 per cent in the early 1870s to about one third in the mid-1890s and 30 per cent by 1910–13.[35] Such a movement is corroborated by statements from some counties in the mid-1890s that rents had fallen as a proportion of total farming costs;[36] and it substantially passes testing at the county level, where rough estimation of the gross agricultural output of a sample of nine counties, county by county, for 1873 and 1911, suggests that rents ranged from 42 down to 30 per cent of output in 1873 and from 40 to 27 per cent in 1911.[37]

In themselves these calculations do no more than suggest that gross agricultural output kept broadly in tune with rent movements, with a tendency to increase relative to rents; they do not prove that farmers' incomes also remained in tune, since these were the residual of gross output when the wage bill and purchased inputs had been met, as well as rent. Agricultural labour certainly became more expensive, but on the other hand less of it was employed. The most acceptable estimates suggest that average earnings were about the same in 1891 as they had been in 1871, while the numbers of regular hired labourers had fallen by a fifth; by 1911 earnings were at least 16 per cent above the 1871 level, numbers 33 per cent below it. Such movements indicate that the total wage bill was about 15 per cent below the 1871 level in 1891, and 22 per cent below it in 1911.[38] Inputs, on the other hand, were substantially increased in volume, but at dramatically falling prices. Estimates of the quantities and values involved are only available for the United Kingdom as a whole, and since the great bulk of the feeding stuffs and fertilizers were imported and hence recorded simply as entering the United Kingdom, it is impossible to disaggregate the figures and arrive at estimates for England alone. It is a fair guess, given the state of farming in the different countries, that English farmers used considerably more of these inputs, in relation to acreage and to output, than did Irish or Welsh farmers, in 1871, but quite likely no more than Scottish farmers; but whether differential usage widened or

113

narrowed over the next 40 years it is difficult to say, since the evident urge of the English to substitute purchased inputs for labour may have been more than balanced by the effects of Irish and Welsh efforts to raise their farming practices from their earlier state of comparative backwardness. The United Kingdom figures show an increase of 67 per cent in the quantities of feeds purchased by farmers, between the early 1870s and 1911, and of 39 per cent in the weight of fertilizers; but such was the fall in prices that the value of the purchased inputs fell by 17 per cent between the early 1870s and the early 1890s, and in 1911 was only 2 or 3 per cent above its 1870 level.[39] The tentative assumption can be made that this pattern of input quantities and values broadly reflected the specifically English experience.

The gross output of English agriculture fell by 13 per cent between 1871 and 1891, but by 1911 it was back at its 1871 level.[40] Putting together the estimates of the relative movements in the several factor shares it appears, taking 1871 as the base, that by 1891 gross output had fallen by a little less than rents, labour cost, and inputs; the difference, of 4 per cent, is not large enough to suggest that any serious shift in factor shares had occurred, but it does at least suggest that farmers' incomes, at the worst, had remained a constant share of output. Unsteady as the foundations may be for carrying any great weight, it is tolerably safe to infer from this that over the classic period of the 'Great Depression' the money incomes of English farmers as a group did indeed decline broadly in step with movements in gross output and in rents; that this decline was markedly smaller (barely half) than the fall in the general non-food price level, so that farmers' real incomes increased; and that regional variations in the size and direction of rent changes reflected similar movements in farmers' incomes, indicating that 'prosperity' was a better label than 'depression' to attach to the experience of some regions. After the early 1890s factor shares appear to have altered radically: by 1911, with gross output roughly back to its 1871 level and purchased inputs only marginally above it, but the wage bill one fifth and rents nearly 30 per cent lower, farmers' incomes must have been substantially larger than in 1871 in order to balance the equation. How much larger cannot be stated with any certainty in the absence of figures for the actual factor shares, except for rents, relating to England; but it is not inconceivable that farmers' incomes were between one fifth and one third larger in 1911 than in 1871.

Part of this improvement was the result of the recovery of agricultural prices from their nadir in the mid-1890s, and it has always been recognized that from about 1895 onwards the fortunes of English agriculture, and of English farmers, began to mend somewhat. Nevertheless, the literature which speaks in terms of a modest recovery, with the situation of farmers in the immediately pre-war years being less miserable than in the depths of the depression, does not exactly convey very clearly the fact that over the period 1871–1911 as a whole, farmers' money incomes definitely increased, and their real incomes rose substantially. There are, to be sure, many reasons why this may not have been appreciated as 'prosperity' at the time. The total amount of gross agricultural output left over to provide farmers' incomes was spread over a remarkably stable number of farmers, so that there was no question of declining *per capita* shares.[41] But there was a great change in the identity of the farmers, so that few individuals can have farmed right through the period and experienced the full benefits of the changes in incomes. One consequence of the decline in the number of hired labourers was that many farmers and their families had to work harder on the land, so that any increase in their incomes would not be viewed by them, and should not be seen, simply as an increase in 'profit'. Above all, however, the benefits of rising incomes were not evenly spread over the whole body of English farmers, but were concentrated in the milk and meat regions at the expense of those where cereal growing continued to be of considerable importance. In the nine counties for which output estimates have been made, output increased substantially, in constant price terms, in Cheshire, Shropshire, and Somerset; remained much the same in Devon and Wiltshire; and declined considerably in Buckinghamshire, Essex, Northamptonshire, and Suffolk. The fortunes of farmers no doubt followed a similar pattern of growth, stability, or decline in counties with similar product mixes.

IV

Farmers came through the period 1870–1914 with mixed fortunes and strongly amplified regional differences; at the end of the day, few suffered any fall in real incomes, but only the men who were in milk or meat became significantly better off. With farm workers something of the reverse happened, as regional variations in wages narrowed, and for all those who remained on the land real wages rose; the pull of higher wages in other occupations of course remained, and the rise in their real wages was scarcely sufficient to bring many comforts or luxuries into the agricultural labourers' homes.[42] With landowners, as with farmers, there were great regional differences in changes in their incomes from rents; but for them there was also a great fall in the capital value of agricultural land to bear, a decline in land values from 30–5 years' purchase to 20–5 years' purchase which applied across the country irrespective of the amount by which rents themselves were reduced. This factor perhaps made them the most genuinely depressed group in the countryside, more certain sufferers from the effects of free trade than the farmers, but quite largely limited in their suffering to the writing down of capital values, and the inconveniences of fixed interest charges on their debts confronting falling money incomes. Free trade helped the decline of the landed classes on its way, but brought something a long way short of disaster to agriculture. Something entirely different, the decline of rural industries and of manufacturing in rural areas, as industry became increasingly concentrated on the coalfields and in the towns, was the main cause of the apparent impoverishment of the countryside. For one brief moment in its entire history, occupying roughly the years from 1870 to 1914, the countryside became a place where little save agriculture was carried on; the countryside found itself more and more denuded of its flow of non-agricultural incomes, and it was not a pleasing experience for the remaining inhabitants.

Notes

1 Perry, 1974, 13.
2 BPP 1884–5 XXII 318–20 (28th Report of Commissioners of Inland Revenue.) The increase between 1852/3 and 1872/3 was 19 per cent; but assessments lagged behind actual rent movements, and the maximum increase in the assessments was that between 1852/3 and 1879/80, of 25 per cent.
3 Bellerby, 1959, 103.
4 Mitchell and Deane, 1962, 349–51.
5 *Ibid.*, 343–4, 471–5.
6 Perry, 1974, 19.
7 E. L. Jones, 1975, 197–8; Perren, 1978, 3.
8 F. M. L. Thompson, 1968b.
9 Morgan, 1979, for techniques of root crop cultivation and extent of root acreages.
10 E. L. Jones, 1975, 197–8.
11 BPP 1884–5 XXII 318–20.
12 In descending order of rent increases: Notts., Rutl., Oxon., Worcs., Northants., Staffs., Derby, War., Leics.
13 Surrey, Kent, Middx., Essex.
14 Sussex, Dorset, Hants., Beds., Bucks., Hunts., Cambs.
15 The East Riding may also have been in this group, but unfortunately the report records Yorkshire as a single county.
16 Hunt, 1973, ch. 1.
17 Ojala, 1952, Table xvii, 209, gives figures for the gross agricultural output of the U.K. at constant prices, which increase in every sub-period between 1867–9 and 1911–13, except for a fall of 3 per cent between 1870–6 and 1877–85. For England alone the growth in gross agricultural output was greater than these U.K. figures suggest.
18 BPP 1882 XVI; Sturge, 1879–80, 23–4.
19 Fletcher, 1961a, 418–20; Fletcher, 1961b.
20 Fletcher, 1961a, 432.
21 Ojala, 1952, 212–3.
22 Ernle, 1961, ch. xviii; Clapham, 1951, 80–1; Ashworth, 1960, 67.
23 Fletcher, 1961a.
24 Perry, 1974, ch. 1.
25 BPP 1894 XVI 51.
26 F. M. L. Thompson, 1976, 60–81.
27 Orwin and Whetham, 1964, 251, 267.
28 Brown, 1978.
29 Taylor, 1976, 590–2.
30 Perren, 1978, 3.
31 Fletcher, 1961b.
32 Leics., Rutl., Northants, Oxon., War., Notts.
33 Hunts., Cambs., Lincs., Berks., Wilts., Essex.
34 BPP 1896 XLIX 245: Schedule B Assessments.
35 Output figures for 1867–71 and 1894–8 from Fletcher, 1961a, 432; for 1909–13, Dewey, 1975, 105; rents from income tax assessments.
36 For example, from Lincs.: Brown, 1978, 88–90.

37 Gross agricultural output was calculated for 1873 and 1911 from the agricultural statistics for Essex, Suff., Northants, and Wilts. in the 'depressed' group; Cheshire, Devon, Shrops., and Som. in the 'prosperous' group; and Bucks. from the 'middling' group. The estimates are rough in the sense that they only value the output sold off farms of wheat, barley, oats, hay, potatoes, beef, mutton, pigmeat, wool, and milk; they thus exclude fruit, vegetables, poultry, and eggs (because adequate statistics are not available at the county level for 1873), and bias the estimates for 1911 downwards since these excluded products had become more important by then. They use the formulae for converting acreages and livestock numbers into marketed output employed in Ojala, 1952, which also bias the 1911 estimates downwards since they assume constant maturity times and killing ratios for the whole period. The resulting product output volumes were valued at current market prices for English produce. The 'rent proportion' rose in Devon and Northants, perhaps because the excluded products were of particular importance there; in the other seven counties it either remained unchanged or fell.

38 Mitchell and Deane, 1962, 350 for earnings; Ernle, 1961, 507, for numbers of hired agricultural workers. Deane and Cole, 1967, 152, give figures for total agricultural wages (including forestry and fishing) of £44.4 million in 1871, £41.8 million in 1891, and £45.8 million in 1911, which cannot readily be reconciled with the behaviour of earnings and numbers employed; given the accuracy of the numbers, they imply an increase in average earnings between 1871 and 1911 of an improbable 53 per cent.

39 Ojala, 1952, 212–13; the value figures include expenditure on imported farm animals, machinery, and 'miscellaneous' farm expenses, as well as on feeds and fertilizers.

40 Figures, in current prices, given by Fletcher and Dewey, see note 35 above.

41 Numbers of farmers in England and Wales, Ernle, 1961, 507: 1871: 249,735; 1881: 223,943; 1891: 223,610; 1901: 224,299; 1911: 208,761.

42 Hunt, 1973, 62–4.

10   The Flight from the Land

W. A. Armstrong

It is a fallacy to suppose that villagers were virtually immobile in distant times, for if their migratory horizons were usually very narrow, every serious inquiry so far conducted points to a degree of movement that is surprisingly high. Likewise the drift of population from the countryside was by no means a novelty brought about by the quickening pace of economic advance from the 1780s. On the contrary, towns of the pre-industrial era had always depended on a net inflow merely to maintain their numbers, and the migratory influx served to reinforce urban growth once the towns began to achieve self-generated natural increases as a consequence of falling mortality, usually during the second half of the eighteenth century. However, the urban population did not clearly surpass that of the rural areas until after 1851, when they were approximately in balance and, absolutely if not relatively, the agricultural labour force of England and Wales stood at its zenith, 1.88 million.[1] By this time, with considerable improvements in the art of census-taking and the advent of civil registration in 1837, materials capable of giving a much clearer view of migratory movements were beginning to be collected. From the original census enumerators' returns it is easy to make a detailed analysis of the birthplace statements observed in any town, village or hamlet, and it is not exceptional to find, for example, that three-quarters of the adult population of an urban area were born elsewhere. As aggregated in the published census abstracts, the returns may also be employed to identify gross and net flows between counties. They do not, of course, throw any light on the intervening stages of migration, its timing, or the extent to which permanent and temporary moves are mixed together. On the side of vital statistics the

118

Registrar–General's *Annual Reports* will yield natural increases calculated at the county and registration district levels, and, when compared with recorded inter-censal population changes, may be used to distinguish the components attributable to natural increase on the one hand and net migration on the other.[2] It is obvious that the migratory trends observed in a particular village do not necessarily represent those of the district or county of which it formed a part, and that alternative arrangements of the material may give rise to dissimilar, sometimes contentious interpretations.[3]

I The Pattern of Rural Depopulation in the Victorian Era

Summing up the basic statistics, which depend finally on the quantitative sources just mentioned, we may reach a number of broad conclusions.

1 Only three English and three Welsh counties (Cornwall, Huntingdon and Rutland; Cardigan, Montgomery and Radnor) recorded absolute decreases between 1841 and 1911. However, such calculations often obscure the factor of urban concentration, so that in Norfolk the aggregate census population of the three main urban centres (Norwich, Yarmouth and King's Lynn) grew by 20.6 per cent and that of the remainder fell by 2 per cent.

2 More revealing are the statistics relating to registration districts (numbering altogether over six hudred), as analysed by Cairncross.[4] In fact the aggregate population of residual rural areas (that is, after subtracting the predominantly urban registration districts and those with extensive collieries) was actually somewhat greater in 1911, by 18.5 per cent in the north and 9.2 per cent in the south, than in 1841. Nevertheless their net losses by migration had been considerable, amounting to some 79 per cent of calculated natural increases in the north and 89 per cent in the south through the period as a whole, whilst, as Table 10.1 shows, the drain was persistent.

Table 10.1 *Net losses by migration from rural residues in England and Wales, 1841–1911 ('000)**

	1841–51	1851–61	1861–71	1871–81	1881–91	1891–1901	1901–11
North	159	229	254	263	349	237	152
South	284	513	430	574	496	423	142

*Derived from Cairncross, 1953, 70. The north includes for this purpose the counties of Herefs., Salop, Staffs., War., Worcs., Leics., Notts., Derby, Lancs., Yorks., Durham, Northumb., and Cumb., together with the whole of Wales.

3 While the phasing of the net outflow no doubt varied considerably among individual districts, Table 10.1 indicates that it was most marked in the south as a whole in 1851–61 and 1871–81, but in the north in 1881–91. There is no obvious

connection with the ebb and flow of agricultural prosperity, for as Cairncross has pointed out, the 'golden age' of the 1850s and 1860s showed a marked increase in migration and the recovery after 1900 coincided with its diminution, whilst in the intervening 'depressed' period the efflux from southern rural areas reached its peak and then subsided somewhat. Likewise Lawton has concluded that in general neither quality of soil nor type of farming were important factors in explaining variations in the intensity or duration of the loss of population, save only from areas of arable land of the very highest quality where it was noticeably lower.[5]

4 Nevertheless, rural depopulation coincided with a substantial absolute decline in the agricultural labour force, which, while the number of farmers hardly changed, fell by some 23 per cent from its mid-century peak by 1911, and as a proportion of the total occupied labour force from 21.5 to 8.5 per cent.

II   The Situation of the Agricultural Labourer

The tendency for the number of employees per acre of land to decrease might appear to offer prima facie support for a theory of labour displacement consequent on increasing mechanization, of the kind envisaged by Hasbach.[6] It is clear that an abundance of cheap labour had tended to militate against mechanical innovation in the years down to 1850 (with the sole, if notorious, exception of the threshing machine) and it is significant that a *locus classicus* of information on the agrarian labour force, the *Reports of the Special Assistant Poor Law Commissioners on Women and Children in Agriculture* (1843), mentions machinery only once. But mowing and reaping machines made their appearance in the 1850s and 1860s under the pressure of seasonal labour shortages, and something of their potential was illustrated by Caird's estimate that 80,000 would suffice to cut the entire harvest of Great Britain in ten days—a number, noted F. G. Heath in 1874, only double that actually used in the previous year.[7] The 1880s saw the advent of self-binding reapers, which, however, were less than satisfactory in dealing with heavy or laid crops. And more difficulties were encountered with the extension of mechanization to other activities. Although steam traction was applied to a variety of tasks, much resistance was met from farmers, not only on account of the expense but also, sometimes, on well-founded reservations about its efficiency. For example, steam-plough sets required a field of at least twenty acres and a terrain free from rocks. In the unpropitious circumstances of the 1880s, the steam-plough works at Dorchester was only saved by switching to the production of road-rollers, whilst well-informed observers on the heavy clays of Warwickshire thought that their use had 'somewhat declined' by 1893.[8]

It is true, reductions in the overall demand for labour were implied also by the shift towards pastoral activities during the 'Great Depression', and small farmers in particular were apt to seek immediate economies of outlay. Among the mountain of impressionistic evidence gathered for the Royal Commission on Labour (1893) the comment from Bishampton (Worcestershire) that not enough labour was employed so that several men had been 'driven away', was by no means an isolated expression of view. Yet the reporter on four northern counties thought that implements were 'often used on account of the dearth of labour, not as a means to enable it to be dispensed with', instancing an encounter with a farmer who purposed a visit to York that very day to acquire a new self-binder 'because he could not get hands enough to do the tying behind his old reaper, except at a ruinous price'. Surveying the whole body of evidence in his general report, W. C. Little was inclined to think that the reduction of working staffs was a consequence and not the cause of migration.[9] Indeed, many witnesses remarked that their brighter young workers had a positive interest in and inclination to work with machines, impressed perhaps by the *hauteur* and high wages of the emerging class of 'agricultural machinery operatives', numerically insignificant though it may have been. In general it seems that where reductions in staffing occurred, they usually reflected either a disinclination to fill all the vacancies arising from death, old age and dismissals, or reduced demand for 'catch' or casual labour.[10] The social implications of the recourse to machinery were accordingly not inconsiderable, particularly in regard to harvest earnings. It was reported from Wiltshire, that owing to the 'perfection' of machinery, the harvest could be secured in as many days as it used to take weeks, given good weather; and that earnings instead of being from £6 to £8, were considered good at £3.[11] Yet all in all mechanization seems to have had little impact in forcing involuntary migration upon the regular labourers, or even in forcing down wages. If it had any such inexorable tendencies they were clearly offset by other factors.

By far the most easily quantifiable contrasts between agricultural and other employment concerned wages and hours of work. Regional variations in farm workers' wages are discussed elsewhere, and here it is necessary to note only that the ratio between agricultural and industrial wage rates remained approximately constant at just under 50 per cent throughout the period.[12] What is more, it is now established beyond any reasonable doubt that gains in money wages arising from migration are unlikely to have been offset by increased living costs. It is true that urban rents were higher, the usual level for three rooms in large provincial towns at about the end of the century being roughly double, and in London perhaps treble, what the rural labourer would normally pay for his cottage, i.e. 1*s*. 6*d*.–2*s*. per week. Otherwise the cost of living was actually lower in the towns as a consequence of the gradual urbanization of wholesale distribution, the growth of imports, and greater competition among urban retailers.[13]

In view of their comparatively low wages, the hours of labour required from farmworkers were excessively long, and came to be regarded as anomalous as hours in factories, mines and workshops shrank characteristically to about 54–56 a week by the 1880s.[14] Farmers in the area of Wigtown (Cumberland) thought their men unsettled by meeting those employed in mines and works where both higher wages and shorter hours could be had; and in Anglesey and in the Pwllheli district during the 1880s contact with weekend sojourners from the Caernarvonshire slate quarries excited the farmworkers to press successfully for a modest reduction in their hours.[15]

But in general they remained remarkably long, and everywhere stockmen were called upon to put in hours which, averaged over a year, were higher even than those of the labourers. Sunday work, in particular, was disliked since usually no compensation was given, and as a consequence it was noticed that, in spite of their higher wages, cowmen were sometimes harder to obtain than ordinary labourers. Resentment at what a Lincolnshire worker called 'constant grind, month in and month out, with never an hour to call their own' was common, but unlikely to be met with much sympathy by employers. From one midland district in 1913 it was reported that farmers voted that the District Council should keep their roadmen at work until 4 p.m. on Saturdays (urban roadmen left at 1 p.m.) 'or else the farm labourer will want to leave also early'.[16]

Much contemporary comment focused on the deficiencies of cottage accommodation. Many horrific details were revealed in the sanitary inquiries of the early and mid-Victorian period, and although Canon Girdlestone, for one, discerned some improvement by the 1880s, inadequate provision remained in 1913 'a potent cause of migration to the towns'.[17] Until the Union Chargeability Act (1865), individual parishes bore the responsibility for their own settled paupers so giving a clear incentive to landlords to strive to reduce the number of cottages wherever possible. But although the Act destroyed the rationale for this, in no way did it encourage landlords to improve cottages or build additional ones. The advent of Sanitary Boards in the rural districts after 1875, and their successors, the Rural District Councils (from 1894), had little impact on the problem, which in the last analysis had economic rather than institutional roots. In a word, cottages were scarce because it was unprofitable to build them for a class of occupiers whose ability to pay rent was so limited. It was agreed that, in general, cottages belonging to major landowners were decidedly superior, but the return on capital expended was so low that the cottage building or improvement was a quasi-philanthropic activity of a kind in which lesser proprietors or the very numerous class of petty 'house-dealers' were unlikely to engage. In 1913 it was estimated that there was an absolute shortfall corresponding to some 6.5 per cent of the existing stock, and that if cottages unfit for human habitation were condemned, a further 5 per cent would be required.[18]

From the labourer's standpoint there was more to the cottage question than amenities or even rents, which by urban standards were very low. Although there is no record of cottages in model villages ever being difficult to let, and indeed testimony comes from Puddletown (Dorset) that news of a vacancy could excite village gossip into convulsions for weeks, such accommodation did not meet with universal approbation. As she passed through one such village, 'Lord so-and-so's place . . . with three bedrooms to every house and a pump to supply water to each group of cottages', Flora Thompson was told by her father that only good people were allowed to live there; a situation corresponding, perhaps, to that on Lord Wantage's Berkshire estate where, if there was no sign of squalor and idleness, 'they daren't blow their noses . . . without the bailiff's leave', in the view of one jaundiced observer.[19] Except where the labourer dealt directly with the landlord or his representative, cottages were predominantly sub-let through farmers and invariably tied to the holder's job. In 23 per cent of the parishes examined by the Land Enquiry Committee, the ordinary labourer received a 'free' cottage as part of his earnings, and where men were in charge of animals, the figure rose to 36 per cent. Not only was this seen as a species of truck, and a factor depressing wages; it implied a lack of independence. A Yorkshire labourer complained: 'There is a feeling about tied houses that it is not your house . . . you know that if the least little thing goes wrong, out you go at a month's notice or less.' The system also curtailed to some extent the freedom of the wife and children who (an Essex witness remarked) felt obliged to assist with housework and occasional work in the fields.[20] By contrast the town labourer, however poor, could usually call his home his own as long as he paid his rent.

The spread of elementary education exerted an influence believed by many employers to be pernicious. In Devon, for example, sixteen schools had been founded, chiefly under the auspices of the National Society, during the 1820s, and by 1870 the total number of voluntary schools in the county had reached 365.[21] Such a trend was general in England to a greater or lesser extent, although it was slower to take effect in Wales, and was matched by a prodigious growth of Sunday Schools. Yet scepticism about the value of education above the barest minimum remained well entrenched among farmers and landlords, and in some respects stiffened as facilities improved. Whether or not the school authorities took 'too scholarly a view of education', and the 'steady grind of book-work' was calculated to give children a distaste for country life and divorce them from their surroundings, as Collings contended, was a moot point; it was certainly an argument capable of being exaggerated, as Richard Heath reflected on encountering youths from Shottery and from Hampton Lucy who did not admit to ever having heard of William Shakespeare.[22] The curriculum apart, a characteristic view was that a lad became accustomed to a warm room and dry feet; 'when he comes out he does not like a cold north-easter with sleet and rain, and mud over his boot-tops'. At Bunnington in the Vale of Wrington parents were drawn to send their children chiefly by the prospect of being able to obtain, by the rector's recommendation, good situations for the more promising of their children, 'sometimes as gentlemen's servants . . . pupil teachers, or clerks in merchants offices [or] porters'. All too often illiterate parents were so proud of their offspring that their sole aim was to 'put them to some trade or occupation other than farming', and from Lincolnshire a schoolmaster reported that he had often heard boys say, 'I'll never be a farmer's drudge if I can help it.'[23]

This comment takes us to the heart of the matter. What was so often decisive in influencing men to move out of agriculture into alternative employment or to the towns was what Acland summed up as a 'want of outlook', or in the words of the *Report on the Decline of the Agricultural Population* (1906) 'any reasonable prospect of advancement in life'. An intelligent labourer might become a master of his craft by the age of twenty-one, 'but after rising to the position of horse-keeper or shepherd, or perhaps, foreman, there is very little further outlook'.[24] Precisely the same point had been made by Sir George Nicholls during the 1840s,[25] and whilst it was no doubt true that 'in no other industry does the workman require more skill, and in few . . . is such a variety of skills needed',[26] this was very evidently insufficiently recognized and rewarded. Thus about Glendale (Northumberland) a mere railway porter would 'consider himself socially superior to a hind, and . . . a hind's daughter would consider that she was bettering her position by marrying anyone not connected with agricultural employment'.[27]

III   The Drift to the Towns

That the movement out of agriculture and migration to towns were related, but by no means synonymous, processes is immediately obvious from the fact that the workforce on the land fell substantially whilst the population of predominantly rural areas actually rose to some extent. Quarrying and brickmaking were common sources of alternative employment, notably in the Peterborough district, whilst in the neighbourhood of Southwell (Nottinghamshire) many young men were tempted to the nearby pit-banks; and in South Wales the remarkable development of the Glamorgan coalfield had caused farmers to become by the 1880s dependent on a regularly renewed influx of labourers from adjacent English counties.[28] Here and there substantial railway workshops presented another alternative. At Crewe, where the works employed 6,800 by 1891, the manager estimated that three-quarters were men who 'would otherwise have been available for neighbouring land', whilst at Ashford (Kent), where 2,000 men worked in the 1880s, the chairman of the Metropolitan Railway Company remarked that their apprentices were as a rule sons of agricultural labourers, adding that 'the labourers themselves come and work and perhaps their sons rise to be mechanics and fitters and moulders'.[29] Leaving aside establishments on this scale, employment at railway stations and in the rural police forces was frequently remarked on. Such changes of employment would necessitate giving up a tied cottage, but they need not entail leaving the village or at any rate going beyond the nearest small town. Similarly the availability of dockyard work at Pembroke and Milford Haven sustained moderate population growth even as numbers in the surrounding rural parishes declined.[30]

The dangers of exclusive emphasis on the condition of the agricultural labourer, and of assuming too close a correspondence between the shift out of agriculture and the drift to the towns, are made apparent again when we bear in mind that a majority of urban immigrants were females. Ravenstein recognized that at least over short distances women were more migratory than men, and it should be recalled that as late as 1911 domestic service remained by far the largest single occupational category. This was reflected in a differential sex ratio, especially in the 15–19 age group which then stood at 864 and 1,044 females per 1,000 males in rural and urban districts respectively.[31] Moreover, a large part of the efflux was made up of rural craftsmen. Saville has examined the case of Rutland, although it should be borne in mind that few if any other counties were so overwhelmingly rural in character, and that variations in census procedures do not permit exactitude.

Table 10.2 *Numbers of rural craftsmen in Rutland, 1851 and 1911**

Craftsmen	1851	1911	% change
Millers	63	22	−70
Brickmakers	38	15	−61
Sawyers	33	10	−70
Cabinet makers	31	10	−65
Coopers and Turners	15	2	−87
Wheelwrights	74	42	−43
Blacksmiths	116	83	−28
Building trades	514	415	−19
Saddlers	31	24	−23
Tailors	173	63	−64
Shoemakers	236	138	−42
Population of Rutland	22,983	20,346	−11

*Saville, 1957, 74.

The factors influencing non-agricultural elements in the rural population to join the drift to the towns have been much less discussed than those relating to agricultural labourers. But it seems clear that the emerging railway system was significant, not as is sometimes naïvely assumed because of its ability to move people from one place to another more efficiently, but on account of its role in fostering a national market. The competitive power of large-scale urban enterprise was powerfully reinforced and brought about the transfer of many rural crafts and small country industries to the towns.[32] Whilst endorsing this view, a recent study has suggested that railways exercised an influence on men's imaginations; excursions, shopping expeditions and similar diurnal mobility may well have made the prospect of living and working elsewhere less painful to contemplate.[33] This must have been more appreciable among non-farm employees, who would have found it much easier to take advantage of such facilities.

The processes involved in the flow from villages into small towns, and from small towns to larger ones, were thus more complex than is generally realized. For example, we have little idea of how frequently movement occurred by stages, and how this related to the declining numbers in agriculture. In the case of mid-nineteenth-century Preston, Anderson discerned a considerable amount of two-step migration in the sense that villages contributing to the growth of the central nucleus in turn drew on places further afield, after the manner described long ago by Ravenstein and by Redford. But there were only slight traces of deliberate two-step migration by the same individuals, except among those born at a distance, who made up only a small proportion of all immigrants.[34] How typical this was is not at present known, and illustrates the kind of behavioural question which existing studies based on aggregative census materials and the analysis of net flows can hardly begin to approach. It is clear that the farm labourers and rural craftsmen came under different

125

pressures. For the former they might be met simply by a change of occupation with or without a move to the nearest town. This would perhaps satisfy many men of limited outlook and ambitions, but some would go further; from Buntingford (Cambridge-shire) it was reported that 'all the quick-witted ones go to London'.[35] Likewise among craftsmen in larger villages and small towns, some would remain and others envisage advancement from removing after completing their apprenticeships. As Llewellyn Smith remarked, 'There are villages and country towns which may be described as breeding grounds for journeymen for the great cities.'[36]

Economic factors apart, we should not overlook the appeal of what the same author described as 'the contagion of numbers, the sense of something going on'. Thus, carters and busmen were apt to say that the busy streets of London were simply more interesting than country roads, and it would be unwise to overlook the temptations of 'the theatres and the music halls, the brightly-lighted streets and busy crowds: all, in short, that makes the difference between Mile End Fair on a Saturday night, and a dark and muddy country lane, with no glimmer of gas and nothing to do'.[37] Then there was the attraction of the girls, who in a sense blazed the trail. To say that at Lark Rise in the 1880s there was no girl over twelve or thirteen living permanently at home may exaggerate but does not mislead. For the vast concentrations of female domestic servants in towns unquestionably served to 'act as a magnet to the lads they leave behind them'.[38]

IV Implications of the Urban Influx

Most of our systematic evidence on the occupations taken up by migratory countrymen relates to the great cities, particularly London, and was collected in response to the re-emergence of the 'condition of England' question during the 1880s and after. In what was by his own admission a 'scattered notice' of the London trades, Llewellyn Smith concluded that in general immigrants from the country were under-represented on the London docks, where labour was recruited from the native-born or those resident for some considerable time. On the other hand, the building trades were 'most overrun by countrymen', whilst they were also employed in large numbers on the railways and abounded on the roads in such roles as carriers or omnibus drivers.[39] More systematic information drawn from the 1881 census by Stedman Jones for the London labour force as a whole shows that while 50 per cent was the general average born in the provinces, this was exceeded among the police (87 per cent), gardeners and railway labour (78), railway service (69), brewery workers (61), carpenters and domestic servants (59), busmen (58), gas works servants (57), builders (56), masons (54) and municipal labourers (52), etc. On the other hand, the most highly-skilled London trades (such as bookbinding, printing, jewellery, manufacture of musical instruments) were dominated by native-born Londoners, along with occupations like dock labour and coal-heaving.[40]

It should be noted that from the metropolitan standpoint, all immigrants (including, let us say, a mason born and trained in Birmingham) were 'countrymen'. No doubt many from provincial towns great and small, and from large villages, came to offer the skills and services in which they already had experience. The former agricultural labourer necessarily undertook an occupational change which, given his starting-point, could hardly fail to be a species of promotion. Llewellyn Smith compared the former and present occupation of some 500 London immigrants born in a group of villages and small market towns in Hertfordshire and south Cambridge-shire, showing that the proportion describing themselves as labourers fell from 640 to 169 per thousand, while the largest gains were made under the headings of military service (+108), railway employment (+87), menservants and grooms (+59), carmen (+49), gardeners (+35), domestic service (+41), police (+34), porters (+22) and soap, gas and chemical works employment (+21).[41] Likewise Wilson Fox, who assembled information on 19,000 regularly employed countrymen in London and 27,000 in the great provincial cities in 1906, found that former agricultural workers accounted for 23, 21, 35 and 37 per cent of the labour force of four London breweries; 25 per cent of the employees of the South Metropolitan Gas Company; 18 per cent of goods porters at the Great Northern Railway Terminus and no fewer than 47 per cent of their stablemen; and 22 per cent of the work people employed by the sixteen largest English Municipal Corporations.[42]

With a large proportion of immigrants undertaking similar work at better wages and others undergoing elevation in the manner described, there is no reason to expect that, even discounting individual success stories, country immigrants would feature disproportionally in the statistics of distress. Indeed, figures brought forward by Llewellyn Smith in the 1880s and by Wilson Fox in 1906 suggested that the overwhelming bulk of those in indigent circumstances were town-born, both in London and the great provincial towns.[43] Stedman Jones has drawn attention to the fragility of such statistics, and emphasized that the oft-repeated statements by employers of a preference for the countryman were based as much on his presumed docility (London men were described as 'shuffling, lazy and know too much' by one brewer) as on his greater vitality and productivity. No doubt, as he suggests, the 'theory of urban degeneration' was an inadequate, incomplete or inappropriate explanation of the weak competitive situation of the London-born, and it seems likely that the superiority of provincials over the debilitated armies of 'pure-bred' Londoners was exaggerated.[44] But at least there is no evidence for the contrary view—that immigrants were especially disadvantaged in the urban labour market, or failed to secure a due share of what work was available, having regard to their background and experience.

Were there not, however, other social costs attendant upon migration? Obviously the inflow must have put pressure on the urban infrastructure and especially on the housing stock, since without it development could have been at a more leisurely pace and the quality of the urban environment might have been higher. Whether it would have been is impossible to say. Moreover, the influx tended to call into being its own supply of housing, especially as real incomes rose more rapidly in the later years of the century. Leaving aside the case of the Irish who patently were left with the dregs of urban housing, it is significant that in London in 1881 a greater proportion of provincials were to be found in the rapidly expanding suburbs than in the central districts such as Bethnal Green, where little more than 12 per cent had been born outside London. All the evidence suggests that the inner metropolitan slums were 'settlement tanks for submerged Londoners' rather than reception centres for provincial immigrants.[45] Even at Lincoln it was apparent by the Edwardian period that most of the working class lived in new housing areas rather than in the older parts of the city.[46] This is consonant with the statistics of distress.

However, it was frequently suggested that migration to the great towns was destructive of personality, family ties and wholesome values. A theme popular in Victorian melodrama was London's 'homeless poor—their crime, drunkenness and nostalgia for the lost life of the village', a scenario which no doubt reflected some actual case-histories but hardly the fate of the majority.[47] Only one element in this stereotype is amenable to examination, namely the supposition that migration was destructive of family ties. Whilst we must allow, the words of a *Morning Chronicle* investigator, 'for a great number of shades of family disruption' and presume that in the long term immigrants would cease to perform important functions within the ongoing family system in their birthplaces, recent research shows that at any rate in the first generation contacts with kin were valued and actively pursued.[48] A new arrival needed a roof over his head, a job and someone to help him to adjust to the new environment, and kin, along with co-villagers, were his main recourse. Among 202 cases traced by Llewellyn Smith, about one half had definitely secured a place in town before leaving the country, and, he remarked, once a country nucleus was established in London, it grew 'in geometric ratio by the importation of friends and relations'.[49] There is also evidence of reciprocal services in the form of numerous examples of migrants seeking assistance from their country relations and sometimes returning there in times of crisis or distress.[50] Not a few, like 'John Jarman' of 'Little Guilden',[51] retired to their villages, so that the flow was by no means uni-directional. Indeed, in every respect including the transfer of people, town and countryside were highly interdependent.

V Overseas Migration

Table 10.3 shows that with the exception of the 1840s, when Irish immigration was in full spate, net losses from the residual rural areas as defined by Cairncross exceeded the net gains by urban districts in every decade from 1851–61 to 1891–1901, and especially in the 1880s. It serves to draw attention to the role of overseas emigration as an alternative to permanent settlement in the towns, although the matter is vastly more complex than might appear at first sight.

Even before the 1834 Poor Law Amendment Act magistrates were looking with favour on emigration as a remedy for the 'surplus population' problem of the southern

Table 10.3   *Urban net gains and rural net losses 1841–1901**

		1841–51	*1851–61*	*1861–71*	*1871–81*	*1881–91*	*1891–1901*
A	Rural losses ('000)	443	743	683	837	845	660
B	Urban gains ('000)	742	620	623	689	238	606
C	Imputed net loss by overseas emigration from rural areas (A−B)		123	60	148	607	54
D	C as a % of A		17	9	18	72	8

*Based on Cairncross, 1953, 70. *N.B.* (i) The rural losses are equivalent to the sum of the 'North' and 'South' figures in Table 10.1 above. (ii) In 1901–11 both the rural and the urban areas showed net losses by migration, i.e. 295,000 and 207,000 respectively. (iii) Colliery districts are included with the urban areas.

counties, for example in Biddenden, Cranbrook and other parishes of Wealden Kent.[52] The authorities charged with administering the New Poor Law espoused this policy, and between 1836 and 1846 assisted some 14,000 persons to emigrate to the colonies, chiefly Canada, from England and Wales,[53] yet the policy was never prosecuted with the vigour that might have been expected. As early as 1837 it had occurred to many guardians in East Anglia that their interests as ratepayers and employers were in conflict,[54] and after 1850 the role of the Poor Law authorities sharply diminished. Another official body was the Colonial Commissioners of Land and Emigration. This was set up in 1842 to aid the emigration of selected persons using funds raised from the sale of Crown lands in the colonies, and by 1869 it had assisted well over 300,000 United Kingdom citizens (including Irish) to emigrate, chiefly to Australia.[55] However, while such sources of assistance were probably crucial in the case of agricultural labourers, it should be borne in mind that, overall, the bulk of British emigration was privately financed and often independent. It also flowed mainly to America, which during the first thirty years of Victoria's reign absorbed some 3.5 million persons from the United Kingdom, against 0.75 million by Canada and 1 million by Australia and New Zealand.[56]

Table 10.3 suggests an apparently much greater rate of loss by overseas migration from rural areas in the 1870s, coinciding with a recorded 140 per cent increase in the number of adult farm labourers, shepherds, gardeners and carters, when the British emigration statistics of 1861–70 and 1871–80 are compared.[57] These years saw the emergence of the first successful agricultural trade unions, which, following precedents set by others, took vigorous steps to promote emigration on the presumption that the bargaining power of those who remained would be enhanced. Thus January 1874 saw the departure of 410 Kentish emigrants at the instigation of the Kent and Sussex Labourers' union, and in 1879, against the background of a lockout, a farewell tea at the Skating Rink in Maidstone was held for a similar number, shortly to depart for New Zealand in a chartered Dutch vessel, the *Stad Haarlem*. 'They wanted to "get on", these gentle civil-spoken southern agriculturalists', commented a *Daily News* reporter. 'There is no blatant mob-oratory ring about their modest aspiration. "We should like to see our children better off than we have been".'[58] Yet the encouragement and assistance of the unions did not endure for more than a few years. Although the funds of the National Agricultural Labourers' Union benefited by 3s. per adult from the Canadian Agent General (a figure more than offset by disbursements in the form of assisted passages), the activities of some of its officials were not above suspicion. Some, such as the chairman of the Oxford District of the N.A.L.U., were in receipt of commissions and retainers, and on a train journey to London Joseph Arch, who had an ambivalent attitude to the matter, was outraged to overhear the comment, 'He's selling them like cattle to the foreigners.'[59] After 1881 there were clear signs of waning interest. Support for the unions was falling and they felt increasingly less able to assist.

Yet the efflux was still more impressive in the 1880s. On the basis of the figures in Table 10.3 Caincross concluded that this was a time when expansion abroad coupled with heavy foreign investment resulted in 'a tremendous rural exodus, not so much abroad as to America and the colonies'. If this view is correct, it would also go far to explain why, in the 1890s, rural emigration was substantially reduced, for as a whole the decade saw a much lower export of capital and a concentration on home investment; whilst after 1900, when overseas lending rose again, net losses from urban as well as rural districts were in evidence for the first time.[60] Such an argument has the appeal of logic and simplicity, but does not reveal everything about the migratory tendencies of the rural population in general, or of labourers in particular. For example, it has been found that farm labourers showed no special propensity to join the flow from Cornwall to New South Wales in 1877–86, and that in 1880–6 emigration from Gloucestershire was very much an urban phenomenon. Moreover, working from American passenger lists of 1885–8, Erickson has shown that almost four of every five men landing in New York gave a principal town as their place of last residence.[61] Apparently the series of net balances which Cairncross relies on, and which is reproduced in Table 10.3, leaves much yet to be discovered about the proclivity of countrymen to emigrate, relative to other social groups. Some direct transfer there undoubtedly was, and at times considerable. For others a move to town might be the first step towards emigration, although in the eyes of the authorities involved the interlude might not improve their acceptability. With some applicants, argued the secretary to the Emigration Information Office (set up in 1889), 'it would turn out that they had been farm labourers five or six years ago, that they had come to London, and had become practically useless for the purpose of emigration'.[62] Thus, in the round, despite a well-marked preference for countrymen on the part of receiving countries, it seems probable that the majority of the labourers who left the land were destined to fill the places of townsmen who at most times showed a greater propensity to emigrate.

VI Remedies

The first signs of concern about the loss of rural population came in the form of sporadic complaints from landlords and farmers about seasonal labour shortages, chiefly from the 1850s onwards.[63] Towards the end of Victoria's reign the rural exodus began to engender more comment, and in the aftermath of the Boer War it featured regularly in discussions of 'national efficiency', with authors such as Arnold White deploring the implications of sturdy countrymen giving place to 'white-faced workmen living in courts and alleys'.[64]

There was, it seemed, no answer to be found. In so far as wages in agriculture were the key, we can discern a definite tendency for the real wages of full-time employees to advance in the later nineteenth century, and the regional wage disparities so evident in Caird's day diminished without disappearing altogether.[65] Yet by any urban or industrial yardstick the labourer remained poorly remunerated. In evidence to the Land Enquiry Committee the secretary of the Agricultural Labourers' Union lamented that 'forty years of experience has convinced me that the labourers cannot get a living wage by Trade Union effort alone', and it is significant that the report of the committee advocated the kind of minimum wage legislation which in fact was first introduced for farm labourers in 1917.[66]

The cottage question continued to generate fitful discussion without much sign of progress, and indeed the last pre-war issue of the *Journal of the Royal Agricultural Society* included yet another essay on the subject.[67] Suggestions that education in rural schools should be re-orientated towards subjects believed likely to contribute to the stability of country life were aired by figures such as the eminent scientist and Liberal M.P., Sir Henry Roscoe, and by school inspectors anxious to develop the 'seemingly instinctive' interest of country children in 'the green earth and its feathered and four-footed tenantry', but to little avail.[68]

The provision of allotments as a means of easing the situation of the labourer had a long history, and, defined as holdings capable of being cultivated by the labourer without help other than from his family and in his spare time, they were already to be found in some 42 per cent of English parishes as early as 1833.[69] Allotments continued to be recommended in various official reports and by sundry publicists throughout the century, yet it would seem were far from being the obvious answer that some of their more enthusiastic advocates supposed. For, if remote from the village, on poor land, or subject to restrictions in use, they were unlikely to meet with the labourers' approval. Thus in Kent the system of 'letting land to the poor at double or treble its value' was reckoned likely 'to exasperate the lower orders still more against their superiors'; whilst forty years on F. G. Heath remarked that around Bridgwater the rents charged by farmers were more than four times those paid to their landlords—a situation, he added, general in the West of England.[70] Although in 1882 the Allotments Extension Act laid down that the trustees of charity lands in any parish should be directed to provide allotments, the issue did not assume any political importance until 1885, when large numbers of rural constituencies were won by the

Liberals (including Joseph Arch in North-West Norfolk) on an agrarian programme which included allotments under the slogan 'Three acres and a cow'. Further legislation in 1887 and after empowered local councils to acquire land compulsorily for the purpose, but they were in many cases very slow to move, being dominated by farmers and landlords hostile to the very idea. Moreover, there is reason to think that among the labourers the desire for allotments was 'very variable'.[71]

Obviously the allotment issue shaded over into the smallholding question and both movements could be said to have originated in a sense of the impolitic social consequences of enclosure. But the aims of the smallholdings movement were quite different, looking to the re-establishment of a class of peasant proprietors wholly occupied on their own holdings. Advocates of such a step, who were especially vociferous in the 1880s, were not infrequently moved by anti-landlord prejudice, by a distaste for the 'monopoly' of land evidenced in the New Domesday Survey of 1870, and by a conviction that continental systems of land tenure were by no means as inefficient as had been assumed by the protagonists of large-scale capitalist agriculture in Britain. Labour leaders thought that such a programme might stem the flow of labour into towns and so mitigate any threat to urban wage-levels, whilst sentimentalists saw it as a step towards the re-creation of Merrie England.[72] More significantly, Tory politicians such as Henry Chaplin and Lord Salisbury came to feel that a peasant proprietary could constitute a bulwark against revolutionary change, their ideas in this respect corresponding with those of the chief author of the movement, Jesse Collings, who freely conceded that his proposals were 'in the true and not in a party sense of the word conservative in the highest degree'.[73]

It was no doubt this coincidence of interest that made possible an Act of 1892 empowering county councils to create smallholdings for purchase by instalments; and that of 1908 which enabled them to provide holdings for sale or for letting. Whatever the merits of peasant proprietorship or of the smallholding ideal (and they did not go uncontested since it was possible to raise some very powerful counter-arguments) comparatively little was accomplished in practice, in part due to the reluctance of county councils actually to use their powers. The general position with respect to the labourer's access to land was reviewed by the unofficial Land Enquiry Committee of 1913. It was estimated that about two-thirds of all villages in England had allotments—a proportion, it should be noted, considerably higher than in the 1830s; whilst since the 1908 Act some 10,000 smallholdings had been provided by county councils, corresponding to 3.3 per cent of all holdings in the range 1–50 acres. There was, the committee maintained, a 'large unsatisfied demand' for both.[74]

Such were the remedies proposed to stabilize rural life and the rural population. It is unlikely that they had any significant impact on the drift from the countryside. Yet in the twenty years before the holocaust of the First World War the efflux showed definite signs of abatement (see Table 10.1) and the number of persons described as agricultural labourers actually rose slightly between 1901 and 1911. No doubt the beginnings of suburbanization had some influence on aggregate rural population changes, and to that extent we have an artificial explanation. Otherwise the

132

hypotheses advanced by Cairncross are plausible and include:

(a) a degree of revival in British agriculture after 1900 as prices improved;
(b) the operation of the law of diminishing returns 'to protect what was left of rural industry just as it was operating to protect agriculture'; and
(c) a pause, albeit temporary, in changes in agrarian structure because the limits of known technique had been reached.[75]

To these explanations an important demographic factor may be added, that is, a much reduced rural rate of natural increase. So far as the agricultural labourers are concerned, this was not due to any marked proclivity to reduce their family sizes, for as a class their fertility in 1911 was exceeded only by coal-miners.[76] Rather, as a consequence of age-selective migration, the composition of the rural population had changed in such a way as to reduce crude birth rates by 1901–11 to 24.5 in the northern and 22.7 in the southern rural residues, compared with 32.5 and 32.3 respectively as recently as 1861–71.[77] The size of the pool of potential emigrants was thus being steadily reduced.

Notes

1 See ch. 35.
2 Thus, where P_1 is the first census population and P_2 that of ten years later, B is the number of births and D the number of deaths occurring in the intervening period, the observed inter-censal increase is P_2-P_1, natural increase is B−D, and the net migration component is $(P_2-P_1)-(B-D)$. Baines, 1972, offers a full discussion of sources and techniques for the study of inter-county migration flows.
3 See, for example, Ogle, 1889, and the critical comments in Saville, 1957, 64–5.
4 Cairncross, 1953, 78. In the main his arrangement of the published source material is relied upon here, but his conclusions do not differ in any important respect from those arrived at in subsequent studies, in particular Saville, 1957, and Lawton, 1973, although both offer more detail.
5 Cairncross, 1953, 74–5; Lawton, 1973, 211.
6 Hasbach, 1966, 256, 258.
7 Heath, 1874, 250.
8 Kerr, 1968, 238–42; Ashby and King, 1893, 6.
9 BPP 1893–4 XXXV [C. 6894–V] 92; [C. 6894–VI] 8; BPP 1893–4 XXXVII [C. 6894–XXV] 40.
10 See ch. 35.
11 BPP 1893–4, XXXV [C. 6894–II] 45; and see Horn, 1976b, 76.
12 Bellerby, 1953, quoted in Saville, 1957, 13.
13 Hunt, 1973, 88–100.
14 Bienefeld, 1972, 82, 122.
15 BPP 1893–4 XXV [C. 6894–III] 144; BPP 1893–4 XXXVI [C. 6894–XIV] 130, 147.
16 Land Enquiry Committee, 1913, I, 16–17.

17 *Ibid.*, 80; BPP 1884–5 XXX [C. 4402–I] 635.

18 Land Enquiry Committee, 1913, I, 132–3.

19 Heath, 1874, 36–7; Flora Thompson, 1954, 335–6; Havinden, 1966, 115.

20 Land Enquiry Committee, 1913, I, 30, 138–9, 144.

21 Sellman, 1967, 25.

22 Collings, 1908, 23–5; Heath, 1893, 235.

23 BPP 1906 XCVI [Cd. 3273] 32, 34; Heath, 1874, 135; Thirsk, 1957, 323.

24 Land Enquiry Committee, 1913, I, xxxiv; BPP 1906 XCVI [Cd. 3273] 11–21.

25 Nicholls, 1846, 3–4.

26 Collings, 1908, 382.

27 BPP 1893–4 XXXV [C. 6894–III] 103.

28 BPP 1906 XCVI [Cd. 3273] 31; BPP 1893–4 XXXV [C. 6894–I] 114; BPP 1893–4, XXXVI [C. 6894–XIV], 8.

29 BPP 1893–4 XXXV [C. 6894–IV] 109; BPP 1884–5 XXX [C. 4402–I] 449.

30 Gilpin, 1960, 3–7.

31 Ravenstein, 1885, 198–9; Saville, 1957, 110.

32 Cairncross, 1953, 75.

33 Hunt, 1973, 266–71.

34 Anderson, 1971b, 21, 25–6; and see Ravenstein, 1885, and Redford, 1926.

35 BPP 1893–4 XXXV [C. 6894–II] 149.

36 Llewellyn Smith, 1904, 141.

37 *Ibid.*, 75.

38 Flora Thompson, 1954, 163; BPP 1893–4 XXXV [C. 6894–I] 18.

39 Llewellyn Smith, 1904, 81–2, 90, 92, 96, 98, 141.

40 Stedman Jones, 1971, 137.

41 Llewellyn Smith, 1904, 140.

42 BPP 1910 XLIX [Cd. 5068] Appendix J, 729.

43 *Ibid.*, 724–7; Llewellyn Smith, 1904, 84–5.

44 Stedman Jones, 1971, 132, 134–5, 143–4.

45 Llewellyn Smith, 1904, 66, 121–2; Dyos and Reader, 1972, 372–3.

46 Hill, 1974, 301–2.

47 See, for example, Dyos and Wolff, 1972, ch. 8.

48 Anderson, 1971b, 66, 152–8.

49 Llewellyn Smith, 1904, 133–4.

50 Anderson, 1971b, 158.

51 Llewellyn Smith, 1904, 131–4.

52 Melling, 1964, 175–9; Johnston, 1972, 99–101.

53 Erickson, 1976, 127.

54 Digby, 1975, 80–2.

55 Erickson, 1976, 122.

56 Woodruff, 1934, 363.

57 Horn, 1972, 100.

58 Arnold, 1974a, 87; and see p. 83 of the same journal.

59 Horn, 1972, 94–5; Arch, 1966, 83.

60 Cairncross, 1953, 209–12.

61 Duncan, 1963, 227, 283; Erickson, 1972, 359–60.

62 Erickson, 1976, 161.

63 Jones, 1964, 328–9, and see ch. 35.

64 White, 1901, 96; and see Stedman Jones, 1971, ch. 6.

65 See ch. 35.

66 Land Enquiry Committee, 1913, I, 42, 67.

67 Allen, 1914.

68 Ausubel, 1960, 200; Collings, 1908, 25–30; and see Land Enquiry Committee, 1913, I, 436–44.

69 Barnett, 1967, 163.

70 *The Labourer's Friend*, 1835, 213; Heath, 1874, 75–6.

71 BPP 1893–4 XXXV [C. 6894–VI] 29.

72 Orwin and Whetham, 1964, 332.

73 Collings, 1908, xxiii.

74 Land Enquiry Committee, 1913, I, 188–9, 191, 229.

75 Cairncross, 1953, 75–7.

76 Innes, 1938, 42.

77 Cairncross, 1953, 82.

11 The Land in Victorian Literature

W. J. Keith

I

A country's literature does not necessarily reflect the historical actualities of the time in which it is written, since writers are influenced by conventions and the traditional practices and expectations of their art as well as by what they see around them. Such conventional forms as pastoral and Gothic romance, for example, may well coexist with realistic presentation and so distort the historical record. Thus readers of Matthew Arnold's 'Thyrsis' or Emily Brontë's *Wuthering Heights* would be unwise to assume that scholar gipsies might be seen on the Cumnor Hills in the nineteenth century or that Heathcliffs habitually roamed the Yorkshire moors. None the less, the Victorian age belongs to what Northrop Frye has called the 'low mimetic' period of literary history, dominated by middle-class values that favoured a realistic art. Consequently, so long as we proceed with caution, Victorian literature can foster and augment our understanding of nineteenth-century attitudes towards the countryside.

Descriptions and evocations of the land abound in the literature of this period, and this profusion of reference dramatically underlines the fact that 'land' is a word embracing numerous shades of meaning. For many Victorians it was automatically associated with concepts of possession and, by extension, of power. A great estate presupposed a great man who owned it. Perhaps because, after the first Reform Act (1832), the landed rural gentry was losing its political dominance over the country as a whole, the continued influence of local families on rural parishes became a favourite subject in fiction, where they could provoke a wide range of responses extending from nostalgic sympathy through ironic amusement to indignant satire. But despite what we can now recognize as the trend of the times, land was generally associated with a sense of permanence and security. Trollope's Barchester series achieved (and has maintained) its popularity not only because of his wittily human presentation of church politics but because of his congenial portrayal of a society which, although threatened by various forces from without, retained an inner strength and basic stability. 'The greatness of Barchester', Trollope writes in the first chapter of *Doctor Thorne*, 'depends wholly on the landed powers', and this is one of many Victorian novels (George Eliot's *Felix Holt* is another) in which the plot turns upon the inheritance of a large estate. The power of land can be used for good or evil, its possessors may prove heroes or villains, but its importance (in the abstract) remains paramount.

This attitude to land favours a panoramic view of rural life, the Victorian equivalent of the eighteenth-century 'prospect' from the high ground in a gentleman's park. Again, the opening paragraphs of *Doctor Thorne* provide a convenient example. Barsetshire is described as

> a county in the west of England not so full of life, indeed, nor so widely spoken of as some of its manufacturing leviathan brethren in the north, but which is, nevertheless, very dear to those who know it well. Its green pastures, its waving wheat, its deep and shady and—let us add—dirty lanes, its paths and stiles, its tawny-coloured, well-built rural churches, its avenues of beeches, and frequent Tudor mansions, its constant county hunt, its social graces, and the general air of clanship which pervades it, has made it to its own inhabitants a favoured land of Goshen. It is purely agricultural; agricultural in its produce, agricultural in its poor, and agricultural in its pleasures.

One wonders, however, whether the working farmers and labourers of Barsetshire would have seen the country in quite this way. For them 'land' and 'earth' become virtually synonymous. The dirt in the lanes, that Trollope mentions self-consciously and with seeming reluctance, becomes central: it is the soil upon which their livelihood depends. In a well-known passage from *Tess of the d'Urbervilles*, Thomas Hardy presents the land from a very different perspective:

> The swede-field in which [Tess] and her companion were set hacking was a stretch of a hundred odd acres, in one patch, on the highest ground of the farm, rising above stony lanchets or lynchets. . . . The upper half of each turnip had been eaten off by the live-stock, and it was the business of the two women to grub up the lower or earthy half of the root with a hooked fork called a hacker, that it might be eaten also. Every leaf of the vegetable having already been consumed, the whole field was in colour a desolate drab; it was a complexion without features, as if a face, from chin to brow,

should be only an expanse of skin. The sky wore, in another colour, the same likeness; a white vacuity of countenance with the lineaments gone. So these two upper and nether visages confronted each other all day long, the white face looking down on the brown face, and the brown face looking up at the white face, without anything standing between them but the two girls crawling over the surface of the former like flies. (ch. 43)

The face of the countryside, then, alters with the perspective from which it is viewed. The land can be a thing of beauty, but also a hard taskmaster. Richard Jefferies, describing a harvest scene in his essay 'One of the New Voters' (*The Open Air*), catches the range of possible response in a single sentence: 'The wheat is beautiful, but human life is labour.'

Trollope's claim that Barsetshire was *'to its own inhabitants* a favoured land of Goshen' is difficult to accept; but most of Trollope's readers, and most readers of other rural literature, were outsiders with no immediate experience of agriculture, and for them the vision of an idyllic countryside proved attractive. It is impossible to over-emphasize the fact that, by half way through Victoria's reign, the majority of the population lived and worked in towns. Understandably, most urban Victorian readers turned to rural literature for the same reasons that they sought the countryside itself—for refreshment and renewal, as a haven from the wearying pace of city life. The usual adjective for such motives, 'escapist', carries negative connotations, but the practice is not (or, rather, need not be) ignoble. A distinction needs to be made between two very different kinds of escape usefully indicated by two of Hardy's novel titles: escape to (*Under the Greenwood Tree*) and escape from (*Far from the Madding Crowd*). The former almost invariably overlaps with pastoral, the positing of a 'golden world' or never-never land remote from what Arnold called, in 'The Scholar Gipsy',

> this strange disease of modern life,
> With its sick hurry, its divided aims,
> Its heads o'ertaxed, its palsied hearts . . . (11. 203–5)

'Escape from' does not imply inferior art, but the value of that art as historical evidence is negligible. This kind of escape is prominent in the novels of Dickens: Dingley Dell in *The Pickwick Papers* provides the most obvious example, its very name suggesting a sheltered warmth and simplicity, but many others could be cited, including the cottage to which Nell and her grandfather come near the close of *The Old Curiosity Shop*, and Betsy Trotwood's home by 'the sacred piece of green' and Peggotty's quaint boat on the beach in *David Copperfield*. Such localities are less important for their own sakes than for their functions as opposite poles to an urban threat typified by Blake's 'dark Satanic Mills' or, more substantially, by William Cobbett's 'great Wen'.

'Escape to' is more positive. The urban reader of George Eliot's *Adam Bede* may first approach the village of Hayslope as if it were a pastoral retreat (once again the name is comfortably lulling), but he quickly discovers that he is confronted here with a community presented in breadth and depth, an alternative way of life which is of interest in its own right. He is introduced not to a world of pastoral ease but to an active society engaged in rural labour. George Eliot offers a remarkably comprehensive view of village life from Squire Donnithorne through the farming Poysers to the artisans like Adam Bede himself. The novel examines the cohesiveness of a rural community, the responsibility of each member to the complete human unit. In writing the book, George Eliot saw herself as a pioneer, presenting realistic truth where her predecessors had offered selective glimpses which led to falsehood. 'I find a source of delicious sympathy', she confides, 'in these faithful pictures of a monotonous homely existence' (ch. 17). Twentieth-century readers, however, are likely to consider the idyllic aspects of Hayslope overstressed. Accustomed to Hardy's Wessex and the dark vision so congenial to the modern mind, we tend to find the landscapes of 'Loamshire' too idealized and simplistic; where, we feel obliged to ask, is the grinding poverty which social historians assure us was widespread? But George Eliot, whatever her omissions, was feeling towards that sense of regional consciousness which is so important and neglected a development in the Victorian period. Advances in communications, the improvement of roads and the establishment of the railway system, had 'opened up' the countryside for exploration and comparison. The Victorians, we might say, learned to recognize not a generalized countryside but a series of different countrysides with their own physical features, history, customs, dialects and ways of living. The Victorian writers, whether of poetry, fiction or discursive prose, had an important role to play in this awakening.

II

Fifteen years before Victoria ascended the throne, William Cobbett initiated his *Rural Rides* (published as a book in 1830) as follows: 'My object was, not to see inns and turnpike-roads, but to see the *country*; to see the farmers at *home*, and to see the labourers in the fields.' He confined his attention, for the most part, to southern England, and so missed the opportunity of observing and commenting on the more dramatic scenic differences in countrysides. Moreover, his socio-political concerns— a major part of his interest—were always in the forefront. None the less, he provides an invaluable record of differences between county and county, differences determined ultimately by the nature of the soil, which in turn affected the kind of agriculture possible in the area, which in its turn influenced the material condition of the inhabitants. Cobbett's viewpoint was essentially that of the practical countryman; he judged the land according to what it produced or could produce, and had little patience with those who looked at the countryside aesthetically or regarded it as a place for relaxation. Such, however, fostered by the 'Romantic' taste for wild nature, was a trend of the times, and later writers were to describe, assess and interpret the countryside for the prospering urbanized middle class (or, in Cobbett's contemptuous terminology, 'the tax-eaters').

A far less important but doubtless more representative writer, William Howitt, produced his panoramic survey, *The Rural Life of England*, in 1838. He explains his intentions in his preface:

> My object in this volume has been to present to the reader a view of the Rural Life of England at the present period, as seen in all classes and in all parts of the country. For this purpose I have not merely depended upon my acquaintance with rural life, which has been that of a great portion of my own life from boyhood, but I have literally travelled, and a great deal of it on foot, from the Land's-End to the Tweed, penetrating into the retirements, and witnessing the domestic life of the country in primitive seclusions and under rustic roofs. (3rd ed., 1844, p. viii)

Howitt writes in full awareness of the new audience for his work. He notes that 'one of the singular features of English life at the present moment is the swarming of summer tourists in all interesting quarters' (p. 37), and later exclaims:

> And what an immensity of new regions will the railroads that are now beginning to stretch their lines from the metropolis in different directions, lay open—*terrae incognitae*, as it were, to the millions that in the dense and ever-growing mass of monstrous London pant after an outburst into the country. (pp. 556–7)

Howitt was both an enthusiast and a sentimentalist: 'The wealth and refinement at which this country has arrived, have thrown round English rural life every possible charm' (p. 11). Although evidence of poverty and degradation among the poor are to be found in his book, these are for the most part offset by complacent generalities about improvement. His middle-class presuppositions are obvious: 'When we go into the cottage of the working man, how forcibly are we struck with the difference between his mode of life and our own' (p. 404), and his rather desperate attempts to equate the evidence of his senses with the 'pastoral' poetic tradition prove revealing: 'In many of the southern counties, but I think nowhere more than in Hampshire, do the cottages realize, in my view, every conception that our poets have given us of them' (p. 411). Howitt writes about everything he encounters, including country sports, scientific farming, farm servants, gipsies, cottage life and education in rural areas. Although his observations are limited by his naïvety, they remain useful in providing a comprehensive and perhaps typically Victorian view of the English countryside.

Howitt's treatment of rural sports reminds us that for many Victorians the countryside was a place not for rest and idle relaxation but for strenuous activity, especially in the forms of hunting and shooting. While many rural commentators indulged in nostalgia for a supposedly simpler past, others looked back to a past that was tougher and more virile. For George Borrow the gipsies, prize-fighters, horse-traders, tinkers, jockeys and roadgirls about whom he wrote represented a sturdy, 'free' England that was fast being superseded by a Victorianism of effeminate pseudo-gentility. In *The Romany Rye*, a sequel to his better-known *Lavengro*, he speaks of 'the wholesome smell of the stable with which many of these pages are redolent' (ch. 25). We have become so accustomed to the stereotype of a Victorian England dominated by Mrs Grundy and the dictates of respectability that we can easily overlook the more vigorous and less inhibited worlds to which numerous youthful Victorians were able (at least temporarily) to 'escape'.

Nowhere is this aspect of the Victorian period better evoked than in the works of R. S. Surtees. The emphasis here is not merely on 'untin', to employ the idiom of his great creation John Jorrocks, the cockney master of foxhounds, but on the vital but rather seedy world of horse-traders, stable boys and all the sporting observers and hangers-on. Jorrocks himself, though it sounds pompous to say so, takes on the status of a symbol. As London tea-merchant he represents that urban enthusiasm for rural pursuits about which Howitt wrote, but he is also a new social phenomenon: the self-made cockney who can infiltrate a sport hitherto dominated by the rural squirearchy. Surtees's ambivalent response to his creation is also significant; he laughs at Jorrocks's ignorance and vulgarity, and makes him a figure of fun whenever he can (in *Handley Cross* Jorrocks falls into 'the dirtiest heap of composition for turnips I ever smelt in my life' (ch 10)), but at the same time Surtees used him to show up the snobbery and conceit of more typical huntsmen and to express some of his own cherished convictions. Surtees was himself a rural landowner, but there is a bluff heartiness and honesty in Jorrocks that he finds endearing. Moreover, although there are few pages of formal description in his books, we gain from them a unique view of the country as seen on horseback from the covert-side, and, particularly, the winter landscape of the foxhunting season rather than the summer of tourists and holiday-makers.

Surtees's best-known works (*Handley Cross, Mr. Sponge's Sporting Tour, Mr. Facey Romford's Hounds*) are officially categorized as novels. But the temporal and causal development central to the art of fiction is not present, and they are continually breaking up into sketches and character vignettes. His contemporary readers were interested not so much in his art as in his subject-matter, not so much in plot progression as in individual scenes and human types. This is a characteristic of rural literature partly explicable in terms of the country writer's dislike of falsification and his commitment to a representative truth. The distinction between fiction and non-fiction is less pronounced here; Surtees's non-fictional *Analysis of the Hunting Field*, with its series of chapters devoted to 'The Master', 'The Huntsman', 'The Whipper-In', 'The Earth-Stopper', etc., bears a closer resemblance to his novels than we might at first expect. The modern reader can find, in novel and essay alike, authentic presentations of rural scenes and rural people.

Richard Jefferies, our best literary guide to gamekeeping, poaching and shooting, discovered his appropriate art form in the rural essay at the same time as he found his true subject-matter. After numerous and generally dismal attempts at novel-writing, he published *The Gamekeeper at Home* in 1878, the first of a series of country books in which information about rural things is tactfully interspersed with vivid evocation of the ways of country life. The average urban sportsman who could devote no more than a week or so to his recreation found in Jefferies's work what he most needed: articles on choosing a gun, accounts of pheasant-rearing, information about natural history, portraits of typical countrymen and a general accumulation of advice about rural things as well as personal accounts of his own experiences in the field which many a frustrated urbanite must have read with a combination of enjoyment and envy. Moreover, the numerous books that flowed from his pen in the decade before his untimely death in 1887—books with such attractive titles as *Wild Life in a Southern County*, *The Amateur Poacher*, *The Life of the Fields*, *The Open Air*—offered the essence of the countryside in book form, works to be cherished and re-read when urban duties prevented the reader's presence in the countryside about which Jefferies wrote. But his most ambitious work of this kind is *Hodge and His Masters*, a commentary on the agricultural state of the country at a time when the 'high farming' of mid-century was giving place to grim years of agricultural depression. Jefferies made his point by means of a series of minutely observed character sketches of farmers, labourers and countrymen. In no other rural work, perhaps, is the human vitality of the Victorian countryside more thoroughly and cogently presented.

'The beauty of English woodland and country lies in its detail', Jefferies wrote in 'An English Deer-Park' (*Field and Hedgerow*). Certainly, his own success at evoking the spirit of a countryside (as distinct from merely amassing facts) stems from his capacity to select and arrange significant details with all the skill of an impressionist painter. A single extract, from *Round About a Great Estate*, must suffice to illustrate his gift for transcending description and communicating what it feels like to move within a specific countryside (in this case, north Wiltshire):

> Upon reaching the foot of the Downs, Cicely left the highway and entered a narrow lane without hedges, but worn low between banks of chalk or white rubble. The track was cut up with ruts so deep that the bed of the pony-trap seemed almost to touch the ground. As we went rather slowly along this awkward place we could see the wild thyme growing on the bank at the side. Presently we got on the slope of the hill, and at the summit passed the entrenchment. . . . Thence our track ran along the ridge, on the short sweet turf, where there were few or no ruts, and these easily avoided on that broad open ground. The quick pony now put on his speed, and we raced along as smoothly as if the wheels were running on a carpet. Far below, to the right, stretched wheatfield after wheatfield in a plain between two ridges of hills. On the opposite slope, a mile away, came the shadows of the clouds—then down along the corn towards us. Stonechats started from the flints and low bushes as we went by; an old crow—it is always an old crow—rose hastily from behind a fence of withered thorn, and a magpie fluttered down the hill to the fields beneath, where was a flock of sheep. The breeze at this height made the sunshine pleasant. (ch. 10)

In Jefferies, informed countryman and creative artist merge. The authoritative references, the range of sense-impressions, the wealth of rural knowledge upon which such a passage depends, are easy to recognize; more difficult to appreciate is the subtle modulation of sounds and rhythms that give the paragraph its grace and eloquence without disturbing the conversational intimacy of the tone. Here the land is recreated by the art that conceals art.

Descriptive accounts of rural England in the nineteenth century run the gamut from formal statistical surveys to artistic evocations of rural scenes in the manner of Jefferies. They include works that emphasize natural history, country crafts, the social conditions of the labourer, the pastimes of the ruling class, etc. These are too numerous to consider here, but mention needs to be made of H. Rider Haggard's *Rural England*. Haggard was an enthusiastic and conscientious gentleman-farmer who used his profits from such exotic fiction as *King Solomon's Mines* and *She* to farm his Norfolk estate. He saw Arthur Young, the late eighteenth-century advocate of land improvement, as his 'great predecessor' (I, p. vii), but for our purposes his book performs a similar function at the time of Queen Victoria's death to that of Cobbett's *Rural Rides* a few years before she ascended the throne.

Like Cobbett, Haggard is conducting an inquiry into the state of agricultural England. He is concerned to examine the dramatic changes that had recently taken place in farming methods, to assess the consequences of the agricultural depression over the previous twenty years, and to gauge the prospects for the immediate future. He favours the method of the interview, which preserves 'an actual record of what a certain number of people intimately connected with English land and agriculture, thought and said on the matter in the years 1901 and 1902' (I, p. xi). Conscious of the extreme variation of conditions from region to region, he organizes his material by counties, and makes a systematic attempt to compare and contrast the state of one area with that of others. Haggard's position as landowner naturally results in a viewpoint very different from Cobbett's, and his clear but unimaginative prose contrasts with the earlier writer's pugnaciously forceful style. Fact and interpretation can be disentangled more readily in *Rural England*, but we do not receive that acutely vivid sense of an observed countryside that is so palpable an effect in *Rural Rides*. None the less, Haggard makes an honest attempt to present divergent opinions. He was assisted in his chapter on Dorset by Thomas Hardy, and his book has a special interest in offering a contemporary non-fiction equivalent to the fictional re-creation of a Victorian countryside in Hardy's Wessex novels.

III

Hardy's writings (the poems and non-fiction prose as well as the novels and short stories) clearly constitute the most important comprehensive presentation in literature of the nineteenth-century countryside. Its local concentration on an area of south-west England (the artistic culmination of the development of regional consciousness discussed earlier) is less limiting than one might expect. Wessex extends over the boundaries of nine modern counties and embraces a rich variety of kinds of countryside from coastal areas to bare upland to sheltered and fertile vales. Human habitations range from the county town of Casterbridge/Dorchester through seaside resorts and several cathedral cities to widely divergent villages, hamlets, isolated farms and cottages. Wessex is, in fact, a rural microcosm, and as novelistic chronicler Hardy covers the broad time-span of the whole nineteenth century from the Napoleonic invasion-scare of 1804 in *The Trumpet-Major* to the bleakly contemporary world of *Jude the Obscure*.

Hardy was in a unique position to represent this countryside in all its detail and complexity. The successful man of letters who wrote his later novels at Max Gate, the solid, gauntly contoured Victorian house he built for himself just outside Dorchester in the 1880s, had been born in 1840 in a small, 'picturesque' but decidedly cramped cottage a few miles away at Bockhampton on the outskirts of 'Egdon Heath'. Though his father was a mason and contractor, many of his local relatives, as Robert Gittings has recently demonstrated in *Young Thomas Hardy*, belonged to the labouring class—a fact that Hardy himself, sharing the social sensitivity of so many Victorians, took considerable pains to conceal. Fortunate in his own education, he moved from Bockhampton to Dorchester, and later to London, broadening his social and intellectual horizons as he went. When he became known as a novelist, he moved (rather awkwardly) in high social circles, and his biographical notes are strewn with references to society dinners and titled acquaintances. Though he was never altogether at ease in portraying the upper classes, his experience enabled him to draw upon a broad social range of rural figures from Mrs Charmond, the lady of the manor in *The Woodlanders*, and the parvenu Stoke-d'Urbervilles in *Tess*, to humbly born characters like Jude Fawley and Tess herself.

Hardy *knew* the countryside about which he wrote from all the viewpoints that I have outlined. And he was acutely conscious of the increasing split between rural and urban in his own age. He could see Wessex through the eyes of the humbly born and intellectually ambitious Jude, eager to escape from the constrictions of his environment; but he could also see it, as a native who had himself returned, through the eyes of Clym Yeobright. He shared the inner knowledge of the realities of rural living that makes his presentations of the poorer countrymen so convincing, but he could also understand the responses of outsiders who came to Wessex and found difficulty in adjusting to local ways. He realized that he lived in two time-schemes; as he wrote in *Far from the Madding Crowd*: 'The citizen's *Then* is the rustic's *Now*. . . . In these Wessex nooks the busy outsider's ancient times are only old; his old times are still new; his present is futurity' (ch. 22). He inherited many of the traditional attitudes of the rural population, yet learnt to come to terms with the up-to-date intellectual controversies of the metropolis. He understood, too, that his readers were, for the most part, these same citizens and busy outsiders eager to explore his countryside as tourists: hence the topographical emphasis of the prefaces and introductions that he later wrote for his novels.

1 *above* A waggon drawn by a
team of oxen, taken in 1870 at
Pepper-in-Eye Farm,
Powdermills, Battle, Sussex
(Museum of English Rural Life)

2 *right* A country carrier on
his rounds at Sibford Ferris,
Banbury, about 1874 (Museum
of English Rural Life)

3 *opposite* Rural transport in late-Victorian
Gloucestershire: (a) newspaper delivery (b) opening of
the Coleford-Monmouth railway, 1883 (Courtesy of
Gloucestershire Community and Federation of
Women's Institutes; the assistance of Mr G. R. Hiatt
and the staff of Gloucester Library is gratefully
acknowledged)

4 *above* Local coaches persisted long after the
coming of the railways. This shows the service running
between Tenterden, Cranbrook and Ashford in Kent
(Professor P. S. Bagwell)

OXLEY'S

IMPROVED PATENT SPORTING CART,

EXEMPT FROM DUTY.

PRICE TWENTY-ONE POUNDS; WARRANTED FOR TWELVE MONTHS.

The Improvement consists of a simple contrivance to move and adjust the body of the Cart over the axle, thereby giving the horse the same weight on his back with either two, three, or four persons. The movement is effected by a neat screw, requiring no key. The Cart is very strong, its weight only thirty stone, and will carry four persons, or six cwt.; has patent axle and lancewood shafts, neatly painted, with cushions, &c.

DELIVERED FREE IN HULL,
From whence they can be forwarded, at a cheap rate, to any part of the Kingdom.

J. OXLEY,
COACH-BUILDER, BEVERLEY, YORKSHIRE.

Jabez Hare, Engraver and Typ., 10, Nelson Square, Blackfriars Road.

TORR'S IMPROVED CARTS.

Awarded a Prize of Five Pounds, by the North Lincolnshire Agricultural Society.

These Carts are made very plain and strong, with wide rungs instead of sideboards. The body of the Carts are broad and short, so as to concentrate the weight as near upon the axle as possible.

	£	s.	d.
One Horse Carts, to contain 22 cubic feet or hold 30 cwt. of gravel, &c. tire 3 inches......................	11	11	0
Two Horse Cart, to contain 30 cubic feet, or hold 40 cwt. of gravel, &c. tire 4½ inches	14	0	0

TORR'S TWO HORSE SPRING WAGGON

Was awarded a Prize of Five Pounds, by the North Lincolnshire Agricultural Society, at Gainsboro', 1845.

INVENTED BY W. TORR, ESQ.
Of Riby, near Grimsby.

This Waggon is constructed with a light broad body and solid rung sides, to carry 2½ tons of Corn in bags, and will load well with Hay or Corn. It is mounted on springs, and Crosskill's Patent Wheels, Patent Iron Axles and Oil Boxes. It is well adapted for speed, to trot to market with ease, at the rate of four to five miles per hour.

This Waggon is intended for carrying out the system of generally working Horses in pairs, only, together with the various Implements of the Farm, as the Plough, Harrow, Drill, &c. In Harvest Work, this Waggon will successfully compete with One Horse Carts, particularly where the distance is great.

---

5 *above* Advertisements for improved carts. Oxley's sporting cart employed a patent device for adjusting the body of the vehicle over the axle according to the number of persons carried; Torr's two-horse spring waggon used Crosskill's patent wheels, patent axles and oil boxes, and was 'well adapted for speed', trotting to market at 4–5 m.p.h. (Dorset County Record Office)

6 *above right* A Welsh sheep-shearing on a mountain farm: the farmer sits astride his horse with his good lady by his side (National Library of Wales)

7 *right* A horse market in a Welsh country town (National Library of Wales)

8 *left*   Two Montgomeryshire drovers pose for the photographer, about 1880 (John Thomas Collection, National Library of Wales)

9 *below*   Llanybydder Fair: A Welsh cattle market about the turn of the century (National Library of Wales)

10 *right*   A scene at the smithy at the Vulcan Arms, Cwmbelan, Montgomeryshire, about 1895. James Morris was the blacksmith standing at the anvil (Welsh Folk Museum, St Fagans)

11 *below right*   A man and a boy cutting peat in Carmarthenshire about 1898. Note the sled used for transporting the peat (Welsh Folk Museum, St Fagans)

12 *above* Haymaking in Wales. Note the large number of women helpers and the universal use of hats for protection from sun and dust. (National Library of Wales, John Dillwyn Llewelyn Album)

13 *below* A party of harvesters seen sharpening their reaping hooks in a field at Llanrhystud, Cardiganshire, in the summer of 1903 (Welsh Folk Museum, St Fagans)

14 David Farquharson, *Tatty Howkers* (Renfrew District Museum and Art Gallery Service)

15 *above*   William Marshall
Brown, *Waling Potatoes* (Renfrew
District Museum and Art Gallery
Service)

16 *above right*   Alan Greive, *A
Perthshire Harvest* (1913) (Renfrew
District Museum and Art Gallery
Service)

17 *right*   William Kennedy,
Harvesters (Renfrew District
Museum and Art Gallery Service)

18 *above left* Duncan McKellar, *Home for the Evening* (Renfrew District Museum and Art Gallery Service)

19 *left* George Smith, *In the Stack Yard* (1923) (Renfrew District Museum and Art Gallery Service)

20 *above* William Pratt, *The Evening Haw* (1903) (Renfrew District Museum and Art Gallery Service)

21 *above* A labourer's cot in the mountain country, Ireland

22 *centre* An Irish cabin built of stone, mud and thatch, and supported at one end by a stone buttress

23 *below* Irish women working in the field— binding corn—about the turn of the century

24 *above* A row of old cottages situated in a village in Ireland, their walls well below the level of the road

25 *below* Ireland at the turn of the century: farmers at a country sheep fair (Nos 21–5 from Michael J. F. McCarthy, *Irish Land and Irish Liberty*, London: Scott, 1911)

26 John Constable, *Arundel Mill and Castle*, 1837. Oil on canvas; 28½ × 39½ in., 72·4 × 100·3 cm (The Toledo Museum of Art, Toledo, Ohio)

27 Joseph Mallord, William Turner, *Norham Castle, Sunrise, c.*1835–40. Oil on canvas; 35¾ × 48 in., 91 × 122 cm (Tate Gallery, London)

28 *left* Frederick Richard Lee and
Thomas Sidney Cooper, *The
Chequered Shade*, 1854. Oil on
canvas; 78 × 66 in., 198·1 × 167·6 cm
(The Forbes Magazine Collection,
New York)

29 *above* Benjamin Williams
Leader, *At evening time it shall be
light*, 1897. Oil on canvas; 30⅛ × 50⅛
in., 76·5 × 127·3 cm (Manchester
City Art Gallery)—reduced replica
of *In the evening there shall be
light*, 1882. Oil on canvas 46 × 79½
in., 116·8 × 179 cm (Ex collection of
Lord Hollenden)

30 *below* Myles Birket Foster,
Children Playing. Watercolour;
13¼ × 27⅝ in., 33·7 × 70·2 cm
(Victoria and Albert Museum,
London)

31 *left*   Robert Walker Macbeth, *A Lincolnshire Gang*, 1876. Wood engraving after the untraced oil painting, publ. *Graphic*, vol. 14, 60–1, 15 July 1876 (The Witt Library. Courtauld Institute of Art)

32 *below left*   John Linnell, *Harvest Home, Sunset*, 1853, exh. 1854. Oil on canvas; 34¾ × 58 in., 88·3 × 147·3 cm (Tate Gallery, London)

33 *below*   Peter Graham, *A Spate in the Highlands*, 1866. Oil on canvas; 47¼ × 69⅝ in., 120 × 176·8 cm (Manchester City Art Gallery)

34　George John Pinwell, *The Shadow*, 1867. Wood engraving; $6\frac{5}{8} \times 4\frac{7}{8}$ in., 16.9×12.5 cm (The Witt Library, Courtauld Institute of Art)

35 *above top* William Small, *An English Ploughing Match*, 1875. Wood engraving; 12¾ × 18½ in., 35 × 47 cm (publ. *Graphic*, vol. 11, between pages 264 and 265, 13 March 1875)

36 *above* Philip Richard Morris, *The Reaper and the Flowers*, 1877. Oil on canvas; 35 × 59 in., 88·9 × 149·9 cm (Ex collection Captain Henry Hill) (engraved by Charles Roberts, repr. *Magazine of Art*, 1902, p. 423)

37 George Clausen, *The Stone Pickers*, 1887. Oil on canvas; 51 × 30 in., 129·5 × 76·2 cm (Laing Art Gallery, Newcastle-upon-Tyne)

All this biographical and social background is necessary, I believe, for an adequate appreciation of the subtleties of Hardy's presentation of 'land'. His landscapes vary dramatically, but in nearly all of them we encounter a distinct sense of unease. This is particularly evident, of course, in Hardy's best-known word-portrait of a tract of country, the description of Egdon Heath in the opening chapter of *The Return of the Native*. We are told that 'civilization was its enemy' but also that it was 'a spot which returned upon the memory of those who loved it with an aspect of peculiar and kindly congruity'. It is 'haggard Egdon', 'a near relation of night', 'the hitherto unrecognized original of those wild regions of obscurity which are vaguely felt to be compassing us about in midnight dreams of flight and disaster'. Yet it is also offered as 'a place perfectly accordant with man's nature—neither ghastly, hateful, nor ugly; neither commonplace, unmeaning, nor tame; but, like man, slighted and enduring'. These are not contradictions; they represent Hardy's most deliberate statement concerning the relation between man and his landscape—or, in more specific terms, between Victorian man and the Victorian landscape.

This same sense of awkwardness and unease recurs, less directly but no less significantly, in other novels. In *The Mayor of Casterbridge*, for example, 'the Ring', a Roman amphitheatre where natural features have been adapted by man to provide a background for human violence through the ages, becomes a suitable meeting-place for Michael Henchard and the wife that he has wronged (ch. 11); the historical associations of the locality are invoked to colour the nineteenth-century human story being played out against it. Frequently, landscape descriptions clash dramatically within a single novel. In *Far from the Madding Crowd* idyllic presentations of sheep-dipping and sheep-shearing stand in contrast to the memorable scene of violent thunderstorm in which Gabriel and Bathsheba fight to save the wheat-ricks from the destructive force of the elements. And in *Tess* the quiet lush beauty of the dairy country at Talbothays is deliberately set against the harsh barrenness of Flintcomb Ash.

Hardy's Wessex is a region undergoing radical and painful change. This can often be seen within the landscape itself (Farfrae's mechanical seed-drill in *The Mayor of Casterbridge*, which will 'revolutionize sowing heerabout' [ch. 24], the Stoke-d'Urbervilles' newly constructed 'country-house built for enjoyment pure and simple, with not an acre of troublesome land attached to it' and the 'red tyrant' of the threshing-machine in *Tess* [chs 5, 47]), and it is paralleled in the uncomfortable and uncertain lives of Hardy's characters. Hardy has often been criticized in the past for his unskilful juxtapositions of documentary reporting and artificial melodrama; but we are coming to realize more and more that the awkward shifts of tone within the novels both reflect and reproduce the jagged patterns of modern experience. In the preface to *Far from the Madding Crowd* Hardy insisted that he was presenting 'a Wessex population living under Queen Victoria;—a modern Wessex of railways, the penny-post, mowing and reaping machines, union workhouses, lucifer matches, labourers who could read and write, and National school children'. Once again the incongruous juxtapositions are noticeable. All in all, Hardy's Wessex novels, read as a series and backed up by his other writings in prose and verse, constitute a profound analysis as well as an unrivalled representation of nineteenth-century rural life and landscape.

IV

Commentators who have grown impatient with the rural positives frequently talk of an idealizing rural 'myth' which distorts and falsifies the darker rural 'reality'. To what extent can such a response be justified? There is, of course, no simple answer to this question. In any age the temptation to idealize is strong, and the Victorian period was no exception. As Bulwer Lytton remarked, 'we can have our real life, in all its harsh outlines, whenever we please; we do not want to see that real life, but its ideal image, in the fable land of art' (quoted in Stang, *The Theory of the Novel in England*, p. 155). It is only too easy, moreover, to fall back upon literary stereotypes. Mrs Gaskell neatly illustrates this process in *North and South* when Margaret Hale, discussing a village in which she used to live, says, 'I am trying to describe Helstone as it really is', but goes on to remark that it is 'like a village in a poem—in one of Tennyson's poems' (ch. 1).

On the other hand, the argument that Victorian literature as a whole offers an excessively rosy picture of contemporary rural life can only be maintained by a selection of evidence as distorting as the supposed idealizing myth itself. Indeed, the presentation of a countryside 'as it really is' is a major preoccupation of nineteenth-century rural writing, and although some of the attempts may have been no more successful than that of Mrs Gaskell's heroine, many are harsh indeed. This is especially true, of course, of the social novels of the period that deal with specifically rural themes. Here, for example, is a passage from Disraeli's *Sybil*:

> The situation of the rural town of Marney was one of the most delightful easily to be imagined. In a spreading dale contiguous to the margin of a clear and lively stream, surrounded by meadows and gardens, and backed by lofty hills, undulating and richly wooded, the traveller on the opposite heights of the dale would often stop to admire the merry prospect that recalled to him the traditional epithet of his country.
>
> Beautiful illusion! For behind that laughing landscape, penury and disease fed upon the vitals of a miserable population. (Bk II, ch. 3)

Similarly, when Lancelot Smith in Charles Kingsley's *Yeast* maintains that 'wherever one goes one sees commodious new cottages springing up', the radical gamekeeper Tregarva replies:

> 'Wherever you go, sir, but what of wherever you don't go? Along the roadsides and round the gentlemen's parks, where the cottages are in sight, it's all very smart; but just go into the outlying hamlets—a whited sepulchre, sir, is many a great estate.' (ch. 13)

Tennyson, stressing behaviour rather than material conditions, expressed comparable sentiments through the speaker of *Maud*:

> Below me, there, is the village, and looks how quiet and small!
> And yet bubbles o'er like the city, with gossip, scandal and spite. (11, 108–9)

Perhaps because the temptation to idealize is so strong and the accusation of it so easy, writers are particularly sensitive on this issue. At any rate, disclaimers are frequent. Even Hardy, for instance, in his 'General Preface to the Novels and Poems' written for the Wessex edition of 1912, felt the need to insist: 'At the dates represented in the various narrations things were like that in Wessex.'

Myths regularly provoke counter-myths. The pastoral tradition, in substituting Arcadia or Eden for the realities of country life, is not likely to pass unchallenged for long, but the concentration upon squalor and misery need be no more accurate than an emphasis on charm and ease. By the same token, Wordsworth's 'natural comfort' (*Excursion*, I, 602) is qualified but not cancelled by Tennyson's 'Nature red in tooth and claw' (*In Memoriam*, LVI, 15). The evidence of literature will admittedly include extremes but it will also offer balance. Once again, Hardy's Tess, ambiguously called 'a pure woman' in the subtitle, provides the complexity of truth. The Tess whom we know and respect by the end of the novel is neither the embodiment of rustic innocence imagined by Angel Clare before their marriage nor the type of guilty impostor that he projects upon her after she has told him her story. If we read *Tess of the d'Urbervilles* symbolically (and this is itself, of course, a partial and so distorting interpretation of the novel's total effect), we can see Tess, torn between the frigidly angelic Clare and the callously satanic d'Urberville, as representative of the middle state of ordinary human nature. And, as we have seen, the landscape in which she moves, the extremes of Talbothays and Flintcomb Ash, reflects this human duality.

The variety possible within literature mirrors the variety within nature and the multiplicity of attitudes, in the Victorian period or any other, towards the land. Examples may be found in the most unexpected places. No one would think of invoking Oscar Wilde as a reliable commentator on the Victorian countryside, but in his love for turning hallowed ideas and commonplaces upside down he should not be ignored. In *The Importance of Being Earnest*, he makes Lady Bracknell observe, while interviewing a suitor for her daughter's hand, 'A girl with a simple, unspoiled nature, like Gwendolyn, can hardly be expected to reside in the country' (Act I). The humour lies in the reversal of customary assumptions, but it still makes its point (Wilde may even have had the current controversy over Hardy's Tess in mind). And paradoxically this master of paradoxes provides an excellent digest of the changes in historical and social attitudes to 'land' in the late nineteenth century. What at first appears a succession of witty epigrams comes to be recognized as significant insight into contemporary trends. It is therefore appropriate to leave the last word with Lady Bracknell:

> What between the duties expected of one during one's lifetime, and the
> duties extracted from one after one's death, land has ceased to be either a

147

profit or a pleasure. It gives one position, and prevents one from keeping it up. That's all that can be said about land. (Act I)

List of Works Referred to

Arnold, Matthew, 'The Scholar Gipsy', 'Thyrsis', in Kenneth Allott (ed.), *The Poems of Matthew Arnold*, Longman, London, 1965.

Borrow, George, *Lavengro* [1851], Murray, London, 1907.

Borrow, George, *The Romany Rye* [1857], Murray, London, 1907.

Brontë, Emily, *Wuthering Heights* [1847], Penguin, Harmondsworth, Middx., 1965.

Cobbett, William, *Rural Rides* [1830], Penguin, Harmondsworth, Middx., 1967.

Dickens, Charles, *The Pickwick Papers* [1836–7], Penguin, Harmondsworth, Middx., 1972.

Dickens, Charles, *The Old Curiosity Shop* [1840], Penguin, Harmondsworth, Middx., 1972.

Dickens, Charles, *David Copperfield* [1849–50], Penguin, Harmondsworth, Middx, 1966.

Disraeli, Benjamin, *Sybil or: The Two Nations* [1845], Penguin, Harmondsworth, Middx, 1954.

Eliot, George, *Adam Bede* [1859], Everyman edition, Dent, London, 1951.

Eliot, George, *Felix Holt* [1866], Everyman edition, Dent, London, 1966.

Frye, Northrop, *Anatomy of Criticism*, Princeton University Press, Princeton, N.J. 1957.

Gaskell, Elizabeth Cleghorn, *North and South* [1855], Knutsford edition, Murray, London, 1925.

Gittings, Robert, *Young Thomas Hardy*, Heinemann, London, 1975.

Haggard, H. Rider, *Rural England*, Longman, London, 1902.

Hardy, Thomas, *Under the Greenwood Tree* [1872]
Hardy, Thomas, *Far from the Madding Crowd* [1874]
Hardy, Thomas, *The Return of the Native* [1878]
Hardy, Thomas, *The Trumpet-Major* [1880] New Wessex edition,
Hardy, Thomas, *The Mayor of Casterbridge* [1886] Macmillan, London, 1974.
Hardy, Thomas, *The Woodlanders* [1887]
Hardy, Thomas, *Tess of the d'Urbervilles* [1891]
Hardy, Thomas, *Jude the Obscure* [1896]

Howitt, William, *The Rural Life of England* [1838], Longman, London, 1844.

Jefferies, Richard, *The Gamekeeper at Home* [1878], World's Classics edition, Oxford University Press, London, 1948.

Jefferies, Richard, *Wild Life in a Southern County* [1879], Lutterworth, London, 1949.

Jefferies, Richard, *The Amateur Poacher* [1879], World's Classics edition. Oxford University Press, London, 1948.

Jefferies, Richard, *Hodge and His Masters* [1880], Eyre & Spottiswoode, London, 1949.

Jefferies, Richard, *Round About a Great Estate* [1880], Eyre & Spottiswoode, London, 1948.

Jefferies, Richard, *The Life of the Fields* [1884], Lutterworth, London, 1947.

Jefferies, Richard, *The Open Air* [1885], Eyre & Spottiswoode, London, 1948.

Jefferies, Richard, *Field and Hedgerow* [1889], Lutterworth, London, 1948.

Kingsley, Charles, *Yeast: A Problem* [1850], Eversley edition, Macmillan, London, 1881.

Stang, Richard, *The Theory of the Novel in England, 1850–1870*, Routledge & Kegan Paul, London, 1959.

Surtees, Robert Smith, *Handley Cross, or Mr. Jorrocks's Hunt* [1843], Bayntun, Bath, 1926.

Surtees, Robert Smith, *The Analysis of the Hunting Field* [1846], Methuen, London, 1904.

Surtees, Robert Smith, *Mr. Sponge's Sporting Tour* [1853], World's Classics edition, Oxford University Press, London, 1958.

Surtees, Robert Smith, *Mr. Facey Romford's Hounds* [1865], Methuen, London, 1921.

Tennyson, Alfred, *In Memoriam, Maud*, in Christopher Ricks (ed), *The Poems of Tennyson*, Longman, London, 1972.

Trollope, Anthony, *Doctor Thorne* [1858], Everyman edition, Dent, London, 1957.

Wilde, Oscar, *The Importance of Being Earnest* [1895], in *Oscar Wilde: Selected Writings*, World's Classics edition, Oxford University Press, London, 1961.

Wordsworth, William, *The Excursion*, in *Poetical Works of Wordsworth*, Oxford University Press, London, 1960.

12   Landscape in Nineteenth-Century Literature

Louis James

A landscape in literature is a view, not only of countryside, but of the moral and social attitudes of writer and reader. In the nineteenth century the upheavals in the intellectual background revealed themselves in attitudes to nature, and in the way nature was portrayed. This was complicated by other developments—geological studies; discoveries by the Pre-Raphaelite painters about the appearance of light and shadow; the popularity from the 1850s of photography, and the changing face of the Victorian countryside itself. But here also one is dealing with ideas. The discovery even of photography led to debates as to how the new medium should be used to select and interpret nature; as P. H. Emerson urged. '[The photographer] must learn, as the painter has to do, to distinguish what in nature is really suitable for pictorial purposes.'[1]

I

Jane Austen (1775–1817) is a transitional writer. Living an uneventful life in the narrow provincial society, she may seem an unlikely choice as a landscape writer. Yet her concern with the moral development of her characters in a precisely charted social milieu gave a sharp edge to the way the country reflected the moral attitudes of those who inhabited it. In *Northanger Abbey* (written from 1798, published in 1818), 'natural' views of the countryside are complicated by the concepts of the 'picturesque' popularized in particular by William Gilpin (1724–1804), author of a

150

series of illustrated tours including *The Wye and South Wales* (1782) and *The Lakes* (1789). Gilpin described the 'picturesque' as 'that kind of beauty which would look well in a picture', and developed the eighteenth-century practice of selecting from the multiplicity of nature its 'ideal' and most perfect forms with his prescription of 'high-colouring' heightening the romantic effect.[2] The heroine, Catherine Morland, is enthralled to discover that, by precepts of the picturesque, 'it seemed as if a good view were no longer to be taken from the top of an high hill, and that a clear blue sky was no longer the proof of a fine day. She was heartily ashamed of her ignorance'—and confronted with a good view, 'she voluntarily rejected the whole city of Bath, as unworthy to make part of a landscape'.[3]

Jane Austen rejected the excesses of the 'picturesque', but this does not mean that she admired landscape as untouched nature. *Pride and Prejudice* (begun in 1796, published in 1813), for instance, concerns the misunderstandings and final reconciliation between the vivacious Elizabeth Bennet and reserved, socially poised Fitzwilliam Darcy. After a letter has shown Elizabeth that she has damagingly misjudged Darcy, she goes north to visit his estate, Pemberley. The landscape may, on first reading, appear natural.

> ... they pursued the accustomed circuit, which brought them again, after some time, in a descent among hanging woods, to the edge of the water, in one of its narrowest parts. They crossed it by a simple bridge in character with the general air of the scene; it was a spot less adorned than any they had yet visited; and the valley, here contracted into a glen, allowed room only for the stream, and a narrow walk amidst the rough coppice-wood which bordered it. Elizabeth longed to explore its windings.[4]

The scene, however, is perfectly 'picturesque'—natural, but with its natural beauty gently accentuated—the valley crowding into the glen, the contrast between the snaking stream and the rough coppice-woods. In particular, the man-made objects are those which perfectly reflect the natural—the bridge is 'simple', in character with the general air of the scene; the walk is narrow to fit in with the glen. Gilpin specified that as nature should have the heightened order of art, so art—including houses, bridges and paths—should reflect the harmony of nature. The scene also has a deeper purpose. Darcy, like Pemberton, balances natural impulse with the orders and restraints of civilization. Observing the estate and the hall—which shows similar qualities—Elizabeth understands his moral character, and is drawn further towards accepting him.

The use of landscape to reflect moral character goes back to the origins of the novel. In Fielding's *Tom Jones* (1749), for instance, Squire Allworthy, who as magistrate, mediates God's wisdom to his community,[5] is introduced in the context of Allworthy Hall, Gothic in its profusion, Grecian in its balance, and built to perfectly harmonize with hill, valley and lake.[6] By the end of the eighteenth century, however, the social upheavals of the French Revolution, war in Europe and the intensifying effects of enclosure and rural poverty at home, all were disintegrating the social image of the estate as an ideal. Jane Austen's *Mansfield Park* (begun in 1812, published in 1814) reflects both disturbance and nostalgia. The order of the park which gives the book its name is being undermined both within and without. The new generation lack the social values embodied in the stern but good-hearted Sir Thomas Bertram; while he is away even the physical order of the house is disrupted and a stage for amateur theatricals is built outside his study. In wider society at the time the debate continued between Edmund Burke's *Reflections on the French Revolution* (1790), defending gradual social change, and Thomas Paine's defence of *The French Revolution* (1791). In *Mansfield Park* the beauty of the English estates that have gradually evolved from Elizabethan times are being wantonly destroyed by the morally shallow characters such as Mr Rushwood, Henry Crawford and even the minor character, Mrs Norris.[7] By contrast the lower-class girl who is adopted into the family and is to emerge as the heroine, Fanny Price, protests against the 'improvers', and Edmund, who is to marry her, puts an argument against rash changes in a form that might have been phrased by Burke. 'I should not put myself into the hands of an improver. I would rather have an inferior degree of beauty, of my own choice and acquired gradually.'[8]

The book also reflects other changes in the attitude to landscape. Compare the experience of Elizabeth Bennet contemplating Pemberley, with that of Fanny sitting in a formal garden:

> [They] sauntered about together many an half hour in Mrs. Grant's shrubbery, the weather being unusually mild for the time of year; and venturing even to sit down on one of the benches now comparatively unsheltered, remaining there perhaps till in the midst of some tender ejaculation of Fanny's, on the sweets of so protracted an autumn, they were forced by the sudden swell of a cold gust shaking down the last few yellow leaves about them, to jump up and walk for warmth.[9]

It is important that it is the lower-middle-class Fanny who is at the centre of the experience: it is not filtered through an inherited cultural awareness. Yet it also reflects a shift in the wider focus of the novel. The objective order of the landscape is retreating; the reader is becoming more directly involved in the subjective awareness of the characters, the senses, atmosphere, the personal reaction to exterior reality.

II

This shift in consciousness of the countryside can be associated with the Romantic movement. This movement is so complex and so well known that it is impossible to say anything incisive about it in a brief compass. Yet as it overshadowed Victorian attitudes to nature—even when in reaction to it—it is equally impossible to ignore. One can do worse than begin with one of Wordsworth's most familiar poems, 'Lines Composed a Few Miles above Tintern Abbey . . . July 13, 1798'. The subject is not a new one—the Wye Valley appeared briefly in Pope's 'Epistle to Bathurst' (1733) as the setting for John Kyrle's benevolent estate, and its beauties were intimately described in one of Gilpin's Tours.[10] Wordsworth's word picture inherits much eighteenth-century diction, and to some extent the compositional eye of the picturesque.

> The day is come when I again repose
> Here, under this dark sycamore, and view
> These plots of cottage-ground, these orchard-tufts
> Which, at this season with their unripe fruits,
> Are clad in one green hue, and lose themselves
> 'Mid groves and copses. Once again I see
> These hedge-rows, hardly hedge-rows, little lines
> Of sportive wood run wild: these pastoral farms,
> Green to the very door; and wreathes of smoke
> Sent up, in silence, from among the trees! (ll. 9–18)

Yet one notices first the date of the poem, thought important enough to be included in the title: the piece was composed mentally by Wordsworth while sitting on the hillside, although it was written down some days later. Like Coleridge's 'Frost at Midnight', written five months earlier to record sitting by the fire on a still winter's night, the lines are about a precise and unique moment. The eighteenth-century view of landscape was concerned with the ideal, the generalized and the timeless. Penetrating beneath the poetic terms—groves, sportive woods, pastoral farms—one finds a sense of exact detail: the apples grown but still green in mid-July; the grass growing over the thresholds of the lonely cottages; the hesitation, encapsulated in the lines, as how precisely to describe the untrimmed hedgerows, and the moment of movement in stillness in the image of the silent, rising smoke. The scene is also interfused with its meaning for the viewer. Landscape becomes more than a giver of heightened sensations: it is an active element working on the individual, a 'medicine' for the soul suffering from the effects of weariness, doubt, and the pressures of an increasingly urbanized society. As 'Lines . . . above Tintern Abbey' continued,

> But oft, in lonely rooms, and 'mid the din
> Of towns and cities, I have owed to them
> In hours of weariness, sensations sweet,
> Felt in the blood, and felt along the heart;
> And passing even into my purer mind,
> With tranquil restoration:—(ll. 25–31)

The experiences Wordsworth is responding to here are those already implanted in childhood, and however much he appealed to Victorian adult nostalgia for the country, his verse essentially linked nature to the child. Although in later life he was anxious to avoid implications of pantheism, his experience of nature was, in a direct way, religious; the soul nurtured in the countryside is in touch with 'the essential passions of the heart',[11] the 'sacred simplicities of life'.[12] In analysing his own

153

experience, Wordsworth recorded that the restorative powers of nature brought both the power of feeling and a mystical sense freed from the confines of dogma.

It was in these terms that he had perhaps his most dramatic impact on Victorian intellectuals. John Stuart Mill records in his autobiography how he suffered a form of mental breakdown as the result of the intensive education to which his father had subjected him from the age of three, when he began to learn Greek. At the age of twenty, in 1826, he read Wordsworth's *Lyrical Ballads*. As he noted,

> What made Wordsworth's poems a medicine for my state of mind, was that they expressed, not mere outward beauty, but states of feeling, and of thought coloured by feeling, under the excitement of beauty. They seemed to be the very culture of the feeling, which I was in quest of.[13]

'Mark Rutherford' (Hale White) had a similar recovery, not from the rigours of utilitarian philosophy and the classics, but from a narrow, nonconformist belief. For him reading the *Lyrical Ballads*

> excited a movement and a growth that went on till, by degrees, all the systems which enveloped me like a body gradually decayed from me and fell away to nothing. . . . Wordsworth unconsciously did for me what every religious reformer has done, — he recreated my Supreme Deity substituting a new and living spirit from the old deity, once alive, but gradually hardened into an idol.[14]

Later in the smoke and crowds of London, he found himself strengthened by his 'early training on the "Lyrical Ballads".'[15]

III

For the mass of Wordsworth's readers, however, he was associated not so much with philosophy and religion as with the Lake District. When his house at Rydal Mount became an object for pilgrimage, Matthew Arnold recorded in 1879, 'I remember Wordsworth relating how one of the pilgrims, a clergyman, asked him if he had ever written anything besides the *Guide to the Lakes*. Yes, he answered modestly, he had written verses.'[16] The specific regionalism of English country literature was one of its features as the century progressed. The most extensive rural poem before Wordsworth's *Prelude* (completed in 1805, published in 1850) was *The Seasons* (1726–30) by James Thomson (1700–46). Thomson covers the whole spectrum of eighteenth-century attitudes to nature, from the tropics to the Arctic, from the theological to the scientific.

Robert Bloomfield was drawn to poetry largely by the example of Thomson. Starting life as a plough-boy at Honington near Bury, he came to London in 1781 and worked as a shoemaker. Making verses in his head as he worked, amid the bustle of the workshop, he composed *The Farmer's Boy* (1800), describing the rural year. In under three years it reputedly sold 26,000 copies. He was praised for writing descriptions 'not like the Poem of Thomson, taking a wide excursion through all the phaenomena of the *Seasons*, but nearly limited to the rural *occupation* and business of the fields, the dairy and the farm yard'.[17] Today the fresh observation of farm life, unsustained by much original talent, does not survive the heavy poetic diction, or Bloomfield's determination to compose his memories into 'pretty' scenes for his readers. But the concern with the actual, not the general, was a new element, reinforced by the detailed woodcut vignettes that accompanied it. The new developments in etching across the grain of boxwood, pioneered by Thomas Bewick (1753–1828), itself brought a new precise awareness of the detail of country scenery, birds and animals to a wide range of readers.

John Clare (1793–1864) at one time a herd-boy, and later a small farmer, had a much greater talent than Bloomfield, both of observation and of the use of language. His *Shepherd's Calendar* (1827) also inevitably echoes Thomson, but one is not simply in an actual countryside, the details are precise, sometimes overloaded—

> Blackening through the evening sky
> In clouds the starnels daily fly
> To Whittlesea's reed-wooded mere,
> And osier holts by rivers near....[18]

Bloomfield's accounts of the farmer's experience—pleasure, fatigue, cold—are poetically distanced. Clare conveys as from within the often exhausting interaction of man, land and nature—

> The ploughmen maul along the doughy sloughs
> And often stop their songs, to clean their ploughs
> From teasing twitch, that in the spongy soil
> Clings round the coulter, interrupting toil ...
> While far above, the solitary crane
> Swings lonely to unfrozen dykes again,
> Cranking a jarring melancholy cry
> Through the wild journey of the cheerless sky.[19]

The scene is experienced through the body of the ploughman. Clare's strength, and his weakness, was his speed of composition: he catches a moment in all its detail, producing a phrase of brilliant clarity, then may lapse into the banal. But his collected work gives a wide-ranging picture of the nature and life of Northampton-shire in the early nineteenth century. From 1835 social and emotional pressures became too intense for him. He was confined as insane, and the nature he had observed objectively became, in a few extraordinary poems, experienced from within. In 'Clock-a-Clay', for example, he *becomes* a ladybird sheltering in a cowslip during a storm:

While grassy forest quakes surprise,
And the wild wind sobs and sighs,
My gold home rocks as like to fall
On its pillars green and tall;
When the pattering rain drives by
Clock-a-clay keeps warm and dry.[20]

Further south in Dorset, William Barnes (1801–86), a country schoolmaster and later parson, combined an empathy with the countryside with a very different temperament. While Clare's insights are intense and luminous, Barnes's lyrical verse is low-keyed, in touch with slower rhythms of everyday farming life. In his poems the art is almost invisible—that is its art.

Well, today then I shall roll off on the road
Round by Woodcombe, out to Shellbrook, to the mill,
With my brand-new little spring-cart, with a load,
To come loadless round by Chalk-hill, at my will:
As the whole day will be dry,
By the token of the sky,
Come to meet me, with the children on the road.[21]

His search for ways to express country life led him to experiment with a dialect to which he was native, although as a schoolmaster he would normally speak standard English. Clare's poetry also often made use of local words.[22] Dialects were an important element in the rural tradition, and did penetrate sporadically into written literature through works such as John Collier's *A View of the Lancashire Dialect*, published as early as 1746, but reprinted and imitated well into the nineteenth century. Tennyson also wrote verse in his native Lincolnshire dialect,[23] and his reading—still preserved on an early phonograph recording—indicates how the rhythms and tones of this lie behind even his verse in standard English. In the poetry of Barnes, consider how the lyrical flow of the above passage is strengthened in the dialect version:

Well, to-day Jeänne is my set time to goo
To the grist-mill out at Sherbrook under Bere,
Wi' my spring-cart out in cart house, vier new,
An' zome grist corn, to come womeward wi' en leer.
Zoo's the whole day will be dry,
By the readship of the sky,
Come to meet me, wi' the childern, on the road.[24]

Barnes's verse had a select but discriminating audience in the Victorian period, including Tennyson, the Brownings and Coventry Patmore. But it was in his influence on and relationship to Thomas Hardy that he made his most important impact. Barnes illustrated for Hardy not only the resources of dialect, the interrelationship of scenery and people, but a sense of the rhythms of country life, of attitudes to experience that were different from those of educated town folk. A central theme in Hardy's work is the conflict between the accepting country culture and intellectual sensibility—Eustacia Vye, Tess, Jude. Barnes gave a voice to the continuing culture of the Dorset folk from which these figures were tragically alienated.

Awareness of the rural condition, however, also brought a sense of the suffering and disruption of rural life. By the fourth edition of Clare's *Poems Descriptive* (1820), 'Helpstone' was docked of ten lines attacking the exploitation of the labourers—'Accursed Wealth, o'erbounding human laws'. His poem 'The Village Funeral' breaks off its description in anger against the effects of the Poor Laws and the general indifference to the 'fatherless' who 'stroll in their rags unnoticed through the street'. 'Helpstone Green' records how the human life and the physical life of the village alike were being affected by the enclosures

> Both milkmaid's shouts and herdman's call
>   Have vanish'd with the green,
> The kingcups yellow, shades and all,
>   Shall never more be seen;
> But the thick-cultur'd tribes that grow
>   Will so efface the scene,
> That after-times will hardly know
>   It ever was a green.[25]

Barnes, too, was drawn into Dorset rural life by his concern with the rural suffering that he saw, and wrote six eclogues, including 'The Commons A-Took In' and 'The Unioners', which explored the effects of enclosure, the Poor Laws and rural depopulation.

For social protest against rural conditions, however, one turns to the tradition begun by George Crabbe (1754–1832) whose poem *The Village* (1783) was an angry rebuttal to Oliver Goldsmith's sentimentalized picture of rural decay, *The Deserted Village* (1770). In the nineteenth century Crabbe published further volumes concerned with country and small-town life in the area of his native Aldeburgh in Suffolk—*The Parish Registry* (1807), *The Borough* (1810), *Tales* (1812) and *Tales of the Hall* (1819). His stories make up a sharply realistic spectrum of country society. He is concerned with landscape in a neutral way; not as a world of beauty, but a grey fen countryside dominated by mudflats, waterweeds, docks and mallow, which stands as an unemphasized background to the often grim life of his characters.

Ebenezer Elliott (1781–1849), a Sheffield master-founder and poet, was best known for his *Corn-Law Rhymes* (1828), which dramatized the plight of the poor who were unable to afford tax-protected bread. In his sympathies he can be seen primarily as a northern town-dweller. Yet, his concern with city life was inseparable from his rural interests. Here he strongly rejected any association with Wordsworth, whom he saw as describing the sufferings of the poor without protesting against the social injustices that caused them, and claimed Crabbe as his model. In *The Village Patriarch* (1829) he uses his image of an old man, Enoch Wray, returned from abroad and revisiting the countryside of his childhood. It is now built over by industry:

> New streets invade the country, and he strays,
> Lost in strange paths, still seeking, and in vain
> For ancient landmarks . . .[26]

As he explores the countryside, he finds there the enclosures denying the peasant his traditional livelihood, and even the rural industries such as the water-mill are ruined and derelict before the competition of steam. In this context nature itself turns malevolent, like the weeds clogging the millwheel and the otter and water-rat chasing the trout through the miller's sunken boat.

> What is this plague, unsearchable and lone,
> Sightless and tongueless, till a wild voice howls
> When nations die?[27]

Like William Morris in *News from Nowhere* (1891) towards the end of the century, Elliott can only look forward to an apocalyptic age in which the forces of industry, 'though their iron roots seem fast', will also pass and the balance of man with nature be recovered.

IV

Clare, Barnes, Crabbe and Elliott are all distinctively linked to the regions in which they wrote. Indeed, a major feature of literature of the country throughout the nineteenth century is the development of a sense of the difference between the English regions. George Eliot becomes associated with the Warwickshire Midlands; the Brontës with the Yorkshire countryside around Haworth; Tennyson constantly returns to the Lincolnshire wolds, Mrs Gaskell comes to be seen as a Manchester writer, Hardy creates Wessex out of the Dorset region. Particularly in the north, the development, with the industrial revolution, of new urban communities created intellectual circles with writers anxious to explore the resources of their local landscape: Robert Story and James Armstrong wrote of Northumbria, John Nicholson of the Airedale Valley, William Heaton published *Flowers of Calderdale* (1844), and a collection such as William Andrews's *North Country Poets* (1888) points to other similar examples.[28]

Where writers were not associated with one area they characteristically spent time detailing specific locales. As Myron Brightfield notes in his monumental compilation, *Victorian England in its Novels, 1840–1870* (1968),

> terrain, altitude, and other geophysical influences were sufficient to produce
> the individual differences which characterized the landscape of various

districts of the island. The Englishman who knew his own country was able
to recognise, within almost every county, the distinctively local
manifestations of natural beauty.[29]

As communications, particularly railways, made provincial areas of the country
more accessible, and as improving standards of living afforded a larger number of
people leisure to explore, the Victorian reader became increasingly interested in
regional characteristics. By mid-century the guide-book and postcard view industries
were beginning to develop.[30] Thus literature used regional locations to give sharper
definition, and at the same time country areas were of interest because of their
literary associations: pilgrims would visit Rydal Mount to see Wordsworth; Reading
and nearby Three Mile Cross were known as the setting for Mary Mitford's stories;
Mrs Gaskell's researches around Haworth, recounted in her life of Charlotte
Brontë,[31] encouraged visits to the Brontë country.

In 1847 the railway opened up the Lake District to the northern cities. As already
noted, many who used it knew Wordsworth's *Guide* better than his poetry, and by the
mid-Victorian age the Romantic interest in nature as a spiritual force had given way
before more secular views. Matthew Arnold, who himself had grown up in the Lake
District under the friendly eye of Wordsworth, loved the area, but rejected its
spiritual influence on the child.[32] John Ruskin had an even more ambivalent attitude
to Romantic views. He held a profoundly religious attitude to nature, and his life's
work was a constantly extending exploration of what he saw as the interconnected
web of God's creation. Yet he was profoundly mistrustful of Wordsworth's tendencies
to elevate created nature itself into an object of worship. For Ruskin one must begin,
not with spiritual or emotional experience, but with a strictly disciplined exploration
of 'the inexhaustible perfection of nature's details'. In a famous passage he called on
the artist to 'go to Nature in all singleness of heart, . . . rejecting nothing, selecting
nothing, and scorning nothing, believing all things are right and good, and rejoicing
always in the truth'.[33]

Equally well known is the work of the diverse group of artists whom Ruskin was to
champion, and who in 1848 formed themselves into the Pre-Raphaelite Brotherhood.
They were also opposed to the numinous, attempting an exhaustive accuracy to the
reality that they saw. They took painting out of the studio to the precise locality, even
though for Holman Hunt when working on *The Scapegoat* this meant a perilous
journey to the Dead Sea, and in order for him to catch a specific effect of dawn for
The Light of the World he had to wait up night after night in a shelter composed of hay
bales. The Pre-Raphaelites spent months on the detail of grasses and foliage. They
discovered new qualities of colour, light and shade. Through their work, and through
their impact on Victorian art and literature, they reinforced a concern with the
specific, the regional. So, Ford Madox Brown recorded in *An English Autumn
Afternoon* still-rural Hampstead in the 1850s; and Holman Hunt's *Hireling Shepherd*
details the scenery on the banks of the Ewell river.

Yet, from the variety of Pre-Raphaelite landscape painting, a particular image of the countryside emerges. it is of a still moment, usually in summer or autumn, heavy with sensations. It is the landscape of Ford Madox Brown's *Pretty Baa Lambs*, John Everett Millais's *The Blind Girl*, Arthur Hughes's *Home from the Sea* or John Brett's *The Stone-breaker*. Nor is this exclusive to painting. To take a few examples at random, it is there in the novel, in the glowing landscapes of George Eliot's *Mill on the Floss* or David's first experiences of Blunderstone in *David Copperfield*; in poems such as Matthew Arnold's *Scholar Gipsy* (1853) and George Meredith's *Love in the Valley* (1851); or in D. G. Rossetti's sonnet 'Silent Noon' (1881):

> The pasture gleams and glooms
> 'Neath billowing skies that scatter and amass.
> All round our nest, far as the eye can pass,
> Are golden kingcup-fields with silver edge
> Where the cow-parsley skirts the hawthorn-hedge.
> 'Tis visible silence, still as the hour-glass.
> Deep in the sun-searched growths the dragon-fly
> Hangs like a blue thread loosened from the sky:
> So, this winged hour is dropped to us from above.

It is a sense of countryside where everything is fertile, secure, small in scale, overlaid with associations. It is recognizably 'English'.

It is relevant to point out, as Raymond Williams does in *The Country and the City*,[34] that it is not necessarily 'England', and that, until Hardy, Victorian novelists of the country were largely out of touch with the realities of rural life. But it is also true that writers were often aware of what they were doing when they portrayed idyllic country scenes. These are often associated with childhood, making the point that, as with Maggie Tulliver or David Copperfield, adult experience will destroy this Eden. Where rural life is asserted as an ideal, as at the end of George Eliot's *Silas Marner*, acceptance of the quiet country life reflects acceptance of Victorian moral values. As George Levine has noted,[35] the Victorian image of the countryside is contrasted with that of mountain or desert. Mountains reflect disquiet, questing, the unreality found by the Dorrit family in Dickens's novel when they visit the Alps. The gentle fields and woods of England image security, balance—a world known and accepted. 'Victorian fiction' (and, one might add, poetry) 'typically lives at low altitudes. . . . Victorian novelists . . . tended to place happiness in bounded human landscapes.'

Under the pressure of materialism and city life, Victorian writers turned to the past or the future to find rural settings. George Eliot characteristically wrote of the earlier years of the century.[36] Matthew Arnold, caught in 'the strange disease of modern life,/With its sick Hurry, its divided aims',[37] recreated in *The Scholar Gipsy* the seventeenth-century Oxford world when an undergraduate could lose himself in rural life. The Victorian quest for the Gothic and the medieval was, among other things, the search for a pre-industrial world in which nature was unspoilt. Thus Thomas Carlyle's *Past and Present* (1843) contrasts Victorian society with that of the twelfth century, when 'the Ribble and the Aire roll down, as yet unpolluted by dyer's chemistry; tenanted by merry trout and piscatory otters; the sunbeam and the vacant wind's blast alone traversing these moors'. William Morris's *News from Nowhere* (1891), a dream of autumn of travelling up the Thames in the twenty-first century, when revolution has abolished capitalist industry, can be read as escapism. Certainly the sun shines continuously. But Morris's rural paradise is constructed throughout from his socialist theory, down to the open countryside which has reasserted itself with the ending of enclosures and capitalist farming. It ends with a rediscovery of his own house near Oxford, whose rural peace has been a foretaste of the possible future.

V

Yet even Morris's ideal world contains doubts—inhabitants unhappy with the new world, unanswered questions about political organizations, human motivation, age and disease. The countryside portrayed by the Pre-Raphaelites, too, rarely could rest in the simple acceptance of nature. Stephens had recommended: 'Believe that there is that in the fact of truth, though it is only in the character of a leaf earnestly studied, which may do its share in the great labours of the world.'[38] Yet their painting characteristically moves away from total objectivity towards moral meanings— telling a story, emblematic details, or, with artists like D. G. Rossetti or Burne-Jones, mystical and symbolic reality. From their first days the Brotherhood debated the nature that they were trying to portray—was it the actual world, or a reflex in the mind of this reality, recreated through art?[39]

A number of their paintings were based on poems by Alfred Lord Tennyson, and his work reflects the same debate. His early poem, *The Palace of Art* (1832), is concerned with the morality of imaginative worlds themselves. It describes the artist who created a pleasure-house of art, only to find that it atrophied and was in need of purgation before it could return to the 'reality' of the world. At the end of the poem, however, the palace is left standing. *The Lady of Shallott* (1832) is even more ambivalent. The story is well known. The lady is doomed to sit in her tower, seeing the countryside only in the reflex in her mirror, weaving this into a 'magic web'. She is 'half sick of shadows', and the beauty of Sir Lancelot draws her to look at him directly: as she dies her body is borne down the river to Camelot and the life she has been denied.

One meaning of the poem is reasonably clear: the lady is like the artist in weaving art from his image of reality. But what are the conclusions? If the artist sees reality as 'shadows', can he do anything else? What is the only reality he can know? In *Mariana* (1830), illustrated by Millais, Tennyson portrayed a moment of stillness and heat close to that characteristic of Pre-Raphaelite painting, and it has become a burden. 'She wept, "I am aweary, aweary,/Oh God that I were dead."' The poem looks forward to D. G. Rossetti's *The Orchard Pit* (1886) where, in a more symbolic image, the spirit of autumn and fruition is linked with that of decay and death.

Questions about the reality of nature were implied in wider questions about the meaning of created nature. A series of works, including Charles Lyell's *Principles of Geology* (1830–3), Robert Chambers's *Vestiges of Creation* (1844) and, later, Charles Darwin's *The Origin of Species* (1859), questioned the biblical account of creation and the centrality of man in nature.[40] Tennyson's *In Memoriam* (1850) was a series of short poems forming a diary of his grief for his intimate friend Arthur Hallam, who died in Vienna from a stroke at the age of twenty-two. Doubts about the Providence that could allow such an irrational tragedy were linked in the poem to wider uncertainty. Science seemed to show that nature was not benevolent, but 'red in tooth and claw'; evolution cried, 'A thousand types are gone: I care for nothing, all shall go.'[41] Nature is independent of the observer: it continues regardless of Hallam's death.

> Unwatched, the garden bough shall sway,
> The tender blossom flutter down,
> Unloved, that beech will gather brown,
> This maple burn itself away. . . .[42]

At the end of the poem, the poet is saved from despair by a religious intimation of the presence of his friend, but the resolution is a precarious one. In his last major work, *Idylls of the King* (1859–74), Tennyson turned to the mythical past, using the break-up of Arthur's Round Table as an allegory for the Victorian loss of moral values. The cycle culminates in a tournament where the court's degeneracy is associated with mist, rain and the dissolution of reality itself.

Towards the end of the century, one main trend of poetry was moving away from objective reality altogether into the man-made aestheticism of art for art's sake. On the other hand George Meredith, notably in *The Woods of Westermaine* (1883), evoked a nature that was hostile to man unless he placed himself in harmony with the created world. For Gerald Manley Hopkins, writing *The Wreck of the Deutschland* (1876), this harmony came through religious faith: to the five shipwrecked nuns drowning off Bremen, their agony was part of the stress that runs through all creation and, accepted, reveals the nature of God. In the sight of the watching Christ, 'Storm flakes were scroll-leaved flowers, lily showers—sweet heaven was astrew in them'.[43] In his sonnet to a falcon, 'The Windhover' (1877), he sees the battle against the wind revealing its inner beauty and being. 'The world is charged with the grandeur of God,' he wrote. 'It will flame out, like shining from shook foil.'[44]

But Hopkins was unpublished until 1918, and unknown to the Victorian reading public. Nineteenth-century rural literature reaches a natural culmination and transition in Hardy. Hardy's childhood in and around Bockhampton laid the foundation of a sense of natural beauty and the seasons which may be compared, in its depth, with that of Wordsworth. Hardy's Dorset was largely untouched by modern developments, and even the town of Dorchester which, when he travelled there as an architect's pupil, boasted railways, telegraphs and daily London newspapers only accentuated the isolation of the villages but a few miles away, where the new 'improvements' still appeared as strange and wonderful.[45] Yet, unlike the lonely hills of the Lake District, Dorset was well populated, and its landscape was a working one, shaped by centuries of agriculture, inhabited by communities living by ancient traditions. It was a palimpsest of history, shaped by generations of farmers going back to the Romans and beyond. In one world Hardy could include kinds of landscape differentiated both by appearance and by their precise impact on those who made a living from them—the rich orchard country of *Under the Greenwood Tree* (1872) and *The Woodlanders* (1887); the wild heath in *The Return of the Native* (1878); the rich pastures of the Vale of Dairies and the bleak, flinty turnip-fields of Flintcomb Ash in *Tess of the d'Urbervilles* (1891).

Hardy therefore could bring together a deep poetic sense of nature with an immediate understanding of the issues of evolution and history that so disturbed Tennyson. The juxtaposition between an individual's aspirations and the impersonality of the natural processes that appear indifferent to man was not a philosophical question, but immediate experience. As Raymond Williams has written, 'Hardy thus achieves a fullness which is quite new, at this depth, in all country writing, the love and the work, the aches of labour and of choice, are in a single dimension.'[46] Hardy's fiction and poetry contain many deliberately composed landscapes; yet, because they are the setting for the lives of country people, their beauty or oppressiveness comes from their working significance. The inhospitable heath of *Return of the Native* dwarfs and frustrates the romantic aspirations of Eustacia Vye; the flat cornfields stretching around Casterbridge, with its straight Roman roads, is the integral setting for Henchard's uncompromising tragedy which brings together his failures in both personal life and in corn-trading.

In this context the 'picturesque' view of the countryside is questioned, not because it is outdated, but because it offers unjustified expectations. 'Men have oftener suffered from the mockery of a place too smiling than from the oppression of surroundings oversadly tinged.'[47] As Hardy's successive works deepened in their pessimism, the sense of man's inevitable tragedy existed alongside a sense of an objective reality of nature from which man, by education, self-consciousness, and changes in agriculture and rural society, was alienated. Hardy is thus profoundly a transitional figure. His power comes from the tension within his writing between early nineteenth-century Romantic and modernist concerns.[48] His poem, 'The Darkling Thrush', written in 1900, deliberately invites comparison with Keats's 'Ode to a Nightingale'. He cannot accept Keats's assumption of eternal natural beauty. Yet he is moved by the 'happy good-night air' to think that in nature there was

> Some blessed Hope, whereof he knew
> And I was unaware.

Notes

1 Emerson, 1887, 13.
2 Gilpin, 1798, 328; Gilpin, 1786, xix.
3 *Northanger Abbey*, ch. xiv.

4   *Pride and Prejudice*, ch. XVIII.

5   *Tom Jones*, ch. III.

6   *Ibid.*, ch. IV.

7   Duckworth, 1971, 38–54, conveniently brings together the themes of 'estate improvement' in the novel.

8   *Mansfield Park*, ch. VI.

9   *Ibid.*, ch. xx.

10   Gilpin, 1782; see also Bloomfield, 1813.

11   Wordsworth preface to *Lyrical Ballads*, 2nd ed., 1800.

12   *Ibid.*

13   Mill, 1873, ch. v.

14   'Mark Rutherford', *Autobiography*, 2nd ed., 1888.

15   *Ibid.*, 1888, ch. I.

16   Arnold, 1879.

17   Bloomfield, 1803, xxxvi–vii.

18   Clare, 1827, 'January'.

19   *Ibid.*, 'March'.

20   Tibble, 1935, II, 447–8.

21   Bernard Jones, 1962, 736–7 (W. Barnes, 'Come and Meet Me').

22   Tibble, 1935, II, 559–67.

23   Ricks, 1969, 1123, 1189–91 (Tennyson, 'Northern Farmer, Old Style' and 'Northern Farmer, New Style').

24   Bernard Jones, 1962, I (2), 532.

25   Tibble, 1935, I, 36.

26   Elliott, 1829, I, stanza xii.

27   *Ibid.*, X, stanza ix.

28   Andrews, 1888–9.

29   Brightfield, 1968, I, 550–1.

30   See, for example, Thomas, 1978, ch. VI.

31   Gaskell, 1857.

32   Knoepflmacher and Tennyson, 1977, 391–425, gives a convenient summary of the issues.

33   Cook and Wedderburn, 1903, III, 623–4.

34   Williams, 1973, especially chs XVI–XVIII.

35   G. Levine in Knoepflmacher and Tennyson, 1977, 137–52.

36   *Adam Bede* (1859), *Silas Marner* (1861) and *Felix Holt* (1866) are Eliot's novels which most centrally use the possibilities of a historically distanced landscape, although she sets other of her fiction in the past.

37   Arnold, *The Scholar Gipsy*, stanza xxi.

38   John Stephens (Frederick George Stephens), 'The Purpose and Tendency of Early Italian Art', *Germ*, no. 2, 58–64.

39   For example, Hunt, 1886, 740.

40   For a discussion of the impact of pre-Darwinian evolutionary theory on English social life see Gillispie, 1951; Henkin, 1963; Knoepflmacher and Tennyson, 1977, 216–30.

41   *In Memoriam*, stanza lvi.

42   *Ibid.*, stanza ci.

43   G. M. Hopkins, *The Wreck of the Deutschland*, stanza 21.

44   Hopkins, 'God's Grandeur'.
45   Williams, 1973, ch. xviii; Williams, 1972, pt II.
46   Williams, 1972, 212.
47   Hardy, *Return of the Native* (1878), Book I, ch. i.
48   For Hardy's concern with the issues raised by evolution see, for example,
     Knoepflmacher and Tennyson, 1977, 259–77.

13   The Victorian Picture of the Country

Rosemary Treble

In the Italian Renaissance the countryside—the landscape and the people in it—was a vehicle for the complex iconography of devotional art; to the French impressionists 500 years later, it provided material for an attempt at the pure perception of light, colour and space. An almost infinite variety of approaches to nature lay between the two extremes and Victorian artists experimented with most of them, for paintings of rural subjects found ready buyers amongst urban patrons nostalgic for a countryside which many of them may only have left within a generation or less, and which represented a pastoral ideal disappearing beneath the onslaught of industrial development. The watercolourists have been exhaustively discussed during this century, above all by Martin Hardie,[1] and this brief introduction is biased towards the artists of the Royal Academy and towards the breakaway groups of the 1860s–1880s.

I Pure Landscape: Naturalism and Romanticism

Queen Victoria received the news of her accession on 20 June 1837 while *Arundel Mill and Castle* (Plate 26) by John Constable (1776–1837) was showing posthumously in the Royal Academy summer exhibition. Around this same time Turner (1775–1851) was working on the last of his studies of Norham Castle, a place he had first painted in 1798 and which, in *Norham Castle, Sunrise* (Plate 27), moved him to the furthest point of abstraction his landscape work achieved, surpassed only by the late studies of storms at sea. The two artists were then the grand old men of the English landscape tradition, but it was a tradition which had had only a comparatively short life of less than a hundred years. Richard Wilson, Gainsborough, Stubbs and the great watercolourists like Paul Sandby and Alexander Cozens created in the second half of the eighteenth century a new category of art, in which the elements of landscape played a major rather than a subordinate part, working on canvas what the landscape gardeners were working on the ground. The picturesque landscape challenged the academic supremacy of history painting and portraiture and made it possible for later artists to explore the full range of possibilities from the naturalism of Constable and the watercolourists to the near-abstract romanticism of Turner. All these developments were rooted in the seventeenth century, when the Dutch— Rembrandt, Van Goyen and Hobbema—and the French—above all Claude— provided the models for their English successors.[2]

The contrast between Constable's *Arundel* and Turner's *Norham* could not be more complete: the *Arundel* is densely worked with a classically structured three-dimensionality, complete with repoussoir (the foreground log), recessional diagonals and the full apparatus of illusionistic landscape perspective. The *Norham* is an exploration of pure light, colour and atmosphere, concerned far more with the luminous patches of palest yellow, blue and green on the picture plane, the surface of the canvas itself, than with any reference to an actual location. Turner's revolutionary painting in both oil and watercolour took him so far beyond the contemporary aesthetic that, in the opinion of some modern writers, it has only recently been fully matched by the American abstract expressionists.[3] Certainly the immediate followers of Turner most often compared with him, James Baker Pyne (1800–70) and Clarkson Stanfield (1793–1867), were unable to pursue his experiments further. Pyne remained content with a golden Claudian glow, deployed to great effect in paintings like *Haweswater, from Waller Gill Force* (1850, Royal Holloway College), while Stanfield worked his landscapes and seascapes into imposing Academy machines, full of sound and fury but with an academic finish and admired by Ruskin as a worthy successor to the immortal Turner.

The search for truth in the representation of nature was the central motivation of both Turner and the Pre-Raphaelite Brotherhood, but the young Millais, Hunt and Rossetti, following in the tracks of the German Nazarenes and of Ford Madox Brown and William Dyce, sought to capture the essence of nature by the minute representation of every visible element in the chosen scene, and totally rejected Turner's abstracted impressions. Ruskin championed both, Turner in the first volume of *Modern Painters* in 1843[4], the Pre-Raphaelites from 1851 onwards, and initially saw no contradiction in his espousal of two such antithetical views of nature. The disintegration of the Brotherhood in the mid-1850s revealed its internal conflicts: at its best it had crystallized a radical movement in English art away from conservative and pedestrian academic views of the landscape; at its most idiosyncratic, the Pre-Raphaelite method, as practised by Hunt and Millais, slipped into a kind of mannered literalism that conveyed only the most specific and subjective experience of nature, rather than uncovering a new universal truth to nature as they had hoped. Millais's *Ophelia* (1851–2, Tate) is perhaps the prettiest as well as one of the clearest examples of this extreme position, which produced work of a novelty, honesty and vitality that, as Allen Staley concludes in his major study *The Pre-Raphaelite Landscape*,[5] made it less important whether it succeeded than that it looked and tried.

The mainstream of landscape art, as with all other forms of painting and sculpture in England, was that shown at the Royal Academy each year. Here the walls, and consequently the viewing public's understanding of contemporary landscape art, were dominated in the early part of the reign by men like Thomas Creswick (1811–69), Frederick Lee (1798–1879) and Thomas Sidney Cooper (1803–1902), who represented the most conservative faction of a conservative Academy. The work of all three was repetitious in subject and composition (Cooper painted such quantities of livestock that he was known as 'Cow' Cooper), and lacked innovative talent, but they also possessed an enviable self-confidence, undoubted technical skill and a genuine interest in the beauties of the English countryside that found a wide market amongst collectors from the most parvenu to the most discerning. Both Lee and Creswick collaborated with Cooper, who painted the cattle and sheep into many of their landscapes, while Cooper's own paintings ranged from the much repeated scenes of cattle grazing on his home ground of the Canterbury Meadows (like that at York, of 1858) to the majestically proportioned *The Halt on the Hills* (1847, Sheffield). Despite Cooper's protestations of disappointment with Paulus Potter's famous *Bull* at The Hague,[6] it is evident that he had been profoundly influenced by the Dutch treatment of animals in landscape during his years in Belgium and Holland in 1827–30, and the monumental forms of the animals in *The Halt on the Hills*, its foreground filled with a pyramidal composition of goats, sheep and long-horned cattle, echoed in the shape of the mountains behind, the whole bathed in a warm golden light, illustrate Cooper at his most opulently arcadian. While Cooper was concerned with an expression of the nobility of the beast, Lee and Creswick produced generally tranquil transcriptions of the English landscape, composed under a limpid light and dotted with ruminating cattle or sheep, like Creswick's *Trentside* (1861, Royal Holloway College). Occasionally they would rise to more dramatic effects: it has been suggested for instance that Lee and Cooper's *The Chequered Shade* (Plate 28), a modern and brilliant exercise in the manner of Hobbema's *The Avenue at Middleharnis*, was a riposte to Holman Hunt's *The Hireling Shepherd*, whose background is dominated by a similar avenue and sheep.[7]

The most popular of their younger successors was Benjamin Williams Leader (1831–1923), an artist who, as Staley points out, synthesized the precision of the Pre-Raphaelites with the subject-matter of the academics and created the instantly recognizable Leader landscape, epitomized by *February Fill Dyke* (1881, Birmingham), highly finished and with a stylized, almost photographic, clarity. *In the Evening There shall be Light* (Plate 29),[8] his Academy picture of 1882, was thought by his biographer[9] to be 'his finest production' and, though not well received by that year's reviews, the painting won for Leader a First Class Medal at the 1889 Paris

Exposition Universelle, where a French critic commented that despite too much contrast and a throbbing colour scheme, it displayed a spiritual quality and a biblical solemnity.

II Sentiment to Social Realism

One of the most powerful images of the Victorian countryside for the modern viewer, and for the Victorians themselves, was provided by scenes of cottage life, featuring rustic simplicity, sometimes in picturesque poverty, sometimes in virtuous and provident though rude comfort. This prettily sentimental view of country life was almost as mythical to its contemporaries as it is to the twentieth century, and seems to have owed its popularity as much to its unattainability as to the evident charm of the paintings it produced. The genre had its genesis in the Dutch seventeenth century with Ostade and Teniers, and in Spain with Murillo, was refined in Gainsborough's 'fancy pictures', and taken to its pre-Victorian limits by George Morland (1763–1804) and his successors, David Wilkie (1785–1841) and William Collins (1788–1847). Collins, for instance, achieved early fame with *The Disposal of a Favourite Lamb* (1813); it was engraved twice that year and some 15,000 of the smaller prints alone were sold.[10] It was clearly a formula that caught the popular imagination, and Collins capitalized vigorously on the fashion with subjects like *Rustic Civility* (1832),[11] showing a child holding open a gate, and its companion, *Cottage Hospitality* (1834), of a child taking broth to a poor traveller. One of his most popular pictures was *Happy as a King*:[12] the apple-cheeked children scramble on a five-barred gate, clean, dimpled and robust despite their rags, innocent and healthy examples of the delights of rural poverty in comparison with the all too evident horrors of urban squalor which presented themselves on every side to Collins's largely urban audience.

Escapism, then, was the principal ingredient in the popularity of this genre, and it reached its ultimate expression in the work of Myles Birket Foster (1825–99). *Children Playing* (Plate 30) was a large, important and typical watercolour: carefree, pinafored children dash down a rolling hillside, pet dog scampering beside them, towards the village pond. The foreground lies in shadow, a favourite Foster device, giving the grass and undergrowth an intense blue-green which complements the hot pink-mauve tones of the girls' dresses in the heat-hazed sunlight. The land and figures are minutely worked with fine stippled touches, while the sky is delicately washed in with pale mauve graduating upwards to palest blue. Birket Foster's country people are children gambolling in nature's garden: they gather flowers or berries, play on stiles or old logs, or, in front of cottages, listen to stories, shell peas or tend chickens. Foster began a highly successful career as an illustrator in the 1840s, turning around 1859 to the watercolours which he continued to paint virtually without change of style for a quarter of a century. They imprinted on the English consciousness an idyllic fantasy of rural existence that was only partly countered by the social realists of the 1870s.

169

Foster's most popular follower was Helen Allingham (1848–1926), a watercolourist of skill and delicacy who concentrated above all on the fabric of the villages and cottages themselves, and who, in a series of exhibitions in London in the 1880s and 1890s,[13] made a practical and committed contribution to the preservationist movement then spearheaded by the Society for the Protection of Ancient Buildings, founded by William Morris in 1878. She was surprisingly impassioned, as the introduction to her 1886 exhibition catalogue (probably written by or with her husband, the poet William Allingham) revealed, and intended her drawings of Surrey cottages to be records of untouched vernacular architecture salvaged on paper as the buildings themselves were being steadily demolished at the rate of some 2,000 a year, or, almost worse, unnecessarily 'done up'. Essential modernization and sanitation were ignored while the landlord, often with a misplaced sense of duty,

> allows the agent to go round with a town architect and settle a general plan
> for doing up the old places (usually described as 'tumbling down' or 'falling
> to pieces'), a village builder makes an estimate and sends in a scratch pack
> of masons and joiners, and between them they often supplant fine old work,
> most of it firm as a rock, with poor materials and careless labour, and rub
> out a piece of Old England, irrecoverable henceforth by all the genius in the
> world and the money in the bank. . . . Whatever else is decided on, no
> uneven tiled roofs, with moss and houseleek, must remain, no thatch on any
> pretence, nor ivy on the wall, nor vine along the eaves, nor wide old
> chimney-places, nor roomy old staircases and cupboards. The cherry or
> apple-tree that pushed its blossoms almost into a lattice, will probably be
> cut down, and the wild rose and honeysuckle hedge be replaced by a row of
> pales or wires. The leaden lattice itself and all its fellows, however perfect,
> must inevitably give place to a set of mean little square windows of
> unseasoned wood—though perhaps on the very next property an architect is
> building imitation old cottages with lattices![14]

What this lament disregarded was the reality of the lives conducted in these picturesque cottages, and it was to this massive problem that the young social realists of the 1870s addressed themselves.

Themes of social concern had surfaced in Victorian art since the earliest years of the reign, most dramatically perhaps in the response to Thomas Hood's *The Song of the Shirt* of 1843,[15] and increased in number with the pressure for social reform. Railways and improving communications made the countryside more accessible and so made the effects of depopulation and deprivation easier for the artist to observe. In the 1850s and 1860s Thomas Faed (1826–1900) took the example of Wilkie and produced for the Academy a series of hugely popular paintings on the theme of cottage poverty (though usually given a literary gloss with lines from Burns), while the *Illustrated London News* invented illustrated journalism and, from its first publication in 1842, printed many drawings of both urban and rural poverty. The quality of its draughtsmanship was, however, generally weak, leaving a gap in the

170

market that was brilliantly filled in the decade from 1869 by the *Graphic*. Its drawings were powerful, the wood engraving was of the highest quality, and a great impact was made on its largely middle-class readership by a young, ambitious and talented stable of artists who made their reputations with often raw and biting drawings, some highlighting aspects of poverty in the country which, while described in print since Cobbett, had not previously received such vivid illustration nor reached so wide an audience. Some of these artists were able to work up an Academy painting from an illustration that had been well received: the most often quoted case is that of Luke Fildes (1843–1927) whose famous documentary painting *Applicants for Admission to a Casual Ward* of 1874 (Royal Holloway College) contributed largely to the success of the first number of the *Graphic* in 1869 as a drawing called *Houseless and Hungry*.

Robert Walker Macbeth (1848–1910) was another *Graphic* artist who, though he never matched Fildes's success, painted a number of interesting East Anglian subjects. The most overtly propagandist of these was *A Lincolnshire Gang* (Plate 31), shown at the Academy in 1876 with the accompanying catalogue note:

> Eight appears to be the ordinary age at which children join the agricultural gangs in the Fens; in some instances they have been known to do so even at four. It is a common practice with parents to stipulate that if the elder children are hired to the gangmaster he must take the younger ones too. The distances they have to walk, or rather run, before the labours of the day begin, are astounding; sometimes eight miles a day. They leave at five in the morning, under the care of the gangmaster, and return at five at night. They work eight or nine hours; and during the last hour they are at work, 'they will ask', said an old gangmaster, 'forty times what o'clock it is.'

The painting, now untraced, was engraved for the *Graphic*, the composition appearing in reverse: it is dawn and the exhausted women and children setting out for the fen look towards the corner of a shed where a child lies collapsed, oblivious to the menacing whip and dogs of the gangmaster, and behind them another gangmaster hauls children from a stable. It was a powerful picture, almost too powerful for the writer of the accompanying text in the *Graphic* who, like many of his contemporaries, was anxious that the subject was too painful to be used for an exhibited painting. This was a complaint often levelled at social realists throughout the reign by over-sensitive critics and by those who may have felt threatened by the potentially revolutionary use that could be made of such images.

These fears were unfounded: apart from the radical circle around William Morris, most Victorian artists were not politically involved, and the hundreds of social subject paintings that were poured out in increasing quantities from the 1850s onwards[16] served as documentary and illustrative material and were not the primary social and political weapons produced by Millet and Courbet in France. Hubert Herkomer (1849–1914) was typical: the depression of the 1870s and his own somewhat self-righteously pious humanitarianism led to a decade of earnest social documen-taries, like *Hard Times* (1885, Manchester), a scene of an unemployed labourer and

171

his destitute family in a country lane. As with Frank Holl and Luke Fildes, however, the very success of the subject pictures attracted portrait commissions which rapidly took all the artists' energies and proved the making of several fortunes.

III Allegory

The heightened awareness of William Blake and Samuel Palmer to the religious and mystical in nature created a visionary landscape of genius that was not matched by any Victorian artist, but outside the Pre-Raphaelite circle there were many artists whose landscapes and country figure scenes included some symbolic elements. John Linnell (1792–1882) was an intimate friend of Blake and Palmer in the early years of the century and lived on to become one of the most prosperous of the Victorian landscapists. He remained a maverick figure outside the Academy because of a dispute with Constable and, with a fierce nonconformism, painted Surrey landscapes and some biblical scenes that bore traces of the religious intensity of Blake and Palmer. *Harvest Home* (Plate 32), shown at the British Institution in 1854, included some of the most potent symbols that can be found in a benevolent countryside—the harvest gathered and the day ended in a radiant sunset. These epitomized the mid-century rejection of the picturesque landscape tamed and distorted by man, and its craving for the expression of man's unity with nature. 'Of all places in the country', Linnell himself wrote,

> parks are to me the most desolate. There seems to be a dearth of intelligence and sympathy with Nature, or rather with the design of the Creator, whose thoughts or intentions are not perceived because men seek to bend Nature to express their sense of their own importance, their riches and powers; and they put Nature as far as they can into a kind of livery, as they do their servants, degrading both with what pretends to be ornament. The landscape is reduced to a toy-shop sentiment on a large scale; everything is denuded of those accompaniments which give the true expression of grandeur or beauty to the scene.
> It is true the trees are left to grow unrestrained, looking like aristocratic 'swells', isolated from all the undergrowth; and, with the ground shaved under them, they look like large toy-trees placed upon a green board. It is not until one gets upon a common, near a forest, or into farmlands, that one begins to breathe again, and feel out of the influence of man's despotism. Man stamps his own thought and character upon everything he meddles with, and, unhappily in most cases, he obliterates the work of God and substitutes his own.[17]

Linnell, however, was prepared to exploit man's ingenuity when it suited him; like many other mid-century artists from the Pre-Raphaelites to Courbet, he is known to have used photographs, and Aaron Scharf suggests that some of Linnell's seething

172

skies and rustic scenes may even have been taken from photographs not of English but of Italian landscape.[18]

The desire to represent God's work in nature at its most unremitting was a sentiment thoroughly understood by Peter Graham (1836–1921), one of a large group of Edinburgh-trained Scottish artists including Orchardson, MacWhirter and Pettie who came south to conquer the Academy in the 1860s. Graham succeeded beyond his wildest hopes with his first Academy picture, *A Spate in the Highlands* of 1866 (Plate 33). Its impressive cataract of water and swirling mists recalled something of Turner's effects, but made specific with the tiny figure of a herdsman driving his animals back from the broken bridge, the brink of the abyss, so that *The Times*'s reviewer felt moved to speak of the subject's 'soul-subduing' impact.[19] Graham strove for an expression of the sublime terror which could confront man in the face of nature; G. J. Pinwell (1842–75), one of the brilliant young illustrators who revived black-and-white wood engraving in the 1860s, had a gift for farmyard and village scenes that bear a curiously claustrophobic weight of foreboding. One of Pinwell's most overtly symbolic drawings was *The Shadow* (plate 34):[20] children drag a calf to slaughter while the farmer stands framed by a grisly gibbet of predatory birds, the final manifestations of man's bloody exploitation of nature.

Pinwell was a member of the circle around George Heming Mason (1818–72) and Fred Walker (1840–75) who between them created in the late 1860s and 1870s what many critics called the first new school in English art since the Pre-Raphaelites. They were eclectic, wildly so to modern eyes, and ranged easily from the modern French realists like Millet and Jules Breton (though eschewing radical politics) to the early Renaissance and classical sculpture. In *The Plough* (Tate) of 1870, Walker placed a ploughing team, drawn from a group of a boy and horses in the Elgin Marbles, against a stratified, mannered landscape which, though taken from a Somerset quarry, has the air of a Bellini background; Walker had prepared himself for the painting by reading Thomson's *The Seasons* and Bloomfield's *The Farmer's Boy*.[21] The curiously still, frieze-like result was far removed from the muscular immediacy of *An English Ploughing Match* (Plate 35) by William Small (1843–1931), engraved for the *Graphic* in 1875. There is sweat on the horses' rumps, the ploughmen are heroic labourers, and the earth curls and crumbles under the onslaught of the blades. It was a dynamic image that anticipated the socialist realism of this century and made Walker's *Plough* seem an effete archaism.

During the same decade, Sir Coutts Lindsay opened the Grosvenor Gallery, his show place for such aesthetic refugees from the Academy as Burne-Jones, Whistler, Tissot and Watts. The first Grosvenor exhibition of 1877 included *The Reaper and the Flowers* (Plate 36) by Philip Richard Morris (1836–1902). It is an odd picture, absolutely English in its sentimental and naïve symbolism, and part of a certain absolutely consistent English idea of the rural idyll. It was hardly surprising, therefore, that those artists who had seen the revolution effected by impressionism in France should have reacted so violently against such a literary view of nature and such an anecdotal kind of symbolism. The New English Art Club, founded in 1886,

173

brought together those young artists like Steer, Sickert and Clausen who in varying ways had found new approaches in France to the whole concept of what a picture should be. George Clausen (1852–1944) was an interestingly transitional figure who, though sophisticated enough to look to France, was led by an inescapably Victorian sentiment to take as his master not Monet or Pissarro, but Millet's academic follower, Jules Bastien-Lepage. Bastien-Lepage was a dogmatic *plein air* painter: that is, as far as possible the whole of his often busy canvases had to be painted on site and in consistent light which, as he worked in Northern France, gave his pictures their characteristic grey tonality. Clausen, in an essay published in 1892,[22] wrote of Bastien's simple acceptance of nature that allowed him to balance the literary and the purely aesthetic elements in his art and supported his purist rejection of studio painting. Clausen also recognized that Bastien took care to choose 'a good type'[23] in his pictures of peasants working on the land—a practice that was thoroughly in sympathy with the Victorian interest in 'types' from Dickens onwards. *The Stone Pickers* of 1887 (Plate 37) shows how well Clausen learned. It is painted with his square brush stroke and restricted, near-monochrome palette, its sombre greys and browns sharpened with acidic green grass out of which the daisies and cornflowers struggle in frail contrast to the pile of jagged grey stones in the foreground. Clausen had made of the girl a grey, ghostly symbol of rural poverty, using the language of the end of the century, but still in an essentially Victorian state of mind.

The 1890s found artists of every persuasion still looking to nature and finding in it the most diverse inspirations. Philip Wilson Steer painted the light and sparkling coast at Walberswick in the spirit of Monet and Renoir; Arnesby Brown and Henry William Banks Davis produced cattle in sun-dappled meadows and fording Welsh rivers with a full range of well-learnt impressionist technique; Arthur Hacker plumbed the depths of silliness with airbrushed nudes in sylvan glades and drifts of leaves; and Robert Bevan painted Exmoor in the spirit of Gauguin. The reign had begun with Ruskin's exhortation to artists to represent nature 'in all singleness of heart';[24] it ended in the decade of Picasso and Braque. In over sixty years, Victorian artists had given their audience many vivid evocations of both a generalized nature and of specific locations, and had also explored social and philosophical issues as they affected rural life. England had not produced a Millet or a Courbet, but the profound nostalgia of the urban middle classes for their rural past ensured the survival, in however changed a form, of the English landscape in art.

Notes

1 Hardie, 1968, III.
2 See Parris, 1973, for a comprehensive survey.
3 Rosenblum, 1961, 350–9.
4 The title continues: 'their superiority in the art of landscape painting to all the ancient masters proved by examples of the True, the Beautiful, and the Intellectual, from the works of modern artists, especially from those of J. M. W. Turner, Esq., R.A.'.

5   Staley, 1973, 185.

6   Cooper, 1890, I, 183.

7   Forbes, 1975, 88.

8   In the collection of Lord Hollenden until 1958, now untraced and represented here by the reduced replica of 1897.

9   Lusk, 1901, 6.

10 'Pictures and Stories', *Connoisseur*, April 1957, CXXXIX, 147.

11 Original picture exhibited at the Royal Academy in 1832; version dated 1833, Sheepshanks Collection, Victoria and Albert Museum, London.

12 The original of this was shown at the Academy in 1836, but was best known from the engraving of 1839 and the replica painted for the collector Robert Vernon, presented with the rest of his major collection of contemporary art to the nation in 1847 and now in the Tate Gallery, London.

13 The Fine Art Society, London, exhibition nos 41, 1886; 66, 1889; 118, 1894.

14 'A Collection of Drawings by Mrs Allingham, RWS, illustrating Surrey Cottages', The Fine Art Society, London, prefatory note, p. 4.

15 *Great Victorian Pictures*, 1978, 71.

16 Rodee, 1977, 307–13.

17 Story, 1892, II, 50–1.

18 Scharf, 1974, 115.

19 *Great Victorian Pictures*, 1978, 41.

20 Engraved by the Brothers Dalziel for Robert Buchanan (ed.), *Wayside Posies: Original Poems of the Country Life*, Routledge, London, 1867, p. 1.

21 Marks, 1896, 192–3.

22 Theuriet, 1892, 111–27.

23 *Ibid.*, 117.

24 Cook and Wedderburn, 1903, III, 624.

II   Agriculture in the Victorian Countryside

14 Agriculture and Industrialization in the Victorian Economy

B. A. Holderness

I

During the nineteenth century British rural society lost much of its former diversity and animation. Agriculture was established as the largest source of employment in the countryside, for its only rival of substance after 1850 was domestic service. Yet the contribution of agriculture in the national economy was on the wane. Its share of national income declined from about one-third in the first twenty years of the century to 5 or 6 per cent by 1900, while the proportion of agricultural workers in the labour force similarly fell from 30 per cent or more in 1801–21 to around 9 per cent in 1891–1911. This declension was matched by a similar contraction in the importance of the agricultural interest in politics and by the depletion of social opportunities in the countryside. By 1880 the majority of Britons lived in towns or cities. Although many were as yet first generation townsmen, the problems and concerns of urban life obtruded upon, and indeed came to dominate, political, economic and social interests in Victorian Britain to such an extent that, although the difficulties of agriculture and the social pathology of rural life were subject to endless discussion and some remedial legislation, preference for policies apt to satisfy urban and industrial needs or interests, even when they were in conflict with agrarian concerns, was always to be expected.

Urbanization of the population was an ineluctable fact of nineteenth-century social development. It proceeded in step with the growth of the great staple industries. Thus the organization of labour and the application of capital in large enterprises came to characterize Victorian industrialization at all its most vigorous growing points. The evolution of the factory system was strongly influenced by the application of steam power to productive processes, and this, coupled with the economies which accrued to entrepreneurs from concentration of production and distribution where both an ample labour supply and an efficient network of communications, especially by rail, could be exploited, tended to encourage the location of industries in the neighbourhood of larger towns or cities. The rise of modern industry certainly defined much more clearly the boundaries between urban and rural, or between industrial and agrarian, than had been possible in the pre-industrial period. Before the age of steam, industrialization had been a much more diffuse process, bound up inextricably with agricultural involution, which revealed itself characteristically in the development of an economic system of dual occupations. Households, that is to say, participated in a combination of agricultural production and manufacturing and mining in a setting which remained rural and agrarian. Rural industrialization came to dominate the development of many regions of pre-industrial Europe, at the same time as other districts, better endowed with fertile soil or easier access to markets, specialized more completely in commercial agriculture. Specialized agricultural and specialized industrial zones formed the basis of economic development in the era of modern industrialization. Most of those districts of Victorian Britain in which the expanding staple industries were located had originated as manufacturing regions far back before the age of steam and of urban agglomeration. South-east Lancashire, the Yorkshire woollen district, the Black Country, the Tyne and Wear district, for example, had become diversified centuries earlier, when spinning and weaving, coal-digging or metallurgy were cottage trades that could be carried on in conjunction with dairying, stock-rearing and even with the culture of barley, oats or potatoes. Before 1830 the 'rural' industries which were to survive into the next century had fallen under the domination of putting-out merchants, and thereafter the transformation from mercantile to industrial organization, by concentration in factories propelled by water or steam power, was a relatively straightforward process.[1]

This latter-day industrialization, however, brought with it much social dislocation. Apart from the often painful social consequences for the labour force of mechanization and concentration within the expansive industrial districts, there also occurred a parallel movement of disindustrialization in many ancient manufacturing communities, which affected not only old industrial or commercial towns such as Norwich, Ipswich and Colchester, but also whole territories once characterized by their dual economies, East Anglia, Essex, south Devon, Wiltshire, Westmorland and the remoter Yorkshire dales. Most of these districts were thrown back, at least temporarily, upon the resources of agriculture. Elsewhere less elaborately commercialized rural manufacture also declined in the nineteenth century for a variety of reasons, only one of which was direct competition for their markets by producers in new towns. We may mention the south midland straw-plaiting industry, needle-making at Long Crendon, Buckinghamshire, paper-making in south Devon and village lace-making in several parts of southern England as examples of long-established crafts in decay by the 1860s or 1870s. In a few cases the process of decline was arrested by the application of industrial techniques to create modern industries—for example the Northamptonshire boot and shoe manufacture and the Chiltern furniture trade, although in the latter instance the traditional chair-making crafts of the area around High Wycombe were still withering as late as 1914.[2]

II

The creeping urbanization of industry in the nineteenth century had the effect of reducing the number and diversity of productive occupations in the agricultural districts. The gradual contraction of the formerly extensive rural manufactures was in due course equalled by the diminution of the crafts and trades that served the self-sufficiency of traditional rural societies. Reduced diversity could lead only to emigration or pauperism, since neither agricultural improvement nor any of the newer sources of employment in the countryside, such as the police service or work on the railways, were enough to supply the deficiency. Migration out of rural districts was persistent throughout the nineteenth century, although until the middle decades natural increase was large enough to prevent depopulation. In some counties, indeed, the increase in numbers before 1841 was almost as great as in the industrial districts, though the reasons for this comparatively high rate of growth, in, say, Lincolnshire or Aberdeenshire, were related to extensive reclamation and colonization of waste land. More generally, however, almost all villages reached their maximum populations at various dates between 1831 and 1871. Thereafter there was a long downhill run to 1911 or later.[3]

The function of excess rural populations as reservoirs of labour in the process of industrialization is a commonplace of development theory. The absorption of farming populations into industrial and commercial occupations is held to be important because migrants from the countryside customarily pass from employment of low productivity to employment of significantly higher productivity, thereby carrying forward the impulse of economic growth. Even in Britain, where the peasant mode was so attenuated by 1830–50 as to be moribund, the shift from rural to urban occupations by the population helped to raise productivity per man in the aggregate economy. Here, however, it was not out of agriculture that any considerable surplus of labour was winnowed before the 1870s. Excess labour in the agrarian districts had not been assimilated by agriculture between 1770 and 1850, especially in those southern counties where disindustrialization had been most marked. The success of the towns and of mining and manufacturing industries in attracting rural migrants contributed more to the relief of pauperism than to the appropriation of established agricultural labour. The persistence of the problems of rural poverty in the southern counties, at least until the 1850s, illustrates the limitation of long-range labour mobility in the early nineteenth century.

181

The demand for labour and the supply of it in the countryside more nearly approached equilibrium in the 1850s and 1860s, thanks both to the increasing momentum of townward migration and to the progress made by agriculture in raising production and creating genuine opportunities for new employment. It is evident, for example, that in 1875–1900 farmers south of the Trent became aware of potential labour scarcity before they were confronted with the consequences for their work force of actual depopulation. In the northern counties agriculturists had come to this pass a generation earlier, for competition for labour between agriculture and industry, or among farmers, tradesmen and coal-owners, was active and at times acute early in the century. Not only did this rivalry force up rural wage levels, but the competitive edge it introduced allegedly brought about a more efficient use of labour in rural, especially agricultural, employment north of the Trent. Late in the century rural employers on both sides of the divide were prone to complain of the shortage and also of the poor quality of their wage-labourers by comparison with the time, thirty or fifty years before, when they had enjoyed a buyer's market. On the other hand, since the attractiveness of town life and of non-agricultural employment had always impressed the abler or more adventurous of countrymen, as well as the failed or destitute, the alleged decline of quality in farm labour during the 1880s and 1890s is difficult to prove conclusively.

The migrants who abandoned agriculture or chose to live in towns in fact formed a heterogeneous group. The majority was composed of men and women drawn from the village poor, whose hopes presumably turned upon a more secure livelihood. How many were actually driven out of their village hovels by hunger, unemployment or severe overcrowding, and how many were attracted by the prospect of better conditions in the industrial districts, is unknown. It is probable that the motives were mixed and the conditions which promoted migration diverse. Of the poor emigrants who fled the countryside a number became labourers or operatives in the staple industries. They entered employment at the bottom and the majority of them remained there throughout their lives. The more intelligent of the one-time agricultural labourers may have risen above the level of the semi-skilled in industrial employment, but the greatest opportunities seem to have presented themselves in the urban service trades. The ubiquity of horse-drawn transport in towns was a continual attraction to countrymen inured to the management of horses. Teamsmen, ostlers, grooms, carters, even cabmen and coachmen were often migrants from the country. Many of the other unspecialized labouring jobs in the transport and building trades were also occupied by recent arrivals from the agricultural parts of England, Scotland or Ireland. The police service, variously instituted between 1829 and 1858, and unskilled vacancies on the railways were filled to a significant extent by former farm-workers or their sons. In other words it was the expanding tertiary sector of the urban, industrial economy which benefited most from the available supply of cheap rural labour. Women migrants, too, often ended up in domestic service or in shop work and the victualling trades.

Even farmers, or farmers' sons and daughters, who drifted away from the land into the towns tended to set up in small retailing businesses. According to Alexander Somerville many of the shopkeepers at Stockport in the 1840s were farmers' children, and there is no reason to think that this was an untypical situation.[4] Some of the farmers or farmers' sons were notably more successful. Several became engineers or industrial entrepreneurs: Richard Hornsby, William Tuxford, Joseph Ruston, James Paxman, William Moore, J. J. D. Paul, the Tangye brothers, J. H. Howlett and Frederick Royce, not all of whom specialized in agricultural engineering. Many of these Victorian captains of industry began with the advantage of a fair education and inherited or parental capital. Examples of men who reached eminence from a very lowly position in agriculture, of destitute farmers or of labourers who became entrepreneurs, are very few; but it is also true that most of the less abject farming families who abandoned agriculture remained in deep obscurity, or even sank to the level of unskilled labourers or servants.

III

The human element in the developing relationship between the agrarian sector and industry is even more evident in the much more celebrated association of land-ownership and industrial and urban development. For a long time the British landed élite had been deeply involved in the exploitation of mineral resources underlying their landed possessions. Less often, but even more significantly, noblemen and landed gentry owned, and sometimes directly managed, industrial plant. In the mid-nineteenth century the pioneering or innovating role of the great landowners in industrialization may have been diminishing, but it was not necessary to go far into an industrial district, old or new, before coming upon a colliery, furnace or smelter which belonged to a local gentleman or to a grandee with immense and far-flung possessions. Fortunately there is now an extensive literature in the subject, so a brief discussion only is necessary here.[5] Colliery ownership and colliery management were the commonest type of industrial entrepreneurship among the landed gentry. Wherever there were coal measures there were estates which derived a large portion of their annual income from coal, often simply as lessors of the sub-surface resources. At the other extreme, however, were several great magnates, such as Earl Fitzwilliam, the Earl of Durham, Lord Dudley, Lord Ravensworth and others, with extensive direct interests in coal-mining. A good example is the Marquess of Londonderry who on his Durham estates not only owned and controlled several valuable pits, but undertook to build a seaport, Seaham Harbour, for the export of his coal. In the Midlands, Lord Dudley was not only an extensive coal-owner, but also an operator of large iron-works, and deserves a good deal of the credit for the development of the western parts of the Black Country.

Another major interest of the landowning entrepreneur was urban development. Several Victorian industrial towns expanded under the auspices of the landed aristocracy. Barrow-in-Furness, for example, was largely the creation of the seventh

Duke of Devonshire to serve his industrial interests in the region. Even more common was the aristocratic involvement in residential development. Many nineteenth-century resort towns grew up under the direction of local landowners: Skegness, thanks to the Earl of Scarbrough; Eastbourne, through the Duke of Devonshire; Bournemouth, through the Tapps-Gervis family; Torquay, through the Palks. Property in some of the larger industrial towns, as well as in London, was owned and developed by families of the same kind. The Duke of Norfolk's interests in Sheffield, for example, yielded a revenue notably greater than the income from his agricultural estates.

We know a great deal about the nature of aristocratic investment in industrial and urban property, about its financial returns and also about the methods and pitfalls of management. So far, however, less attention has been devoted to the question of its *economic* results for the economy at large. It is probable, but not certain, that the flow of funds, at least by the nineteenth century, was out of industry and into agriculture, and that much of the ostentatious rebuilding of farmsteads and villages by landowners was paid for in many instances out of revenue obtained from urban rents, from coal-owning or from industrial enterprise. With few exceptions the super-rich among the Victorian aristocracy held their position because of extensive non-agricultural incomes. They were certainly less vulnerable to the effects of agricultural depression than landowners who depended only upon farm rents. Even so, it is difficult to overestimate the importance of certain leading aristocratic entrepreneurs in the development of their own regions: the half dozen magnates who dominated the Durham coalfield, for example, or the barons and earls of Dudley in the west Midlands, the Fitzwilliams around Barnsley and the Leveson-Gowers in north Staffordshire and Shropshire.[6]

IV

The growth of a large industrial population laid a considerable strain upon domestic agriculture. This may not have undermined the economic strength of the landed interest before the 1870s, but landlords, farmers and labourers were placed under pressure to raise both the output and the productivity of agriculture in order to feed the burgeoning numbers. To an increasing degree the Victorian economy relied upon foreign supplies of foodstuffs and raw materials, but large as primary imports had become by 1900, their increase went hand in hand with increments of domestic production, at least in the century before 1875 during which period Britain first became a net importer of foodstuffs. The stimulus of industrialization affected agriculture at first through extension and modification of demand schedules for its products. Thus whereas the population in Britain increased by 230 per cent between 1760 and 1860, output from agriculture possibly grew by about 110 per cent. British farmers could by the last date still supply four-fifths or more of this population with its basic food requirements of carbohydrate and protein materials, even allowing for some *per capita* improvement in dietary standards since the early years of the century. In 1840–60 we imported only about 15 per cent of our cereals and below 10 per cent of our meat and dairy produce in domestic consumption. Despite a marked deceleration of the rate of population growth in the next half-century the share of imports in human dietary needs much increased, reaching about 60 per cent in 1900–10, i.e. 85 per cent of bread grain and 45 per cent of meat.[7]

This scarcely reflected a failure on the part of British agriculture, since within the limitations imposed by the effects of free trade in foodstuffs, the industry showed itself capable of much adjustment. Long before the fall in cereal prices brought about in the later 1870s by the supplies of cheap overseas grains, British farmers had begun the process of diversifying out of wheat, and even out of potatoes, into the production of protein-rich consumables, or into the forage crops and grains that supported livestock husbandry. A greater concentration upon the régime of 'high feeding', as a response to urban patterns of demand, was in train by the 1850s at least, on ordinary working farms in the eastern counties. Naturally, in the drier, more fertile eastern lowlands wheat cultivation was still an object of commercial production (and on a smaller scale so remained in the 1890s). Out of the grain surplus districts, from Strathmore to Dorset, the metropolis and the western counties where much of the industrial population lived were fed. The inter-regional grain trade, however important qualitatively, was not a major element of exchange in the context of Victorian internal commerce. Hawke has demonstrated that even in 1865 only about 630,000 tons of wheat (about 30 per cent of available domestic production) were carried by rail, that is to say, about 2 per cent by weight of railway freight in that year. Hawke also discusses the traffic flow of livestock by rail at the same period, and draws the same conclusion that railways were not essential to the growth of the trade, and that the benefits to the railway companies of capturing this already substantial traffic were not considerable. On the other hand, rail-borne fatstock kept its condition better, despite some bruising, than driven fatstock; and the same advantage probably applied to the leanstock brought into the lowland region from highland or moorland breeding areas.[8] In the distribution of perishable commodities, especially of liquid milk by rail into the towns which gathered momentum in the last thirty years of the century, the effects of railway extension upon dairy production were not geographical, except for the gradual rehabilitation of dairying in south-eastern England. Liquid milk replaced butter and cheese-making as the chief interest of dairy farmers in the traditional milk-producing districts, from Ayrshire to Devon, particularly under the influence of developing mass distribution through companies like Express Dairies and the C.W.S., which organized the supplies of Wiltshire and Cheshire for urban consumption.[9]

However, the contribution of the railways in joining together surplus and deficit zones of agricultural production in nineteenth-century Britain was not innovative. Railways increased the tempo of economic life but cannot be said to have brought about the commercialization of agriculture. They speeded rural emigration but did not cause it. Although railway services cheapened the transport of farmers' goods inwards and outwards, they also introduced to consumers a range of commodities which competed, in price, quality and availability, with home-based primary production. The concentration of agricultural processing, and equally of the farmers' distributive trades, was also influenced by the spread of the railway network. Whether this development was beneficial for the farmers is a moot point, but for the majority of country craftsmen—for millers, maltsters, smiths, brewers, brush-makers—the access which later Victorian farmers had to industrialized or mass-produced commodities was a serious check to their livelihood. The railways should not be blamed for the decay of rural society, although they doubtless contributed to it by undermining the self-sufficiency of agricultural communities.

The function of British agriculture as supplier of raw materials to industry declined in relation to the total consumption of the industrial sector throughout the century. More and more of the materials processed in manufacturing industry were imported. This was partly the consequence of technological changes, as when a tropical or sub-tropical commodity was preferred to a domestically produced commodity, or when an inorganic substance was substituted for an organic one. But it was also partly the result of a much greater commitment to the import of primary products from regions where conditions of plant growth were very similar to those in Britain. The high import content of the processed foodstuffs consumed in late Victorian Britain—bread, butter, cheese, bacon, tinned meat, tinned milk—was not the only threat faced by farmers after 1850. A good deal of the wool, a considerable part of the leather, much of the flax and hemp, all of the jute, coir, esparto, rubber and other fibres employed in the production of cheap fabrics for industrial use, much also of the oils and fats used in manufacturing, were imported by the late nineteenth century. British farmers suffered hardly at all from the discovery of chemical dyestuffs and stearin, since little of the organic substances eventually replaced by these new commodities was produced in Britain by the middle of the century. Even when industries in traditional fibre-, oil- or tallow-using businesses increased their dependence upon imported materials, the effect upon British agriculture was minimal because domestic production of these commodities had either become too small to be significant or was maintained at something like the old absolute level in the midst of a substantial enlargement of total industrial output.

Wool, however, presented a different case. The wool-using industries were already large by 1830, and they continued to grow thereafter. The British supplied perhaps 90 per cent of the domestic requirements of the woollen industries in 1830, that is to say, about 120,000,000 lb, but only 20 per cent or 130–140,000,000 lb at the end of the century.[10] This comparative decline reflected the changes which affected the sheep–corn husbandry of the eastern districts, as it marked the emergence of new world, especially Australasian, wool production. More subtly, however, the change mirrored the progress of fashions and techniques of production in the woollen textile industries. Particularly affected were long- and coarse-staple wools, because the fashion for fabrics made of combed-wool fibres diminished from the middle of the century onwards. The demand for fine- or short-staple wools held up much better, and this, as much as the inherent competitiveness of southern hemisphere sheep stations, accounts for the success of merino or merino-cross sheep-rearing outside these islands. By 1900 Australian flockmasters provided British woollen manufacturers with 220,000,000 lb of their needs, and wool was also imported into Yorkshire and Gloucestershire from New Zealand, Cape Colony, Argentina and central Europe.

Woollen manufacturing was the only great industry in Great Britain which still processed a fair share of its raw materials out of domestic resources. At a lower level, the growing dependence upon imports by industries which had once relied heavily or wholly upon domestic raw materials is exemplified in the development of milk processing. Against the background of a sustained increase in liquid milk distribution by rail from dairying districts into the larger towns, the manufacture of secondary milk products, butter and cheese above all, declined or stagnated. Thus imports of butter, chiefly from continental Europe, rose from 1.05 lb per head in 1840 to 9.05 lb in 1900, and of cheese, from Europe and America, from 0.92 lb per head to 7.21 lb.[11] Irish dairy produce, too, entered largely into urban patterns of consumption. The establishment of co-operative creameries, and of factories operated by firms with substantial interests in mass-distribution, marked several attempts to retaliate against foreign penetration, but before 1900 these were minor efforts. Social investigators at the end of the century frequently noted the consumption of American tinned milk by the poor of both town and country, so that even the expansion of the market for liquid milk produced in Wiltshire or Cheshire was restricted at the lower end of the scale. Another limitation upon the buoyancy of late-nineteenth-century dairy-farming was the small-scale but ominous developments in the field of butter substitutes, in which British oil mills played a pioneering part, although it fell to the Dutch and Germans to exploit their commercial possibilities before the Great War. From 1880 to 1914 margarine occupied a much larger share of the market for edible fats in Germany than it did in Britain, but, as with condensed milk, margarine had entered the diet of the poorest in Britain by the end of the century. Even when manufactured in Britain margarine was a compound of imported oils and fats, and therefore, even if only marginally, it sliced into the traditional market for domestic agricultural produce. By 1900 consumption of dairy produce, excluding liquid milk, amounted to 10,735 cwt in 1896–1902, to which retained imports contributed about 57 per cent.

Modest new industries processing agricultural primary products grew up in various parts of Britain. Preserve-making, typically in small, modern factories, which made use of soft fruits grown in the home counties, the Vale of Evesham, Clydesdale or the Carse of Gowrie, was an invaluable outlet for market gardeners bedevilled with problems of seasonal gluts. Most of the firms famous subsequently for their jams originated in the later years of the century. In the case of Wilkin of Tiptree, the culture of soft fruits and the production of preserves began as an integrated enterprise, significantly on the farm which J. J. Mechi, extreme exponent of high farming, had cultivated in the 1860s, and upon which he had gone bankrupt. A similar history can be sketched for food canning. The first developments in the trade date back to the early years of the century, but it was only after the 1870s that the canning of surplus food became commonplace and cheap enough to attract mass consumption. By 1900 the importation of tinned foods, especially from North America, was already well established, and British manufacturers were well set to capture a fair portion of the market for tinned fruit and vegetables and, if not in the same degree, for tinned meat, fish and condensed milk. No doubt in the face of overseas competition the newer food-processing industries in Britain grew more slowly than they might have done, but the comparatively small home base of commodities suitable for preserving set a limit upon the development of jam-making, canning, pickling or dehydration processes until well into the present century. The world-wide character of the Victorian trade in foodstuffs affected those who specialized in fruit and vegetable production less than the producers of wheat or wool, but the expansion of food-preserving across the world in the late nineteenth century did interfere with the delicate balance between supply and demand upon which producers of perishable and traditionally seasonal commodities have always depended for success. Even British canners and jam-makers sought supplies of their essential raw materials abroad for much of their regular business, and this tendency was growing by the turn of the century.

V

Of course much of the produce of British agriculture still found its way into the diets of men and animals within Great Britain. Most was sold fresh or in a semi-processed state, such as flour or meal, but all the traditional trades devoted to processing—bacon-curing, flour-milling, malting, brewing and distilling—flourished as never before in Victorian Britain. The immense growth of population after 1770 kept these traditional industries buoyant and expansive. Far-reaching changes affected them both entrepreneurially and technologically, and the difficulties of regeneration frequently obscured the success of transformation. The movement towards large-scale production, indeed the trend in some trades towards cartelization, brought ruin to many small, backward or old-fashioned businesses, but the large and persistent fall in the number of millers or brewers, say, in each census from 1851 to 1901, is a sign of industrial rationalization rather than decay, though at various times the inflow of commodities such as ready-milled flour from North America appeared to threaten even the livelihood of enterprising British firms until the market leaders responded by out-marshalling their overseas rivals.

The history of grain-milling in nineteenth-century Britain has until recently been inadequately researched.[12] It forms, however, one of the most important components in the changing relationship between agriculture and industrialization, since the raw material has for centuries been the principal commodity—by weight—produced on farms, and one or other of the bread-grains has since the beginnings of cultivation been the staple of human diet. Traditionally, farmers produced their grain, had it milled for local consumption or, in areas of substantial grain surpluses, sold it to corn merchants who then distributed it about the nation. Mills were usually small and localized, for in all but the very biggest towns the large urban demand for bread flour was typically satisfied by a multitude of low-capacity mills. Steam-milling enabled some economies of scale to be achieved, but the technology of grinding by mill-stones inhibited the development of large-scale production. Hence the very numerous millers, 37,268 returned in the census of 1851, none of whom could claim to be a capitalist comparable with any of his contemporary captains of industry. Cornmilling remained very much a traditional industry in the middle of the century. It was much affected by vigorous competition, especially in the towns, and a few milling entrepreneurs had already begun to safeguard their profits by product specialization, or by attempting to stabilize prices through horizontal integration. The millers' problems increased *pari passu* with those of the arable farmers, as the trickle of high-grade imported bread grain, milled or unmilled, turned into a steady stream. Wheats grown in better climates and producing the widely favoured high-white flour came to be regarded as indispensable for bread-making. Moreover, the Americans, by developing techniques of grinding based on inventions made in hard-wheat producing districts of central Europe, had achieved a quality of flour, which only the very best contemporary British millers using stone-grinding could emulate in the 1860s and 1870s. The three-fold necessity of acquiring easy access to imports of hard grains, of beating off the threat of foreign millers unloading flour on the British market, and of coming to terms with the new techniques of roller-grinding concentrated the efforts of the more businesslike and far-seeing mill-owners upon the accomplishment of economies of scale without loss of quality. It was inevitable that by 1900 much of the expansion in British flour-milling should have been concentrated upon the greater towns, especially upon the seaports, since no firm aiming to produce for a mass market could ignore either the inflow of foreign supplies or the urban location of demand for its product. Location of flour-milling in East London, in Hull, Manchester, Bristol, Liverpool, Glasgow, Newcastle or Leith preceded the adoption of roller-grinding, of which the pioneers, in the 1870s, were to be found in eastern England, in Colchester, Ipswich and Nayland, Suffolk for example, although nearly all these early mills using soft wheats were failures. In 1879 the first automatic roller-miller was opened in Manchester and its success ensured the future of roller-grinding in Britain. By the late 1880s most of the future market leaders such as the C.W.S., Joseph Rank & Company, Henry Leetham & Company, Spillers and Bakers Ltd, had embraced roller-milling with large plant to handle an immense throughput of both imported and home-produced wheat. Smaller firms still situated in the agricultural districts—Clover of Halstead, Essex, Quinton of Needham Market and Ingleby of Tadcaster, for example were also converted to roller-grinding and continued to market successfully in their own hinterlands, although in every case success seems to have depended upon access to port or railway facilities. According to one estimate, the capacity of the port mills increased from less than 30 per cent to about 50 per cent of total consumption between 1890 and 1906, and there had been an absolute fall in the capacity of the inland mills, not all of which were small wind- or water-driven enterprises, of about 3 million sacks per year (or 17 per cent) from their already somewhat shrunken output in 1890.[13]

Mergers and agreements had begun to influence the domestic grain trade, and the emergence of a comparatively small number of dominant firms in flour-milling during the last twenty years of the century affected the bargaining position of the farmers, since they were not only faced with the buyers' preference for imported bread grains, but with increasing oligopoly in the organization of the trade.

For British wheat producers the saving grace lay in the growing demand for biscuit flour, since British soft wheats remained suitable for biscuit-makers and pastry-cooks. The growth of a confectionery industry on a comparatively large scale is as characteristic of late Victorian society as the development of commercial brewing, patent medicine production or cigarette manufacture. As important in this development, although not so widely celebrated as Cadbury or Rowntree, are firms such as Carr of Carlisle, Meredith & Drew, Huntley & Palmer and Macfarlane Lang which specialized in biscuits and similar confectionery products utilizing home-produced wheat flour or oatmeal. Imported flours were used by these firms, but their products were characterized by a larger admixture of soft flours than was appropriate for bread-making. The same remark applies to household flours which before the end of the century were already being distributed through retail outlets in bags bearing the brand names of particular mills or firms.

Except that it was somewhat less susceptible to foreign competition, the domestic production and processing of barley experienced vicissitudes similar to but less pronounced than those which affected wheat. Malt was the chief product of barley, although not all barley was of malting quality, and beer and whisky were the most important end products. Both of these were subject in Victorian Britain to far-reaching entrepreneurial transformation and minor technological modification. The industrialization of brewing, in particular, was a complex development. It was influenced by several changes, including the application of steam power to manufacturing procedures, the proliferation of public houses tied to particular breweries, the concentration of capital and management, and the establishment of extensive commercial relationships which turned leading breweries into regional or even national, rather than local, concerns. The result of these changes affected the position of the maltsters and the farmers who supplied them. Large-scale maltings, some controlled and built by brewing or distilling firms, others erected by specialists in the field, such as Paul of Ipswich or Sanders of Gainsborough, increasingly concentrated the production of malt at places convenient for the brewers, just as steam-milling had revolutionized the production of flour and meal. Small-scale malthouses survived, as wind- and water-mills survived, but theirs was very much a declining role. Moreover, despite the reputation of East Anglian and Scottish malt, maltsters and brewers found that foreign supplies were not only often cheaper but, in the case of Californian and some River Plate barleys, of equal or superior quality. Thus the malt used in brewing by 1900 consisted as much of blended grains as the flour used in biscuit-making. To add insult to injury, some maltsters were developing mashes containing other cereals, such as maize, which technically could not be malted. Nevertheless, before the Great War most of the grain used in brewing, and all of that in whisky distilling, was British barley, the chief limitation being apparently the insufficiency of supplies, particularly in poor years, rather than the superiority of overseas produce. Technical changes in malting were not spectacular after 1830, but a series of minor amendments, especially to kiln design, improved both quality and extraction, so that the industry was certainly more efficient in 1900 than it had been a century before.[14]

To sum up the position of British farmers as suppliers of raw materials to manufacturing industry we can say that although they more or less maintained the absolute volume of deliveries, the immense expansion of almost all the industries in Britain processing temperate raw materials or their tropical substitutes far outstripped supplies available from domestic sources. British farmers were less important to the woollen manufacturers, rope-makers, millers and brewers than they had been in 1800 because what they contributed to their input of primary materials was by 1870–1900 only a fraction of total demand. To this relative diminution of the farmers' commercial influence the free trade in primary produce added another layer of difficulties. The cheapness and superiority of much produce brought from overseas, the development of substitute materials to replace those traditionally used in a wide variety of products—from rubber and petroleum to maize, soya beans, locust beans, palm-oil and cottonseed—must not be underestimated both in their impact upon crop selection in Britain and the rate growth of the many new industries based on the processing of agricultural commodities drawn from across the world.

VI

Although the contribution of British primary produce to manufacturing industries was diminishing, the role of farmers as consumers of industrialized products remained one of great importance. The development of processes which concentrated production in factories or large workshops changed the relationship of farmers, as consumers of manufactured goods, with their suppliers as much as in respect of farmers as suppliers of primary products to industry. The consumption of manufacturing by-products—malt dust, brewers' grains, hoof and horn, wood ashes, shoddy, oilcake—increased notably, although the use of the organic waste of industry for feeding stock or for dressing the soil was already two centuries old. A greater scientific knowledge of the properties of such 'artificial' fertilizers led to better efficiency of application and, in some cases, to improvements achieved through compounding or processing. The farmer's dependence upon industry in his business was, before the middle of the nineteenth century, essentially marginal. That is not to say that the part played by agriculturists as consumers of manufactured goods was inconsequential. In the middle of the eighteenth century, for example, agriculture was judged to have consumed up to two-thirds of the output of the British iron industry, and the quantity of bricks and timber used in the construction or repair of farmsteads was also very important even during the residential building boom after 1770. The impact before the middle of the nineteenth century, however, was diffuse, because of the multiplicity of blacksmiths, wheelwrights, carpenters and builders who supplied the farmers' wants. From about 1830 the emergence of large-scale industries in agricultural engineering, feed-compounding, oil-milling and fertilizer-processing, and the greater concentration of production in trades like brick- and tile-making, and hand-tool manufacture, began to set on foot important changes in the relationship of farmers with their suppliers. These changes were slow-acting in the generation before 1870, but the pace quickened notably in the last thirty years of the century.

In this context, the milling industry had a new and important part to play. From the point of view of agriculture the most important change was the development of feed-compounding, which apparently began in about 1850 when Joseph Thorley of Hull began to produce 'Thorley's food for cattle'. What was new in Thorley's product was the mixture of grain, vegetable oils and spices (and later of minerals) in a particular formula. The close association of compounding with seed-crushing was inevitable, especially since one of the most valuable by-products of the vegetable-oil industry of the Humber and the Mersey was oilcake, long since used by discerning farmers both for stockfeed and for fertilizers. The oilcake was manufactured out of oil-rich plants imported for processing—colza, linseed, cottonseed, sunflower, palm-oil—and remained in great demand throughout the century although, as after about 1870 the more specialized régimes of dairying, calf-rearing, poultry-keeping and bacon-pig rearing assumed greater relative importance, the character of this demand began to change and offered new opportunities for compound formulae. Many firms sprang up before 1880, drawn by a process of diversification both out of flour-milling and malting and out of seed-crushing. The successful ones came to command both roller-mills and oil-presses, for by 1900 compounding had became a complex industrial process. The subsidiary character of the business in 1860–70 was soon supplanted by the emergence of large specialist enterprises attracted by the considerable size of the potential market for ready-mixed feedstuffs. The firm of Bibby, easily the largest in the field in 1914, first produced compounds in about 1876 at a grist-mill in rural Lancashire. During the next thirty years they acquired an oil-mill and the two components of their business were joined together to produce their famous Cakettes and Cakelettes. R. & W. Paul of Ipswich, corn merchants and maltsters, also turned their attention to animal feeds, and in addition to a standard range of products they built a plant to process cooked, flaked maize, 'Kositos', which made them nationally famous by 1914. The seed-crushing combine, B.O.C.M., formed in 1899, also entered the market for feeds early in this century, using formulae contributed by some of the member firms. By 1900 feed-compounding had become so lucrative to the market leaders that it attracted both the flour-milling giants, Rank and Spillers, whose success was limited, and many small and often hard-pressed country-town millers and maltsters, like Clarke of Framlingham, some of whom attempted to undercut the dominant suppliers to the trade by marketing cheaper but inferior products bearing brand names. By 1900, also, many compounds had become exotic, blending home-ground barley, oats or wheat tailings with millet, maize, locust beans, fenugreek, and dill, compressed with oil obtained from a wide variety of plants. Each mixture was reputedly specific for each kind and age of livestock. Late in the nineteenth century another stand-by of the modern stockbreeder was introduced, the synthetic milk powder that could be given to calves weaned early from the cows' milk which was needed for sale.

How many farmers made regular use of the 'sack-feeds' marketed by Bibby, Paul, Silcocks or B.O.C.M. is unknown. The firms mounted large and expensive advertising campaigns, published 'scientific' reports on the efficacy of pure, well-balanced compounds, offered discounts to distributors and issued grave warnings against imitations or adulteration. Bibby's output of feedstuffs in 1902 exceeded 1 million tons, and that of their half dozen principal rivals apparently varied between two-fifths and two-thirds of this total; while Spillers already claimed to sell 60 per cent or more of all purchased poultry feeds at the turn of the century. Bibby's production apparently trebled in the fifteen years before 1901–2, and doubled again in the next dozen years to 1914. Some of their rivals languished but most of them could show a curve of growth at least as impressive as that of the market leader. Bibby's Cakettes and Paul's Kositos, at least, were roaring successes in Edwardian Britain.[15]

The importance of agricultural demand for processed materials is reflected also in the development of industries concerned with the supply of fertilizers. Theoretical and industrial chemistry here played a fundamental part, for it was in the production of phosphates and synthetic soda or potash materials that the most far-reaching improvements occurred. The long tradition of making use of industrial waste and the residual materials of everyday life had brought about the establishment of processing plants to prepare the more important of these by-products for fertilizers, especially oil-cake and bones. By 1830 farmers could buy oil waste, crushed bones or bone-dust from firms operating in many parts of the country, but especially from plants situated along the Humber and Trent. Experiments were going ahead to find a convenient means of handling human excrement for agricultural purposes, and the application of town sewage on the land was to have many advocates in the nineteenth century. Most of the non-farm manures available in 1830–40, however, had serious drawbacks, particularly in the fact that they were very slow-acting. The introduction of Peruvian guano, and sometime afterwards of Chilean nitrates, began to change this, for there is no doubt that good quality guano was an excellent organic fertilizer. Imports increased from 26,000 tons in 1841–3 to 165,350 in 1851–3, but crucial as it was for the maintenance of soil fertility in the nineteenth century, reliance upon guano brought about no great technological breakthrough of the kind adumbrated in Liebig's *Agricultural Chemistry*. That came only with the development of superphosphates, accurate knowledge of the chemistry and physiology of plant growth and the industrial means of translating theoretical certainties into a practical framework of production.

The translation of Liebig's researches in 1840 was portentous, although he had already begun to influence some British experts like J. B. Lawes, Lyon Playfair and J. H. Gilbert before the English version was issued. Liebig's work, although original, was in essence the culmination of a long sequence of observation, field trials and theorizing. Forerunners such as Francis Horne, George Winter, Lord Dundonald, Humphry Davy and J. B. Boussingault deserve at least to be mentioned by the historian in this context. Liebig's work, however, was more than preceptory; it was also catalytic. The 1840s saw not only a spate of experiments on principles laid down by Liebig, but the establishment of agricultural chemistry as a profession in the appointment of scientists and lecturers of the calibre of Lyon Playfair, T. B. Way, A. Johnston and, later, of Augustus Voelcker and Andre Aitken to several agricultural and university institutions. As important for Britain as Liebig's theoretical apparatus was J. B. Lawes's discovery and patenting of a method to produce superphosphate of lime in 1842, which owed something to Liebig but not less to a course of experiments on his Rothamsted estate.[16]

The principle of making neutral phosphate of lime soluble by sulphuric acid was applied in field trials to the culture of roots and gave striking results. The chief source of phosphates was bones, for which an extensive trade and manufacturing process already existed, but the addition of sulphuric acid linked agriculture firmly to the heavy chemical industry. The use of vitriol to activate dormant or slow-releasing plant nutrients was one of the most important elements in the growth of the British chemical industry after 1850, and its production formed the basis of the practical development of agricultural chemistry. Firms grew up which specialized in this new line of production. Lawes himself opened an establishment near London in 1843 for the manufacture of superphosphates, and almost simultaneously factories were set up or converted to produce chemical fertilizers at Blaydon, Durham, and in the west of Scotland. A new element was introduced with the discovery of coprolites in East Anglia in about 1840, for not only did a new mining industry develop in parts of east Suffolk, Cambridgeshire and Hertfordshire, but the use of coprolites instead of bones allowed chemical manufactories to be situated in places remote from the bone-mills. Three large enterprises established at Bramford and Ipswich in 1843–56 first developed their agricultural chemical interests in the processing of coprolites. They were Joseph Fison & Company, Edward Packard & Company and Prentice Brothers, and others came in to the business from commerce, especially from the distribution of guano, bone-dust or nitrates.

The production of superphosphates, which were most valuable as a dressing for root crops, reached its Victorian peak in about 1880, by which time it had become but part of the agricultural chemical industry of this country. Ammonia, the importance of which lay in the fact that it was the only cheap, synthetic material containing nitrogen that could be absorbed by non-leguminous plants, was in 1880 already a significant component in the production schedules of many firms. It was a by-product of the gas-works, and its usefulness was not confined to the dressing of top-soil. Somewhat later another industrial by-product, basic slag from the Thomas open-hearth furnaces, was discovered to be useful for dressing grassland, although its general application had barely begun by 1900.

Having described the development and the industrialization of processes devised for refining inorganic fertilizers in the nineteenth century, I must end by stressing that these new products did not supplant ancient varieties of manure and top-dressing. Yard dung, composts and materials such as lime and chalk, clay and even marl continued to be preferred by the majority of farmers, who professed to believe that purchased synthetic fertilizers, however desirable, were too expensive for regular application by ordinary husbandmen. It had not yet become commonplace for agriculturists to rely heavily upon synthetic materials as manures, and most of the inorganic fertilizers mentioned above tended still to be used sparingly for particular purposes at the end of the century.

Other trades supplying agriculture and estate management were subject to some process of industrialization during the middle and later nineteenth century. Pipe-drainage and the widespread use of bricks and tiles in rural building were encouraged by improvements in process technology which reduced costs and enlarged output. Brick-making was most highly developed as a mass-production industry in or within the orbit of towns. Elsewhere the exploitation of seams of brick-earth resembled more nearly the older form of cottage industry. Nevertheless, the mechanization by 1850–60 of production of machine-wrought bricks or drain-pipes, especially in the eastern counties, marks a point at which industrialized manufacturing had begun to overtake the craft-centred trade in brick-ware, even though it was to be many years before the immense brick-fields of Peterborough or Bedford came to dominate the industry. Pipe-making after 1840 was perhaps the best example of extensive industrialization in this context. The selection of building materials, however, was subject to constant modification. By the 1880s new materials, mild steel, concrete, galvanized steel sheets, all the products of heavy industry, were coming into favour among farmers and landowners. We might say very much the same about the adoption of new fencing materials, wire netting, in which the Norwich engineering firm of Boulton & Paul had a large interest by 1880, and barbed wire, which supplemented rather than replaced post-and-rail and quick fences in the British agricultural landscape. Both commodities were necessarily machine-made, and were produced as a rule by firms with large plant and highly mechanized equipment.

VII

During the middle of the nineteenth century many firms were founded to produce implements or engineering equipment for agriculture. The origins of most of them lay in the blacksmiths' shops of villages and small towns that had for centuries served the interests of farmers and landowners. Inventive or enterprising smiths, like Richard Hornsby of Grantham or John Brand of Lawford, Essex, became renowned for their skills as innovators in the new technology of agricultural engineering, and, perhaps even more notably, by acting as the artificers of well-found and influential amateurs of agricultural progress, gained both a clientele and an extensive reputation. Obviously not all succeeded; the roll of failed blacksmith-inventors is as long as the catalogue of unsuccessful inventors among the agriculturists. A large group of 'agricultural mechanics', moreover, remained tied to a confined locality or were restricted by their inability to embrace the techniques or capital requirements of industrial iron-founding. In 1800 the adaptable and adaptive smith or wheelwright was an old mutation of their species, but the restraints of inherited traditions were still very powerful in the country districts. Local preferences for tools and implements, formed partly no doubt by the exigencies of terrain or prevailing techniques, were not broken down easily, even when improved performance could be shown to result from a new or modified piece of equipment. In this respect, the 'mechanics' were as likely to be as conservative as their farmer clients, and many an innovating entrepreneur not only failed but also suffered the ridicule of his neighbours. The successful transmutation from blacksmith to engineer (or iron-founder) depended upon several factors often external to the intrinsic skills or technical soundness of particular entrepreneurs. Success was perhaps more likely to attend upon those who set up in business in areas of rapid industrialization, where supplies of necessary raw materials and skilled labour were plentiful, but the development of agricultural engineering in Bedford, Ipswich or Lincoln, and even more in Dursley, Leiston and Earl's Colne, suggest that several other factors were also at work.[17]

Agricultural engineering was widely dispersed in Britain by 1870. Leaving aside the purely local smithies or wheelwrights' shops which still had a part to play, the firms classified under the industrial heading of iron-founders (and later of engineers or boiler-makers) whose interests were largely or wholly agricultural, were located in every region of Britain except the Scottish Highlands. Most districts contained market towns or larger villages with foundries and forges producing ploughs or chaff-cutters, seed drills or threshing tackle, and everywhere were to be found undertakings which specialized in a particular invention or patented artefact—like, for example, James Smyth's patent Seed Drill, manufactured at Peasenhall in Suffolk, or Richard Boby's Corn Screen (of Bury St Edmunds), or Bentall's Goldhanger Plough (in Essex). None the less this special line of production was seldom exclusively pursued by such firms, for each of those just mentioned offered a wide range of iron products for sale by the middle of the century. Sometimes the high reputation of a particular product—Smyth's drill, Crosskill's patented clod-breaker, Ransome's steel plough or Howards' horse-rake—permitted firms to develop not merely a wide range of equipment but a national network of distribution for all their products. The emergence of Ransomes of Ipswich as the dominant, but not unchallenged, leader among mid-Victorian agricultural engineers owed much to the quality of its products, but more to its marketing organization and the goodwill which it obtained from the encomia of influential landowners and affluent arable farmers. But Ransomes was fortunate also in its location, for Ipswich, although remote from the iron- and coal-producing regions of Britain, was accessible to both the arable heartlands of the country and the wider world by means of the wet dock excavated at the head of the Orwell navigation and the railway network that serviced it. Elsewhere it was the railways which assisted enterprising firms to acquire a national system of distribution. One test of this contention is to examine the records of the implement exhibition at the annual Royal Agricultural Society's Show, which since the show was peripatetic is a fair reflection of the penetration by particular firms of the national market for agricultural implements. What is evident from the annual lists of exhibitors is that many of the smaller firms that did not command a special line of production sent equipment only to show-yards which were comparatively close at hand, partly no doubt because of expense, but partly also because they were concerned to maintain existing custom or to attract new clients in an area which they could adequately serve. It is with a comparatively small number of firms that we can demonstrate a nation-wide system of distribution.

Of these national and international businesses Ransomes of Ipswich apparently exercised the greatest influence. By 1860 Ransomes probably offered the largest variety of implements. It had by that date fully diversified out of plough- and harrow-making into seed drills, threshing tackle and, significantly for the future, steam engines. It also had some interest in grinding implements and mowing machines of various kinds. It had many local rivals in the production of tillage implements, where Crosskill and Howard also had a national reputation. Moreover, in the development of the seed drill, threshing-box and reaping-machine, as in the adaptation of steam power to agricultural uses, Ransomes, in spite of its healthy share of the market, was not in the forefront of innovation. New firms were rapidly emerging among the nation-wide exhibitors of agricultural machinery by the 1860s and 1870s, and Ipswich was being overtaken as the centre of agricultural engineering by other places conveniently located at the intersection between agrarian and industrial Britain: Lincoln, Leeds, Grantham, Gainsborough. Ransomes was probably unchallengeable in the diversity of products, but in particular segments of the engineering business, Clayton & Shuttleworth, Foster and Ruston of Lincoln, Fowler of Leeds, Marshall of Gainsborough and Hornsby of Grantham were beginning to compete effectively with the older enterprise. Even in East Anglia, Garrett of Leiston, Savage of King's Lynn and Burrell of Thetford, were also coming into prominence as specialist engineers by 1870–80.

The correlation between the market for agricultural machinery and the demand for comparable products in sectors such as civil engineering enlarged the scope of firms like Ransomes or Ruston, and created, side by side with their agricultural production, an interest in earth-moving, drainage or pumping equipment. Ruston in due course diversified even further into marine engineering. Hornsby had earlier been involved (to their financial embarrassment) in the development of the Ackroyd oil engine, and another Lincoln firm, after 1914, was implicated in the evolution of the tank. Lincoln, and to a less extent Ipswich, Peterborough and Grantham, had by 1900 established an intricate network of iron-founding, boiler-making and ancillary trades, supplying an interlocking system of markets, agricultural and industrial.

The large firms commanded the biggest share of the market for engineering products in agriculture, but even in the field of steam technology local firms—Allchin of Newbury, Burrell of Thetford or Tasker of Andover, for example—still managed to find outlets for their products, at least within their own regions. This was in spite of an increasingly comprehensive ramification of dealerships and agencies controlled by the market leaders throughout the country. Depots, manned by salesmen and service engineers employed by the firm, were established at strategic points by several of the more enterprising businesses even before 1850. Smyth of Peasenhall, for instance, maintained branches in Paris, London and Witham, Essex. More widespread was the use of commission agents. Many a village blacksmith held a commission to supply and repair the factory-made products of one or more engineering firms, and to judge from the evidence of contemporary advertisements it became increasingly commonplace after about 1870 for retail ironmongers to accept agencies for particular brands of implements. At times the marketing of ready-made implements was complicated and apparently illogical, as when the whole range of Bentall's products was offered for sale by rival manufacturers, Smyth of Peasenhall and Hughes of Bishop's Stortford, from their own depositories.[18]

The evolution of the British firm of agricultural engineers, which with few exceptions passed from workshop to factory within a generation after 1830–40, was evidently much influenced by the general process of industrialization in the domestic economy. The relationship between agricultural demand and industrial resources, more specifically between agriculture and the application of engineering technology to the cultivation of the soil, to the management of crops or to the modernization of dairying, was a two-way process. Industrialization was a necessary concomitant of technological progress in agriculture but this was not an association of cause and effect. In the context of agricultural engineering another element requires to be discussed. The penetration of American firms, largely but not exclusively in the field of reaping equipment, was significant chiefly because the American engineer introduced a new concept to the manufacture of agricultural implements. The principle of interchangeability of parts, which was characteristic of the engineering industries in nineteenth-century America, reduced production costs, at the expense of durability, and therefore made their prices very competitive with those of British engineers whose production methods were much more labour-intensive. The McCormick reaper, especially in a form suitable for British conditions and built under licence by British firms, eventually triumphed over most of the types invented and patented in the United Kingdom, many of which had evolved out of the prototype introduced by Patrick Bell in 1827, but the interest of British firms in the technology of mechanical reaping (and binding) persisted throughout the century.

VIII

Many examples of the complex and various connections which existed between agriculture and agrarian society and the urban, industrial economy during the nineteenth century have been quoted in the preceding pages. The diversity of this relationship makes summary generalization extremely difficult. It is clear, however, that industrialization affected agriculture in rather contrary ways. The benefits which flowed to agriculture from the adoption of industrial technologies in the manufacture of feedstuffs, fertilizers and implements cannot be offset directly against the losses which were caused by dependence upon imported primary products, or which resulted from the decline of political influence, from rural emigration or from the decline of village self-sufficiency. The agricultural sector was forced increasingly to fit itself into an economy and a social structure in which it played a very minor theme. It was obviously a painful adjustment but the integration of rural and urban life made possible by improved communications and confirmed by the reticulation of systematic mass distribution offered some compensation for the decay of isolation in the countryside. To strike the balance of the reckoning is essentially a matter of judgment, although there seems little doubt that articulate opinion in late Victorian times was remarkably consistent in the belief that the events of the past century or so had produced some kind of social disaster in the rural world.

Notes

1 E. L. Jones, 1968; Mendels, 1972; Fischer, 1973; Kellenbenz, 1974; and Parker and Jones, 1976.
2 Saville, 1957, 20–30; Sturt, 1912; Graham, 1892; Sturt, 1923, 17–19, 153–4; Green, 1915; *Victoria County History: Essex II*, 356; *Victoria County History: Suffolk, Buckinghamshire, Gloucestershire, Cambridgeshire II*; Shorter, 1938; BPP 1919 I 24.
3 Redford, 1926; Saville, 1957, chs 2–3; Welton, 1900; Ravenstein, 1885; Longstaff, 1893.
4 Somerville, 1852, 89.
5 For example, Ward and Wilson, 1971, 16–62.
6 Raybould, 1973; Mee, 1975; Richards, 1973; Spring, 1952; Pollard, 1955.
7 Lawes and Gilbert, 1868; Burnett, 1966; Fairlie, 1969.
8 Hawke, 1970, 101–56; Perren, 1978.
9 Fussell, 1966, 260.
10 Porter, 1912, 328, 333.
11 Porter, 1912, 433.
12 Collins, 1975; Booker, 1974; Burnett, 1945; Janes, 1955; Barty-King, 1977.
13 Burnett, 1945, 158; McCrosty, 1903, 324–34, 536–43.
14 Vaizey, 1960; Steel, 1878; Stopes, 1885; Corran, 1975.
15 Brace, 1960; Bibby, 1978; Hooper, 1963; Reckitt, 1951.
16 Clow, 1952, ch. xxi; Fussell, 1962; Mathew, 1970.
17 Fussell, 1952; Spence, 1960; Stephens, 1858; Wright, 1959; Booker, 1974, 12–48; Newman, 1957; Hill, 1974, 118–21; Whitehead, 1964; Grace and Phillips, 1975; Rolt, 1969.
18 Booker, 1974, 30.

15 The Age of Machinery

E. J. T. Collins

I

Mechanization came late to English agriculture and was a vital force there only at the tail-end of the agricultural revolution. Indeed, mechanical aids played little part in the raising of agricultural output and productivity in the eighteenth and early nineteenth centuries. Machinery, like chemical fertilizers and purchased feeding stuffs, was a feature of what is sometimes called the 'second agricultural revolution', which broke the closed circle of English farming by the insertion of new types of input supplied by manufacturing industry or through the expansion of overseas trade.[1] The 1830s were an important watershed in the history of farm mechanization for, although the first machines were developed in the eighteenth century, there is clear evidence that the source of supply—the agricultural engineering industry—did not begin significantly to expand and to assume a modern form until the late 1830s. The zeal of the Board of Agriculture's reporters exaggerated, perhaps, the scale of mechanization in the Napoleonic Wars. In the post-war period neither farm accounts, company records, farm sale notices, nor the contemporary literature, suggest that machines were at all widely used in southern Britain. That achievement properly belongs to the reign of Queen Victoria.

In agriculture the prime function of machines is to save time and labour. The need to use labour more efficiently and hold down labour costs became more pressing after 1835 when the supply of labour became less elastic and wages increased. Between 1830 and 1880 agricultural output rose by 60–80 per cent, whereas the permanent

200

agricultural workforce rose by only about 17 per cent between 1831 and 1851 and fell by about 20 per cent between 1851 and 1881[2] The extent of the decline in the third quarter of the nineteenth century was probably greater than that indicated by the occupational censuses by reason of a sharp (but unrecorded) fall in the numbers of casual and migrant workers, whose effort had been, and to a large extent still was, essential at the summer work peaks.

The need to save labour was most apparent in arable farming, whose labour requirement using traditional methods was uncommonly high. In corn harvesting, for example, between 4.5 and 5.0 worker-days were needed to cut, sheaf and stook an acre of wheat using the saw-edge sickle, and between 2.5 and 2.0 worker-days using the scythe. Between 5 and 6 bushels, or roughly a quarter of an acre of wheat, was threshed in a day by means of the flail.[3] Roots were the most labour-intensive crop, needing as many as 10–15 worker-days per acre. Before the seed drill and horse hoe were generally introduced vast quantities of hand labour were used for thinning and cleaning; two or three hoeings were the general rule by the 1830s and the average work rate of the hand hoe was 0.25 to 0.33 acres per day.[4] Where, as in the case of mangolds, the crop was also lifted, another large input of labour was needed in the autumn. It is recorded that on one farm 47 man worker-days and 133 woman and child worker-days were spent in harvesting 30 acres of mangolds and 10 acres of swedes.[5]

These example serve to illustrate the extreme labour-intensiveness of mixed arable farming in the pre-machine age. By the late 1830s some farmers in the low-wage districts of southern England were beginning to learn the wisdom of the adage that the *sine qua non* of productive mixed husbandry was a cheap and elastic supply of labour, and when it failed there was instantly created a demand for work saving over a wide range of tasks. Labour requirements in corn harvesting increased by at least 50 per cent between 1800 and 1850, and more than doubled in root growing. The greater emphasis on livestock production meant more work during the winter months supervising the fold and preparing animal feed. Thus not only did the size and diversity of farm workloads increase, but the tasks, especially in the summer months, tended to overlap.

The position in the 1860s was summarized by J. C Morton, editor of the *Agricultural Gazette*:

> and yet limited as to quality as is the labour now required upon the farm, the quantity needed of it is enhanced so much more by the more vigorous cultivation which the land now receives, that more labourers are needed now than when nearly all the work was done by men alone. So much more land has now been broken out of pasture; so much less of the arable land is each year in clover and grasses; so much more of potatoes, and of mangold-wurzels, and turnips, and crops of that class, all of them laborious, are grown . . . over whole counties the extension of potato culture has created an increased demand for labourers. Over the whole island the introduction of guano and other concentrated manures had induced a more profitable and

therefore more laborious cultivation. In many districts the change of rotation—as for example, the retention of grass and clover only one year down instead of three, and the substitution of wheat and perhaps mangold-wurzel for a second and third year's pasture—has created more need of steam power to thresh the increased produce, of horse power to cultivate the increased arable land, of hand power to superintend and manage the detailed cultivation of the crops, their ingathering and consumption. There is much more grain grown now than used to be, but the food for stock upon a diminished extent of land has much more rapidly increased than even that of grain; and the labour now required is that of men whose competency and skill may be trusted rather than whose mere brute strength may be wielded.[6]

The process herein described—progressive intensification within mixed farming—reached its apogee during the final surge of the 'high farming era' in the early 1870s, when there was a serious shortage of labour and, with the rise of trades unionism, a spell of labour unrest. Labour requirements in arable farming fell during the great depression as the tillage acreage declined, but there was a selective demand for machines, especially on grass and dairy farms where shortages of hay makers and milkers began to develop after 1890.

The demand for labour-saving methods in the Victorian period has been demonstrated, but the event of mechanization was dependent on a supply of cheap and efficient machines. This in turn awaited a revolution in mechanical engineering and the transformation of machine and implement manufacture from a workshop into a factory trade.

II

The agricultural engineering industry was still in the embryonic stage in the mid-1830s.[7] Few if any firms then employed more than thirty workers and only a handful such as Ransomes of Ipswich (ploughs) and Smyth of Peasenhall (seed drills) enjoyed a national reputation for their products. The period from Waterloo to the accession of Queen Victoria was a difficult one for machine makers. Demand was sluggish and diminished further in the wake of the Swing Riots. Not surprisingly, few firms listed in the Board of Agriculture *Reports* as active in the Napoleonic Wars long survived the peace.

In 1835 the making of implements and machines was a workshop trade and at most points scarcely distinguishable from that of the smith, or ploughwright. Yet inside a few years, indeed by the time of the Great Exhibition, it had become a major industry containing a number of factory firms. The demand for improved implements and machines recovered strongly in the later 1830s at the start of the era of high farming. This was matched on the manufacturing side by dramatic advances in mechanical engineering science and the production of machine tools, which together with a fall in the price of iron gave rise to a new generation of farming tools, more reliable and cheaper than hitherto. 'The present age', wrote James Slight in 1844, 'is perhaps the most remarkable that time has produced from the perfection of almost every kind of machine or tool required in the various departments of art and manufactures.'[8] Many leading firms of agricultural engineers were launched on the tide of the first railway building boom in 1835–46, and for a time at least were as famous for their railway work as their agricultural products. One of the mottoes of Ransomes of Ipswich was 'Success to plough and rail', and as late as 1851 non-agricultural work, mostly railway parts, accounted for over 60 per cent of the total output.[9]

The importance of agricultural engineering at the middle of the century is testified to by the large area of space which it occupied at the Great Exhibition, where more than 300 firms exhibited in the class. Between 1840 and 1860 many new firms were established out of country foundries and blacksmiths' shops, or as wholly new enterprises. From the outset the industry was dominated by a handful of large firms, and with odd exceptions the hierarchy was already established by 1855. To some extent firms vied with each other as to the variety of their products. In 1851 Garrett of Leiston, for example, was producing steam engines, seed drills, horse hoes, ploughs, harrows, threshing machines, chaff-cutters, barley-humellers, oat-mills, cake-crushers, corn-dressers and reaping machines.[10] Other firms also produced a wide range of cast-iron goods for use in the home, such as mangles, stoves, kitchen ranges and garden furniture. In practice, however, most firms concentrated on a few products, a trend which became more pronounced in the 1860s and 1870s when the rising costs of product development led to a narrowing of competition. The structure of the industry was also influenced by the growth of the export trade which centred upon a smaller range of products than that for the home market. Another factor was the development of steam power, which became the fastest growing, most technically complicated and most capital-intensive branch of the industry. By the 1860s most of the large firms—including Ransome, Garrett, Fowler, Burrell, Clayton & Shuttleworth, and Barrett, Exall & Andrews—were heavily involved with steam. Ploughs and cultivating implements could be made in country workshops, but the manufacture of steam engines and engine parts required elaborate plant and more advanced engineering skills.

The small firms lost ground to the larger manufacturers and were obliged to concentrate on just one or two main products or, as was often the case, they became purely agents and service engineers. By 1862 the most common ploughs in use in Dorset and Somerset were those manufactured by Suffolk, Lincoln and Bedford firms.[11] The small manufacturer was not completely eclipsed, but new entry costs were very much higher in the 1870s than in the 1850s when the home market was growing so quickly as to be able to absorb virtually all new production. By the time of the great depression up-to-date plant was the key to survival. The new owner of the Barnstaple Foundry in north Devon, for instance, installed in 1884 a 20 h.p. steam engine to drive the machinery in the fitting shop and to supply blast to the smithy and cupola. The machine shops were equipped with planing machines, a large boring machine capable of handling up to 18-foot wheels, a lathe for heavy shafting, a large screw-cutting machine. Typically, the greater part of the output then consisted of general engineering work such as street lamp pillars, water wheels, axle boxes and verandahs.[12]

The agricultural engineering industry grew rapidly and continuously between 1835 and 1875 but thereafter lost momentum. The demand for tillage equipment declined, and this, combined with the fact that the home market was in large measure already saturated by the 1870s, meant that the industry had to adjust to lower levels of demand and a slow turnover in replacements. Many small firms ceased manufacturing and turned to non-agricultural work, while the survival of the large firms depended as never before on export. With the western European market enclosed by tariff walls, attention became focused on eastern Europe and the Empire. In 1913 upwards of 70 per cent of British production was exported.[13]

Throughout the Victorian period most of the largest manufacturers were located in the eastern counties, although the West Riding, industrial Lancashire and the west Midlands became relatively more important after 1870. In 1913 twenty-four principal firms employed between 40 and 45 per cent of the total workforce. Ransomes of Ipswich had 2,500 hands in 1911, Clayton & Shuttleworth of Lincoln 2,300 in 1907, Marshall of Gainsborough 4,500 in 1900 (550 in 1870), and Bamford of Uttoxeter 400 in 1893 (only 30 in 1876).[14] The overwhelming majority of the 900 or so firms of agricultural engineers in being at the end of the nineteenth century employed fewer than fifty workers, and probably less than 50 per cent were engaged in actual manufacturing. Activity was spread between agricultural engineering, general engineering, repairs and sales, and was so diverse that it is quite impossible to define the 'typical' firm.

During the course of the nineteenth century agricultural engineering became a major exporting industry. In the middle decades it was one of the fastest growing branches of the engineering industry and an important market for machine tools. Its inventiveness failed, however, in the 1870s. The Americans were the dominant force in harvesting machinery, and the Scandinavians in dairying equipment. Britain held her own only in steam engines, steam ploughs and threshers. In 1908 agricultural steam engines accounted for over 50 per cent of total output; the implications of this became clear after 1920 when the internal combustion engine took command and the traditional export markets declined.[15] This great industry, which had made the transition from workshop to factory production before 1850, failed also to develop techniques of mass-production along American lines, which it might have done had the home market been larger and the pattern of demand more homogenous as to the type of machines in use.

III

It is difficult to generalize about the course of development of farm mechanization in the Victorian period, but notwithstanding the variety of local and individual experience three main stages can be identified.[16] In the first stage, 1835–50, the generality of farmers in southern Britain began to demand, and on a limited scale to adopt, more sophisticated tools. Their interest focused on improved designs of tillage and cultivating equipment; on simple machines, such as corn-dressers, chaff-cutters, root-slicers, bean-mills, and oat-crushers; but also on seed drills and mechanical (mostly horse-powered) threshers. By 1850 many farmers were re-equipped with iron-frame ploughs fitted with cast-iron shares. Tined cultivators began to appear after 1830; the modern zigzag harrow evolved in the 1840s, and the two famous rollers, the 'Crosskill' and the 'Cambridge', soon to become the standard forms, were patented between 1841 and 1844. It was claimed of seed drills that 'no class of implement has been more abundantly multiplied in the land within the past few years'. As memories of the Swing Riots began to fade so mechanical threshing came back into favour, and the development of new and more efficient designs of travelling machine did much to popularize the technique in the arable districts of eastern and southern England after 1840. The first 'combined' threshing and dressing machine was produced by Burrell of Thetford in 1848.

The pace of innovation visibly quickened after 1850, but the second stage, 1850–80, was dominated by two particular items, the steam thresher and the mechanical harvester. The latter spread quickly after the début of the American reapers by Hussey and McCormick at the Great Exhibition, and by the late 1870s at least two-thirds of all corn was cut and threshed by machine. In southern Britain the portable steam thresher was then the rule, while fixed installations (mostly horse- or water-powered) were commoner in the north and west.

The final stage, 1880–1900, was one rather of consolidation than of radical departures. With minor amendments the pattern of mechanization established in arable farming at the end of the high farming period endured up to the Great War. Where farmers could afford it, tools were upgraded; self-binding reapers and double-furrowed ploughs became commonplace, and in large-scale potato growing, for instance, more specialized equipment was devised and introduced.

IV

Writing in 1899 of the changes in rural life that had occurred in the previous sixty years, the agriculturist, Joseph Darby, noted the extent to which mechanical inventions had lightened human toil in almost every department of field work and 'made the entire business of farming more pleasant and less slavish'.[17] There were, he went on, persons still living who could remember when the thump of the flail was heard at almost every farmstead, and when no other ploughs were in use but cumbrous wooden ones 10 or 12 feet in length, fitted with wrought-iron points which had to be dressed now and then by the village blacksmith.

Traditional tools and methods survived especially in the upland zone and on small farms and allotments, while on the average dairy farm the régime had changed little since early Victorian times. The overall trend, however, was progressive. By the late nineteenth century all but a small proportion of harvesting and barn work was performed by machine; most crops were sown by the drill and cleaned by the horse hoe; steam was the predominant force in the threshing and dressing of grain; and most horse-drawn implements were recognizably industrial in design and construction.

The process of mechanization was, however, complex. The pace and pattern varied not only between regions and farming systems but often between adjoining farms in the same parish. Choice of technique was influenced first and foremost by availability; by, that is, the historical sequence of invention and product development. It was also determined by the physical geography of the farm, by the terrain and the size and layout of fields. The steam plough, for instance, was difficult to manoeuvre and uneconomic except in large rectangular fields, and to accommodate it many farms had to be entirely re-modelled, hedges grubbed up, and new roadways constructed. Often whole fields had to be cleared of stones and the ridge and furrow ploughed out to allow the use of a reaping machine. Physical considerations apart, the vital question was whether the machine was the cheaper method. As a rule, the larger and more expensive the machine the greater the amount of work it had to perform in order to cover the capital and depreciation costs. Small farms could normally justify the purchase of inexpensive machines yielding modest gains in work output. In the third quarter of the nineteenth century hand-operated chaff-cutters cost only £6. 8s., turnip-cutters £4. 5s., horse-hoes £4. 6s. and simple seed drills £6. 12s; and much less when bought second hand. Scale of use was a major constraint on the adoption of high-cost, high-work output machines. In 1870 a two-horse self-delivery reaper cost between £30 and £36, a 10 h.p. portable steam engine upwards of £240, a double-blast threshing and finishing machine £100–130 and, most expensive of all, a double-engine steam-ploughing set about £2,600. Automated dairy equipment was also expensive: in 1895 a horse-powered cream separator cost £55–£60, and a milking machine £50–£100 excluding the power unit.[18]

By the 1870s simple barn machines were profitably employed on most arable farms; 12–15 acres of corn would repay the use of a reaping machine, but only the very largest farmers growing at least 800 bushels of corn would normally have purchased a steam-threshing set for their exclusive use. Reapers and mowing machines were not only cheaper but tended to be needed everywhere at once. Steam-threshing and steam-ploughing sets, on the other hand, were normally owned by firms of contractors, their workload spread over a large number of farms, some of them situated at a considerable distance, up to twenty miles away from the depot.

Between 1850 and 1880 relative costs shifted dramatically in favour of machines as wages began to rise, farm workloads increased and machines became more efficient, more reliable and in real cost terms progressively cheaper. The impact of mechanization, however, was greater in arable than in pastoral farming, a result partly of differences in the tasks, and partly of differences in the average size of farm (that of pastoral districts being normally much smaller), and in the structure of the labour force. As Fussell remarked, labour-saving machinery on the dairy farm did not play so important a role as did good, cheap (i.e. family) labour.[19]

On the farm itself different levels of technology were applied to different tasks. Within the space of thirty years some farms went through the entire range of power sources, commencing with hand tools, and graduating via hand-operated then horse-operated machines to the apex of steam. In the 1870s a common mix on the normal arable farm was a steam-threshing machine (hired), a horse-powered chaff-cutter, two or three small manually operated machines for preparing feed, and a flail for separating clover seed and beans. The sequence of technological change in corn harvesting is especially interesting as it affords one of the best historical examples of what is nowadays termed 'intermediate technology'. In the early nineteenth century the faster-working scythe and bagging hook took over from the sickle and reap hook as the standard corn-harvesting tools, and on many large corn-growing farms continued to predominate during and after the third quarter of the century when reaping machines were available.[20]

Social considerations played an important part in determining the choice of technique. Farm workers were hostile to machines which threatened to reduce income and employment, as was shown in 1830 when large numbers of threshing machines were destroyed in central and southern England. Machine wrecking by no means ceased with the Swing Riots and could be subtle as well as violent. All manner of devices—iron spikes in the field and sand and grit in the bearings—punctuated the advance of the reaping machine. And where sabotage was not direct, it was often indirect: labourers pretended not to understand mechanical things and were uncooperative.

For their part, employers understood only too well the connection between the supply of labour and the scale of technique. As James Caird explained in 1851: where there were large numbers seeking work, to adopt a machine and raise the productivity of the few must diminish the employment of the many for whom work must be found.[21] Mechanization was easiest in parishes where there was a shortage of resident labourers and a large part of the summer work was performed by migrant and casual workers whose services could be dispensed with. Otherwise, employers trod warily for fear of a collision with their regular staffs, who 'looked with an evil eye on what they considered . . . an interference with the rights of labour'.[22]

Where a farmer was expanding production the men displaced by machines could be redeployed in some other activity, and the material position of the labourer was not affected, or was even improved. As Harleston Farmers' Club was quick to point out in 1842:

> the employment of machinery in agriculture, where there is sufficient capital at the occupier's command is not opposed either to the employment or to the moral condition of the labourer, but where it is employed for the purpose of extinguishing labour, then it is most baneful from every point of view. . . .[23]

Thus after 1850, when winter work became more plentiful, the threshing machine soon replaced the flail, hand threshing being reckoned the most arduous and punishing of all the farm tasks; and the reaping machine soon became established when labourers were convinced it would not seriously affect their harvest earnings. The keeping up of employment in what was traditionally regarded as the key earnings period was a factor underlying the adoption of faster hand tools instead of reaping machines. Here, and elsewhere, hand tools were retained deliberately to create work. As late as 1914 farmers were still being advised to pause before substituting machines 'when men are available and wages are not too high'.[24]

V

To the Victorian mind steam was the symbol of technical progress, and was reckoned to be the means whereby fortunes could be made out of land in the same way as in a factory or a mine. The feasibility of steam power was enhanced by a succession of technical improvements in engine design and construction, which made for lower working costs and greater efficiency combined in a portable power unit. The eighteenth-century beam engine was too expensive and immovable for agricultural purposes. Between 1800 and 1830, however, a high-pressure engine was developed, and a number of these had been installed, mostly in Scotland, before 1835. An efficient portable steam engine adapted for agricultural purposes appeared in 1840. This was followed in the 1850s by the self-moving engine, and later in the century by the 'compound' engine which employed a two-stage expansion process to reduce heat loss from condensation in the cylinder.[25]

After 1850 the steam engine became widely used for 'belt work', mostly threshing and winnowing, but also chaff cutting, root pulping and cake crushing. Stationary engines were preferred in northern Britain, but in the south portable engines operated by firms of specialist contractors were the general rule. In about 1860 J. C. Morton calculated that 10,000 horse power was then being added annually in steam alone 'to the forces used in agriculture', and by 1868 the leading manufacturer, Clayton of Lincoln, was said to be making about 500 engines a year, many of them for export.[26] By 1890 at least two-thirds of all corn produced in England was threshed by steam. A 7–10 h.p. portable engine working a full-sized thresher with a 54-inch smooth drum, double dressers, awner and polisher, and rotary screen, became the standard type of set. Already by the 1870s the annual visitation of the travelling steam thresher had become as much a part of the farming year as the harvest itself.

By the 1850s it had been demonstrated that steam was an economic proposition for barn work, especially threshing. The logical development from the portable engine was the self-propelled engine, which in turn opened up the possibility of steam cultivation. For a while the steam plough was looked to as a panacea for the ills of clayland farming and as the complete answer to the age-old problem of waterlogged soils. But the technical problems were insuperable, and much ingenuity, and a good

38 *above* Essex farmyard in the mid-nineteenth century. This illustration appeared on a certificate presented by the Brentwood Labourers' Friend Society to James Dear of South Weald with a prize of 10s. for long service. The farm has a highly romanticized and antiquated appearance, the farm buildings wooden and thatched, and the labourers threshing with the flail long after the threshing machine had become commonplace in southern counties (Essex County Record Office)

39 *right* An improved hand-powered threshing machine, made by Barrett, Exall and Andrews of Reading in 1843. Many hundreds of this machine were sold in the following years (*Farmer's Magazine* XIII, 1846)

40 *above* Steam power comes to the farm: a threshing machine driven by a Hornsby's portable steam engine in 1851. Farmers hired such machines and engines from contractors who supplied the men to work the steam engine (*Illustrated London News*)

41 *below* Smith's steam cultivator, patented in 1855, was made by J. & F. Howard of Bedford. A combined double-breasted trench plough and subsoiler was hauled via a separate windlass and snatch blocks arranged in a rectangle. Any portable engine of at least 7 h.p. could be used to provide the power, and by 1859 more than fifty sets of the apparatus had been sold (John Donaldson, *British Agriculture*, 1870)

42 *left*   Announcement of the Thetford trials in 1857 of the Boydell traction engines manufactured by Burrell of Thetford. Early locomotives proved unsatisfactory for direct traction of farm implements owing to the high initial cost, heavy fuel consumption and defects in operation (*The Engineer* LXXIX, 1896)

43 *below*   Fowler's patent steam ploughing apparatus as manufactured and advertised by Ransomes and Sims of Ipswich about 1859 (University of Reading Institute of Agricultural History, Trade Records Collection RAN PZ/A 32)

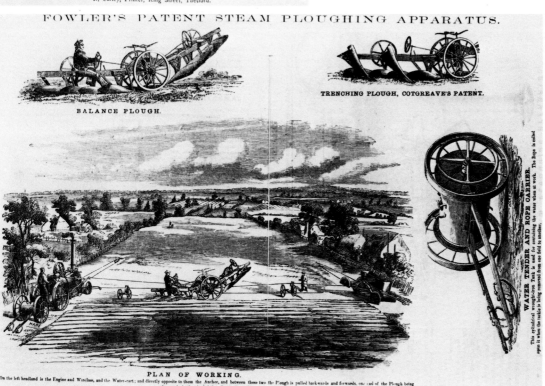

FOWLER'S PATENT STEAM PLOUGHING APPARATUS.

BALANCE PLOUGH.

TRENCHING PLOUGH, COTGREAVE'S PATENT.

PLAN OF WORKING.

On the left headland is the Engine and Windlass, and the Water-cart; and directly opposite to them the Anchor, and between these two the Plough is pulled backwards and forwards, one end of the Plough being alternately in the air and the other in its work.

44 *above* The age of elaborate factory-made machinery: Fowler's patent four-furrow plough, designed to be used with steam haulage, as shown at the International Exhibition of 1876 (*Illustrated London News*)

45 *below* A somewhat fanciful impression of the well-equipped farm as illustrated in Samuel Copland's *Agriculture, Ancient and Modern*, 1866. By the 1860s an extensive variety of barn machinery was being made by numerous firms

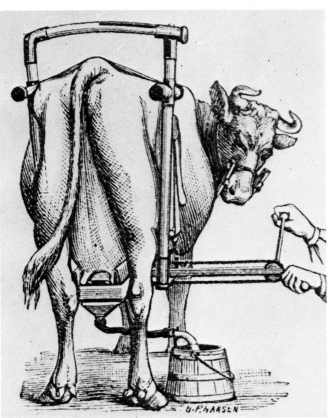

46 *left*   An early milking machine, invented in Denmark and shown in England in 1892. Even the cow seems astonished at the crudeness of the device, which required as much or more labour as did hand milking (*Journal of the Royal Agricultural Society*, 1892)

47 *below*   Steam threshing with a portable engine, in use in north Berkshire about 1900 (Museum of English Rural Life, Nalder Collection)

48 *far left* William Drury of Laceby, near Grimsby: he was an agricultural engineer and proprietor of steam-powered threshing gear (Hallgarth Collection)

49 *left* Overhauling a binder at Riplington Farm, East Meon, Hampshire at the turn of the century. Mechanical harvesters were simple machines and could be maintained by skilled labourers, though local blacksmiths and implement dealers carried out complicated repairs and supplied spare parts (Museum of English Rural Life, Mrs Luff Collection)

50 *above* A section of the new plough and implement shop at Ransomes, Sims and Jefferies' Orwell works, Ipswich, about 1904. In 1901 the firm sold 9,549 ploughs, 12,077 lawn mowers, 284 threshing machines and 488 steam engines (Museum of English Rural Life)

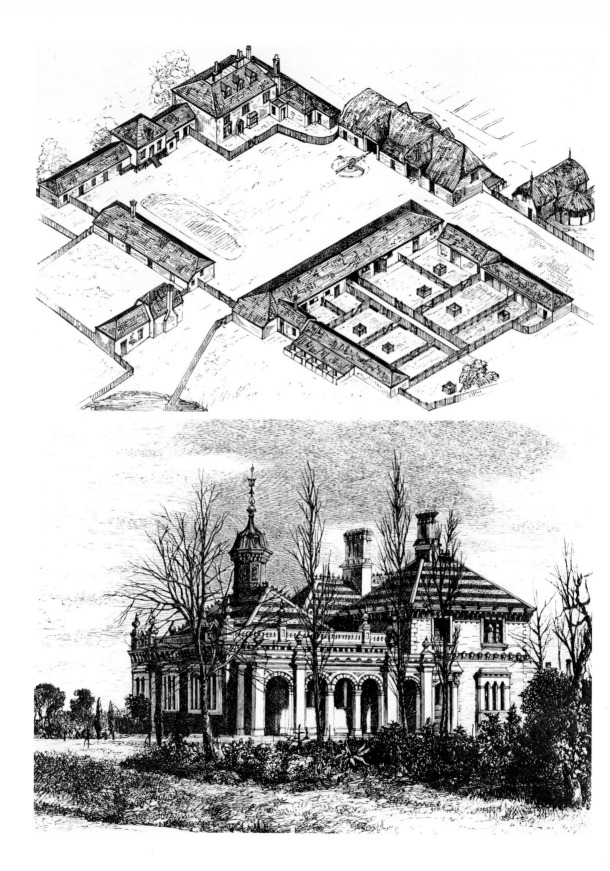

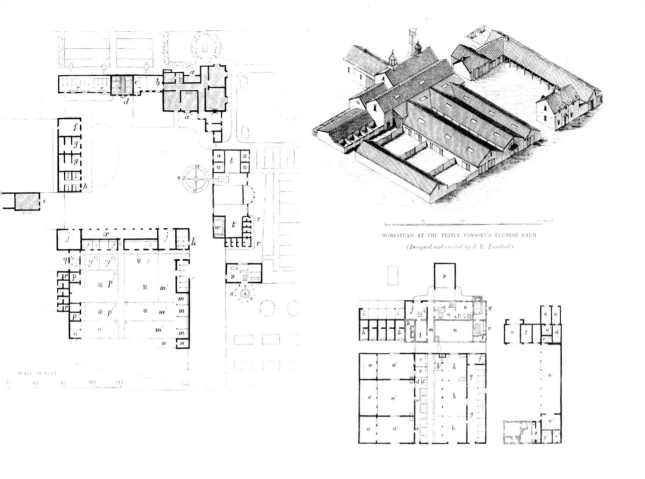

HOMESTEAD AT THE PRINCE CONSORT'S FLEMISH FARM

(Designed and erected by J. R. Turnbull)

51 Model farms built by the Prince Consort at Windsor: (a) *opposite above* and (b) *above left* the Norfolk homestead; (c) *above right* the Flemish farmstead completed in 1858, designed to house the royal herd of champion Herefords; (d) *left* the royal dairy at Frogmore, an extraordinarily elaborate building in renaissance style constructed at the same time as the Flemish farm (J. C. Morton, *The Prince Consort's Farms*, 1863)

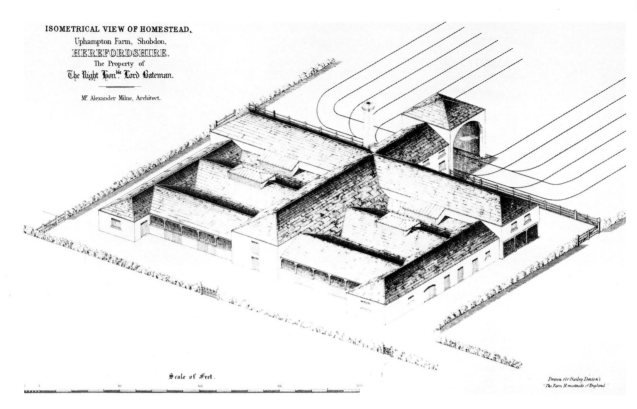

ISOMETRICAL VIEW OF HOMESTEAD.

Uphampton Farm, Shobdon,

HEREFORDSHIRE.

The Property of

The Right Hon.ble Lord Bateman.

M.r Alexander Milne, Architect.

Scale of Feet.

Drawn for Bailey Denton's
"The Farm Homesteads of England."

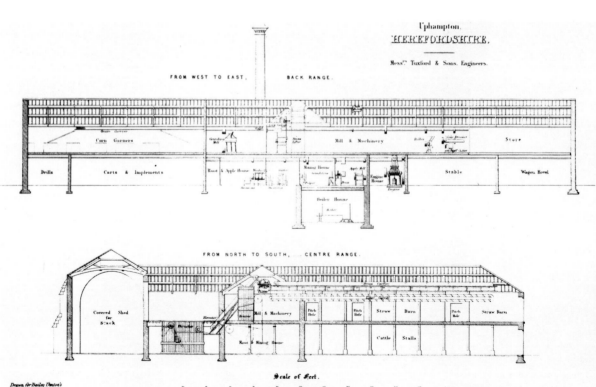

Uphampton.

HEREFORDSHIRE.

Mess.rs Tuxford & Sons, Engineers.

FROM WEST TO EAST,   BACK RANGE.

Grain Garner   Corn Garners   Grinding Mill   Stone Lifter   Mill & Machinery   Roller   Cake Breaker   Chaff Cutter   Store

Drills   Carts & Implements   Root & Apple House   Mixing House   Apple Mill   Engine House   Stable   Wagon Hovel

Boiler House
Boiler

FROM NORTH TO SOUTH,   CENTRE RANGE.

Covered Shed for Stack   Elevator   Engine   Mill & Machinery   Straw Garner   Pitch Hole   Pitch Hole   Straw Barn   Pitch Hole   Straw Barn

Root & Mixing House   Cattle Stalls

Scale of Feet.

Drawn for Bailey Denton's
"The Farm Homesteads of England."

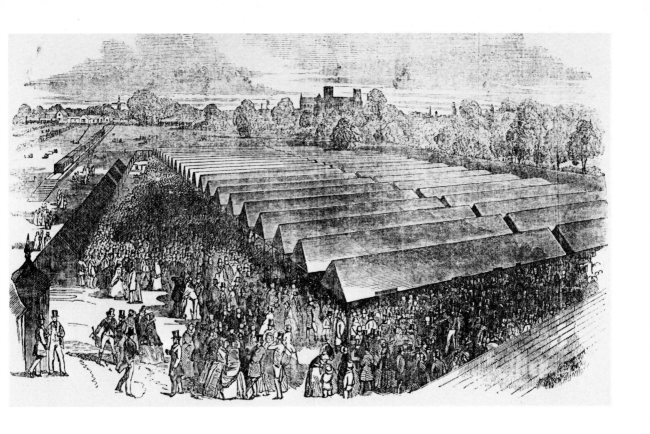

52 *opposite*   Lord Bateman's model farm at Shobdon,
Herefordshire, built in 1861, incorporated a 12 h.p.
steam engine and a railway network (J. B. Denton, *The
Farm Homesteads of England*, 1864)

53 *above*   This view of part of the Royal Agricultural
Society's 1848 Show at York gives a good impression of
the scale of the exhibits and the extent of popular
interest within a few years of the Society's beginnings
(*Illustrated London News*, 15 July 1848)

54 *above* The 1848 Council
dinner, an integral part of the
Royal Agricultural Society's
annual meeting, was held in the
Guildhall, York, with the Earl of
Yarborough presiding and Prince
Albert as guest of honour
(*Illustrated London News*, 15 July
1848)

55 *above right* A view of the
Smithfield Club's annual Cattle
Show held in December 1848. The
Club, founded in 1798, had a
strongly aristocratic membership,
and at this date had as its president
the Duke of Richmond (*Illustrated
London News*, 9 December 1848)

56 *right* An impressive view of
the 1881 Show of the Royal
Agricultural Society, held at
Windsor, with field trials in the
distance and the Castle in the
background. The Shows began in
1839 and from the beginning
aroused enormous interest
(*Illustrated London News*, 19 July
1881)

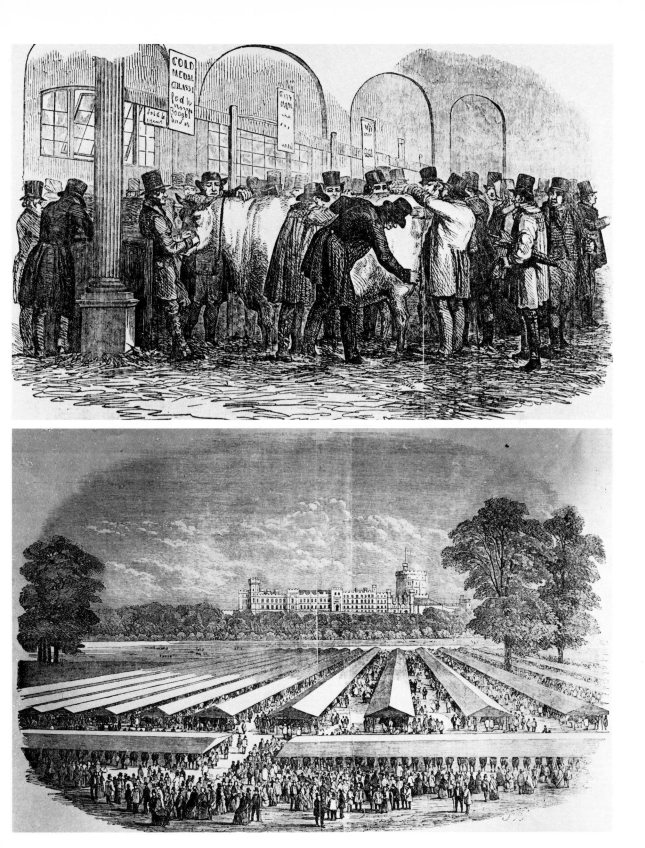

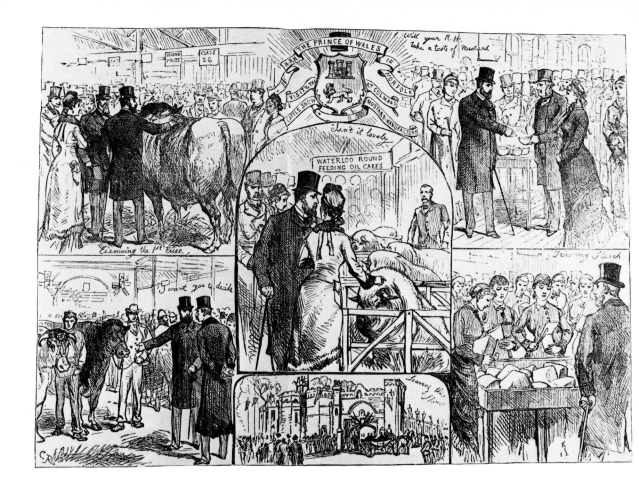

57 *above* Agricultural Shows attracted much royal patronage. Here are scenes from the Prince of Wales's visit to the Norwich Fat Cattle Show, held at Messrs Colman's Mustard and Starch mills in the autumn of 1880. The royal interest extended to the factory as well as the cattle (*Illustrated London News*, 27 November 1880)

58 *opposite and overleaf* Plans and drawings of the Lawes Testimonial Laboratory (a) *above right* exterior, (b) *right* interior, (c) *overleaf* ground plan. The laboratory was built in 1855 and it is believed that these drawings were made about 1857–9, probably as a presentation to subscribers to the building fund (Lawes Agricultural Trust, Rothamsted)

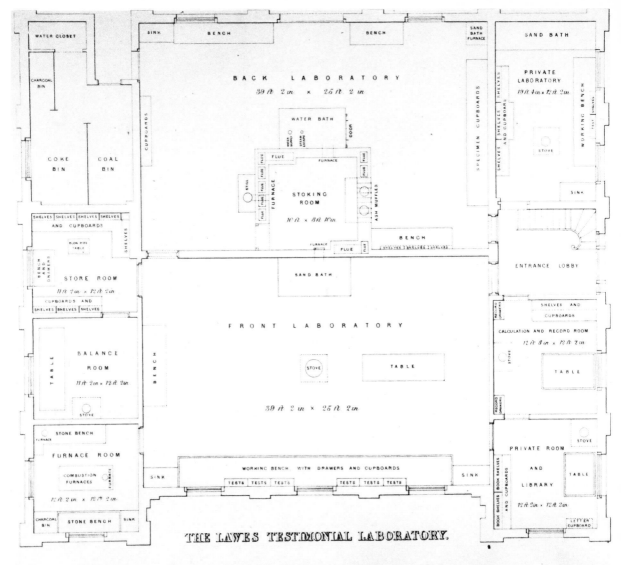

THE LAWES TESTIMONIAL LABORATORY.

GROUND PLAN

many fortunes were wasted trying to overcome them. Neither the 'rotary cultivator' nor 'digger' types of steam ploughs were successful, although the latter produced a succession of 'fearful and wonderful' machines culminating in the famous 'Darby Digger', thirty of which were manufactured between 1877 and 1898 at a total cost of over £100,000.[27]

The preferred and more practical solution was to employ a steam engine to winch implements across the field, a proposition that was realized in the 1850s when the mobile 'road' engine was adapted for that purpose. Most steam ploughs were operated by contractors, and the sets were also employed for mole draining, trenching and land clearance. Though invaluable in special situations such as on run-down farms, or in potato growing where deep tillage and timeliness were of the essence, the steam plough was too cumbersome and expensive for use by the average farmer and was at most but an auxiliary to the horse. At the peak of their popularity steam ploughs could be numbered only in hundreds, whereas portable steam-threshing engines numbered many thousands. Indicatively, between 1880 and the Great War Fowler of Leeds, the leading British manufacturer, sold fewer than 100 sets to the home market.[28]

VI

The impact of machines on work output during the Victorian period was not as dramatic as is sometimes supposed. As R. E. Prothero observed in 1901: 'It is in harvesting, preparing and forwarding crops to market that mechanical invention has proved most useful.'[29] Numerous tasks about the farm were then still performed, in part or exclusively, by horse and manual labour using traditional tools. In ploughing, for example, output was largely determined by the speed of the horses (1.5 miles per hour), and 0.75–1.0 acre was still the normal daily rate of work in the late nineteenth century. The same was true of hedging and ditching, cartage, lifting work and also dairying. Steam power was employed mainly for threshing: in 1907 there were fewer than 9,000 (mainly portable) steam engines servicing 300,000 or so farms.[30] Indeed, the opportunities to save labour diminished somewhat after 1880 when farmers switched away from cereals into dairying and market gardening, areas which did not so easily lend themselves to mechanization. Nor during the Victorian period was there a significant change in the farm size structure; larger farms would have meant greater economies of scale in the use of machinery, though it is true that about 70 per cent of the cultivated area was organized in farms of more than 100 acres which allowed greater scope for mechanization than in other European countries.

In some arable operations the gains afforded by mechanization, or as in corn harvesting by the use of improved hand tools, could be very substantial, though in practice they were rather less impressive than the crude work rates of the faster methods might suggest, chiefly on account of the larger numbers of workers required in linkage and ancillary tasks. Table 15.1 shows work rates and labour requirements for hand tools and machines in harvesting, threshing, hoeing and shearing.[31]

Table 15.1 *Work rates and labour requirements for hand tools and machines*

WHEAT HARVESTING

	Acres per day	Worker days per acre
Hand tools		
Sickle (cut low)	0.33	4.8
Scythe	1.15	2.4
Bagging hook	1.0	3.0
Machines		
Manual delivery reaper	10.0	1.1
Self-delivery reaper	10.0	1.0
Reaper-binder	10.0	0.5
WHEAT THRESHING	*Tons per day*	
Flail	0.2	5.0*
2-horse threshing machine (excluding winnowing)	5.0	1.6
12 h.p. steam-threshing machine (including winnowing and dressing)	15.0	0.8
HOEING	*Acres per day*	
Hand hoe	0.3	3.3
Horse hoe	4.0	0.25
SHEEP SHEARING	*Sheep shorn per day*	
Hand clippers	25–30 (large)	
Shearing machine	30–8	

*30 bushel (0.75 ton) crop.

In harvesting and threshing wheat, machinery yielded a saving in labour of approximately 70 per cent, but in barley and oats much less, and smaller again over the entire sequence of operations from the first ploughing to the final dressing. Overall, in 1900 about 7.5 worker-days were needed to produce an acre of corn using horse plough, seed drill, reaping machine and steam thresher, compared with about 11.0 worker days (wheat) and 10.0 worker days (barley) in the 1840s using all hand tools. Labour requirements per acre in corn growing fell by about 30 per cent over the period, but in British agriculture as a whole the gain was smaller, of the order of 20–5 per cent. The saving in labour costs was also modest because of the expense of purchasing and maintaining machines, and in the use of horses to haul and drive them. It is estimated that despite a decline of 18 per cent in the area under tillage the number of horses employed in British agriculture rose from about 1.7 million in the early 1870s to over 2.0 million in the 1890s.[32]

Output per worker in British agriculture improved by upwards of 70 per cent between 1840 and 1900, reflecting partly the growth in farm output and partly the more productive use of labour. Work spreading and seasonal unemployment had been the rule in the low-wage districts of southern and midland England in the second quarter of the nineteenth century. One source of higher labour productivity, therefore, was a fuller and more efficient use of the existing workforce, in summer, but especially in winter. The benefits of mechanization were most evident at the summer work peaks—at hay and corn harvest and in cleaning row-crops—where there were acute shortages of labour in the 1850s. The chief advantage of machine threshing was that able-bodied males who previously had spent upwards of three or four months each winter chained to the flail were freed for more productive work in and around the farmyard, supervising and feeding livestock, or in the fields, under-draining and carrying roots. By using machinery farmers became less dependent on casual and part-time labour during summertime, and were able to spread their workloads more evenly over the year. In 1921 just over 200,000 seasonal workers were employed in British agriculture, mostly in market gardening and fruit and hop picking; half a century earlier their numbers were much greater and most of them were engaged in arable farming.[33] By the end of the century a higher proportion of farm work was performed by the permanent staff, and a variety of tasks which had once been done 'by the piece' were now done 'by the day'.

The effect of mechanization on the financial structure of farming is difficult to measure. Fixed capital was substituted for labour, but this assumed major significance only on the largest farms. The investment in machinery was small compared with that in farm buildings, while throughout the Victorian period changes in the stock of working capital (for example, livestock, seed, tillages, manures and feeding stuffs) were more significant than changes in fixed capital. The simple machines and improved implements used on the generality of farms were comparatively cheap and had a long working life. Steam engines, steam ploughs and combined threshing machines were owned by large farmers (and hobby farmers) or by firms of contractors. Of the first there were only about 8,500 in use in 1900; of the second probably fewer than 350; and together they represented a new-cost investment of no more than £2·8 million. The numbers of implements and machines then employed is indicated by the estimate of principal requirements on the different sizes of farm made by Primrose McConnell in 1910 and shown in Table 15.2.[34]

The tabulation implies that on a 300-acre farm the investment in machinery (as against vehicles and implements) was less than £140, and on the average farm less than £80. The expenditure on tools and equipment was larger in 1901 than in 1837, but the proportion of farm capital which it represented was probably very little different. A survey of 1,000 farms carried out in the eastern counties in 1931–3, when tractors and oil engines were already employed on the larger holdings, showed that machinery and equipment accounted for only about 18 per cent of total capital of farms between 100 and 300 acres (less than £2 per acre): and annual maintenance and running costs accounted for only 11.5 per cent of gross costs (just over 80p an acre).[35] In the country at large expenditure on machinery was put at less than 10 per cent of total costs in 1938–9.[36] This does not detract, however, from the Victorian achievement. During this, the first stage of mechanization, the emphasis was on

Table 15.2 *Estimate of principal implements required on a mixed-husbandry farm*

Implements	\multicolumn{6}{c}{Acres}
	100	150	200	300	500	800
Carts—one-horse	3	4	4	6	8	10
Lorries or wagons	–	1	1	1	2	2
Liquid manure cart	1	1	1	1	1	1
Clod-crusher	–	1	1	1	1	2
Iron roller	1	1	1	1	2	2
Horse hoe	1	1	1	1	1	2
Drill-harrows and grubbers	1	1	1	1	2	2
Ploughs	1	2	2	3	5	8
Double-mouldboard plough	1	1	1	1	2	2
Light grass harrows and chain harrows	1	1	1	1	1	2
Heavy seed harrows	1	1	2	2	3	4
3-horse grubber and scarifier	1	1	1	1	2	2
Corn drills	–	1	1	1	1	2
Grass-seed sowing machine	–	–	1	1	1	1
Drag-harrows	–	–	1	1	1	2
Turnip drill and clod-crusher	1	1	1	1	1	2
Turnip-scufflers	–	–	–	1	1	2
Mower and reaper	1	1	1	1	2	3
Sheaf binder	–	–	1	1	1	2
Horse rake	1	1	1	1	2	2
Tedder	–	–	1	1	1	2
Horse fork or elevator	–	1	1	1	1	1
Potato-raiser	–	–	1	1	1	1
Chaff-cutter	1	1	1	1	1	1
Turnip-cutters	1	1	1	1	2	2
Winnowing machine	1	1	1	1	1	1
Oat-bruiser or millstones	1	1	1	1	1	1
Oilcake breaker	1	1	1	1	1	1

simple mechanical devices offering modest but acceptable savings in time and labour at least cost. The benefits of the most expensive machines were diffused through hiring. The labourer was spared at least some of the toil and drudgery with which farm work had been always associated. The next stage of advance awaited the fuller development of the tractor and oil engine, a further half-century of rural migration, and the renewed expansion and recovery in farming fortunes which began in the Second World War.

Notes

1 F. M. L. Thompson, 1968b, 62–77.
2 Deane and Cole, 1967, 142–4.
3 Collins, 1969a, 140; Collins, 1972, 21.

4 McConnell, 1910, 71.
5 Morton, 1868, 71.
6 *Ibid.*, pp. 70–2.
7 For brief accounts see Grace and Phillips, 1975; Collins, 1974, 23–5; and for detailed studies: Blake, 1974; BPP 1920 VIII.
8 Stephens, 1871 edn, I, 404.
9 Grace and Phillips, 1975, 3.
10 Whitehead, 1964, 52–7.
11 Fyfe, 1862, 321–60.
12 Strong, 1971, 2–9.
13 Saul, 1967, 119.
14 Blake, 1974, 159–60.
15 Saul, 1968, 192.
16 The best general account of technical developments is Fussell, 1952.
17 Darby, 1898–9, 95.
18 Royal Agricultural Society of England Show Catalogues; David, 1971, 145–214.
19 Fussell, 1966, 199.
20 Collins, 1969a, 453–73.
21 Caird, 1852, 515; Hunt, 1967, 280–92.
22 Clutterbuck, 1869, 10.
23 Harleston Farmers' Club, 1850, 112–13.
24 White, n.d., VII, 226–7.
25 Fussell, 1952, 152–79.
26 Collins, 1972, 20–1.
27 Bonnett, 1972; Spence, 1960; Tyler and Haining, 1970.
28 Institute of Agricultural History, University of Reading: Fowler Records, TR/FOW.
29 Prothero, 1901, 15.
30 BPP 1908 [Cd. 6277].
31 Collins, 1969b, 9; other data, McConnell, 1910, 42–75, and contemporary sources.
32 Bellerby *et al.*, n.d.
33 Ministry of Agriculture, 1968, 62.
34 McConnell, 1910, 60.
35 Carslaw and Culpin, 1936, 11.
36 Ministry of Agriculture, 1968, 79.

16   Model Farms

Stuart Macdonald

The model farm in Victorian Britain has largely escaped the attention of historians, and probably for good reason. The concept was admirable: in theory the landlord's model farm provided a local paradigm of the latest and best agricultural techniques from which it was only reasonable to assume that emulation would follow. Consequently, the tenants, and eventually the whole farming neighbourhood beyond, would—to use a cliché of the day—profit by example. Indeed, so advanced was the example to be that the tenantry was destined—to use a cliché of a later age not wholly inappropriate to the new era of scientific agriculture—to make a quantum jump as it deserted time-worn traditions and entered the new age of agricultural enlightenment. While the more calculating landlords might have considered that better farming produced fatter rent rolls, it seems that most of those who favoured model farms did so for much the same reason that they sponsored Sunday Schools—a feeling of responsibility incumbent upon those of high social standing. Model farms were much more a product of Victorian morality than of Victorian materialism.

I

Victorian model farms had their eighteenth-century precedents,[1] but their spiritual origins were in the experimental farms and sheep-shearings of the late eighteenth and early nineteenth centuries, the age of adventure in agriculture. The early experimental farms were a recognition of the feeling that a degree of rigorous trial

214

and error was necessary to distinguish between good ideas and bad ones. Such farms were a rejection of mere book-learning and pure theory, a reaction against agricultural authors who had no farming experience.[2] Unfortunately, such farms all too often existed only in theory themselves. In principle, experimental farms seemed a fine idea:

> Public farms, in every county, conducted by proper persons, would tend more towards forwarding the perfection of Agriculture in all its branches, than any other measure that has ever been suggested; and as the Gentlemen of large landed property would be the most interested in the results of such an institution, they certainly ought to be the guardians and supporters of it.[3]

Several groups of county gentry and farmers seem to have toyed with the idea of experimental farms.[4] In County Durham, for example, detailed plans were made in 1796 for such a farm of 200 acres, to be managed by no other a personage than Dr Anderson from Edinburgh and organized by a committee of practical farmers as well as landowners. Some emphasis was placed on the importance of practical farmers; in fact, apology was made to the landowners for the necessity of enlisting working farmers before soliciting the county's subscriptions. Perhaps this was why the venture came to nothing, or at least resulted in no more than the usual well-patronized agricultural society a few years later.[5] Northumberland also mooted the idea of an experimental farm in 1797, but the whole project was deemed too expensive and it too was abandoned.[6] It is, perhaps, not surprising that this was a common fate of experimental farms. Everyone appreciated their theoretical benefits, but run by farmers they were socially unacceptable, and run by landlords they were of little agricultural value.

It appears that only Norfolk retained its eighteenth-century experimental farm well into the nineteenth.[7] Norfolk, however, was the home of Thomas Coke, the apotheosis of improving landlords. It used to be fashionable to expound a view that Coke was personally responsible for a great deal of the nation's agricultural improvement. By taking over the running of farms from reluctant tenants, Coke was said to have been both inspiration and example to the remainder: the best breeds of sheep and cattle, barren wastes replaced by acres of rolling wheat, modern farmsteads, and the rent increased ten-fold.[8] Coke was the enthusiastic expert and the local farmers the indolent idiots;[9] but such an heroic picture is no longer regarded as realistic.[10] Instead, there is a universal tendency to adopt what seems to have been Coke's own opinion rather than that of his admirers. Improvement there certainly had been on the land where two rabbits had previously fought over a single blade of grass. Yet, though the rabbits no longer quarrelled and Coke had became a national celebrity, improvement did not spread at more than a mile a year.[11] Nor did attempts to leapfrog resistant areas to influence more adventurous regions meet with much success.[12] Had Thomas Coke really been the unique influence it has been said he was, enlightenment would only now be reaching some of the more remote parts of the home counties.

While Coke's agricultural innovations found but slow acceptance, his social influence, like his reputation, was much more widespread. From about 1790 until 1821, Coke held an annual sheep-shearing during which farmers and landlords were invited to examine the latest agricultural techniques. Long before 1821 the event had become of national importance and had been copied by other landlords, notably the Duke of Bedford.[13] There were other imitators; for example, Frank Sitwell, of Barmoor in Northumberland. In 1806 it was reported: 'The Show of Sheep at Barmoor was very numerously attended. Mr. Sitwell has built a large House & Hovel etc in imitation of the Duke of Bedford at Woburn. The House holds about 150 persons at dinner. . . .'[14] The same Sitwell was also said to be 'quite Wild about establishing an Experimental Farm' but could get no support from the farmers.[15] Now why should Coke's agricultural improvements have encountered resistance when his concept of a week-long garden party with sheep was so eminently acceptable? The answer is, of course, that the latter merely occupied a man's leisure while the former posed a threat to his livelihood.

The single basic objection to nineteenth-century model farms—and it was posed by their advocates as well as their opponents—was that they did not have to be economic. A normal farm, above all else, did have to be a profitable proposition. The landlord could experiment if he wanted, but the farmer had his living to earn.

> The farmer . . . is the least likely of all men to pursue . . . experiments to an impartial and accurate conclusion. His practice is founded upon the custom of his vicinity and his own observation and experience . . . and were his knowledge and acquirements equal to the task . . . it might not be venturing a very rash conjecture to suggest that he would not be the first to attend the summons on rent day.[16]

Some even went so far as to argue that it was the landlord's duty to experiment, in that he alone was free to do so. Catch 22, however, was that any improvement emanating from the landlord was almost bound to be regarded as useless for the working farmer, because there had been no regard for economic constraints. To paraphrase Arthur Young, the old husbandry, unlike the new, was tried and tested. Tenants, therefore, acted wisely in refusing to dabble in experiments and book husbandry. 'Would they not be prodigious fools to meddle with all the fashionable whims that are every day started in farming? . . . Let the landlord try experiments.'[17]

Arthur Young, though not a landlord, was unrivalled as agricultural experimenter and publicist. At Bradfield in Suffolk he operated, if not exactly a model farm, certainly an experimental one. As experimenter, Young inevitably made mistakes: as publicist, equally inevitably, he made enemies. Understandably, the enemies criticized him for what they saw as incompetence,[18] but more interestingly, so, too, did many of his friends. Well-disposed visitors to Bradfield seemed to leave Young's farm in a state of shock.

> At Mr. Young's I did not see much worth attention, indeed there my disappointment was great—in reading his Annals he immediately discovers

the smallest fault in any other person's management, from that I imagined to find an example of the old Arcadian Agriculture—instead of that I met with a hodgepodge of everything without arrangement or system—Chicory the chief production.[19]

Deserved or not, Young's reputation was that of the worst practical farmer in the county,[20] a view probably reflecting the average farmer's attitude towards the proprietors of model farms in general.

The Hon. J. C. Curwen was responsible for a model farm in Cumberland, the Schoose Farm, from which it was said much of the agricultural improvement of the county emanated. The improvement was also variously attributed to the example of a Mr Watson who actually farmed some 1,400 acres for a living, to Mr Curwen's specially imported bailiff, hotfoot from his training under George Culley in Northumberland, and, more mysteriously, to the Durham ox.[21] Presumably, agricultural progress in Cumberland, or anywhere else, had no single progenitor. There were no doubt innovation leaders, and these may have been landlords, such as J. C. Curwen, with model farms. However, such men, even with model farms, were not well equipped for the role.

It would be unfair to think meanly of Mr. Curwen's management as a farmer, because it is still inferior to that of many professional men in our more improved districts . . . the example of one who is a good farmer, and nothing more, must have a much more beneficial effect in his neighbourhood, than that of a great landholder, however successful his practice may be.[22]

There was the rub. The 'farmer paying rent, and acting at his own risk'[23] was a professional, and was influential because he was automatically taken seriously. The landlord with his model farm, no matter how successful his methods, was an amateur. If a single characteristic more than any other distinguished the mid-nineteenth-century farmer from his mid-eighteenth-century counterpart, it was his sheer professionalism.

II

High farming involved the calculated use of expensive agricultural techniques to produce the greatest possible yield, and its practice distinguished much Victorian agriculture from what had preceded it. From late eighteenth-century Dorset it was reported: 'He is esteemed here the best Farmer, who gets the most Money, & which is generally done, where there are least out goings . . . .'[24] But increased input did not lead automatically to increased income, and farmers were understandably suspicious of those zealots who suggested it did.

> People in their zeal for a Cause they've espoused generally think they can never point out the advantages too strongly—but by over doing it, they often hurt it. . . . I had much sooner know *how to make the most* of any land, than to be told *how much* can be made of it. If I know the former, the latter will follow of course, & *the farmer* not hurt.[25]

In other words, the farmer was interested in better agriculture and not particularly in the best possible agriculture, a situation not dissimilar to that existing in many developing countries today. The growing importance of science in agriculture did nothing to alter the general demand for the most appropriate technology rather than for simply the latest technology. That was a demand for which model farms simply did not cater.

What then was high farming? Basically it was the achievement of high production by the widespread application of new knowledge and equipment. Land was drained to grow more grain and other food for more and fatter stock, yielding in turn more manure and heavier crops. To add greater impetus to the cycle, maize and cattle cake were imported and Peruvian islands stripped of centuries of accumulated bird droppings. To house valuable stock, preserve its manure, and promote efficiency in the working of the greater complexities of the system, new buildings in new configurations were required. Implements of unprecedented complexity and dedication to individual tasks became increasingly common, and steam power invaded first the barn and eventually the field. The result was increased production, freighted by rail to hungry urban mouths.[26] The change was impressive, and certainly significant enough to fascinate contemporary observers. In short, farming had developed from a largely extractive industry to a manufacturing one.[27] The farm, as nineteenth-century commentators never tired of noting, was now a factory.[28] But a factory is expected to produce a profit, and it was solely to this end that the Victorian farming factories used the new techniques. Model farms, on the other hand, displayed the latest agricultural techniques not necessarily because they were profitable, but because they were remarkable. Some examples may illustrate the difference between high farming in the real world and high farming in the protected environment of the model farm.

III

Probably the best-known model farmer in Victorian England was the Prince Consort himself. At Windsor, such farms as the Shaw and the Flemish continued the royal tradition of showing the nation the latest in agricultural fashion. By 1860, however, the Norfolk Farm, the pride of George III, was beginning to show its age (Plate 51(a) and (b)). The homestead was largely of wood and thatch, picturesque and rambling. In particular, the arrangement of the buildings was logistically offensive because so much time and effort were required to move straw and litter from the farm to the

218

cattle sheds. The absence of special arrangements and undue exposure to the elements made the collection of farmyard manure difficult and expensive, which both restricted cropping options and necessitated the purchase of large quantities of artificial manure. Much of the land formerly in turnips had been turned to permanent pasture, but the light turnip soil refused to show off the full advantage of drainage and steam tillage.[29] The Flemish Farm was much more impressive (Plate 51(c)). The old farm buildings having become unseemly for the herd of champion Herefords they housed, plans were made for a completely new farmstead based upon the most advanced models in England and the whim of Prince Albert. Work was completed in 1858, and the result was a farmstead of brick rather than timber, buildings which would 'enhance every modern improvement that might be suitable for the farm, . . . by the convenience of arrangement and plainness of finish, they should recommend themselves to farmers as a model to be copied'.[30]

Indeed, the new Flemish Farm was something of a masterpiece in its incorporation of the most approved principles of the day. The stockyard was now the central feature, with the stables on one side and an open yard on the other. Separated from this complex by a covered cart-way was the barn with its associated machinery and sheds for preparing and storing food and litter. Implements were housed to one side under cover and drainage from the whole complex led to a single underground tank where the liquid manure was pumped to the fields beyond. The farmstead would have been the delight of any time and motion man. For example, horses emerged from their stables (g), picked up their carts (from w), then carried corn from the stack through the gangway between the sheaf-barn and the threshing-barn (p and o). After threshing, the grain went up to the granary and the straw through to the straw-barn (n). The straw was then alongside all the areas that needed it (at a, b, c, g and h). After use as litter, soiled straw from the stables (g) and the cow stalls (e) was shoved through openings to the adjacent yards where it was trodden down before being applied to the fields.[31] Without a doubt, the farm was impressive, an agricultural showpiece crammed with the latest implements, useful or not, and with stock as well-bred as its owner.

It is worth remembering that at the very time Prince Albert was presiding over the building of the new Flemish Farm, he also supervised the construction of the new Royal Dairy at Frogmore (Plate 51(d)).[32] The exterior style was Renaissance: the interior beggars decription. The floor looked like a Turkish carpet; the walls were white and green with mauve stars, and contained bas-reliefs on agricultural themes as well as medallions supported by sea horses and dolphins. There were fountains, too, one with a nymph pouring water from a jar, and the other 'a fountain of majolica ware, designed by the late Mr Thomas, rising from a shell supported by a heron and bulrushes'.[33] But excellent as the royal model might occasionally have been (and the vast expanse of tiling reflected a concern for hygiene), serious consideration by the professional farmer must often have been wanting.

Another model farm extravaganza was that created by Lord Bateman at Uphampton, Herefordshire, in 1861 (Plates 52(a) and (b)). The hub of this industrial complex was the 12 h.p. steam engine, complete with Doric frame, which powered not merely the threshing machine, but whole production lines of other machinery. Once threshed, grain and straw went their separate ways to be processed, classified and appropriately stored. The engine also provided power for the fodder unit, which cut, ground, mixed and otherwise prepared food for the cattle. Perhaps the most ambitious feature of this rural factory was the railway network, which brought the stacks to the threshing machine when required.[34] As an exhibition piece Uphampton was fascinating, but as an example for the farming community to follow it was a nonsense. So too, was the home farm planned for the Lowther Estate in Cumbria (Figure 16.1). A monstrosity, with its pigsties just outside the front door of the farm house, it was, like other estate follies, designed to be admired from afar and had nothing to do with farming.[35] Even Coke's estate at Holkham was not entirely free of agricultural structures that were more decorative than functional.[36]

There were, of course, other people with model farms of some renown; for example, Philip Pusey, M.P., in Berkshire, Mr Hewitt Davis in Norfolk and the Rev. Anthony Huxtable in Dorset.[37] John Joseph Mechi, with a model farm at Tiptree Hall in Essex, was one of the best known. Mechi was an entrepreneur who had made his fortune by inventing and selling Mechi's Magic Razor Strops. When the fashions of the Crimean War obviated the necessity for regular shaving, Mechi turned his attention to gas lamps. He patented a device for removing the noxious fumes and made a second fortune. But it was his first fortune that allowed Mechi to indulge his agricultural fancy and to buy Tiptree Hall in 1840.[38]

Having purchased Tiptree Hall for £3,250, Mechi proceeded to spend £6,200 on improvements between 1843 and 1844 alone. In less than eighteen months, he cut some eighty miles of drains on his 130 acres, removed 5,000 yards of banks and fences, made new ditches and roads, removed two or three hundred trees, carted 60,000 bushels of stones, 300,000 drainage pipes, 400,000 bricks, 200 loads of building material, and demolished farm buildings in order to erect more convenient ones. By the end of 1845 Mechi had spent some £13,500 on improving the farm.[39] Its value trebled, but Mechi never succeeded in convincing the farming world that he was making a profit as his own tenant. As he travelled the country addressing agricultural societies, he waved his latest balance sheet, boasting (if it showed a profit) that his improvements were responsible or (if it showed a loss) explaining that the improvements would produce their profit next year or that, though the methods were good, he and his bailiff were too busy displaying them to actually make money. One cannot help but admire Mechi's energy and pluck. Not only did he speak at meeting after meeting at which professional farmers heaped good-natured scorn upon him, but he actually published reports of the proceedings. Perhaps his efforts were of value, but not among the class which actually farmed. 'I do not hold up my farm as an example for the ordinary class of landlords and farmers, for it is quite clear that their general capital is totally inadequate to similar proceedings.'[40] Such a caveat was probably implicit in all Victorian model farms, but it was hardly well calculated to achieve the widespread adoption of an innovation. In short, Mechi's steam ploughing

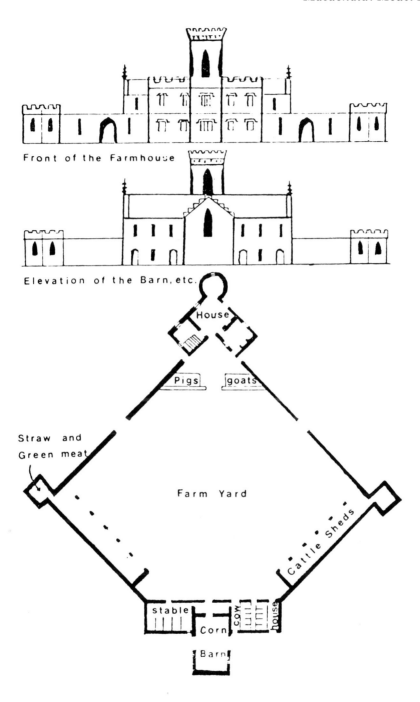

Figure 16.1 Plan for the home farm of the Lowther Estate, Cumbria. An example of the *ferme orné*, with Gothic features to match those of Lowther Hall. The plan placed the pigs inconveniently near the front door but included a cowhouse with individual stalls and a feeding passage (Carlisle Record Office, Lowther Estate Collection)

and manure irrigation caught the attention of those who mattered least, and merely entertained those who should have benefited most.

> I believe I was the first who attempted to send out all the manure in this way [by pipe to the fields]. Last year I had 20 dead horses and some dead cows, besides the puddings [dung] in my tank; I had 30 feet of solid stuff. . . . Luckily it dropped into my head to apply the air-pump. . . . All those dead horses, except the large bones, have gone through a hole the size of my finger.[41]

Mechi died in penury in 1880.

IV

It is easy to make the mistaken assumption, as Mechi and probably other model farmers did, that nineteenth-century agriculture was an entirely industrial process which reacted immediately to inputs of capital, energy and science. That was not the case. The land, its stock and its caretaker, the farmer, reacted slowly to change, and the farmer most slowly of all for he had first to be convinced that change was both safe and profitable.[42] Not only did the model farm ignore the importance of safety and profitability, it also ignored the farmer. There were other ways in which the farmer found out about agricultural improvements and became sufficiently interested to try them. Model farms were merely a subject for discussion within that medium and not an integral part of it. At best they were a catalyst rather than an active agent of agricultural improvement; at worst they were an entertaining example of how not to do things: 'cases there have no doubt been, where, from careless management and untidiness, or from the opposite extreme of lavish and improvident expenditure, "his Lordship's farming" has only proved a by-word and an example to be avoided'.[43] It is a tribute to Victorian positive thinking that even the most disastrous model farms were reckoned to have their uses. They allowed the landlord to sympathize with the difficulties and losses encountered by his tenants.[44]

It is hard to escape this conclusion that model farms were ineffectual in their primary purpose. In 1853 Andrews declared that 'many new farmeries are erected and called *model farms*, but very few can be considered as proper examples to be copied by others'.[45] At the beginning of the twentieth century Hall recalled that 'the model farms that were not uncommon a generation ago were justly discredited as only instructive in their expensiveness . . .'.[46] Exactly what was and what was not a model farm is not absolutely clear. In 1880 Brodrick estimated that most country gentlemen retained a home farm 'for the purpose of breeding pedigree stock, conducting agricultural experiments, or otherwise setting a good example to their neighbours'.[47] But, as Thompson has succinctly explained, the home farm 'was not generally regarded as a business enterprise and when one was run at a profit for a few years it was worth writing a book on the case'.[48] When one model farm was found by a visitor to actually make money, he recorded the fact in italics and described it as a miracle.[49] Of all the classes concerned with the tilling of the soil, the landlord was probably the most agriculturally ignorant[50] and worst equipped to proffer agricultural advice. His role in agricultural improvement—and it was of crucial importance—was in establishing the conditions under which that improvement could take place.[51] The landlord set the scene for progress: length of lease, convenants, size of farm, rent level, the financing of major improvements such as drainage, building construction and repairs, and whatever there was of tenant right, were largely under his jurisdiction. He could initiate or inhibit agricultural improvement, but even with a model farm he was unable to act as an example of it.

There were two model farms of a rather different sort; from 1843 John Lawes's research station at Rothamsted, and from 1845 the agricultural college at Cirencester.[52] The first sought to put science, and especially chemistry, into agricultural practice: the second to implant the new knowledge in the minds of the young. In Britain, though not in Europe, both were pioneering institutions in the mid-nineteenth-century and their very survival indicates a fair measure of success but, as with other model farms, neither exerted much direct influence on the ordinary farmer. After more than half a century of agricultural chemistry at Rothamsted, it was noted that

> We are greatly in need of more experimental work on the operations of cultivation, this being one of the subjects with which local experimental farms well might occupy themselves, instead of with the permutations and combinations of nitrogen, phosphoric acid, and potash which seem to bound the imagination of too many of our agricultural teachers.[53]

Cirencester attempted to teach agriculture by means of an experimental farm, a method thought most inappropriate for those who would have to earn their living by following ordinary methods of cultivation.[54] In fact, it hardly mattered; of the seventy pupils in the class of 1849, not one was a farmer's son.[55] The best farmers had long sent their sons to farms run by distinguished farmers in the most progressive districts. There the professional taught not agriculture as a diversion for gentlemen, but farming as a business for farmers.[56] If Cirencester were to be effective, it would be as a supplement to the existing system.[57]

The golden age of British agriculture, from the 1840s to the 1870s, was one of growing markets and profitable prices which permitted high farming. Those conditions were not present during the last quarter of the century when imports of agricultural produce burgeoned. As farmers struggled for survival, it became starkly obvious that technical efficiency was not the equivalent of economic efficiency in a world of free trade.[58] The maxim of the depression—'the better you farm, the more you spend, and the more you spend, the more you lose'—contrasted vividly and ironically with those of the golden age;[59] and those farmers and landlords who had refused to entertain the extremes of high farming as demonstrated on the model farms could have had no more convincing vindication of their caution. The model farms of the closing decades of the nineteenth century were of a different sort altogether. They were models of ideal smallholdings, set in the midst of limited and scattered colonies of such units and run by such unlikely agriculturalists as the Salvation Army. This back-to-the-land movement, was shortlived and, on the whole, unsuccessful. Its driving force, like that of the model farms of the golden age, was social rather than strictly agricultural—but who is to say that the demonstration of how to farm with a plot of cabbages and a single cow was any more futile than that of the use of a railway network on the farmstead?

Even at the height of the golden age, most farmers were not high farmers.[60] Most lagged well behind the innovation leaders and waited for tangible, and generally local, proof of profitability before forsaking the old for the new. That proof came from the example of successful neighbours, as it long had done and largely still does. Such leaders—often newcomers themselves—obtained their knowledge and interest from a variety of sources, such as local newspapers or letters from colleagues, or by travelling or hiring especially skilled men.[61] Apparently the only way to learn anything useful at the famous Dishley Grange, the ill-mannered Bakewell's farm, had been to bribe or hire his workers.[62] The relative importance of each medium changed, of course, and so, too, did the sort of message it conveyed. During the era of high farming the agricultural press and farmers' clubs seem to have been of special importance, and their message was particularly concerned with manures and fertilizers. After 1880 the press probably grew in importance, but with a new concentration on livestock and agricultural machinery.

Always the individual progressive working farmer, whatever his source of information, remained the prime originator of local agricultural innovation. Even on model farms the amateur was advised of 'one certain test by which he may know whether a practice he adopts be an improvement or not: the test of the practice of the best farmers'.[63] There was no shame in this: the method was that by which the professionals themselves learned most of their techniques. Even the mighty Coke anxiously welcomed such visitors: 'It is from them I gain the little knowledge I have, and derive the satisfaction of communicating improvements amongst my tenantry.' That order of events is fundamental and has too often been ignored.[64] At no time was the model farm of any great significance as a means of influencing even the effective innovation leaders, never mind the mass of the farming community. Most model farms were essentially a fashion, and exhibited the characteristics typical of a fashion in that they were expensive, trivial and, ultimately, ephemeral.

Notes

1 Mingay, 1963, 163–4.
2 Fussell, 1929, 148–51; 1947, 1–8.
3 Bailey and Culley, 1805, 192.
4 See suggestions in *Annals of Agriculture*, IV, 1785, 111, 459.

5 Durham CRO D/Sa/X/68; *Newcastle Courant*, 23 and 30 July 1786, 7 January 1787; *Annals of Agriculture*, XXVII, 1787, 204–6; *Farmer's Magazine*, IV, 1803, 283–6.

6 Newcastle Central Library: L630; Alnwick Castle Library: 187A/31, shelf 43/2; *Newcastle Courant*, 16 September, 11 November, 30 December 1787.

7 Hall, 1913, 85.

8 For example, Spencer, 1842, 1–9; Stirling, 1912, 190; Ernle, 1961, 217–23; Caird, 1968, 164–6; Orwin, 1949, 123–5.

9 Prothero, 1888, 79–81.

10 Parker, 1975.

11 Fussell, 1948, 91.

12 Riches, 1937, 113–14.

13 Russell, 1966, 67.

14 Northumberland CRO: 2DE/4/60/24, John Carr to George Culley, 21 June 1806; *Newcastle Courant*, 14 July 1804.

15 Northumberland CRO: ZCU/28, Frank Sitwell to George Culley, 24 June 1806; ZCU/31, George Culley to Frank Sitwell, 24 June 1806.

16 Northumberland CRO: ZHE/34/16, John Grey, 'An Account of Some Experiments with Guano and Other Manures on Turnips', 1843.

17 Quoted in Marshall, 1929–30, 53–4.

18 One of Young's most bitter enemies was Thomas Stone, the superseded Reporter for the *General View of the Agriculture of Lincolnshire*. Stone opens one delightful diatribe with 'If we turn our observations to Bradfield Hall Farm, in Suffolk, the seat of your improvements, the most useful lesson of practical husbandry may be instantly learnt by adopting the contrary to your example.' Stone, 1800, 20.

19 Northumberland CRO: ZCU/18, William Mure to George Culley, 31 March 1783. See also Mingay, 1975, 9–11.

20 For example, Bell, 1871, 250.

21 *Farmer's Magazine*, X, 1809, 466–8; XV, 1814, 467; XX, 1819, 249, 375.

22 *Farmer's Magazine*, XXI, 1820, 480.

23 'Obituary of James MacDougal', *Farmer's Magazine*, XXIII, 1822, 512.

24 Northumberland CRO: ZCU/12, George Boswell to George Culley, 9 September 1787.

25 Northumberland CRO ZCU/14, George Boswell to George Culley, 6 April 1789.

26 Chambers and Mingay, 1966, 170–97.

27 F. M. L. Thompson, 1968b, 64.

28 Ernle, 1961, 214.

29 J. C. Morton, 1863, 81, 150–60. See also Spearing, 1860, 25–9.

30 J. C. Morton, 1863, 246.

31 *Ibid.*, 83, 136–40.

32 *Ibid.*, 104–11.

33 *Ibid.*, 108.

34 Denton, 1864, 56–9, 92–5; Harvey, 1970, 162–3.

35 Messenger, 1975, 343–5.

36 Robinson, 1974, 1557.

37 On Huxtable's farming see Ruegg, 1854, 410–12.

38 Scott Watson, 1951, 86–96.

39 Mechi, 1859, 28, 35, 141.

40 *Ibid.*, 183.
41 *Ibid.*, 153–4.
42 Beresford, 1959, 2, 4.
43 Bowick, 1862, 247.
44 *Ibid.*, 266–7.
45 Andrews, 1853, 60.
46 Hall, 1913, 437.
47 Brodrick, 1881, 199.
48 Thompson, 1960, 392; Habakkuk, 1953, 92–3; Colyer, 1975, 406–13.
49 Chambers and Mingay, 1966, 173–4.
50 Caird, 1968, 491–3; 1878a, 316–17.
51 McCulloch, 1837, I, 547.
52 Chambers and Mingay, 1966, 170.
53 Hall, 1913, 29.
54 Stephens, 1871, I, 60–1.
55 Morton, 1856, I, 745; Vallentine, 1866, 12.
56 Morton, 1856, I, 745–6; *Farmer's Magazine*, VII, 1806, 153–6; Macdonald, 1976, 139–45.
57 Lawrence, 1865, 1–9; Morton, 1865, 447–8.
58 Chambers and Mingay, 1966, 177–81.
59 Harvey, 1970, 172–3.
60 See, for example, Trow-Smith, 1959, 234; or, perhaps, Hennell, 1934, 1–5.
61 Macdonald, 1979, 30–9.
62 Northumberland CRO: ZCU/9, George Culley to Matthew Culley, November 1784.
63 Pusey, 1850, 438.
64 Quoted in Parker, 1975, 115. See also Pusey, 1842, 185, 215.

17 The Victorian Farmer

B.A. Holderness

I

Agriculture in nineteenth-century Britain was not a single industry but a combination of several, and the men (and women) who cultivated the soil were no less heterogeneous. The term 'farmer' was used to describe a rather residual occupational class. The holders of land who were not labourers, market-gardeners, landowners, graziers, millers, innkeepers and so forth, were 'farmers'. Thus the category included capitalists occupying 2,000 acres and smallholders with but 5 or 10 acres whose common interests, except perhaps as tithe- or rate-payers, were minimal. So indeed had long been the case, but earlier generations had made a useful if inexact distinction between 'yeoman' or 'husbandmen'. By 1851 farmers were readily differentiated only by the size of their holdings, but the diversity of agriculture was such that mere acreage was an inadequate indicator of social status. The standing, wealth, education and life-style of farmers in different categories bore few marks of uniformity. At the top, farmers and their families almost, but not quite, merged with the professional classes and even with the lesser country gentry; while at the lowest level, the condition of the poorest farmers differed little from that of the better-off labourers and small village tradesmen. It is difficult, therefore, to discuss the 'place' of farmers in Victorian society. The larger capitalist farmers enjoyed most of the limelight and held nearly all the political and social authority vouchsafed to the Victorian farming community. The 'two-horse' occupier or the man without a team had about as much voice in public affairs as the labourer, and elicited less sympathy.

Only in a few anachronistic districts such as the Pennine moorlands or the Isle of Axholme was there a kind of rough agrarian democracy in landholding, compounded of a peasant-like tenacity and an approximate equality of wealth.

Subsistence farming in the full sense scarcely existed by the second half of the nineteenth century, although it is probable that half or more of Victorian farmers consumed more of their own produce than they sold. The capitalist farmers were in a small minority in the whole body of British agriculturists. Not all were men with 300 acres or more. The marginal productivity of the soil established different criteria for the optimum size of holdings in particular circumstances.[1] Some market-gardeners were as affluent and commercially successful upon 50 acres or less as many cereal producers on 600 acres of scarp land. Moreover, as the century developed the bases upon which agricultural prosperity were founded changed significantly, and this shift not only transformed the practice of agriculture but wrought a number of important changes within the agricultural community. Victorians tended to understate this diversity and the process of change in favour of an ideal of progressive 'high farming', and in due course became entangled in the web of their own propaganda. The message of the depressed 1880s, received and understood by an intelligent minority in the eastern counties, was spelled out in the changed pattern of demand for farm holdings, for smaller farms were let more easily than large. The small family farmer, however, remained a rather shadowy figure in the 1890s, but the ability of his kind to survive both the mania for amalgamation and improvement and the new regime of 'low farming' after 1875 was demonstrated repeatedly during the century.

Victorian statistics indicate the numerical importance of the small farm. There were 19,400 holdings occupying 300 or more acres, chiefly in the eastern counties from East Lothian to Wiltshire, while the class of farms of 5–50 acres accounted for two-thirds of all the holdings above 5 acres returned in the enumeration of 1885. Even where, as Samuel Sidney suggested, the choice lay between 'large farms, much manure and numerous stock or no cultivation', farms of 50 acres or less were still to be found, clinging like moss to an ancient wall. In the Lincolnshire wolds, for example, there were 665 holdings of 5–20 acres and 216 holdings of 20–50 acres recorded in an official survey of 1890. The districts of greatest *morcellement* lay in the rich fens, especially in Axholme, and in the Pennine fringe regions of Lancashire and the West Riding near the growing industrial towns. The median holding in the pastoral west of Britain, where only Cheshire, Cumberland and Somerset possessed a considerable number of farms in excess of 300 acres, was 65 acres in 1885, by comparison with 120 acres in the arable and stock-feeding districts of the east and south-east. The heavy clays, which were found everywhere but were characteristic of broad river vales or great plains, had a different profile, being neither fertile enough to support a thriving peasantry nor sufficiently friable to promote the cause of high farming. The clays were typified by holdings of middle size (50–200 acres) devoted to stock-raising or to an often rigidly traditional regime of mixed husbandry.[2]

II

Two obvious facts had a deep influence upon the structure of British agriculture. First, in spite of the pronounced dichotomy between large and small holdings, farm sizes in Britain, on average and in the lowest quartile of classification by acreage, were greater than anywhere else in western Europe. There were, for example, more 'agriculturists' assessed to Schedule B of the income tax in Ireland than in Great Britain.[3] Second, the overwhelming majority of farmers, except the gentlemen 'farmers-in-hand', were tenants. This was no less true of the far from negligible number of affluent owner-occupiers of farm land, nearly all of whom also rented holdings from other proprietors. The investment of savings by farmers, millers, maltsters, agricultural engineers, like that of the *nouveaux riches* of the towns, is a neglected theme, perhaps because it seldom affected the aggregate relationship between owner-occupied and *rentier* land in Britain before 1900. Every county could provide evidence of a few well-found ancient 'yeoman' families, like the Spurrells or Primroses in east Norfolk, or the Waights at Crawley in Hampshire, who survived or even prospered in Victorian times. In most regions of Britain, however, owners occupied only 10–15 per cent of their cultivable land after 1850.[4] The gains which may have been made by smaller landowners before 1815 were partly or wholly lost in the following twenty years. Tenancy, however, was a complicated institution. Not only were tenants often part-owners of their lands, but many held of more than one *rentier* proprietor. The large estates frowned upon the practice of hiring land from several owners, but less exalted proprietors had perforce to accept the divided loyalties of a tenantry, especially in difficult times such as the 1830s or 1880s. Many of the smallest estates depended upon the letting of land not equipped with buildings in order to maximize their net incomes from rent.

After 1850 there remained about a quarter of a million individuals admitted as farmers by the General Register Office, a slight fall from the numbers existing in 1831. The difficulty is to relate the data of the Census, the Agricultural Statistics and the Inland Revenue. It is evident, although the numbers are uncertain, that Victorian agriculture supported a substantial body of part-time farmers. There were perhaps 100,000 holders of land whose occupation or social position was not that of farmer. On the fringe of the industrial districts, and in rural communities of complex social structure, smallholders and even 50-acre men could supplement their incomes by cartage, poultry higgling or milk-selling, and, conversely, many of the petty tradesmen and even some labourers also occupied plots of ground upon which they grew cereals and vegetables or kept nags, asses, cows or swine. At the other extreme of the social spectrum, businessmen, solicitors, clergymen, as well as landowners, were often part-time farmers. Hobby-farming, as it was called, was quite fashionable in the nineteenth century. A few were like John Joseph Mechi, the London alderman who bought and cultivated Tiptree Hall estate in Essex, and spent many of his best years teaching and urging others how to farm profitably, but the majority had few such ambitions.[5] The variety of dual occupations in late-nineteenth-century Britain is surprising after a century or more of industrialization and urban expansion. In districts of distinctively small holdings, Axholme, the southern fenlands, parts of Lancashire and the West Riding, for example, it was apparently common for 'peasant' landholders to go out to work leaving wives and families to manage their holdings.

Although the numbers engaged in cultivating the soil of Britain were comparatively stable, a good deal of change occurred in categories of farm size. In the districts in which 'high farming' predominated by 1850—the scarp-and-vale and former heathland landscapes of the east and south, from Strathmore to Dorset and Wiltshire—the work of arranging holdings of optimum size for maximum exploitation of cereal and livestock production had largely been done by the time of Repeal. Minor adjustments were made thereafter, although the trend towards amalgamation was less marked than before, and some of the bigger holdings were actually divided, even before the 1880s. Large-scale capitalist farming prevailed, chiefly because of the scale economies which could be achieved in light, dry soils, but most of the more enlightened estates, at least from Yorkshire southwards, operated a system of large, small and middle-sized holdings. This encouraged some degree of upward social mobility among the tenants, and its social purpose was generally acknowledged by landlords like Lord Monson or the Earl of Yarborough. It was, however, also a consequence of the mixed soils which were to be found on the larger estates, for on the clayland arable the movement towards larger capitalist farms before 1850 had been slower and more hesitant. Even after a generation of heavy expenditure upon the clays, especially upon under-drainage, the obstacles to large-scale amalgamation remained. In the pastoral region of the north and west large farms of more than 300 acres were relatively less common. Even so it was in this area, especially in the north-west of England, that consolidation was most marked after 1820. The disappearance of the Pennine 'statesman' had been in train for a very long time before 1820–50, but the process was not complete even in the 1860s. In Cumberland, the Graham, Lowther and Carlisle estates had undertaken to 'rationalize' their farm holdings by the middle of the century, as a result of which the number of their tenants was much reduced. Thomas Farrell cited an example of one 300-acre farm which had been formed out of eleven former holdings.[6] In the more fertile plain districts of the west from Solway to Somerset the engrossment of farms in the interests of a successful mixed husbandry or of a more efficient dairy industry was active in the nineteenth century as a result of better superficial and sub-soil drainage and of the re-alignment of much of the farm layout of the region. Consolidation was not a constant theme of agricultural change in the nineteenth century: its progress and effects depended upon geographical and technical differences in the structure of British farming.

A larger question is raised if we turn from the number of farmers to consider the constancy of particular farming populations. Questions of inheritance, migration, recruitment and upward (or downward) social mobility are difficult to answer from the surviving records. A study of particular populations at different periods suggests that there was a fair degree of volatility among British landholders.[7] A surname analysis in parts of East Anglia, for example, reveals that between two-fifths and two-

230

thirds of the inhabitants described as farmers in each sample community had changed from about 1850 to 1890–1900, although many of the names recurred at different points in the same district during the later period. The census enumerations of 1851–71 tend to confirm this inconstancy. In a random sample of twelve English villages the number of farmers who were not born in the villages where they lived in 1851 averaged over two-fifths (40.8 per cent). Fewer than one quarter of these were not demonstrably the sons of farmers themselves, but there is evidence from a variety of sources that men were drawn into farming on their own account, from the ranks of labourers and servants and from the sons of clergy, tradesmen, auctioneers or innkeepers. The opportunities for the farm labourer were slender but not completely closed, partly because even in the 1850s some landlords actively favoured ambitious, diligent and frugal labourers or retainers in allocating small farms, but chiefly because in periods of low prices holdings were generally difficult to let, and many proprietors tended to encourage labourers with experience and small capital to take up tenancies. The successful were then able to progress up a ladder of promotion, and were not infrequently mentioned by agricultural writers of the time. In the farm prize competition of 1881, for example, one of the candidates, on a 70-acre holding, had himself risen from being a labourer. Even some of the bigger holdings in counties such as Lincolnshire or Northumberland were occupied by men who had begun as labourers during the last two decades of the century. However, it is difficult as yet to decide whether cases quoted in contemporary sources were representative of the general experience.

The pattern of geographical mobility is clearer. A minority of farmers migrated to seek better opportunities in other regions, and several of the most famous estates constantly received applications from far afield for vacant holdings. The best-known case is that of the Scots, from Ayrshire and Clydesdale, who descended upon East Anglia after 1880, to take farms which local men would not, or could not, occupy and, by their expertness in dairying, by their frugality and hard work, they rehabilitated many rundown farms.[8] This migration was exceptional only in its long range. Everywhere new tenants can be found moving in upon an alien landscape, and several estates, dispersed in different soils, actually encouraged good men to move from forward to backward districts.

III

The ubiquity of tenant farming in Britain signified that the most important of the relationships which existed between farmers and the rest of society was that which bound landowners and landholders. Tenant farming was not unique to Britain, but the symbiosis which developed between the two parties was regarded as the outstanding characteristic of British agricultural progress. Landlordism was not necessarily popular in the period, but more authoritative voices were raised in its defence than were deployed to attack it. The farmers apparently accepted the obligations and the benefits of the system in good grace. That is not to say that the history of landlord and tenant in Victorian times was uneventful or tranquil. On particular issues tension often ran high, but except in areas where ethnic or religious differences divided proprietors from occupants, in Ireland, Wales, the Western Highlands or Shetland, disputes seldom flared up into conflict. Landlordism was an aspect of rural social order which, in some minds, was associated with traditions of hierarchy. The squire at the head of his little world of farmers and retainers, of shopkeepers and other clients, demanded a measure of deference or subservience which bore the colour, variously, of paternalism, feudalism or tyranny (the point of view depended upon political judgment). But even squirearchal villages, graded in strata of social order, were seldom regimented in a recognized chain of command. The estate was a miniature social universe, orderly and patriarchal, but only a minority of British villagers, even of tenant farmers, lived near the pale of a great country house. Many farmers were tenants of more than one proprietor, and more than half of Victorian village communities were not directly under the influence of any great landowner. Indeed it was sometimes the farmers and village businessmen who formed the real elite of country society, not the landed gentry. As a political and social force the constituency of more affluent farmers had always been powerful enough to disturb the pattern of rural aristocracy. With their higher social standing and additional political power after 1830 capitalist farmers enjoyed a degree of public independence not matched since the apogee of the yeomanry before 1650. Thus while before 1900 there were villages which could be classified as feudal, and estates in which the will of the proprietor or the disposition of his agent were important in the ordering of social relations, obedience, except to the demands of good husbandry, was not necessarily a requisite of tenantry.

Deference is a different matter, for it appears that most farmers accepted the premise of the social superiority of the gentry and regarded deference as a natural element of good grace. On the other hand the social institution of tenant farming was regarded by most Victorians as a political instrument. Political disobedience could be punished by recourse to eviction, as was the case in Ireland and sometimes in Wales, but this was a sanction sparingly used. It caused too much disturbance and adverse publicity, and often resulted in the loss of an excellent batch of tenants. The furore which surrounded evictions in Merioneth after elections in the middle of the nineteenth century, and the even more famous scandal of that superlative farmer, George Hope of Fenton Barns, East Lothian, who had the temerity to stand for Parliament against his landlord's interest, and was subsequently dismissed when his lease ran out, were lessons which the majority of landlords heeded. The risk of dismissal for the average tenant farmer in Britain was less than the risk of bankruptcy or the risk of eviction for execrable husbandry.[9]

Victorian tenant farmers paid for access to the resource of land itself. Applications to occupy farm land generally outreached its supply, and in most agreements to hire land a premium was levied, latently or quite openly, on its scarcity value. Offering holdings to tender was disapproved of by many agents and proprietors, but before the late 1870s it was a successful method of raising the level of rents in several instances. In the buoyant years from 1853 to 1873 most of the larger or better managed estates enjoyed a waiting list of promising applicants, so that sitting tenants had to be circumspect in their dealings with the estate administration, particularly in chaffering over rent and expenses. This sellers' market was seldom exploited to the full, and during the 1880s across the lowland zone of the island its metamorphosis to the tenants' advantage reinforced the message that good relations between owners and occupiers depended upon trust and fair dealing. Rents for the most part were determined by the soil, by the state of prices and the nature of production rather than by the simple willingness of tenants to pay a particular sum of money.

Interest on landlords' capital was a major element in rent. Interest, indeed, probably accounted for at least three-fifths of average rents in the middle and later nineteenth century.[10] The landlord's provision of buildings, drains and fences was the principal justification in contemporary eyes for his control over farm land. Without his contribution the need to improve fixed equipment must have been met from other sources, from central government or from the banks, since the majority of occupants would have had insufficient funds from savings for such extensive capital formation as was achieved before 1914. Landlords were regarded by many farmers as desirable creditors, partly because the latter benefited directly from the fashion for conspicuous investment in agricultural estates, but chiefly because estate administrators were generally less exacting in their terms than institutional lenders. Between 1840 and 1880 the fashion for expensive buildings and drainage was such that few freeholders could have matched even by borrowing. Needless to say many tenants did not enjoy the almost perfect amenities offered by a Bedford, a Leicester or a Yarborough, but between 1850 and 1875 even the more backward estates began the process of modernizing their fixed equipment.

The formal distinction between landlord's and tenant's capital was seldom maintained in practice. The system was essentially flexible. Some landlords preferred low rents and little investment, leaving most of the improvement to the occupier; others shared the costs of fixed investment by providing materials while requiring their tenants to pay for the labour. There were, however, many variations of practice, most of which allowed the farmers some initiative or charged them for part of the expenditure. A legal impediment (quidquid solo plantatur solo cedit), whereby a tenant's fixtures became the property of the landlord, did not hinder their efforts, because landlords seldom demanded their full rights at law, even against yearly tenants. This was important because with the decay of lease-holding, except in Norfolk and the Lothians, farmers' capital investment was largely unprotected. In due course systems of tenant right, by which outgoing tenants were recompensed for unexhausted improvements, developed outside the common law, especially in progressive regions such as Yorkshire and the east Midlands. Eventually the law was brought up to date, in 1875, 1883 and 1906, after which sitting tenants enjoyed enforceable rights against landlords or their successors. Yet without their contribution to estate capital formation the quantity and quality of fixed equipment would have been less impressive. The landlords played the leading role before 1880, and in the last twenty years their need to retain sound tenants compelled them to shoulder almost all the burden of new investment. At the same time, landlords resumed another responsibility as creditors, that is, of supporting their farmers' business by remitting or abating rents, which had seldom been necessary in the 1850s and 1860s.[11]

Owners and occupiers were also enmeshed together in the observance of rules which governed the cultivation of the soil. The landlord's long-term guardianship of his estate led him to limit the liberty of the farmer to manage his holding as profit or short-run advantage might dictate. The long lease devised in the eighteenth century had laid down the ground rules of good husbandry, but fell into disfavour in the early nineteenth century. By 1850 the majority of British tenants were governed by yearly lettings. The effective difference, however, was insignificant, despite James Caird's opinion that the best husbandry depended upon the institution of long leases.[12] The essential point is that most annual tenants enjoyed security of tenure, even from one generation to another. For example, the stability of tenants on the Yarborough estates in Lincolnshire between 1815 and 1914 was almost exactly the same as on the Leicester estates in Norfolk, where lease-holding was maintained. Moreover, annual tenants were often bound by the same rules of management as lessees. Some husbandry clauses were regarded by many farmers as being too rigid, and several landlords certainly preferred standardized régimes of husbandry to arrangements to suit individual tenants.

IV

Central as was the relationship between farmers and landlords, it was not all-consuming. The countryside was still densely populated, and the farmers' connections with the clergy, trades people and professional advisors, and above all with the rural poor, were equally involved and significant in their daily lives. Most British rural parishes reached the peak of their population in 1851 or 1861, and although the decline before 1901 was often quite marked, rural society even in Edwardian England was occupationally and economically more diverse than has been the case since motor transport and commuter living altered the demographic balance of the countryside. The farmers were outnumbered by their labourers, and in many rural districts even by the rest of the gainfully employed population, but the largest proportion of the merchants and professional persons who still lived in the villages and small towns depended upon the prosperity of agriculture for their own livelihood. The wheelwrights, blacksmiths, millers, innkeepers, auctioneers, land agents and solicitors of Britain's villages could not have flourished as they did without the business generated by the farmers. Early Victorian Britain in its rural setting was still essentially dependent upon handicrafts. Distributing and processing the produce of agriculture remained trades of major importance because so much of the goods and raw materials consumed in nineteenth-century Britain was still obtained from British farms. That the share supplied by foreign producers increased notably after 1850 is significant both for the development of domestic agriculture and for the changing structure of the agricultural service industries, but even in 1890 the connection between production and distribution or processing in British agriculture remained close. In 1850, however, farmers still sold their produce at local marts or to local dealers, and still also acquired their leanstock, seeds, horses or tools within a similarly restricted horizon. Smiths were still called upon to make or alter implements or hand tools. It is naturally not an accident that the majority of the agricultural engineers who set up in business on a larger scale between 1770 and 1870 had begun as blacksmiths.

Farming families were also important consumers of retail goods, and in every village there were grocers, shoemakers and tailors, even, in a few, drapers, wine merchants and furniture brokers, whose businesses throve upon a clientele of farmers. Even country butchers depended upon slaughtering other men's fatstock for a good part of their income. The entirely self-sufficient farmer still existed in 1850 but he represented a dying species of peasant. During the period of fairly general prosperity from 1853 to 1873 much was achieved in rebuilding or modernizing country towns or large villages. New houses, shops, workshops, warehouses and public buildings were erected in such profusion, especially in eastern Britain, that the outward appearance of many of our small towns is essentially mid-Victorian still. The process continued much more circumspectly after 1880. The local vitality of rural society was ebbing, for with the decline of population, the small world of traditional economic and social relations passed away. Decay, however, was matched by a trend towards business concentration, with economies of scale that broke down the old, disaggregated pattern of village economic connections. The common complaint that village shops were full of foreign products was interpreted as part of this malaise, but it should be taken equally to represent the first triumph of mass distribution in the British countryside.[13]

The emergence of large commercial firms handling milk, malt, bread-flour, and on the other side of the equation, producing and marketing fertilizers, feedstuffs or agricultural machinery, affected the whole framework of rural society, modifying farmers' relations with their suppliers or merchants and undermining the livelihood of small country tradesmen. In milling, for example, two influences were at work from the 1860s, first the ever-increasing proportion of British bread-grains imported from overseas, which tended to concentrate the new industry in seaports near the chief centres of consumption; and second, the introduction into Britain of roller-grinding by entrepreneurs such as Joseph Rank, who not only stole a march upon competitors but were better able to exploit the supplies of hard Indian, American and Canadian wheats. By 1900 flour-milling in Britain was becoming concentrated in the mills of a few large firms, to which specialist corn merchants such as Quinton of Needham Market or Brooks of Manningtree were delivering great quantities of British grain. Furthermore, many middle-sized corn dealers, like R. & W. Paul of Ipswich, were also maltsters and feed compounders in quite a large way by the end of the century. A town like Ipswich, indeed, represented the new order of agricultural merchanting very well. It contained millers, maltsters, agricultural engineers and milling engineers whose activities were very far removed from the millers and blacksmiths of Suffolk but a generation before.

The mechanization of British farming after 1860, and especially after 1880, was carried out through the agency of a few large firms and several smaller ones, whose interests were technically diverse and often international in scope. The small village craftsman survived the onslaught of British and American engineers, chiefly because he had adapted to repair or modify implements in the field. Whatever the farmers' views of machinery—and many resented it because of the high cost of mechanization relative to labour—machines and the network of distribution to supply and service them were part of the life of the larger commercial farmers by 1890. Moreover, the spread of expensive machinery gave rise to another rural occupation, that of the contractor who offered the use of cultivating or harvesting machines, particularly threshing boxes, and thereby spread the influence of mechanization further down the social scale.

The reorganization of the agricultural service industries did not coincide with a further bout of farm amalgamations. Big commercial farmers who had dominated the market for their produce and by their requirements in 1840–50, were less well placed by 1890–1900 to make bargains with their merchants. Co-operation was slow to take root in Britain, partly because of the prop of landlordism, but chiefly because there was little official encouragement for, and a good deal of individual apathy or opposition to, conjoint marketing. Only in 'residual' peasant areas, especially in the pastoral highland zone, did co-operative creameries become established before 1900, although the Irish example and Danish competition were constantly reiterated by enthusiasts such as Sir Horace Plunkett.[14] The problem was less serious than it might have been because the extension of rural railways and the growth of large firms in the processing industries tended to increase the demand for farm produce, even for cereals. In the particular case of potatoes, indeed, the decline which was observed about 1870 amid rising living standards was reversed by the efforts of entrepreneurs such as William Dennis of Kirton, Lincolnshire.

The influence of the railways upon the farmers was not completely beneficial. Rail transport did more than any other innovation of the age to create a national and international market for primary products. Without cheap rail transport in the New World the possibilities opened up by the free trade in grain and wool, and subsequently in meat and other products, would have been much more limited. Nevertheless, the economy of free trade which so aggrieved farmers was assisted by, not dependent upon, the innovations made in international transport, though home producers confronted with better or cheaper imports often confused cause and effect. Moreover, rail transport at home not only speeded up the process of rural depopulation, taking many of the better labourers and their families away from the land, but it also offered employment to countrymen. Again, railways were not the cause, merely the most effective means, of townward migration. The positive contribution of railways within Britain was particularly marked in the re-organization of the distributive network of the agricultural economy. Rail transport made it possible for producers quite remote from centres of consumption to concentrate upon perishable commodities—liquid milk, vegetables, soft fruits—so that specialized areas of production—fruit farming in the Carse of Gowrie, around Wisbech, and in the Vale of Evesham, for instance, or market-gardening in the Fylde or the fens—developed to supply the extensive new market for protein-based or green foodstuffs after 1860. Furthermore, the business of grazing, or livestock feeding and breeding, was changed with the expansion of rail carriage for live animals. Not only were the ancient droving trades modified by the railways, but new opportunities were opened up, as in the growth of the trade in Irish, and even in Canadian, leanstock after 1870. Farmers accepted the railways as a necessary adjunct of progress in Victorian Britain. There was little adverse criticism expressed about their economic role, for on balance railways probably improved and even cheapened the supply of farmers' goods; but in the case of particular railways local farmers were found in opposition to companies' construction plans, for permanent ways occupied useful agricultural land, and the farmers were as shortsighted as most in defending their vested interests.

The commercialization of agricultural marketing was obviously not complete by 1900, but the widening of the farmers' relations with merchants as well as with landlords was generally tempered by the influence of the proliferating army of representatives and local agents. The personal element was valued particularly because too few farmers kept adequate accounts and they seldom entered willingly into correspondence. The travelling salesman and the local dealer thus acted as a direct personal link in the lengthening chain of economic relationships between primary producer and distributor. Rural life retained much of the personal and parochial character which had distinguished village society for centuries. The social intercourse of farmers and labourers, tradesmen, clergy and so forth was bounded by a restricted horizon as late as 1900. Contact with church, chapel or school, interest in the affairs of the vestry or a local club, parochial alliances and antipathies, were the sum of the social activities of the majority of British agriculturists.

V

Victorian farmers were socially too diverse for a completely valid generalization to be made in a few words about their relationship with the church. Relations with the established church were sometimes very strained, especially in regions where the general population belonged to a religious denomination different from that of the official incumbent or minister.[15] This 'Irish' problem was rooted also in parts of Britain, in west Wales, in Shetland and in the Catholic parts of the Highlands, and was aggravated by ethnic differences. In Wales, for instance, the Anglican clergy represented an alien elite whose demands affronted the Nonconformist traditions of the common farmers and others. Thus, those issues which everywhere were contentious, such as church rates and tithes, in Wales became matters to divide communities bitterly and even violently. Even in England many farmers were staunchly Methodist, and a few were Baptist or Congregationalist, their relationship with the Church of England uneasy if not antipathetic. In country districts the congregations of Wesleyan or other dissenting churches were frequently dominated by farmers whose authority resembled that exercised by their social peers in the parochial vestries. The wrangling over the control of education, over disestablishment or parochial organization took place in rural England as much as in the towns, while in Scotland the dissensions which rent the kirk also disrupted the rural calm of many agricultural districts. Even within the Church of England the conflicts between High and Low, between Tractarians and Evangelicals, had much the same effect of suspicion and acrimony. Farmers, as a group, allegedly also held serious reservations about the social role of many of their parish priests. The gentrification of the English church, almost complete by 1850, in itself caused difficulties of communication beneath the sacramental level, however loyally and selflessly many country priests laboured to serve their flocks. The strong feelings which many parsons expressed about the plight of the rural poor alienated them from the farmers, so much so that William Johnston believed the parson's hat was more often to be seen hanging in a cottage than in a farmhouse.[16] The parson's championship of rural education, his agitation for, or provision of, allotments, and at times his partisanship in such matters as the agricultural strike of 1872, were resented by many farmers, even indeed when they were loyal churchgoers. But the division among the farmers themselves on political, social and, above all, on religious lines reduced the threat of an open breach based merely upon class interests. It may be true that most Anglican farmers belonged among the better-off, socially pretentious strata of village society, while the bulk of Methodists, however rich, were less easy to assimilate into the traditional pattern of the rural hierarchy, but as a generalization it is deficient in most of the finer shades of social distinction which were well understood in the Victorian village.

Anticlericalism, nevertheless, was not strongly marked in English or Scottish rural society. Most of the conflicts were about particular issues or over personalities. Of the great issues, the duty of Nonconformists to pay church rates and the general obligation of tithes were the most important. Tithes posed a problem which the early Victorians purported to have solved, although since tithe charges were not exonerated before 1900 their payment continued to cause discontent in parts of rural England and Wales throughout the century. The Tithe Commutation Act of 1836 was intended to offer a standard system of levying tithes, to replace the variety of payments in kind or in money operated by local agreements. The commission established to discharge the provisions of the Act had largely completed its work by 1851. The plan was to commute tithe dues into an annual rent charge calculated on the basis of average prices over seven years. In operation it worked to the advantage of the farmers, for the base prices were low by the standards of the century, but in certain areas, notably in Wales, allegedly unfair assessments aggrieved the farmers and caused much unrest which culminated in the Rebecca Riots of 1842–3. But even in England the Tithe Commission could not smooth all anomalies. Before 1836 some parishes were already tithe-free, partly as a result of special dispensation but chiefly as a consequence of parliamentary enclosure, since numerous villages had solved their tithe problems by allocating land in lieu of the charge. After 1850 the ancient complexity and diversity of the tithe system had been amended to such an extent that during the years of general prosperity before 1880 conflict fell away. At the end of the century, however, the relative burden of the tithe rent-charge increased, especially in eastern England, and a new agitation for reform or exoneration began. This culminated in the so called 'tithe wars' of the 1920s and 1930s in counties such as Suffolk, from which emerged a plan for gradual exoneration after 1936. In Wales, where agriculture suffered less from the 'depression' of prices after 1873, the slow-burning antagonism between farmers and clergy or lay impropriators also flared up again towards the end of the century and led in its turn to disestablishment in 1914.

The parson's role as first or second gentleman in the Victorian village was not challenged by the majority of farmers. More often his position and his pretensions were ignored or disregarded. The average Victorian village had so many conflicts or suppressed discontents to divide or incense its people that the uneasy relations which existed between the parson and so many of his leading rate-payers were a matter of regret but not of surprise to contemporaries. Harmonious parishes did exist of course, but often only because the landlord had induced good feelings by force of his authority or by careful selection of the incumbents. Religion was too much a part of everyday life to be divorced from political or social differences.

The spread of rural education which was particularly active in the 1840s and 1870s owed little to the active support of farmers in general. Some farmers involved themselves in the building, equipping and staffing of parochial schools, and the denominational battle over control of rural schools brought a number of farmers into the fray who were perhaps uninterested in the principles of education. Rural education, however, was dominated by parsons and ministers, by aristocrats and gentlemen, by exceptional men whose passion for progress and reform was unbounded, not by the generality of country rate-payers. The well-to-do farmers educated their own sons (and daughters at times) within the established network of schools, especially in the country grammar schools, while before the 1870s the poorest farmers often vouchsafed no book-learning to their children whatsoever. Comparatively few farmers appear to have felt strongly that parish schools were an asset which would serve their interests. Indeed, for many the amenity of elementary education for their own kind was outweighed by the fact that educating the poor would give labourers false ideas of their worth and position in life. The majority of the farmers who ventured an opinion on the subject were scornful or even strongly antipathetic.

VI

Although we know comparatively little about the social life of Victorian farmers, for few have left accounts of their entertainments and opinions, most certainly revelled in outdoor activities.[17] Hunting, shooting and fishing were the most important pursuits, and despite the arrogation by the gentry of the best sporting amenities during the century, the increased leisure, social pretensions and access to inexpensive sporting equipment of the more affluent farmers encouraged their participation in field sports. The Game Laws, which had reserved to gentlemen of substantial means the right to kill both wild and preserved game, were modified in 1831, but even then few tenant farmers expected to receive the privilege of shooting over their own holdings unless they were so far from the headquarters of the estate that their game was not required by the gentry. In 1846 a select committee was informed that most of the bad feeling between landlords and tenants arose from game preservation, especially of rabbits and hares which damaged crops. It required another bout of prolonged agitation in the 1870s to produce the Ground Game Act of 1881, which authorized farmers to destroy rabbits and hares without their landlord's permission. Ground game, which caused so much strife between gamekeeper and poachers, between the rural poor and the country constabularies, was nevertheless of slight importance to many gentlemen, and long before the 1880s tenants were often allowed to take rabbits freely on their own holdings. Around mid-century the acquisition by farmers of sturdy and trustworthy guns, often of American manufacture, suggests that shooting, legally or illicitly, was a quite widespread pastime. A few of the most opulent were even invited to *battues* by enlightened landlords, such as the Earl of Yarborough. Exclusive rights attached to fishing, but since it was a less fashionable sport, licences to take fish in estate waters, except perhaps in the best trout or salmon streams, were more promiscuously granted.

Hunting was the great nineteenth-century field sport. It was, as some writers alleged, the cement which bound together countrymen of almost all ranks, one of the sturdiest props of the landed interest. Victorian fox-hunting was well organized, dominated by coteries of landed gentry and precisely stratified in social ranking. The great hunts of the Midlands were fashionable and attracted many scions of the beau-monde, but almost all hunts permitted or encouraged well-appointed farmers to ride with them. Throughout the hunting counties of England and Scotland, farmers and their peers, sometimes dressed properly in 'pink' but often in less aristocratic colours, turned out when they could. So many Midland and Yorkshire capitalist farmers bred hunters and carriage horses that a day's riding was an opportunity for self-advertisement as well as pleasure. But there was never a genuine freemasonry of the hunting-field in the fashionable hunts, and hence the characteristic mid-Victorian development of farmers' hunt societies, open to gentry and others, but not dominated by them. Hunting retained its hold on even the foot-weary followers who could not afford to turn out mounted, the smaller farmers and labourers for whom drawing a local covert was great entertainment.

Field sports unified Victorian countrymen in a common pleasure. Other leisure activities are less easy to select, for farmers differed as much in personal inclinations as they did in wealth and social standing. Gentlemanly households, like that of John Pullett in *The Mill on the Floss* or even that of Farmer Boldwood, resembled those of the country gentry or *haute bourgeoisie* of the age. Such farmers' daughters were young ladies, and their sons were often educated to the law or the church. Card parties, musical entertainments, refined reading, were part of their lives, as they were elsewhere in the upper reaches of Victorian society. But there were other rich farmers, like Tennyson's 'Northern Farmer' or Richard Jefferies's John Hodson, of simpler, more vernacular stamp, who had neither polite manners nor elevated tastes. Most farmers belonged in this class, and their free-time activities resembled those of the labourers and village tradesmen. For some, no doubt, the public house was their Mecca, for others the chapel, and the narrowness of their lives was a matter of condescending observation among gentlemen, journalists or large farmers. On the other hand, reading was certainly more extensive by the end of the century than it had been at the beginning. Country newspapers proliferated after 1855, and their attention to agriculture and local politics gave them a circulation which ran deeply into the rural population. Once upon a time, said J. C. Atkinson, the *Yorkshire Gazette* was passed from hand to hand among his farming parishioners until each copy fell to pieces.[18] By 1890 not only newspapers but magazines and broadsheets, some of them very lurid, could be found in even the remote farmhouse and cottage.

The newspaper merely reinforced what another custom among farmers had begun. The farmers' ordinary, offered at public houses in the country towns on market days, had long been used to make acquaintances and discuss prices and politics, and writers from Young onwards attended ordinaries to discover agricultural opinion. As an institution the ordinary was organized by the innkeeper and one or two leading farmers, so that it was easily converted into a vehicle of propaganda or persuasion. But market-day dinners were also enjoyable and companionable, and their influence in forming farmers' opinions deserves more attention from historians.

The social life of the Victorian farmer depended not a little upon the outward appearance of his life-style. Diet, dress and, above all, housing distinguished farm families as much as any other social group. The house, in some sense, exemplified the family. Nineteenth-century farmhouses varied from the picturesque antique to the most modern brick boxes. A rage for rebuilding on many of the greatest estates from about 1840 to 1870 was transmitted to less affluent properties in due course, but even in the 1860s many leading estates still contained farmhouses of old-fashioned pattern and inferior materials. Vernacular styles had all but ceased after 1750, except in the remoter regions, in favour of brick or dressed stone with tile- or slate-hung roofs, but everywhere in Britain there survived weatherboard, wattle-and-daub, cob, black-and-white and roughstone houses with thatched or shingled roofs which dated from an earlier period of extensive rebuilding between 1500 and 1700. Many of the smaller farmhouses were indistinguishable from cottages, cramped and inelegantly laid out. Indeed in the pastoral regions and the fenlands, where small farms still pre-

241

dominated, the accommodation of farmers was a matter of quaint curiosity or downright condemnation.

This, however, was only part of the story. On the soils adaptable to Victorian high farming a rebuilding programme of major importance was accomplished before the 1850s, whereas in the clays the comparative poverty of the arable farms did not warrant extensive expenditure by farmers or landlords until the next generation. On the other hand, one noteworthy result of large-scale parliamentary enclosure, especially in the midland counties, was the construction of new farmsteads in the 'ring-fence'. That is to say, the old village-centre sites were abandoned in favour of a new, more efficient layout. Many Victorian farms bore names redolent of their epoch of construction, Quebec, America, Bunkers Hill, Salamanca, Talavera, Waterloo, Balaclava. We need go no distance to find a splendid example of Victorian agricultural brick or stonework. The farmhouse, 'commodious and convenient', surrounded by sturdy foldyards, cart-houses, barns and stables built to last several life-times, was an emblem not only of agricultural prosperity but also of proprietorial pride and ostentation. The farmhouses occupied by affluent tenants at Woburn, Holkham or Brocklesby were fit for gentlemen. They typified an age in which well-to-do farmers had a large household of family and servants, and one in which material distinctions in standards of comfort and riches were no longer dependent upon the social order. Farmers were not gentlemen, but they could live like them. The reverse applied at the other extreme. There was no special cachet attached to being a farmer if you were poor.

It is probably best to assort British farmhouses into four categories from the standpoint of the late nineteenth century. First came the large, but diminishing, class of vernacular buildings, some of which were big, well-appointed and comfortable, especially in the 'wood–pasture' regions. Many old farmhouses had been converted into cottage tenements by 1850, partly as a result of consolidating holdings and partly because of the relocation of farmsteads after enclosure. Others had been modernized, refaced or rerooffed to increase comfort or reduce fire risks. In 1850 the majority of British farmhouses were in this category; by 1890 the proportion had fallen significantly. Next came eighteenth and early nineteenth-century houses in new materials, many built after enclosure but some merely the consequence of agricultural prosperity or landlordly concern in the years between 1690 and 1820. Third were the splendid and often extravagant houses built on the larger estates from 1830 to 1880, costing anything from £1,000 to £1,800. This fashion for 'high building' diminished after the 1870s as less money was available, but the visible remains of such work are still one of the most obvious features of Victorian farming life. Lastly, there was a large, undifferentiated class of more modest buildings, some constructed for small farms; others the work of particular owner-occupiers or tenants active in their own interest; yet others merely an expression of estate caution or poverty in providing new fixed equipment. Modest newly built farmhouses are everywhere in evidence from the period after 1830, as they were put up to replace dilapidated buildings or to satisfy the needs of medium-sized or small farmers. Such a farmhouse probably cost about £300 in 1850.[19]

By 1880 villages in which the farmyards still abutted onto the street in medieval style were few, as ring-fence farming became accepted as the standard of efficient management. But on clays or in backward areas generally, the impulse to remove the farmers out of the centre of parochial life was less potent, and old-fashioned villages such as Kirk Smeaton, Yorkshire, or Brooke, Norfolk, still retained several features of their ancient inheritance into the twentieth century.

VII

The position of farmers in Victorian society at large changed as the prospects and contribution of agriculture changed. From its place at the head of the British economy in 1837, agriculture had declined sharply in relative importance by 1901. The contraction of agriculture owed something to the setbacks which afflicted arable husbandry after 1875, but it was chiefly the result of steady expansion in other sectors of the economy. The number of farmers indeed remained surprisingly stable after 1851 while the number of labourers declined significantly, a development which had a direct bearing upon the cultivation of the soil. The area of agricultural land had fallen by at least 1.5 million acres between 1830 and 1900, chiefly because of the spread of the built-up area. More important, however, was the much enlarged dependence upon foreign produce, even of products from temperate climates, which weakened the political and social significance of the farmers of Britain. Caird believed that about 21 per cent of our food supplies were imported in 1876, whereas forty years before the figure was probably only about a quarter of this. By 1909–13, 60 per cent of all British food consumption was imported.[20] Victorian agriculture continued to be efficient to the end, and the farmers were able to conduct a successful political lobby on many minor issues which concerned them. But on the great questions of protection and rural education the farmers' interest had been ignored or discounted in favour of larger political issues. This was not simply the outward sign of decay. It betokened a much more fundamental shift from a rural and agricultural to an urban and industrial society, in which the place of the farmer, in every sense, was bound to change. More remained of the lineaments of Victorian farming society in 1900 than the relative position of agriculture in the economy implies, for the complete absorption of agriculture into the framework of an industrial society was delayed until the Second World War; but the rural economy of the 1890s was no longer essentially hand-wrought and personal.

Notes

1   Colin Clark, 1973, ch. 3.
2   Census of 1851, 1854; BPP 1886 [C. 4848]; 1890 [C. 6144]; Sidney, 1848, 4; Craigie, 1887; Grigg, 1963; Whetham, 1968; Phillips, 1969.
3   James Caird, 1878a, 300.
4   Sturmey, 1968, 283–6.
5   Mechi, 1845; 1859.
6   G. P. Jones, 1962; Farrell, 1974, 418.
7   From author's unpublished data.
8   McConnell, 1891; Lorrain Smith, 1932.
9   Davis, 1972; Olney, 1973; Crosby, 1977.
10 R. J. Thompson, 1968, 79–81; Bellerby, 1968; Clark, 1973, ch. 6.
11 F. M. L. Thompson, 1963, chs 9–11; R. J. Thompson, 1968, 79–81; Holderness, 1972a; Perren, 1970; Grigg, 1963; Perkins, 1975a.
12 Caird, 1968, 27, 145, 347.
13 Graham, 1892; Haggard, 1906b; Sturt, 1912.
14 Digby and Gorst, 1957; Coleman, 1871; Pratt, 1906.
15 G. Kitson Clark, 1973; Evans, 1976, chs 6–7; 1975; Dunbabin, 1974; Johnston, 1851, II, 48; Ward, 1965.
16 Russell, 1965–7; Hurt, 1961; 1968.
17 F. M. L. Thompson, 1963, 137–50.
18 Atkinson, 1891, 16.
19 Barley, 1961; Harvey, 1970; Peters, 1969; Denton, 1864.
20 James Caird, 1878a, 283; Flux, 1930, 541.

18 Agricultural Societies*

Nicholas Goddard

I

Institutional means for the promotion of agriculture originated, in England and Wales, during the second half of the eighteenth century, although the Royal Society, founded in 1660, had given attention to agriculture in its early years.[1] The Society for the Encouragement of Arts, Manufactures, and Commerce—generally known as the Society of Arts—was established in 1754, and the fostering of agricultural innovation was one of its prime objectives well into the nineteenth century.[2] At the national level the first institution to be devoted entirely to agriculture and allied topics was the Board of Agriculture (1793–1822). Best remembered for its county reports, the board engaged in a variety of projects connected with rural economy.[3] Despite its official status and government financial support, the Board acted as a private body; it failed to give any marked direction to agricultural progress, having insufficient resources, and lacked the confidence of the agricultural community, which distrusted its links with government, however tenuous these may have been. Its successor was the Royal Agricultural Society of England, established on rather different lines in 1838, and the premier agricultural institution in Victorian England. The Smithfield Club, founded in 1799, was concerned with stock. Its principal activity was the annual pre-Christmas show, an important event for many farmers as, indeed, it still continues to

*I am grateful to Dr H. S. A. Fox of the Department of English Local History, University of Leicester, for allowing me to see the text of his paper 'Local Farmers' Associations and the Circulation of Agricultural Information in Nineteenth Century England' in advance of publication, and to Mr C. J. Warne, Map Librarian, School of Geography, Cambridgeshire College of Arts and Technology, for cartographic assistance.

245

be.[4] The London Farmers' Club, founded in 1842, provided modest club accommodation and held monthly discussion meetings on agricultural topics with particular regard to matters affecting the interest of tenant farmers.[5] In addition to these national institutions, there were numerous local agricultural organizations in Victorian England. These originated in the late eighteenth century, but underwent a remarkable expansion in early Victorian times; the nearly one hundred local societies recorded in 1835 (Map 18.1) experienced four-fold increase over the next ten years, and by 1855 the number of local agricultural institutions was put at seven hundred.[6]

The national and local agricultural organizations of Victorian England had the same general objectives, but there were differences in emphasis. The Society of Arts had been concerned with invention, innovation and improvement which it sought to secure by offering prizes—'premiums'—for items specified on annual lists, and by promoting the spread of information by publication; and the Royal followed this pattern. Local organizations also offered premiums, but these were more usually for excellence than invention. Prizes awarded at the shows, their most important activity, were given for stock, crops and skills, and extended to farm servants as well as the members. The acquisition and evaluation of information was an important function of local agricultural bodies, and they also had a strong social role, their shows, gatherings and dinners being a much valued part of Victorian rural life. Organizations at both national and local levels had the political objective of influencing the legislature which was generally seen as hostile to the agricultural interest, and towards the end of the nineteenth century farmers' organizations with commercial functions became established.

II

The Royal Agricultural Society of England was the outcome of a suggestion made by Earl Spencer at the annual dinner of the Smithfield Club in 1837.[7] Much of the credit for the foundation of the English Agricultural Society (as it was styled until 1840) belongs to William Shaw, who had consistently advocated such an institution through the medium of the *Mark Lane Express*, the main agricultural publication of the day, which he edited. He had approached Spencer in 1837 through Brandreth Gibbs, secretary to the Smithfield Club,[8] and Shaw acted as secretary of the new society until 1840. Although a number of objectives were published by the English Agricultural Society,[9] the fundamental concern was the application of science to agriculture, embodied in the motto 'Practice with Science', prompted by a realization of the great potentialities of science for raising agricultural productivity. Spencer considered that agriculture in 1837 was still in its infancy, while Henry Handley, one of the chief promoters of the new society, declared that science was the pilot that must steer them into those 'hitherto imperfectly explored regions'.[10]

The Royal held an annual country meeting, and the publication of its *Journal*

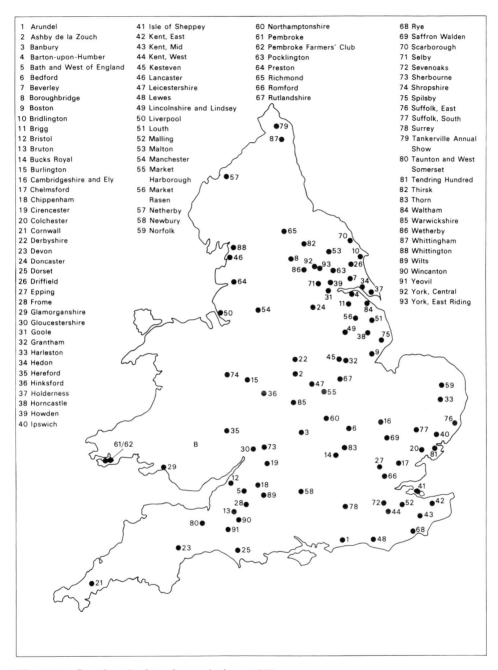

1 Arundel	41 Isle of Sheppey	60 Northamptonshire	68 Rye
2 Ashby de la Zouch	42 Kent, East	61 Pembroke	69 Saffron Walden
3 Banbury	43 Kent, Mid	62 Pembroke Farmers' Club	70 Scarborough
4 Barton-upon-Humber	44 Kent, West	63 Pocklington	71 Selby
5 Bath and West of England	45 Kesteven	64 Preston	72 Sevenoaks
6 Bedford	46 Lancaster	65 Richmond	73 Sherbourne
7 Beverley	47 Leicestershire	66 Romford	74 Shropshire
8 Boroughbridge	48 Lewes	67 Rutlandshire	75 Spilsby
9 Boston	49 Lincolnshire and Lindsey		76 Suffolk, East
10 Bridlington	50 Liverpool		77 Suffolk, South
11 Brigg	51 Louth		78 Surrey
12 Bristol	52 Malling		79 Tankerville Annual
13 Bruton	53 Malton		Show
14 Bucks Royal	54 Manchester		80 Taunton and West
15 Burlington	55 Market		Somerset
16 Cambridgeshire and Ely	Harborough		81 Tendring Hundred
17 Chelmsford	56 Market		82 Thirsk
18 Chippenham	Rasen		83 Thorn
19 Cirencester	57 Netherby		84 Waltham
20 Colchester	58 Newbury		85 Warwickshire
21 Cornwall	59 Norfolk		86 Wetherby
22 Derbyshire			87 Whittingham
23 Devon			88 Whittington
24 Doncaster			89 Wilts
25 Dorset			90 Wincanton
26 Driffield			91 Yeovil
27 Epping			92 York, Central
28 Frome			93 York, East Riding
29 Glamorganshire			
30 Gloucestershire			
31 Goole			
32 Grantham			
33 Harleston			
34 Hedon			
35 Hereford			
36 Hinksford			
37 Holderness			
38 Horncastle			
39 Howden			
40 Ipswich			

Map 18.1   Local agricultural associations, 1835

Source: *Agriculturist*, 2 January 1836
Note: This source is incomplete, the Brecknockshire Society (B) founded in 1755 and the Faversham Farmers' Club (F), being examples of local associations omitted.

began in 1840 under the editorship of Philip Pusey. The show was held on a peripatetic basis, a centre being chosen each year from a series of nine districts established in 1841 which were visited in rotation; Brandreth Gibbs was director of shows until 1875. That the annual show be held away from London was seen as essential in order to achieve the identification with the rural community that the Board of Agriculture had lacked, to bring innovations to the attention of those who would not otherwise come in contact with them, and to generate enthusiasm for improvement. Thus it was hoped that the first meeting, held at Oxford in 1839, would 'rouse the spirit of emulation in Oxfordshire and adjoining counties the beneficial effects of which will . . . be markedly perceived long ere the period for holding another meeting in that neighbourhood shall arrive'.[11] The award of prizes was seen as a key means of stimulating advance, especially in agricultural engineering.

Table 18.1 *Location and attendances at the Annual Show of the Royal Agricultural Society, 1860–1902*

1860	Canterbury	42,304	1882	Reading	82,943
1861	Leeds	145,738	1883	York	128,117
1862	Battersea	124,328	1884	Shrewsbury	94,126
1863	Worcester	75,807	1885	Preston	94,192
1864	Newcastle	114,683	1886	Norwich	104,909
1865	Plymouth	88,036	1887	Newcastle	127,372
1866	No show—cattle plague		1888	Nottingham	147,927
1867	Bury St Edmunds	61,837	1889	Windsor	155,707
1868	Leicester	97,138	1890	Plymouth	97,141
1869	Manchester	189,102	1891	Doncaster	111,500
1870	Oxford	72,053	1892	Warwick	96,462
1871	Wolverhampton	107,519	1893	Chester	115,908
1872	Cardiff	85,185	1894	Cambridge	111,658
1873	Hull	104,722	1895	Darlington	100,310
1874	Bedford	71,989	1896	Leicester	146,277
1875	Taunton	47,768	1897	Manchester	217,980
1876	Birmingham	163,413	1898	Birmingham	98,278
1877	Liverpool	138,354	1899	Maidstone	68,393
1878	Bristol	122,042	1900	York	87,511
1879	Kilburn	187,323	1901	Cardiff	166,899
1880	Carlisle	92,011	1902	Carlisle	88,895
1881	Derby	127,996			

Upwards of 20,000 people attended the Oxford meeting, but the Royal Show really blossomed as a mass spectacle in the 1870s and 1880s. Table 18.1 indicates the location and attendance at the shows from 1860 to 1902; in 1903 the peripatetic principle was abandoned for three years in an unsuccessful attempt to establish a permanent London showground. The attendances demonstrate one of the problems of the Royal:

as the shows became more complex, a good attendance was essential to guard against financial loss; this could be secured by holding the show near a large urban centre, but most benefit would accrue if it were held in a rural district. Success tended to depend on the location of the showground with regard to transport and accessibility, and also upon the weather. In this latter respect it was a disaster that the third largest attendance was achieved in the notoriously wet year of 1879. As Joseph Darby reminisced in 1902,

> Everyone who visited Kilburn retains vivid recollections of its incessant downpours; of the planks laid down in the leading avenues and without which they would have been perfectly impassable . . . one man slipped and falling between two of the planks, was so tightly wedged that it was difficult to pull him out . . .[12]

As the size of the shows increased—the twenty-three implement stands at Oxford had increased to 11,878 exhibits at Kilburn—organization became a problem. A particular difficulty surrounded the question of implement trials: new ploughs were not the best for demonstration, and trial grounds were not always representative of field conditions. Ill-conducted demonstrations could have a negative effect. Thus an open letter to Spencer from a 'Plain Derbyshire Farmer' in 1843 complained that ploughing trials had shown crooked furrows of irregular width and depth leading to ridicule by those hostile to improvement:

> 'Well, we are satisfied with our old ploughs now, eh, mates?' was a constant question, 'Why, I think we shall go home contented' the nearly uniform answer, whilst at every turn some lusty sexagenarian was seen instructing his chubby-faced nephews in the danger of novelty.[13]

Various remedies were tried to improve the arrangements, such as deferred and extended trials, but the problems were extremely difficult to resolve and were exacerbated when steam tackle underwent evaluation in the 1850s and 1860s.

Dissatisfaction with the trials, together with criticism of the prize system, led to strained relations between the Royal and implement manufacturers which reached a peak when most major firms boycotted the Canterbury Show of 1860. They claimed that the necessity to compete led to considerable expense, the prize system had outlived its usefulness and there was too much stress on novelty.[14] Awards made too great a distinction between the winner and the rest, and the variations between the ploughs of the major firms were so small that it was impossible 'to fish out the microscopic differences that may exist'.[15] Competitive trials were said to produce implements that won prizes but were unsuited to normal work,[16] and the degree to which the awards of the society could be considered a guarantee of excellence was questioned.[17] This point was forcibly illustrated by J. C. Morton who cited the case of a manufacturer who had seen his sales fall yearly despite receiving the highest accolades, only to regain sales when he reverted to the old, pre-prize, pattern, having been told by his workmen that he had been 'bamboozled' by twenty years of false leadership.[18] Most agriculturists preferred to keep the system; in its defence it was claimed that prizes allowed small firms to come to public attention and gave a degree of protection to buyers, a doubtful justification.[19] Above all, the Victorians relished the spirit of competition; of the larger societies, the Bath and West abolished competitive trials, the leading implement firms promising, in their place, to make up the finest collection of implements ever seen. Decreased attendance was thought to be a result of this change: 'Wells [1862] *was* the finest collection that was ever seen—and nobody came to see it!'[20] Absence of prizes meant a lack of spice; thus the Bath and West ploughing match at Taunton (1870) was like 'a salad without the dressing, an opera without the orchestra, or a battle fought with blank cartridge'.[21]

Stock exhibits were also an important feature of the Royal Shows as well as of the Smithfield Club and its provincial counterparts, such as the Birmingham Agricultural Exhibition Society and the Leeds Smithfield Club. The utility of these shows was restricted by the fashion for large, over-fed beasts, whose carcase value was limited while the generative powers of breeding animals were frequently damaged through over-feeding. 'Whoever saw a well-made giant?' a writer asked in 1845;[22] but forty years later Thomas Plowman could still comment that 'prizes are frequently awarded to over-fed animals'[23] and the Royal was considered to have an undesirable influence in this respect.[24] There were notorious abuses, such as falsification of the age of pigs (by breaking and filing their teeth) at the Lincoln Show in 1854, and these proved very difficult to eradicate.[25]

The Royal was at the centre of much of the agricultural progress of the nineteenth century, though its record does not reveal that the full expectations of its founders were realized. In its early years the immense enthusiasm of men such as Spencer, Pusey, Handley and others saw the Royal through a variety of problems—organization of the shows, dissatisfaction with the stress on science[26] and criticisms of those who looked for a political stance. Thus the *Guide* to the Exeter Show of 1850 observed that

> those whose task it has been to guide its footsteps across the ploughed field
> of public opinion . . . have been astonished at the undeviating line that it
> has followed . . . pressing with equal ease over the clayey surface of bigotry
> and calumny and the light sandy alluvium of scorn and jest.[27]

However, after the death of Pusey in 1855, much of the pioneering spirit was lost. Charges of mismanagement were made, coming to a head in 1859 when James Hudson, secretary since 1840, was dismissed for embezzlement. It was considered that the proceedings were directed by aristocratic elements rather than the tenant farmers who had been among the chief supporters in the early 1840s. The council was dominated by too many 'dilettante' farmers and not enough 'practical men' and the society had become 'a comfortable club of fashionable amateurs';[28] this was the sort of criticism that had contributed to the demise of the Board of Agriculture.[29] Distance from the membership was manifested when P. H. Frere, almost unknown, was appointed *Journal* editor in 1860 (instead of J. C. Morton, the first choice of the agricultural community), and again when H. M. Jenkins was appointed joint secretary/editor in 1868 on the death of Frere, a move which involved the summary dismissal of Henry Hall Dare, who had acted as a most efficient secretary since 1860. The low value put upon the proceedings of the Royal at this time is illustrated by a report of a 'Wednesday Afternoon' at the society's headquarters, these being monthly occasions for members to present communications on agricultural topics:

> Nine out of ten of these Wednesday meetings resemble the Protestant Church in Ireland where Dean Swift began the service with 'Dearly beloved Roger'—members of the council . . . depart in haste and trepidation: for there was a rumour that Mr Edwin Chadwick was waiting . . . when he might report for the hundredth time . . . the value of sewage. The Journal Committee were . . . the first to vanish . . . Sir Watkin W. Wynn mounted his weight-carrier with the grim satisfaction of a man who has 'escaped'.[30]

It was fortunate that Jenkins exceeded the expectations of those who had criticized his appointment: in 1877 C. S. Read observed that 'the Society had woken up to its responsibilities'.[31] The prize for the best farm in the district of the show was a popular innovation in 1870, and libel actions connected with the society's condemnation of sub-standard animal-feed mixtures won sympathy.[32] The Royal engaged in a valuable series of experiments at Woburn after 1876 and the work done for members by the consulting chemist and botanist expanded. Membership, which had been at little more than 5,000 in the 1850s, exceeded 10,000 by the end of the 1880s. Despite this, the Royal lacked the intimate association with agriculture envisaged by the founders, and Sir Ernest Clarke, who succeeded Jenkins in 1887, was primarily concerned with its standing as a great national institution.[33] The shows tended to be fashionable society occasions, and the decision to establish a permanent showground was bitterly resented by the agricultural world, being attributed to the influence of the 'clique' who ran the society's affairs.[34]

III

Complementary to the Royal were the numerous regional and local institutions, ranging from major provincial societies to the humble village root-show. The Bath and West, founded in 1777, is the best-known of the provincial societies, revived in the 1850s by Thomas Dyke Acland after a period of decline in the early nineteenth century. Its annual show, held on a peripatetic basis throughout southern England, usually attracted attendances of around 50,000, with 110,000 at Bristol in 1874.[35] One of the most important features of the show was the working dairy, and dairy education was a significant part of the work of the Bath and West. Under the direction of T. F. Plowman the shows had considerable popular appeal in the 1880s and 1890s, and profits generated at centres such as Bristol were used to subsidize shows at more remote localities in southern England, enhancing their utility.[36] The northern provincial counterparts of the Bath and West were the Yorkshire, founded by Spencer in 1837,[37] which for some time had a larger premium list than the Royal, and the Royal Lancashire, founded in 1767, which held one of the largest provincial shows in Victorian England.

Although a visit to such events could be an important occasion to the Victorian countryman, the activities organized by the county or local society were of more immediate significance. Their phenomenal extension in early Victorian England has already been noted: in addition, institutions styling themselves farmers' clubs became popular. Before 1837 the only institutions with this name seem to have been at Pembroke and Faversham, but their number was estimated at over 150 in 1845.[38] The earliest were in east Suffolk where J. Allen Ransome gave encouragement to their formation;[39] the rapidity of their creation can be seen as a response to a desire to acquire information on rapidly changing techniques, and to assess the widely differing opinions in farming books and periodical publications by which 'many practical men are confused'.[40] The spread of farmers' clubs was given much encouragement by full reports of their proceedings in the press; so frequently did William Shaw stress their merits, that there were protests from the readers of the *Mark Lane Express*.[41]

In an important recent survey of the role of local associations in the spread of agricultural information in Victorian England, H. S. A. Fox has argued that the distinction between clubs and societies was not fundamental;[42] the clubs operated within a smaller compass and with more modest resources than the societies. While it is true that there was considerable overlap between the functions and methods of clubs and societies, the distinction between them recognized by contemporaries, who termed clubs 'another class of institution', is worthy of note.[43] As Charles Poppy, chairman of the Ashbocking Club in 1837, and a contemporary and correspondent of Arthur Young and Sir John Sinclair, observed: 'societies were established by the aristocracy for cattle shows, ploughing matches and for premiums to servants', and clubs could spread information to a 'tenfold degree' compared with such activities.[44] Farmers' clubs saw themselves as the rural equivalent to the urban mechanics' institutions, a manifestation of a desire for self-improvement[45] on the part of tenant farmers, often of very modest means. Tenants, it is true, belonged to societies and owners to clubs, but the latter served particularly to advance the cause of the tenant farmer. There were many variations in their character but regular discussion meetings and maintenance of agricultural libraries were the most important part of their activities in the 1840s while visits to well-known farms were sometimes arranged:[46] for example, the Maidstone Club visited Tiptree in 1847.[47]

Some societies also engaged in similar activities, but their emphasis and tenor could often be profoundly different. In one sense, they could be a means of maintaining the *status quo*, especially when dominated by landed proprietors, as they often were. Their paternal role in early Victorian England is typified by the award of premiums not only for labouring skills but also for good conduct: a usual prize was the award of a guinea or so to the labourer who had brought up the largest family without recourse to parochial relief. The *Mark Lane Express* was especially critical of what it termed the 'Tickle-me-Toby and I'll tickle you' system of the societies in which 'noble lords occupied valuable time lauding each other', although it perceived a more practical element coming into their proceedings during the 1840s.[48] This seemed to be lost again in the next decade when the clubs, as opposed to societies, were thought to be much more useful.[49] Long lists of toasts at dinners were especially criticized: 'some people feel that a great man cannot be made welcome without you give him a speech ... officious nobodies run in and out announcing that Lord Longyarn is in the yard or the rev. Mr Rigmarole is "coming" and down he goes for a speech accordingly'.[50] The *Mark Lane Express* looked to the day when such gatherings were presided over by practical farmers with 'County members and magistrates left and right if you please'.[51]

Premiums awarded at local shows were subject to much criticism; they could too often go to the man with the greatest resources, the gentleman or amateur[52] or the person who bought an ox one Christmas and could 'put it in an attic and show it for a prize next Christmas'.[53] The award of prizes by patent manure manufacturers, begun in the 1860s, could also have adverse effects, leading to the production of 'a huge overgrown monster root, consisting mainly of water and woody fibre, that will decay on the appearance of frost'.[54]

Despite such criticisms, the local show was a much-loved feature of the Victorian countryside. In October 1860 there were

> few country towns but are cognisant of some little bustle ... county people come rolling in ... the glimpse of an honourable M.P. is caught ... rosy, rural-looking clergymen hail each other from the opposite side of the street. There is obviously something going on, though not exactly in the town itself ... a well bred bang-tailed horse swings by ... following this ... at the entrance to a goodly sized close you are brought to stand and deliver—a shilling for the sight of the anniversary show of the Shire Agricultural Society.[55]

These shows were

> more than merely a display of fat beasts or the echo of fine speeches. The tastes of all are consulted. The use of a band is secured. There is a flower show in the next field and a poultry show in one corner of this ... 'the best dairy maid' has made up her mind to be married forthwith on the proceeds of her premium, and every young lady you know, with two or three hundred you don't, is going to the dinner![56]

There was such a proliferation of shows of all sorts in early Victorian England that there were calls for amalgamation, the established trend from the late 1850s onwards,[57] and the newer, larger societies often adopted the peripatetic principle. As some societies declined others came into prominence, and new societies were founded in the 1880s and 1890s, either out of defunct organizations or as completely new institutions; comparatively few had an unbroken existence throughout the period.

As for the clubs, these tended to have a more ephemeral existence, and it was often difficult to sustain them when the favourite discussion topics were exhausted.[58] J. C. Nesbit, an agricultural chemist, observed in 1854 how he had helped to form some fifteen or sixteen clubs but it was difficult to keep them going after the novelty had worn off, and half had failed after a year or two.[59] Morton observed in 1863 a decline in the number of clubs over the preceding twenty years.[60] Those that remained tended to broaden their activities, and responded to calls to embrace political topics in their discussion meetings.[61] Many of the seventy or so clubs that existed in 1900 offered local club accommodation and services to members such as coal and manure at discount prices and the maintenance of stud animals.[62]

Initially, the rules of clubs and societies often precluded discussion of political topics, though some societies were manipulated for political ends and affiliated with the Central Association formed in 1835. This apart from calling for continued protection, attributed much of the low prices for agricultural produce to Peel's Currency Act of 1819. The Central Association bitterly opposed the formation of the Royal,[63] whose rules excluded political matters from consideration; but those who looked to improved techniques rather than protection to secure adequate remuneration for agriculture were equally opposed to the Central Association, that 'political abortion, off-spring of a confederacy of bankrupt landowners, mercenary speculators, and merciless currency-mongers'.[64] Many local protection societies came and went; after the repeal of the Corn Laws in 1846 protection became a dead issue for a time, although longstanding grievances such as the malt-tax and hop-duty remained. There were also new issues, and questions raised by the outbreak of rinderpest in 1865 prompted the call in the following year for a farmers' league[65] to look after the political side of agriculture. The chambers of agriculture which resulted from the efforts of Charles Clay and others to secure this came to embrace the major political topics of the late nineteenth-century countryside, such as government policy on animal diseases and agricultural depression, local taxation and adulteration. Although there was occasionally alignment with farmers' clubs—the Central Chamber and London Farmers' Club held a joint annual dinner after 1894[66]— it was seen as desirable to maintain a division of function. As C. S. Read observed, farmers' clubs were 'chambers of the field', and chambers of agriculture 'chambers of the state'.[67] Chambers were often perceived to be dominated by landlords, an important motive for maintaining the separate identity of clubs,[68] and gave little attention to those matters that were of particular concern to tenant farmers, such as tenant-right and game laws. It was in response to this that the Farmers' Alliance was founded in 1879, particularly concerned to secure better representation of tenant farmers in Parliament.[69] In the face of increasing depression and dissatisfaction with the treatment of agriculture by both major parties, an Agricultural Union was launched by Lord Winchelsea in 1893 as an attempt to unite all agricultural classes to a common cause. After the death of Winchelsea in 1898, however, this organization became more concerned with co-operation. Although the Central Chamber gave consideration to the formation of a national agricultural party, it was not until the foundation of the National Farmers' Union in 1910, where voting membership was confined to tenant farmers and owner-occupiers, that a significant political voice emerged for agriculture.[70]

IV

The final type of farmers' organization in Victorian England was those with commercial objectives. In the twentieth century, co-operation in farming has become commonplace, to achieve economies of scale by the bulk-buying of farm inputs, in sharing machinery, and in the organization of marketing. A form of co-operation was pioneered by a farmers' club on the Scottish Borders in the late 1850s, which engaged in the bulk-buying of fertilizer,[71] and in England the Agriculture and Horticultural Association was founded by E. O. Greening in 1867, and the Aspatria Co-operative Society in 1869. In general, however, co-operation made slow advance. Lord Winchelsea founded the British Produce Supply Association in 1896, but progress in co-operation was most marked in the early part of the present century under the auspices of the Agricultural Organisation Society, founded in 1901.[72] Farmers preferred to act individually, and particularly disliked shared business arrangements, but organizations to promote the interests of particular branches of agriculture were well-established by 1900; among the more important of these were the British Dairy Farmers' Association (1875) and the Central Association of Dairy Farmers (1892) with local affiliated associations in most of the dairying districts, the National Hop Growers' Association (1894) and the National Fruit Growers' Association (1902), again with affiliated bodies in the fruit districts such as north-west Kent, Evesham and Wisbech.[73]

Map 18.2 shows the local associations in existence at the end of the nineteenth century; the impressive total of societies, clubs and chambers underestimates the continued vitality of agricultural organizations of all kinds for those of a more specialist interest, such as dairy farmers' associations, have been omitted, and most counties had several horse show societies and a bee-keepers' association. Co-operation made tardy progress, and farming lacked a strong political voice in Victorian England, as shown by the late abolition of the malt-tax as a budgetary measure rather than a concession to agriculture.[74] It is therefore to the broad educative and social roles of agricultural societies that we must look for their greatest achievement and influence in Victorian England. This is illustrated by some of the reaction to the early Royal Shows. In 1863 J. C. Morton cited a correspondent who wrote that he considered that the 1855 Carlisle meeting of the Royal

> was instrumental in opening the eyes of many of our Cumberland
> mechanics. Previous to 1855 our county was wont to boast of her
> ploughmen, but when it came to the test in Carlisle, we were well beaten on
> our own soil; not that our ploughmen were deficient in skill, but they had
> not the implements to work with.[75]

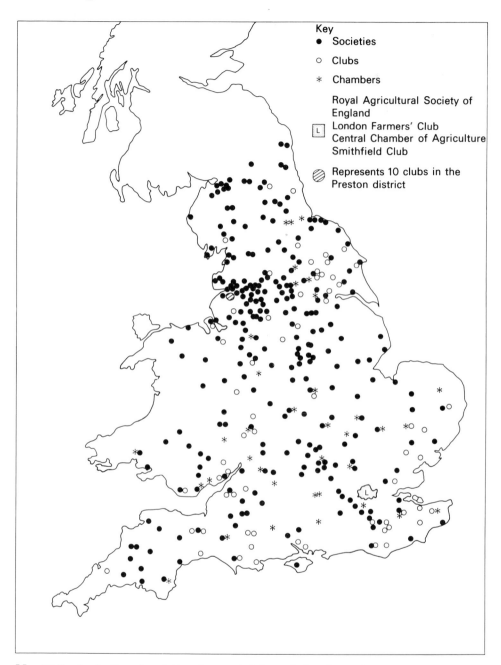

Map 18.2   Agricultural societies, farmers' clubs and chambers of agriculture *c.* 1900

Source: *British Yearbook of Agriculture*, 1908
Notes: 1 Area associations by residence of secretary
2 Regional federations:
(a) Lancashire and Cheshire Federation of Agricultural Societies, 1903
(b) Staffordshire Farmers' Association, 1897
(c) Yorkshire Union of Agricultural Clubs and Chambers of Agriculture, 1890

Again, looking back on Royal Shows in 1902 Joseph Darby, who first attended the Exeter show of 1850, could remember how the

> Party of Agricultural Young Englanders . . . looked to the Royal Shows with heart-thrilling enthusiasm for improved stock, machinery, and implements . . . at Salisbury [1857] there were feats of engineering to excite the emotions of the marvellous almost as much as magic.[76]

The influence of Royal Shows later declined with changing conditions: by the end of the century it was stressed that

> the man of to-day expects a great deal more for a shilling than did his father and grandfather before him. He is so accustomed to cheap excursions, both to seaside and country, that he is apt to laugh at the thought of paying a shilling for the privilege of walking about all day to inspect a lot of stock tied by their heads in sheds.[77]

Local shows, however, continued with unabated vigour, and although any consideration of local societies must not neglect their negative aspects, local associations of all types had a key role in the spread of information on agriculture, as recently outlined by Dr Fox. They could do much to raise the general level of farming in particular districts; the force of example, stressed the *Mark Lane Express*, was never so great as when brought to a man's own back door.

> When Smith sees what Browne who is only a tenant farmer like himself can do, he begins to consider if he, too, should not do a little more. By next year he will have a ram to show, a prize heifer to sell, or a speech to make, as a successful exhibitor, at the annual dinner.[78]

Participation by all classes in the varied activities of agricultural societies was a striking, indeed essential, feature of the Victorian Countryside.

Notes

1 For a survey of early institutional attempts to promote agriculture, see Middleton, 1912.
2 Wood, 1913, 114–42; Hudson and Luckhurst, 1954, 57–85.
3 Clarke, 1898; Mitchison, 1959.
4 Bull, 1926.
5 Fitzgerald, 1968.
6 Plowman, 1855, 380.
7 For a report of the dinner, see *Farmer's Magazine*, 1838, VIII, 47–8. For an account of the formation of the English Agricultural Society, see Clarke, 1890.
8 Bull, 1926, 10–11.
9 See Watson, 1939, 18–19; Hudson, 1972, 59.

10 Handley, 1838, 6.
11 *Mark Lane Express*, 30 July 1838.
12 Darby, 1902, 22.
13 *Mark Lane Express*, 24 July 1843.
14 Day, 1857; 'A Manufacturer', 1857.
15 J. C. Morton, 1863, 64.
16 *Ibid.*, 65.
17 Ransomes and Sim, 1862, 6.
18 Morton, 1863, 64–5.
19 H. S. Thompson, 1864, 13.
20 *Farmer's Magazine*, 1862, 3rd ser., XXII, 527.
21 *Farmer's Magazine*, 1870, 3rd ser., XXXVIII, 12.
22 Hincks, 1845, 14.
23 Plowman, 1886, 171.
24 *Farmer's Magazine*, 1861, 3rd ser., XIX, 299.
25 Watson and Hobbs, 1937, 207.
26 Peel, 1976, 11–12.
27 Jewitt, 1850, vii.
28 *Mark Lane Express*, 28 February 1859; S. Sidney at the half-yearly meeting of the society, *ibid.*, 28 May 1860.
29 Mitchison, 1959, 61.
30 *Farmer's Magazine*, 1861, 3rd ser., XIX, 495.
31 *Farmer's Magazine*, 1878, 3rd ser., LIII, 60.
32 For a report of the best-known case see *Journal of the Royal Agricultural Society*, 1872, 2nd ser., VIII, 481–685.
33 Watson, 1939, 167.
34 Stanton, 1902, 82.
35 Hudson, 1976, 230–1.
36 *Ibid.*, 150.
37 Fairfax-Blakeborough, 1936.
38 Plowman, 1855, 380.
39 *Farmer's Magazine*, 1857, 3rd ser., XI, 1–2.
40 Hincks, 1847, 17.
41 *Mark Lane Express*, 15 February and 1 March 1841.
42 Fox, 1979.
43 *Mark Lane Express*, 11 February 1839; Morton, 1863, 62–3.
44 *Farmer's Magazine*, 1838, VIII, 333; 1858, 3rd ser., XIII, 306–7 for memoir of Poppy.
45 *Maidstone Gazette*, 2 February 1841; *Mark Lane Express*, 15 February 1841.
46 Morton, 1863, 63.
47 Goddard, 1974, 81.
48 *Mark Lane Express*, 21 October 1839; 15 September 1845.
49 *Farmer's Magazine*, 1859, 3rd ser., XVI, 466.
50 *Ibid.*, 388.
51 *Mark Lane Express*, 14 March 1859.
52 'Agricola', 1842, 6.
53 Finney, 1860, 95.

54 *Farmer's Magazine*, 1863, 3rd ser., XXIII, 245.

55 *Mark Lane Express*, 8 October 1860.

56 *Farmer's Magazine*, 1861, 3rd ser., XX, 436.

57 *Mark Lane Express*, 8 October 1860.

58 *Ibid.*, 14 March 1859.

59 *Farmer's Magazine*, 1854, 3rd ser., V, 28.

60 Morton, 1863, 62.

61 *Farmer's Magazine*, 1852, 3rd ser., I, 431; 1861, 3rd ser., XX, 489.

62 *British Year Book of Agriculture*, 1908, 98–163.

63 Moore, 1965, 548.

64 *Mark Lane Express*, 22 January 1838.

65 Matthews, 1915, 392–4.

66 Fitzgerald, 1968, 99.

67 *Farmer's Magazine*, 1868, 3rd ser., XXXIII, 74.

68 *Farmer's Magazine*, 1869, 3rd ser., XXXV, 432–3; 1871, 3rd ser., XXXIX, 141.

69 *Farmer's Magazine*, 1879, 3rd ser., LVI, 28–9.

70 Orwin and Whetham, 1964, 314.

71 *Farmer's Magazine*, 1874, XLVI, 200.

72 Agricultural Co-operative Association, 1954, 2, 27; 1966, 3–4; Pratt, 1906; 1912.

73 *British Year Book of Agriculture*, 1908, 82–9.

74 Fitzgerald, 1968, 91.

75 Morton, 1863, 64.

76 Darby, 1902, 22.

77 Stanton, 1902, 80.

78 *Mark Lane Express*, 20 September 1858.

19   Agriculture and Science

J. D. Sykes

I

The alliance of science with farming practice became an established fact during the Victorian era. Much had gone before to establish the necessary foundations. The agricultural improvers had provided a convincing and extensive demonstration of the practical significance of new farming techniques during the eighteenth century and the more perceptive leaders of the agricultural and landed interest groups looked forward to the time when the 'principles of agriculture' could be established. As early as 1779 the Bath and West of England Society had commenced field experiments, the first in Britain, and by 1805 had formed a Committee for Chemical Research. Thus the first steps towards a scientific basis of agriculture were taken.

Scientists, too, were beginning to make progress. In France, Lavoisier (1743–94) had established a basis for the development of modern chemistry. His careful qualitative experiments destroyed the phlogiston theory and opened up the way for Dalton's atomic theory (1807) and for the eventual study of organic chemistry. In Geneva, De Saussure (1767–1845) was able to demonstrate the basic relationships between plant growth and oxygen, carbon dioxide, water, light and mineral requirements. The cause of agricultural science in Britain was advanced by botanists such as Erasmus Darwin (1731–1802), whose *Phytologia or The Philosophy of Agriculture and Gardening* was published in 1799, and by chemists such as Sir Humphry Davy (1778–1829). In a brilliant series of lectures given at the Royal Institution between 1803 and 1812 and published under the title of *Elements of*

Agricultural Chemistry (1813), Davy brought together much widely scattered information. He also developed a method of soil analysis which, despite its shortcomings, remained in use for several decades. In Davy's view the study of agricultural chemistry would elucidate the problems of 'the growth and nourishment of plants, the comparative values of their produce as food; the constitution of soils; the manner in which lands are enriched by manure, or rendered fertile by the different processes of cultivation'. He could neither foresee how long it would take to discover answers to these important questions nor appreciate the wide spectrum of scientific knowledge which would be involved in their solution.

Virtually a quarter of a century was to elapse between the publication of Davy's book and the beginning of the modern period of agricultural science. Lack of progress prior to Queen Victoria's reign was largely due to lack of organization and leadership and the severe depression which afflicted British agriculture with the ending of the Napoleonic wars. Just how science could meaningfully contribute to farming practice was uncertain.

Within a few years much had changed. The Royal Agricultural Society of England was founded in 1838 with 'the object of perfecting the System of English Agriculture the union of practice with science'. Able and energetic leaders emerged, such as Philip Pusey (1799–1855), landowner, editor of the society's *Journal*, and enthusiast for agricultural science. He believed that British agriculture could flourish without protection if it took advantage of all the new knowledge available to it. By 1845 systematic instruction in the principles of agricultural science, combined with practical aspects of farming, had become available following the founding of the Royal Agricultural College at Cirencester.

Whilst some may have expected that the application of 'science' was likely to provide ready answers to the problems of agricultural production, others remained sceptical. Liebig considered that many farming problems were 'capable of easy solution by well-known facts'.[1] Hudson more wisely informed the R.A.S.E. in 1842 that whilst the principles of inorganic chemistry were 'well established' and could confidently be expected to lead to a knowledge of the properties of soils, 'organic chemistry, a less perfect branch of the science—ultimately promises the most important results'.[2] Generally speaking, there was a lack of clear understanding of the nature of science and scientific method and of their inter-relationships with agricultural technology.

The depressed state of British farming in 1837 is vividly portrayed by Ernle. 'In gloom and depression', he says, 'agriculturalists entered upon a new reign', but, he continues,

> the new alliance of science with practice bore rich and immediate fruit. Science helped practical farming in ways as varied as they were innumerable. Chemists, geologists, physiologists, entomologists, botanists, zoologists, veterinarians, bacteriologists, architects, mechanics, engineers, surveyors, statisticians, lessened the risks and multiplied the resources of the farm. . . . The general level of agriculture rose rapidly.[3]

261

What science contributed to the early development of 'high farming' may be disputed. Perhaps the major part of the rise in output may be attributed more properly to technological advance, arising from the activities of practical innovators and the growth of experience based on trial and error. Many sought to develop more intensive farming practices, relying heavily upon purchases of feeding-stuffs to increase livestock numbers and the supply of farmyard manure. Caird observed that they were greatly encouraged by the 'general prosperity and growing trade and wealth of the country'.[4] He considered that much of the great expansion of agricultural output which occurred during the 1850s through to the 1870s was primarily due to mechanization, followed by the greater use of fertilizers and purchased feeding-stuffs. The real benefits of scientific research were yet to be realized.

II

The meeting of the British Association for the Advancement of Science held in 1837 at Liverpool was attended by Dr Justus von Liebig, Professor of Chemistry at the University of Giessen from 1824 to 1852. The discovery by Friedrich Wöhler in 1828 that urea, a typical organic substance, could be synthesized by purely inorganic reactions had shown that no 'vital force' was involved. Liebig had subsequently undertaken extensive investigations into organic compounds, and three years after his visit to Britain he published a book entitled *Organic Chemistry in its Application to Agriculture and Physiology*, dedicated to the British Association. It was an event of singular importance for the development of agricultural science and as a consequence of its wide circulation the book's influence was to be felt for several decades. As Hall observed, 'Liebig's brilliant essay excited universal attention and to a very large extent we can date modern agricultural science from this.'[5]

Liebig stated that the plant assimilated carbon from the air in the form of carbon dioxide and derived its hydrogen and oxygen requirements from the soil water. Nitrogen, he asserted, which was present in the air in the form of ammonia, was made available to the plant through rainfall. Since these elements were available in nature it followed, he argued, that organic fertilizer matter, such as farmyard manure, was superfluous. The mineral constituents of plant ash, such as potassium, sodium, calcium and phosphate, however, were insufficiently available to the plant due to slow weathering processes in the soil. Thus supplements were required which should be provided in the form of inorganic fertilizer matter. The exact requirements of each mineral could be determined, Liebig postulated, by comparison of the chemical constituents of the soil with plant ash. These views, later proved to be invalid in many important respects, yet propounded by one of the foremost men of science, clearly were of significance to farmers. They afforded a view of agriculture as a precise activity regulated by and responding to the exact rules of science. Moreover, they appeared at a time when new fertilizers were becoming available and drainage and improved cultivations gave promise of intensifying production to meet the growing market demand for food. 'The most urgent problem which the present day has to solve', Liebig himself said, 'is the discovery of the means of producing more bread and meat on a given surface to supply the wants of a consistently increasing population.'[6] 'Farmers already knew soot, bones, salt, saltpetre, hoofs and horns, shoddy and such substances as marl, clay, lime and chalk', Ernle observed. 'But they knew nothing of Nitrate of Soda, of Peruvian Guano, of superphosphate, Kainit, nitrate of potash, rape dust, sulphate of ammonia or basic slag.'[7] It fell to scientists, in particular John Bennet Lawes (1814–1900) and Joseph Henry Gilbert (1817–1901), working in partnership at Rothamsted, to establish what were sound manurial practices and eventually to explore wider dimensions of the role of chemistry in the service of agriculture. Inevitably they clashed with Liebig. He had shown what elements a plant requires and had prepared a catalogue of existing knowledge. But in attacking the humus theory through the exposition of his mineral theory, Liebig opened up an area for intense controversy.

J. B. Lawes, who owned an estate at Rothamsted near Harpenden, had studied under Dr Charles Daubeny (1795–1867), Aldrichian Professor of Chemistry and Sibthorpian Professor of Rural Economy at Oxford. As early as 1836 he had observed the use of bone dust on turnips; in 1839 he commenced studies on the use as a fertilizer of soluble phosphate, which had been derived from bones and mineral phosphate treated with sulphuric acid. Encouraged by the results he obtained patent rights covering the production of superphosphate of lime and of ammonia, etc., and he established a factory for their production at Deptford in 1843. When in the same year J. H. Gilbert joined Lawes at Rothamsted, the scene was set for a unique scientific partnership which lasted for fifty-seven years and which established Rothamsted Experimental Station as the foremost centre for agricultural science research.

Gilbert, who had studied chemistry at Glasgow and London and had worked with Liebig at Giessen, was almost a perfect foil to Lawes. According to Russell, 'he was a born student, much devoted to detail and meticulously accurate',[8] and he was somewhat of a martinet. He travelled extensively and regularly attended scientific meetings. His methodical approach ensured that the details of crop yields, chemical analyses and meteorological data were a complete record throughout the time he was at Rothamsted. Lawes, on the other hand, was gifted with shrewd scientific insight, was a capable organizer and business man, but was impatient of detail. He was a practical person with extensive experience of farming and field experimentation who found only limited interest in travel and public meetings. Both men were keen controversialists and soon were in dispute with Liebig.

Lawes mistrusted Liebig for his lack of experimental knowledge and of practical farming experience. 'The contempt which the practical farmer feels for the science of agricultural chemistry', he told the Royal Agricultural Society,' arises from the errors which have been committed by its professors.'[9] In 1849 he succeeded Liebig on the Chemical Committee of the Society. The principal grounds for dispute between Lawes and Gilbert and Liebig were: firstly, that atmospheric ammonia was insufficient to meet the plant's requirements for nitrogen; secondly, that the supply of mineral elements required for plant growth was not necessarily indicated by the ash content of the plant. Careful experimentation at Rothamsted had shown that the availability of mineral constituents in the soil was a variable but determinative factor. Similarly, it had been demonstrated that the provision of nitrogenous manures played a major part in determining crop growth except in the case of leguminous plants. Organic matter had a complex role affecting soil structure and the availability of nutrients required for plant growth.

The partnership of Lawes and Gilbert was productive over a wide field yet, as Dale observes, although 'the programme of Lawes and Gilbert in theory covered all branches of agriculture ... it was in fact confined to very definite problems—especially soil and crop problems; the source and fate of the nutrition of vegetation remained in one form or another the dominant interest'.[10] Close on two hundred scientific papers were produced, many representing years of continuous field experimentation. The classical experiments in Broadbalk Field on the manuring of wheat long outlived their initiators. According to Russell twenty years had passed before the first results of work which began in 1844 were published, and fifty years before a full account appeared.[11] It was considered essential to observe strict experimental procedures and—somewhat of a novelty—for plots to be of adequate size, as well as for trials to be repeated over a run of years. Inevitably the cost was appreciable, and by 1853 Lawes had spent some £10,000 on experimentation, according to Russell.[12] There was no state aid though some support was provided by the agricultural societies. Much of the work of analysis and recording was dull in the extreme but it was rigorously supervised by Gilbert. It took many years for many of the findings at Rothamsted to become widely known. Incorporation into farming practice was often slow and uncertain and this was increasingly so as farmers struggled against the deepening agricultural depression after the mid 1870s.

Towards the end of the nineteenth century, however, it had become evident that Lawes and Gilbert had made major contributions to the science of agriculture. Sir Henry Rew stated that 'the effect of the careful and patient labours of Sir John Lawes and Sir Henry Gilbert upon British Agriculture is beyond estimate. Their work has permeated farm practice and has influenced every phase of the cultivation of the soil and the treatment of livestock.'[13]

It fell to Daniel Hall (1864–1942), who succeeded Gilbert in 1902 as the new director of Rothamsted, to pronounce on the scientific achievements. In *The Book of The Rothamsted Experiments*, published in 1905, he brilliantly summarized the detailed work of the preceding sixty years. There existed, he wrote, 'records of the most astonishing completeness', and there was 'hardly any part of the science of the nutrition of the plant on which [the work] cannot be made to throw light'.[14] Section by section the experimental work was reviewed and its practical importance outlined with exceptional lucidity. Most of the research had been concerned with manurial and rotational investigations involving cereal crops, but there were also important trials on turnips, potatoes and sugar-beet. Much of the work was designed to disprove Liebig's mineral theory, but there were also studies of crop varieties and of the composition of wheat grain, barley and malt. Studies into problems of nitrogen availability had focused upon the process of nitrification in soils and the loss of nitrates in drainage waters. Attention had been given to leguminous crops though the Rothamsted research had not identified the process by which atmospheric nitrogen was 'fixed' by microorganisms living symbiotically with these crops. Hall also reviewed the work on grass crops, which had become increasingly important as demand had increased for livestock products and arable farming had declined in profitability. There had been pioneering work, too, into the chemical composition of cattle, sheep and pigs and into the value of different foods for livestock production. Although subsidiary to the work on crops and of less practical significance than studies eventually to be undertaken by scientists overseas, the results proved of great practical value for assessing the manurial residual value of foods fed to animals. The work of Lawes and Gilbert on the residual values of fertilizers was also of particular significance, providing a systematic approach to the compensation entitlement of farmers at the end of a farm tenancy. Hall concluded that

> the great object . . . of the Rothamsted experiments [was] to obtain knowledge that is true everywhere, and to arrive at principles of general application, leaving the farmer himself, through his more immediate advisers to adapt these principles to his own practical conditions and translate them into pounds, shillings and pence.[15]

Sir E. John Russell (1872–1965), who followed Sir Daniel Hall as Rothamsted's director, considered the period between 1855 and 1875 'the Golden Age of Rothamsted'. 'Lawes and Gilbert', he wrote in 1942, 'had amassed quantities of analytical data and set them out in a series of papers which have become classic and remain the best we have on their subject.'[16]

III

Although the veterinary arts had changed little between Roman times and the eighteenth century, considerable progress had been made towards the establishment of a veterinary profession by the time of Queen Victoria's accession. The need for a more enlightened approach to the diagnosis and treatment of disease and for a more extensive knowledge of animal physiology had become apparent by the mid-1700s. The farriers and cow leeches, men of limited education and often of mean status, proved increasingly less capable of treating the better bred and more valuable horses, cattle, sheep and pigs.

Although a farriery school was created at Knightsbridge in 1778, the early veterinary schools were established on the continent, the first being the college at Lyons founded in 1762. Between 1769 and 1798 no fewer than five schools were founded in Italy and seven in Germany.

The London Veterinary College was established in 1792. It largely came into being as a consequence of the activities of the Odiham Agricultural Society whose members sought 'to put a stop to the progress of . . . the quackery of farriery and to obtain . . . those real services which medical skill is capable of rendering to our cattle'.[17] The government provided generous financial support; no less than £25,000 was contributed between 1796 and 1813. Subsequently the college was financed by the fees of students, of whom there were about seventy in 1830, and by subscriptions from its members. Queen Victoria became the college's patron in 1838, from which date the name was changed to the Royal Veterinary College. Support came from the Royal Agricultural Society of England also, amounting to £200 in 1840. In Scotland, similarly, the Highland and Agricultural Society assisted with the financing of the Edinburgh Veterinary School, which had been established with William Dick as its principal. The schools each had similar problems besides finance. They were criticized for the type of students recruited, the shortness of their courses, their examination methods and the failure to teach certain subjects. Thus as late as 1829 the London course, which ran for one year, did not cover the diseases of cattle, sheep, pigs or dogs.

Improvements really date from the establishment of the Royal College of Veterinary Surgeons in 1844 which created a profession open only to the graduates of the London and Edinburgh schools. Certificate examinations conducted by the Highland and Agricultural Society and the Royal Agricultural Society of England were continued for several years, but they eventually disappeared as the professional courses became more scientific and of longer duration. The course for membership of the Royal College of Veterinary Surgeons was extended to three sessions in 1873, with an oral examination at the end of each. It was not until 1895 that a course lasting four sessions was introduced and a written examination also instituted.

The marked expansion in livestock numbers during the Victorian era, the development of new methods of production, such as in dairying, and the increased attention to the nation's health created important fields for the development of veterinary science and practice. More intensive production methods had proved conducive to the spread of disease, and growing imports of livestock added urgency to the need to control disease outbreaks of epidemic proportions. Foot and mouth disease, traced back to an importation to the Zoological Gardens at Regent's Park in 1829, had within twelve years spread throughout the kingdom. Pleuropneumonia, long known to exist upon the continent, made its first appearance in this country in the winter of 1842–3. Rinderpest, or cattle plague, reached epidemic proportions in 1865–6 and legislation became vital for its control. The Cattle Disease Prevention Act of 1866, instrumental in reducing the number of infectious cases reported from 120,000 in January to only 300 in June, showed the way. In 1870 the Veterinary Department was established by the government to administer legislation such as the Contagious Diseases (Animal) Act. Further legislation followed, not only aimed at preventing disease amongst livestock but at improving the standards of hygiene and quality relating to milk and other foodstuffs for human consumption.

In a paper presented to the Farmers' Club in 1882, Professor J. Scott of the Royal Agricultural College observed that 'a strong opinion is growing up amongst scientific men that the communicable diseases have a similar origin. It has been proved that the contagion of disease consists . . . of . . . minute animal and vegetable organisms.'[18] Pasteur had identified the anthrax bacillus and had produced a vaccine for its control. 'The virus of the contagion pleuro-pneumonia has also been cultivated and this pestilence . . . has also been found to be capable of extermination by means of its own germs.' Sceptics, however, still felt that 'although we know so much more about these diseases . . . we do not advance very much in the practice of curing them'. It was early days still and considerable time would elapse before the results of the work overseas of Pasteur, Koch and Ehrlich could be extensively applied. Nevertheless, substantial progress was often the result of less spectacular happenings. Thus, the increasing use of the microscope, stethoscope and clinical thermometer after 1870 greatly improved veterinary practice. Antiseptics and anaesthetics became important in the 1860s.

IV

The role of the agricultural college in the advancement of farming was first seriously discussed during the seventeenth century. Samuel Hartlib produced well-developed ideas for the founding of a 'Colledge of Husbandry' in 1651, and Abraham Cowley in 1664 proposed that one college at each of the universities should be devoted to the study of agriculture. In 1790 William Marshall advocated the creation of local colleges of agriculture, or 'rural seminaries' as he called them. As Dr Charles Daubeny informed the Royal Agricultural Society in 1842, Britain lagged behind France and Germany in the provision of agricultural education. A college with an estate of no less than 1,000 acres had been founded in 1817 at Hohenheim near Stuttgart; an even earlier college was established at Keszthely in Hungary.

When the Duke of Wellington's patronage was solicited by Lord Mahon in 1838 for the foundation of 'a College of Agriculture for the sons of farmers and yeomen in Kent', he received a terse reply. The duke would have none of it. 'If there is one thing in the world of which I know positively nothing it is agriculture; then observe that I have not an acre of land in Kent.' He went on to add, 'the theory of agriculture is one thing; the practical application of the theory in what is called agriculture wholly different. . . . The practice of agriculture . . . must depend upon experience.'[19] Some of the aristocracy, however, held different views.

In April 1844 Earl Bathurst presided at a meeting of the Fairford and Cirencester Farmers' Club which led to the founding of an agricultural college at Cirencester in 1845. He offered a 400-acre farm on a favourable lease and generously advanced the funds required to build the college. Able, indeed outstanding, persons were appointed to the staff. Through their experimental work, consultancy activities and publications, as well as their teaching, they contributed significantly to the development of scientific farming. Dr Augustus Voelcker (1822–84), who held the Chair of Agricultural Chemistry, established an unequalled reputation as an analytical chemist; Professor J. T. Way (1821–84), of whom Russell wrote 'no other worker of his time . . . opened up so much new ground', was also a chemist gifted with exceptional originality. Many of the staff moved on to important positions. One became director of the Royal Botanic Gardens at Kew, another became president of the Royal Veterinary College. No fewer than six were elected to Fellowships of the Royal Society and three gained knighthoods.

Punch showed its interest at the proposed establishment of the college and wrote,

> we can see no difficulty in organising a College of Agriculture, and we can suggest a few of the probable professorships. Of course there will be a chair of new laid eggs, which the professor of poultry would be well qualified to occupy. Degrees will be conferred in guano: and a series of lectures of making hay when the sun shines would, no doubt, be exceeding popular.[20]

Early in its history Caird rather critically observed that 'the College was originally founded in order to furnish a sound education in scientific agriculture for the sons of tenant farmers . . . [but] the sixty students at present entered on the books [1850] are all the sons of solicitors, clergymen, officers or landed proprietors'.[21] Yet Charles Dickens, whose son was at the college in 1868, wrote with evident satisfaction: 'the college founded . . . not by Government, but by working farmers, when a fashion had grown up recognising the need of scientific farming . . . has not received one farthing of public money'.[22] Although finance proved troublesome throughout, new facilities were added even during the depression of the 1880s and 1890s. The college became the Royal Agricultural College in 1880. It was finally established as the oldest and best known, and eventually sole survivor, of the several independent and privately-owned colleges, which included Downton in Wiltshire, active from 1880 to 1908, and Aspatria in Cumberland, which functioned between 1874 and 1914.

Although a Chair of Agriculture had been created in 1790 in the University of Edinburgh, there was no degree in agriculture until the late 1880s.[23] William Somerville, later to become a distinguished professor, was the first to graduate in 1888. Early occupants of the chair mainly concerned themselves with research and publication, giving only occasional lectures. A somewhat similar position existed at Oxford[24] where not until 1840 were funds available to fill the Sibthorpian Chair in Rural Economy, founded in 1796. Although the professor was required to give only twelve lectures annually, the first occupant, Dr Charles Daubeny, a man of rare ability, culture and distinction, did much to promote the early development of agricultural science. He was Liebig's greatest advocate, yet counted Lawes amongst his pupils and sought to reconcile their conflicting views. Between 1884–90 Dr J. H. Gilbert of Rothamsted held the Sibthorpian Chair, lecturing, according to Russell, to sparse audiences on the principles of crop nutrition, the composition of the soil and the feeding of livestock.[25] The Board of Agriculture made proposals in 1891 for more systematic and regular instruction to be offered, but these were not fully taken up. Indeed a statute proposing the institution of an honours degree was defeated by 47 votes to 45 in 1898. Not until 1907 was a full-time professorship established, with Dr

William Somerville as the first occupant. Oxford's main contribution to agricultural education during the late Victorian era came through extension lectures organized by the Oxford Delegacy for Local Examinations with the assistance of the Board of Agriculture and the newly established county councils.

A somewhat similar pattern of development occurred at Cambridge. Proposals were received for courses of instruction from the Board of Agriculture in 1890, but were not acceptable to the university despite the recommendations of a review syndicate. It proved possible, however, to establish a diploma course in agriculture in 1893, despite considerable pressure on funds. The first of two important benefactions, the endowment of the Gilbey Lectureship in the History and Economics of Agriculture, dates from 1896. In 1899 the Worshipful Company of Drapers provided funds for the establishment of the Drapers Chair in Agriculture, whose first occupant was again Dr William Somerville. Despite considerable opposition, the university in turn formally established a degree course in agriculture in conformity with the terms of the Drapers' Company bequest. However, some £1,500 was raised through public subscription towards the establishment of a university farm at Impington in 1900. Close links were maintained with Cambridgeshire County Council, and in 1899 investigational work was in progress on no fewer than fifty sites.

Appreciation of the part agricultural education could contribute towards increasing the competitiveness of British farming grew after the mid-1870s. Britain lagged well behind its overseas competitors and the Royal Commission of 1881 recommended the provision of technical instruction in agriculture. There followed the Departmental Committee Report of 1888, which recommended that state aid should be made available for the establishment of local agricultural education centres. County councils, created in the same year, were required to provide facilities for instruction under the Technical Education Act. The Board of Agriculture, re-established in 1889, contributed £2,160 towards the financing of agricultural education in England and Wales, and £2,425 in Scotland. More appreciable funds became available in 1890, however, when the residues of the beer and spirits duties, known as the 'whisky money', which had been collected without Parliamentary sanction, were handed over to local authorities for use for technical education purposes. By 1894–5 expenditure on agricultural education had risen to £78,000 in Great Britain as a whole.

The University College of North Wales, founded at Bangor in 1884, was associated with agricultural instruction from the outset.[26] In 1888 it received from the Agricultural Department of the Privy Council a grant of £200 for agricultural education and instruction in dairy farming. This had increased to £800 by 1890–1 and public subscriptions produced a further £500. A Chair in Agriculture together with a bachelor of science degree course were established in 1895.

A similar pattern was followed elsewhere, modest funds derived from the Board of Agriculture being supplemented with locally subscribed funds. Much individual energy and effort went into establishing the various founding institutions. The Yorkshire College at Leeds established its Agricultural Department in 1890, followed by the colleges at Aberystwyth and Newcastle-upon-Tyne in 1891, and Reading and

Nottingham in 1893. Horticulture was studied by men at Swanley College from 1889, and by women at Studley Horticultural College from 1898. Although several colleges lacked internal students, the departments worked intensively at their extramural tasks thereby establishing important links with the farming community.

When the South-Eastern Agricultural College was established at Wye in Kent in 1894 some fifty-six years had elapsed since Wellington's curt reply to Lord Mahon. It was in the very depths of the depression, and it seemed that the 'only evidence likely to remain in that district [of] what had once been the mainstay of English farming' was, according to Hall, the wheatsheaves in the medieval glass window depicting the arms of the college's original founder, John Kempe.[27] Under the youthful and inspired leadership of Daniel Hall, however, the college quickly established itself as a leading centre for scientific study and for progressive farming. The farm was to be first and foremost a teaching institution but it was to be conducted 'as much as possible upon strict business principles'. Although Daniel Hall was by upbringing a chemist he developed an understanding that economic knowledge was essential for the real improvement of British agriculture. He quickly gathered together a brilliant team of lecturers including J. Percival, the agricultural botanist, 'a born teacher and incomparable field naturalist', F. V. Theobald, 'the rising economic entomologist of the time', and E. J. Russell, the chemist, who was destined to follow Daniel Hall to Rothamsted and eventually succeed him as director. Student numbers rose steadily and several went on to make major contributions to the development of scientific farming in the present century. Others established careers overseas, many in the Colonial Service, but the greatest proportion went into practical agriculture as managers, land agents or farmers. In sharp contrast were the aims of one respected Kentish member of the governing body who, Hall reports, had declared that the college should be 'a place from which we can get a really good ploughman or shepherd'.[28] In 1900 the college became a school of the University of London, and under Hall's wise leadership it branched out and developed interests in hops and fruit and horticultural crops. His own work was a pioneering study into the agriculture and the soils of Kent, Surrey and Sussex, undertaken with Russell.

V

The intensity of competition to which British agriculture was subjected during the last quarter of the nineteenth century had considerable scientific and technical consequences. It largely destroyed the leadership which had come from the landed classes and a generation of 'high farmers'. Frugality and flexibility became the order of the day. Yet some were able to adapt well. George Baylis, who farmed some 400 acres in Berkshire in 1870, was farming nearly 3,500 acres by 1900. He applied the basic lessons of the Rothamsted experience and used only artificial fertilizers to grow continuous corn crops, without any recourse to farmyard manure or livestock.

Although funds were short for experimentation, some stimulus to innovation derived from the introduction of legislation providing tenant farmers with compensation for improvements. Increasing pressures were put on the newly established county councils and the Board of Agriculture to extend experimental and educational facilities. However, only limited progress had been achieved by the end of the century. More and more the contrasts with overseas countries were seen to be wide. The land grant colleges in the U.S.A. had a head start in the advancement of farming technology, giving attention to farm management and agricultural economics as well as to applied science.

In the main stream of agricultural science it also appeared that British achievement had tended to lag behind the progress made in countries such as Germany. Russell records the feelings of Daniel Hall on succeeding Sir Henry Gilbert as director of Rothamsted in 1902: 'I was not aware of the rigidity of the outlook which had been maintained for many years at Rothamsted . . . but I will confess that my heart sank when I did come to take possession of the laboratory . . . it was . . . like a museum.'[29] All the energy, wisdom and breadth of vision of men like Hall and Russell were needed to revitalize the scientific scene. 'Agricultural science was at a low ebb . . .,' states Russell, 'its future looked very gloomy.'[30]

However, a new vista was opening up which was to take Rothamsted forward to outstandingly important work on soils, crops and fertilizers. Within a decade or so, with help from sources such as the Development Commission, new specialist institutions would be established with facilities for research into subjects such as fruit growing, dairying and economics. Furthermore, able and well-trained men were beginning to come forward and new disciplines were brought into use. There was a more rigorous approach to experimentation and more exact scientific methods were imposed. The rediscovery of Mendel's work on breeding in 1900 and its publication in the *Journal* of the Royal Horticultural Society was of fundamental importance. The conference on hybridization held in 1899 'was undoubtedly the most significant and important in the Society's history', according to Fletcher.[31] New and improved varieties of grain crops and disease-resistant and better quality crops such as potatoes were the result. Similar improvements were made with fruit and market garden crops for which there was an increasing consumer demand.

Veterinary science was also on the point of major advances as diseases were more exactly described and means of treatment developed. Many of these improvements resulted from the development of medical studies. The last outbreak of pleuro-pneumonia occurred in 1898, and rabies was eliminated in 1902. As livestock production grew in importance there followed an increased interest in experimentation. 'Protein and energy standards based on feeding trials . . . were pretty well established by 1900', according to Byerly, due mainly to work overseas.[32] The work in England had been rather less successful, although from 1876 onwards the resources of the Woburn Abbey Home Farm had been placed at the disposal of Lawes and Gilbert for investigations into livestock feeding and the laying down of permanent pasture.

The late Victorian era saw the real beginnings of modern agricultural science and education. Much progress was made by pioneers such as Lawes and Gilbert, and farming practice developed towards a more rational use of resources despite the difficulties created by the intense growth of competition from overseas food supplies. Yet it is evident that the real dimensions and complexities of agriculture were not adequately understood by scientists or by practising farmers. The trained manpower and the financial resources available were still woefully inadequate as the century ended. But a new era was shortly to dawn, typified by Hall's appointment to Rothamsted and his later work for the Development Commission. His vision was of 'development . . . based on scientific research; the results of which were to be carried to farmers, through advisory and educational agencies'.[33] By this means was science with practice achieved.

Notes

1   Rossiter, 1975.
2   Peel, 1976.
3   Ernle, 1961, 356, 364.
4   J. Caird, 1878b, 29.
5   Hall, 1905, 3.
6   Little, 1874.
7   Ernle, 1961, 369.
8   Russell, 1966, 103.
9   Lawes, 1847.
10   Dale, 1956, 56.
11   Russell, 1937, 4.
12   Russell, 1966, 144.
13   Rew, 1897, 33.
14   Hall, 1905, viii.
15   *Ibid.*, ix.
16   Russell, 1942, 180.
17   Pugh, 1962.
18   Scott, 1882.
19   Stanhope, 1938.
20   Boutflour, 1938.
21   Caird, 1852, 37.
22   Boutflour, 1938.
23   Shearer, 1937.
24   Scott Watson, 1937.
25   Russell, 1966, 167.
26   White, 1939, 1.
27   Hall, 1939, 1.
28   *Ibid.*, 5.
29   Russell, 1937, 6.
30   Russell, 1966, 181.
31   Fletcher, 1969, 249.
32   Byerly, 1976, 226.
33   Russell, 1942, 183.

III   Country Towns and Country Industries

20 Country Towns

C.W. Chalklin

The agricultural and pastoral character of the people upon whom the town depended for its existence was shown by the class of objects displayed in the shop windows. Scythes, reap-hooks, sheep-shears, bill-hooks, spades, mattocks, and hoes at the ironmonger's; beehives, butter-firkins, churns, milking stools and pails, hay-rakes, field-flagons, and seed-lips at the cooper's; cart-ropes and plough-harness at the saddler's; carts, wheelbarrows, and mill-gear at the wheelwright's and machinist's; horse embrocations at the chemist's; at the glover's and leather-cutter's, hedging-gloves, thatcher's knee-caps, ploughman's leggings, villager's pattens and clogs.

Thomas Hardy, The Mayor of Casterbridge[1]

'Will you tell me what is sold in this general market?' 'All sorts of things. Anyone may have a stall for boots if he likes as long as he pays the toll. There are a good many people who sell crockery, and then there are butchers, and fishmongers, and those people who sell anything in the nature of provisions.'

Report of the Royal Commission on Market Rights and Tolls, 1888,
concerning Newbury[2]

I

Nineteenth-century urban historians have tended to give their attention to London, the metropolitan industrial and commercial cities of the Midlands and the north, and the lesser manufacturing centres that were rising in their wake. In view of their importance, size and pace of growth this is natural enough. Yet the several hundred market towns and small regional centres in the countryside, whose basic role was to provide a variety of services for the farming communities, are equally worthy of study. In the Victorian period, as in earlier centuries, the country town was the basic English urban type.

Most of these country towns were essentially of local importance. Through their markets and fairs, a growing variety of shops, a wide range of crafts, and a few professional men, they were service centres for a rural hinterland of perhaps no more than three or four miles in radius. Many of them had some cottage industries, and some had workshops and small factories; if they lay on the coast, fishing, seaborne trade or summer visitors provided an additional livelihood. A minority of country towns were small regional centres; in comparison with the average market town they had many more different tradesmen and craftsmen, larger markets, and their shops stocked a wider range of goods. Some had a sphere of influence covering several market towns: in addition to their local trade and commercial links with other parts of England, their regional importance was often symbolized by an administrative function as a county town or as the headquarters of a see of a diocese. As in the smaller country towns industry was sometimes an important subsidiary means of livelihood.

There was thus some variation in the size of the country towns. At the opening of the Victorian period the typical market town had a population of between 1,000 and 3–4,000. As an example let us look first at the towns of the western part of Sussex in 1841. There were four small inland market towns, Arundel (population of the parish 2,624), Petworth (3,364), Midhurst (1,536) and Steyning (1,495). The parishes of Petworth and to a lesser extent Arundel and Steyning had a considerable rural acreage and the population of the market towns alone was probably much smaller. Worthing was primarily a seaside resort, but Littlehampton combined the function of small market town, port and seaside resort. In the north west of the county the town of Horsham, the major trading centre in the western Weald, had less than 5,000 people (parish population 5,765). Chichester (8,512) was the regional centre of west Sussex, an important market town and see of the diocese of Chichester. All the country towns differed from the villages in their hinterlands in that the majority of the occupied inhabitants of the latter were directly involved in agriculture as farmers or labourers, and that the trades and crafts in the towns were far more varied and specialized. The likely size of the hinterlands of the market towns may be illustrated by the case of Midhurst. The market towns of Petersfield and Haslemere in adjoining counties lay eight miles to the north and west respectively; Chichester lay ten miles to the south and Petworth only six miles to the east. The difference between the commercial importance of a town such as Midhurst or Arundel and, say, Horsham was visible partly in its occupations. While there is no evidence that the markets at Midhurst or Arundel were of more than local importance, according to *The Post Office Directory of the Six Home Counties* (1845) at Horsham 'large quantities of corn and poultry are sold here for the London supply'. In the same directory 109 tradesmen, craftsmen and professional people were listed for Midhurst, representing fifty-one different occupations; Horsham had 235 people listed, representing ninety-one occupations. Horsham clearly served a bigger rural hinterland than did Midhurst.

As a second and to some extent contrasting example, Oxfordshire in 1841 may be chosen. Oxford, with 30,000 people, was an important regional centre, linked to the Midlands and London by water. It was a county town and see of the diocese, with the university providing an important additional livelihood for its inhabitants. With one exception the nine or ten other urban centres in the county were small. Unlike the towns of western Sussex nearly all had some manufacturing in various states of prosperity, in addition to the agricultural processing industries to be found in all country towns. At Burford (population 1,644), where the market was held on a Saturday,

> the making of saddles, and a considerable trade in malt and wool, that formerly flourished, have much declined: this, added to the diversion of the line of road, which now avoids the town, instead of passing through it as before, has reduced it from a flourishing condition to a state of comparative poverty.[3]

The neighbouring market town of Witney (3,419), seven miles away, was exceptional in the presence of an important and flourishing local industry, blanket-making, the greatest source of employment in the town. In 1852 it was said that every year about 93,000 blankets were made, the six chief manufacturers in the town using weekly 120 packs of wool.[4] At Charlbury (1,526 in 1851) it was reported in 1852 that the weekly market was almost in disuse, but was hoped to improve after the opening of a railway. It was still a minor trading centre: 'owing to its being surrounded by about twenty villages within a circuit of a few miles, a considerable trade is carried on at Charlbury'. Glove-making was an important employment: 'here is the largest glove manufactory in the county'.[5] Probably, apart from Oxford, only Banbury had importance as a centre for the supply of goods and the collection of agricultural produce greater than that of the typical market town. Its population in 1841 was 6,753. In 1843 there were said to be 'one hundred and forty places within a circuit of ten miles' for which Banbury was a 'metropolis'. Plush-weaving was a special minor industry, in about 1850 a steam-powered factory for worsted and mohair spinning was built, employing fifty workers, and shoe-making served more than purely local needs.[6] Altogether in the market towns of Oxfordshire in the mid-nineteenth century, as in some neighbouring counties, textile and other manufactures were an important means of livelihood.

Some country towns grew rapidly in the Victorian period (though not at the pace of the majority of towns in the big industrial regions); others practically stood still. Some prospered as better communications brought by the railways attracted the agricultural trade of a wider area, or with the development of local industry; others stagnated as the population of the rural hinterland ceased to grow, or even declined, as the developing railway network passed them by and drew trade away to neighbouring market towns or regional centres, or as existing cottage industry faded in the face of factory competition. Thus in Sussex Horsham's population more than doubled between 1841 and 1901 (5,765 to 12,994). With the help of favourable rail communications its role as the major marketing and agricultural processing centre in the western Weald expanded; in the 1890s it was noted for its important corn, poultry and cattle markets, corn mills, malthouses, breweries, iron and brass foundries and coach factories.[7] In contrast, the trading centres of Midhurst, Petworth, Arundel and Steyning hardly grew at all. Steyning, as Kelly's directories indicate, was the most thriving of them with, in 1891, two breweries, a fatstock sale on alternate Wednesdays and a corn and cattle market on alternate Mondays; it grew from 1,495 in 1841 to 1,752 in 1901. The population of Petworth parish decreased from 3,364 to 2,503, and that of Midhurst rose by barely a hundred (1,536 to 1,650); and while they retained their function as minor shopping centres, their markets had disappeared by the early 1900s.[8] In mid-Sussex important rail communications helped to create a new town, Hayward's Heath, with, by 1891, an important agricultural trade, 'the largest cattle sale in Sussex being held here'.[9]

The pattern of urban development in Oxfordshire, as in other counties in the south Midlands, was influenced by the differing fortunes of the local industries which had been so important in the economies of the market towns in the early nineteenth century. By 1900 Oxford with its 50,000 people had been transformed into much more than a county town. Banbury (10,012 in 1901) had grown slowly, helped by good rail communications and the consequent development of the manufacture of agricultural implements and engines.[10] Wtih the exception of Chipping Norton, the population of the other market towns had not increased at all owing to the slow decline of the neighbouring agricultural population which they served and the stagnation or decline of the little cottage or workshop industries, such as the making of gloves, lace and shoes.

II

Victorian England inherited three types of market from previous centuries, the general retail markets for the sale of many sorts of perishable provisions and cheap household goods, corn markets, and livestock markets. The fortunes of individual markets of all three types fluctuated during the course of the later nineteenth century. Some gained trade, others lost it. A few disappeared altogether, particularly general and corn markets, as trade was diverted to neighbouring towns or was carried on by other means. Some new markets were created as a result of local initiative, perhaps encouraged by the arrival of favourable rail communications. Many retail markets continued to prosper. In 1888 when the Royal Commission on Market Rights was investigating the market at Market Drayton, Shropshire, it found that farmers' wives were continuing to bring provisions for sale to the market place as they had done for centuries.[11]

Nevertheless, the number and importance of these retail markets was declining. Some country towns lost them altogether, in others little trade was done. Village and town shops were absorbing more and more of the business in perishable foodstuffs formerly done in the markets. As consumption grew there was increasing need for more regular outlets for farm produce than the weekly market could provide, and hawkers as well as shopkeepers helped to satisfy this growing demand. In 1888 the lessee of the Helston, St Austell and Penrhyn markets in Cornwall complained to an assistant commissioner: '[Helston] market is decreasing very much, the trade being diverted to the shops; in fact in most of the country towns the market has gone . . . every village has its butcher's shop and vegetable shop.'[12] In many towns hawkers with vegetables, fruit, poultry and eggs toured the streets every day, though not every market was much affected by them. According to an assistant commissioner who visited Hereford market in 1888: 'there is no doubt tradespeople do more and more go out with their carts, and a great many markets that I have been to suffered from it, but I do not find that this market has'.[13] In some towns, such as Guildford in Surrey, shops selling perishable foodstuffs tended to cater for the well-to-do, while the working class continued to patronize the market.[14]

The numerous corn exchanges created up and down the country are a witness to the fact that market trading in corn (generally by sample) remained active and their importance is supported by contemporary evidence.[15] In fact, in many towns dealing in corn, trading outside markets tended to limit profits from market tolls. Much corn was sold in inns, in open streets or by direct conveyance from farm gate to mill. At Banbury two corn exchanges were erected in 1857 as a result of competition by rival companies. One was still in use in 1888 with about forty corn stands let to dealers at £1 a year, but it was not a financial success because much dealing was still done in the yard of the Red Lion Inn in the High Street and later at the Crown Inn in Bridge Street.[16]

Livestock markets, involving particularly lean and fat cattle and sheep but also horses and pigs, were perhaps the most important form of market trading in the Victorian period. By the 1880s and 1890s they had tended to absorb the great annual fairs in cattle, sheep and horses, leaving fairs, if they were held at all, for merrymaking and, still in many towns, for the traditional hiring of farm servants. At Banbury in 1888 fortnightly market sales were said to average 1,000 sheep and 1,200 cattle.[17] Many cattle markets were created or developed as a result of new facilities which captured trade from neighbouring towns, or because railways replaced the traditional transport 'on the hoof'. In 1888, for example, the livestock market at Sevenoaks was said to be not so important as it had been formerly. One reason was that in 1849 the neighbouring town of Tonbridge, in addition to its existing market, had set up a second cattle market on the third Tuesday in each month, which competed with Sevenoaks' existing Tuesday market; another cause was the construction of the South Eastern Railway:[18]

> Sheep from Romney Marsh and that district were brought to this market by
> hundreds; they came here through Tonbridge instead of stopping at
> Tonbridge to be sold as they do now. Instead of sending sheep to Sevenoaks
> market they now sent them to Ashford or Tonbridge for dispatch to London
> by rail.

Despite the varying fortunes of individual markets up and down England, market day remained by far the most important day of the week for most country towns. This may be seen in the large number of carriers that poured into the towns on their market days. The Ditchling, Sussex, carrier transported 'pork from farms in Wivelsfield, hides for Lewes tannery, rabbits on poles, vegetables by the bushel, butter in chocolate boxes, baskets of laundry, razors, scissors, and ploughshares for sharpening, also numerous parcels, contents unknown'.[19] Most, though not all, of the services were on market day. At Melton Mowbray, Leicestershire, a town of nearly 6,000 people in the 1880s, four-fifths of the services run to the town by carriers in no less than sixty neighbouring villages were on the single market day, Tuesday.[20]

III

In addition to the markets, the towns served the surrounding countryside by means of their various crafts, distributive trades and professional men. Towns which lacked an important industry had a relatively similar occupational pattern. A typical example is Ashby de la Zouch, a Leicestershire market town with just under 4,000 people in 1861 (see Table 20.1). Particularly in the smaller towns those earning a livelihood directly from the land—farmers, market gardeners and numerous agricultural labourers—who tended to live near the edge of the built-up area comprised a significant minority of the working population, perhaps 10, 15 or 20 per cent. Another large group were the domestic servants. The numbers of those working in transport (such as railway workers, carriers, canal boat hands) or in services (such as hairdressers or chimney sweeps), and general labourers, were smaller but still significant. Yet it was not uncommon for the various craftsmen (with their apprentices and skilled assistants), retailers and professional people to comprise about half the working population.

By far the most numerous group were the craftsmen. Many of the master craftsmen retailed the goods they produced in their own shops. So many goods which are today supplied from a distance, typically from a factory, were made locally. This was particularly true of clothing and shoes, always important in providing work for townspeople. For example, in 1857 at Tadcaster, a market town in the Vale of York, of

Table 20.1 *The occupational structure of Ashby de la Zouch according to the 1861 census (individuals)*

	Percentage
Crafts	35
Domestic servants	15
Trades	13
Agricultural workers	9
Services	6.5
Labourers	6
Professions	5
Innkeepers	4
Independent	3.5
Farmers and graziers	1.5
Clerical workers	1.5

Source: Page, 1974, 86.

2,516 inhabitants, 99 people, or just about one-third of the 297 masters, journeymen and apprentices working at all the skilled crafts, were tailors, shoe-makers and cordwainers, and dress-makers. Much of the work was done, as one might expect, for the inhabitants of the neighbouring parishes. An eighty-year-old lady living in Tadcaster in 1970 recalled how her shoe-maker grandfather in his old age thought nothing of walking a twelve-mile round trip to deliver his shoe repairs to customers in the villages.[21] If there was no tailor in a country parish, a man might travel from a nearby country town with made-to-measure or ready-made clothes. One tailor and draper from Stowmarket, Suffolk, used to travel round villages at harvest time when the men had received extra pay, collecting orders which he executed in the family workshop.[22] Many of the tailors in the country towns were also drapers, and sold ready-made clothing in shops. This was the case at Tadcaster, which had two hat manufacturers, five stay-makers, five milliners and three bonnet-makers. Another numerous occupational group in all the country towns was the building trades. At Tadcaster there were 109 people in building and allied occupations. They included thirty-eight joiners, carpenters and cabinet-makers, nineteen stone-masons, eleven bricklayers, twelve house painters, nine sawyers, four plasterers, two plumbers and glaziers, and several men in brick- and tile-making. It was not uncommon for a few master craftsmen in these trades each to employ up to a dozen or even a score of skilled workmen as well as apprentices, and to turn their hand to a variety of work. In 1851 John Rodwell of Tadcaster was employing six men and two apprentices. Seven years earlier a local directory described him as a 'cabinet maker, upholster, builder, turner, picture frame maker, undertaker etc.', and he announced as his speciality 'all kinds of fancy work and needlework mounted. Cane and rush bottom chairs manufactured and repaired'. In an economy which remained dependent on horse-drawn vehicles for local transport, saddlers, blacksmiths and wheelwrights were

281

naturally numerous in both town and country. Tadcaster had ten people working at the saddlers' craft, six wheelwrights, and three smithies employing eleven men. In addition all towns had an assortment of craftsmen who did not fall into any of the categories so far mentioned. They included braziers, turners, clock-makers, coopers, curriers and many others.

In every town in the mid-nineteenth century those working at crafts, many of whom sold their wares direct to the customer, greatly outnumbered the inhabitants who were merely retailers. The most common tradesmen included butchers, grocers and drapers, and every town had a variety of more specialized retailers. Among the 4,000 inhabitants of Tonbridge, Kent, in 1851 were numerous butchers, beersellers, grocers and drapers, and there were also greengrocers, fishmongers, milkmen, coalmen and clothiers. The more specialized tradesmen included stationers, a bookseller, a wine merchant, and as many as four tea dealers.[23] A special group were the publicans. In Banbury there was one for every 110 of the population in 1851, and one for every 131 in 1871.[24]

In the later nineteenth century it is likely that the number of shops, shopkeepers and shop workers grew faster than the population. By the 1880s, if not before, shops were taking over trade in perishable goods previously handled by retail markets in some towns. Furthermore, the growing volume and variety and cheapness of factory-made goods restricted the work of craftsmen-retailers and increased the sales of those tradesmen who were just shopkeepers. Towards the end of the nineteenth century more and more factory-made boots, watches and clothes were being sold. New types of shop were appearing in the country towns, reflecting the widening range of goods available and new tastes on the part of more well-to-do customers. In 1898 Huntingdon (population 4,349 in 1891) had a dealer in antique furniture, a firm of photographers and an agent and maker of cycles. Rising real incomes among the mass of the population led to the appearance of multiple shops particularly in footwear and provisions: thus Huntingdon in 1898 had its Freeman, Hardy & Willis, and its International Tea Company.[25]

As the volume of machine-made goods manufactured outside the district grew, the number of craftsmen in the country towns began to decline.[26] In Devon the number of shoe-makers was nearly 6,000 in 1871, but had fallen to 3,000 by 1901.[27] Nearly all the traditional crafts of the country town still existed at the beginning of the twentieth century, but they were drawing increasingly on the factory or large-scale industry to supply half-finished goods—iron axles, saddlers' ironmongery, lead piping, sawn planks and sewing thread—and employment opportunities for young townsmen in these trades were becoming more and more limited.

Professional services were also an important feature of every country town. Apart from the clergy, Anglican and Nonconformist, there were various teachers, solicitors, medical practitioners, bankers, accountants and surveyors, among others. Thus Tadcaster in 1851 had five clergy, comprising the vicar and his curate, two Wesleyan ministers and one Inghamite, four doctors, two governesses, fourteen teachers at various types of school (four men and ten women), four solicitors, three opticians, three bookkeepers, an inland revenue officer, an auctioneer, two artist painters, and a professor of music.[28] Although relatively few in number, only a tiny proportion of the occupied population, the professions were an essential part of the functions of the country town.

IV

There was some industry in nearly every country town. Often it merely comprised the processing of agricultural produce by millers, maltsters, brewers and tanners. But many country towns made agricultural equipment, machinery and engines, or manufactured goods with no direct connection with agriculture, such as woollens, lace, gloves, straw plaits or furniture. In coastal towns fishing, boatbuilding and sometimes the provision of accommodation for summer visitors, provided additional employment.

Among the industries closely linked to agriculture milling had always been ubiquitous. In the middle of the nineteenth century nearly every town, however small, had its windmill or watermill run by a miller and one or two assistants; the larger towns and those in fertile corn-growing districts which supplied London or one of the industrial regions often had several windmills and watermills. Where grain supplies and demand were sufficiently large some relatively big enterprises emerged. For example, mid-nineteenth-century Gloucester, in the centre of a grain-producing area, supplied increasing quantities of flour to industrial south Wales. In addition to its many small windmills and watermills, there were a number of large mills, sometimes owned in conjunction with other businesses. In the late 1830s a man named Healing took over the Abbey Mills in Gloucester, operating them as well as the Quay Mills at Tewkesbury and Cox's Mill at Evesham, the total output being about 700 sacks of flour a week. In the 1860s he increased his business by building a steam mill at Tewkesbury and adding further capacity until his output was over 3,000 sacks a week.[29] But with the increased use of steampower, machinery, and the growing reliance on imported wheat entering the country through the great ports, many of the small watermills and windmills in the agricultural regions were abandoned or converted to other uses. Bridlington, a market town, port and resort on the Yorkshire coast, had no fewer than seven windmills and three watermills in 1853. But only one watermill and two windmills appear to have been still grinding corn at the beginning of the twentieth century. One watermill had been converted for the manufacture of manure, and the third had become by 1882 a steam saw mill.[30]

In the early nineteenth century every country town had at least one malthouse to supply the local brewers. Some towns in barley-growing areas or with access to imported barley, and with good water communications to large markets, were well known for numerous maltings, such as Newark on Trent in Nottinghamshire or Saffron Walden in Essex. Later many small malthouses became disused because local breweries obtained their malt from their own malthouses, or because they lay distant from rail communications suitable for the carriage of malt to large urban markets. In 1877 Thaxted in Essex witnessed 'huge maltings and granaries falling into decay. To such a state of inactivity does seven miles from a railway station reduce a once thriving borough.'[31] At Newark, on the other hand, the railways gave access to both coal and distant markets; many more malthouses were built and several large businesses emerged.[32]

During the course of the later nineteenth century the more successful breweries tended to become bigger as premises were enlarged, plant was modernized, amalgamations took place and public houses were bought. Typical of the more successful enterprises in its steady expansion was the brewing business of Henry Michell of Horsham (died 1874), whose diary over thirty-nine years recalls the major achievements of each year. When he began business in 1835 he brewed only about 400 quarters of malt in his first year and 600 quarters in his second year. In 1868 he brewed 3,075 quarters; in the interval he had acquired a new brewery (which he enlarged twice and adapted to the use of steam), a new malthouse and a succession of public houses in the district. As early as 1837 he noted in his diary: 'this year I bought the Jolly Tanner at Staplefield Common for £400. . . . This proved a great bargain, as it has always yielded £5 per cent interest, besides a good beer trade.'[33] In Banbury, Hunt's brewery was enlarged between 1850 and 1866; after an additional partner joined the firm in 1872 his capital was used to buy sixty-four tied houses between 1874 and 1876. Four more breweries were taken over before 1900 and fifty public houses acquired in the 1890s.[34]

Yet another industry involving the processing of a farm product was the manufacture of leather. Nearly all country towns in the mid-nineteenth century had a tanyard drawing on cattle hides from local slaughterhouses, run by a tanner with perhaps five or six assistants. Usually, too, there was at least one master currier in the town who handled the final dressing and trimming of the leather. By the 1880s some of the small tanneries were closing down as local supplies of hides dwindled. Production tended to concentrate in the larger works using steampower, often relying on hides drawn from markets in the industrial cities or from abroad.[35]

Iron works were a feature of many country towns from the beginning of the nineteenth century. The typical small foundry of the 1830s made agricultural implements, general castings such as grates, range backs and pipes, and sometimes structural ironwork such as bridges. Later agricultural machinery, various types of engine, boilers and pumps, and sometimes railway equipment were made. Diversification often developed rapidly. In Buckingham the Castle Iron Foundry was set up in 1857 to make ploughs and harrows and other implements; within a few months it was producing a steam locomotive cultivator, and later it was making steam road cars. In 1860 the manager announced that he was taking orders for cars costing £180 and £200, and five years later he was building traction engines for hauling omnibuses.[36] In a few towns, generally those served with good rail communications, such as Banbury and Newark, large works emerged employing not tens but hundreds of men. In Banbury the largest works in the mid-nineteenth century, that of Bernhard Samuelson, had 27 workmen in 1846; by 1861 it was employing 380 men and boys.[37] The ever-widening demand for metal goods outside agriculture brought more and more firms into being in the more important country towns in the last decades of the century. In Essex firms were set up in the 1890s to make metal windows, accessories for motor and cycle trades, gramophones and pianos, and many other products.[38] Various textile industries were flourishing in the middle of the century in some of the predominantly agricultural regions, bringing much extra work to the country towns. Most of them were cottage industries, though in a few instances (as in the case of the silk manufacture of Essex) the work was carried on in small factories or workshops in the towns. For many, both employers and employed, these gave additional means of livelihood. Thus in the small market town of Castle Donington, Leicestershire (3,508 in 1841), where hosiery manufacture in the mid-nineteenth century was carried on in small factories, workshops and particularly in the workers' homes, one hosiery manufacturer was also a farmer with 60 acres, one kept a grocer's shop, and a third had not only a general shop but was also a boot- and shoe-maker; rather later, in 1870, the publican who kept the King's Head in the Market Place was also a wholesale manufacturer of baby linen.[39] Some manufacturers employed women and girls in particular, providing additional income for families in which the head of the household worked at a craft or trade. The glove industry of Woodstock near Oxford was said to employ about 100 men and no less than 1,500 women in the district in 1852.[40]

During the course of the Victorian period the nature of employment in the textile industries sometimes changed, and in other cases disappeared altogether. Local factories using machinery gradually took over some of the processes previously done by outworkers, while cottagers continued to handle the remaining processes. At Woodstock in about 1900 the glove-making firm of R. & J. Pullman employed about 60 people in a factory and about 150 or 200 people in the neighbouring villages, presumably cottage workers engaged on sewing.[41] In other cases the local textile industry declined or disappeared as a result of competition from machine production in other regions or changes in fashion. In Bedfordshire the pillow lace industry, a cottage manufacture carried on in both town and country, was declining from the 1880s through the competition of production by machine.[42]

A few specialized industries developed in a particular country town and its district in response to the growth of a national demand for its products. Redditch in Worcestershire gained a national reputation for needles, Tonbridge in Kent for cricket balls. At High Wycombe in the early Victorian period the manufacture of chairs grew 'from a semi-rural craft of local fame to an industry of national importance'. The local products, with interwoven cane seats, were quite distinctive. In 1875 about seventy chair manufacturers employed nearly 700 householders in the district, and many young men, boys, girls and women.[43]

The momentous economic and social changes of the Victorian period all left their mark on the country towns. A few, such as Lincoln, Reading and Swindon, were transformed into important industrial or railway centres while retaining links with the surrounding countryside; a small number, particularly in the home counties, were swallowed up by the expansion of a large city. The majority altered slowly over the decades. In general the larger towns which were already of regional importance in the 1830s, or those which received the benefit of good rail links in the mid-nineteenth century, gained trade at the expense of the majority of country towns which were only of local importance. For many country towns market trading was ceasing to be so significant, and in a few it disappeared altogether. In most of them there was a greater variety of shops, and everywhere the range of goods sold in them was becoming larger. On the other hand, by the end of the century goods produced in other areas were slowly but surely restricting the work available to local craftsmen. So far as industry was concerned, cottage and small workshop industries were tending to decline or disappear, though with some exceptions; and, where manufacture survived in the town, it was tending to concentrate in larger works, mills or factories. Yet in its essentials, as a trading centre for a primarily agrarian hinterland, the country town survived into the twentieth century.

Notes

1   Hardy, 1926, 33.
2   BPP 1888 LV, 74.
3   Lewis, 1840, 378.
4   *Victoria County History: Oxfordshire II*, 251.
5   Gardner, 1852, 637.
6   *Victoria County History: Oxfordshire X*, 13, 64–6.
7   Kelly, 1891, 2253.
8   Kelly, 1905, II, 509, 526.
9   Kelly, 1891, 2243.
10 *Victoria County History: Oxfordshire X*, 13, 67.
11 BPP 1888 LVII 481.
12 BPP 1888 LIV 169.
13 BPP 1888 LIV 124.
14 BPP 1888 LV 83.
15 BPP 1888 LV 174.
16 *Victoria County History: Oxfordshire X*, 60.
17 *Ibid.*
18 BPP 1888 LIV 87–8.
19 Greening, 1971, 172.
20 Everitt, 1973, 232–5.
21 Brewster, 1970, 1–16.
22 Horn, 1976b, 101.
23 Chalklin, 1975, 17.
24 Rogers, 1972, 225.
25 Kelly, 1898, 32.
26 Clapham, 1932, 125.
27 Horn, 1976b, 101.

28 Brewster, 1970, 18–21.
29 Freeman, 1976, 84–5.
30 *Victoria County History: Yorkshire: East Riding II*, 56–7.
31 Booker, 1974, 74.
32 Cooper, 1971, 103–12.
33 Neale, 1974, 32, 38–40, 51, 56–7.
34 *Victoria County History: Oxfordshire X*, 86.
35 Jenkins, 1972, 61.
36 Elliott, 1975, 235–7.
37 *Victoria County History: Oxfordshire X*, 66–7.
38 Booker, 1974, 22.
39 Lee, 1956, 62.
40 *Victoria County History: Oxfordshire II*, 258.
41 *Ibid.*, 258.
42 *Victoria County History: Bedfordshire II*, 123.
43 Ashford, 1960, 290, 311.

21   Country Professions

Barbara Kerr

Towards the end of the eighteenth century many professional men, particularly lawyers, doctors, and those with a mechanical turn of mind, began to realize that the countryside could offer as rewarding a sphere of activity as the city. Also those sections of rural society which had prospered during the French wars were offering new candidates for the professions, including the Church. The determination of rising men to be heard in local matters and the concern of those from long-established professional families to maintain their authority were not, however, always conducive to the harmonious management of local affairs. Though a façade of public order was maintained, Victorian society was rent with alarms and dissensions. To the public controversies no small contribution was made by professional men, who entered the arena armed with all the authority imparted by specialized knowledge and with the self-confidence of a thrusting age.

Of the many controversial issues two were literally matters of life and death: sanitation and the control of zymotic, or infectious, diseases. The obsession with these topics was not due to national hypochondriacal tendencies, as often asserted by foreigners, but to the rapid growth of villages and towns without any provision of sewerage or supplies of unpolluted water. The scene was set for epidemics, and cholera, typhoid and typhus duly made their appearance. In such menacing times confusion and contention were the keynotes at meetings of vestries, local boards of health and town councils. Here clergymen and doctors often took the lead, as men of authority if not of omniscience. Their prolonged arguments often delayed urgent matters of public health; and in these procrastinations lawyers played a major part.

Questions such as 'Does anyone know a great drainage company ... who are not continually before the Law Courts, or indulging in costly parliamentary struggles?' were seldom answered in the affirmative.[1] Besides the hazard of disease, another phenomenon was unsettling rural communities. Though in the mid-nineteenth century Kersal Moor still dominated the smoking chimneys of Manchester, the city had started its onslaught on the countryside. Many villages in the propinquity of developing industrial activities throughout England and Wales were overshadowed by a sense of doom.

I

The urban onslaught on the countryside and the spread of Darwinism caused many rural incumbents to adopt a brisker and more scientific attitude towards their time-honoured interest in the flora and fauna of their parishes. Whatever their pastimes, the majority of country parsons retained their generally accepted position as the apex of the village triangle until the end of the nineteenth century. This ascendancy was due to an education which enabled them to play many parts, and due also to the stable social hierarchy which persisted in the village until the townward trek intensified in the latter part of the century.

A university degree followed by a course of theological study rendered a man eligible at the age of twenty-three for ordination, but in no way ensured that he secured a living. This designation was a misnomer when, at the end of the century, incumbents of four hundred benefices earned less than £50 a year, and of 3,500 less than £100. The stipend of a curate often determined his survival, while that of an incumbent regulated his social relationships within the parish. A competency enabled him to enjoy the satisfaction of intercourse with his equals in education and also that of helping those in need. The expectation that the parson should be the village factotum owed much to the spanking pace set by Sydney Smith. As rector of Foston in Yorkshire (1808–21) he wrote that he was playing his part 'in the usual manner, as doctor, justice, road-maker, pacifier, preacher, farmer, neighbour, and diner out'.[2] Time, and the proliferation of local authorities, relieved incumbents of some of these activities, such as poor relief and the maintenance of roads; but they remained eligible to sit on the Bench and continued to act, with or without qualifications, as doctors. Some parishioners felt the parson's doctoring 'was like hedge-carpentery—not neat-like, but everlasting strong'.[3]

In 1836 the commutation of the tithes freed incumbents from prying inquisitions into their parishioners' barns, and enabled them to experiment on their own land, and act as agricultural advisors. Farmers would have done well to heed John Stevens Henslow, vicar of Hitcham in Suffolk (1839–61) and author of *Letters to the Farmers of Suffolk*, one-time mentor of Charles Darwin and assistant to Sir Joseph Hooker at Kew. They justifiably hesitated to follow the lead of Anthony Huxtable, the farming rector of Sutton Waldron in Dorset (1834–83). Though the yearly value of his living was only £205, private means enabled Huxtable to embark on factory-farming with steam-driven machinery and with sewage piped on to the fields. Like many agricultural innovators, Huxtable never revealed the working of his 'rural sums'; but his concern for his parishioners was manifest.

Huxtable's steam-driven machinery was a far cry from farming by hand-labour and prayer as described by Elizabeth Gaskell in her rural idyll, *Cousin Phillis* (1863–4). To survive, many Nonconformist clergy were forced into the harness of small-scale farming and regular teaching. But aid came from the tradition of 'helping the minister', which was general in Wales and not uncommon in England.[4] This help, whether in the form of labour or of kind, forged a link between the minister and congregation that was not always found in Anglican parishes.

Many incumbents were dogged by an 'Aggrieved Parishionership'.[5] Though the term was applied to Deddington in Oxfordshire, this state of irritation was endemic in England and Wales. Resentment in the Principality was chiefly aroused by the English-speaking parson and extended, according to George Borrow, to his cat. In England, if parishioners were not complaining about the over-elaborate part played by the choir, as in the harvest procession of 1868 at Haydock in Lancashire, they were deprecating, as at Deddington, the expulsion of the choir by a Low Church incumbent who wished to seat his family in the stalls.

Vestries, where plural voting in favour of the man of property was established early in the century, were the storm centres for all parochial discontents. This was particularly the case at Easter when the church expenditure was examined by all ratepayers including, until 1868, the Nonconformists. At this time the vestry became both a political forum and a boxing ring.[6] When the vicar of Orton in Warwickshire arrived ten minutes late he found a radical installed in the chair. And as the vicar of All Saints, at Sudbury in Suffolk tried to leave a meeting with poll book he was forcibly detained, and had some reason to declare that abuse was the vestryman's 'vocation'.[7] Muscular Christianity was often the expression of a physical rather than a theological need. The most serious clash occurred at Halberton in Devon. The vestry refused to vote the rate because Edward Girdlestone, the vicar (1862–72), wished to drain the village sewage which was seeping into the wells, and because he had assisted miserably paid agricultural labourers to emigrate to the more prosperous midland and south-eastern counties. Taken to the Queen's Bench Division the dispute resulted in a victory for the vicar, who soon left the parish, and for the lawyers. The sewage remained undrained.

A solution to this problem was found by Henry Moule, vicar of Fordington in Dorset (1829–80). Having worked in his parish throughout the cholera outbreak of 1849, Moule evolved the earth closet. This was an invaluable stop-gap until greater improvement could be effected by the water closet system. Besides being costly, the water closest was often faulty. In the 1870s 'the lives of a family [were] made to depend on half an inch of water in some inscrutable hole or upon a grating not getting choked with street mud'.[8]

Like Moule, Charles Kingsley, vicar of Eversley in Hampshire (1844–69), was active 'in thundering in behalf of sanitary reform'.[9] A strong interest in natural history and a living worth £500 a year encouraged Kingsley to embark on a campaign to save wild life from pollution and from the onslaughts of the naturalists, with many of whom seeing was collecting. *The Water Babies* (1863), perhaps Kingsley's most effective book, was written to draw attention to the depredations of naturalists. Though not guiltless of collecting moths and butterflies, Francis Morris, rector of Nunburnholme in Yorkshire (1854–93), defended foxes from the huntsmen, pheasants from *battue* shooting and every sort of bird from the insatiable demands of milliners. To protect birds massacred for decoration, Morris was to the fore in founding the Plumage League (1885) and also in prohibiting the sale of native song birds. As a parson often without a cure, John George Wood (1827–89) lived chiefly on the proceeds from his lectures and his books on natural history. These were mostly published by the S.P.C.K., and were frequently awarded as prizes at boys' schools. Wood's wide range of subjects included *Feathered Friends* (1856), *Houses without Hands* (1863), *Bible Animals* (1871) and 'Unappreciated Insects' about which he lectured in Ireland. Wood was an earnest and accurate observer who did much to encourage other clerical naturalists and to popularize wild-life studies. All the natural history honours did not go to the clergy of the established Church. The zoologist with the most influence on the nascent enthusiasm for marine life was Philip Gosse (1810–88). He had been a Congregational minister before introducing the public to the wonders of the microscope, under which could be seen 'the *dear* animalcules and infusoria, about which Mr. Gosse writes so charmingly'.[10]

II

The superabundant energies of Victorian parsons active in promoting sanitary improvements, the diffusion of knowledge ranging from earth worms to ethics, and the more mundane provision of village reading rooms and allotments, ensured a clerical hegemony in many rural parishes. Nevertheless, a shrewd observer of village life considered the apothecary 'one of the most important personages in a small country town. . . . He takes rank next after the rector and the attorney, and before the curate; and could be much less easily dispensed with than either of those worthies.'[11] The trust placed in the apothecary was due to his antecedents, and because his cures, mostly herbal, were well known to the village community. That he might have been a licentiate of the Apothecary's Society in London, and so legally recognized as a medical man, had little weight in a country community.

The net of examination and certification was less easily evaded by physicians and surgeons after the mid-nineteenth century, when it seemed clear that cholera, typhoid and typhus had come to stay. The fearful suddenness with which cholera struck and spread engendered the belief that 'the timid and fanciful' were particularly vulnerable.[12] The man who contributed most towards allaying this terror was William Budd (1811–80), who pointed to exposed sewage and not to the imagination as the source of both cholera and typhoid. Though he had studied in London, Edinburgh and Paris, the latter being the Mecca of those seeking to see beyond the accepted cures, Budd learnt most from the typhoid outbreaks in his home, North Tawton in Devon. This was a small wool town noted for the 'rare healthiness of its site'.[13] Here a serious outbreak of typhoid in 1871, with repeated sporadic visitations in the west of England and in south Wales, enabled Budd to study the disease. He deduced that typhoid, 'like malignant cholera, dysentery, yellow fever and others', was an infectious disease often spread by uncleared sewage.[14] While sanitary work remained a hit-or-miss affair, Budd could only advise 'disinfection by anticipation'. This injunction was unwittingly carried out by villagers throughout the country; for, as the *Sanitary Inspector* (3 March 1877) pointed out, male adults drank beer, the females tea, and only the children took water. From the knowledge he gained at Tawton Budd was able in 1866 to contain an outbreak of cholera in Bristol, where seventeen years earlier the disease had carried off 444 souls. That Bristol was the Black Hole of disease was largely due to the frequency and virulence of political disputes among the city authorities.

As a student of outstanding ability and the son of a doctor with private means, Budd was able to choose his niche in the medical world. Many newly qualified doctors, however, were obliged to start their careers in workhouses, lunatic asylums and local hospitals. During the vacations the Poor Law guardians accepted student labour for out-patients; and they exerted a rigid control over their fully qualified doctors. Despite the plea of Dr W. M. Torrens in the House of Commons that Poor Law medical officers as 'educated gentlemen ... ought to be respectfully and honourably treated by the Legislature', the reverse was the case.[15] In 1868 a qualified practitioner was receiving £55 a year at the notorious Farnham Workhouse; two years later the guardians at Kingsbridge in Devon appointed a 'medical officer for one year at £20 per annum'.[16] Conditions were no better in the more prosperous north, where at Berwick the authorities offered £25 a year for a doctor who was to supply his own medicines—except cod-liver oil, which the guardians could buy cheaply in bulk. At the same institution the porter was to receive £20 yearly with lodging found. But even a workhouse doctor could turn. In 1866 the medical officer of the Sherborne institution ransacked the stores for alcohol to keep alive a 12-year-old servant girl who had been half killed by her employers.[17] They appeared later at the assize court.

Workhouse scandals generally provided the neighbourhood with news; but the refusal of the Board of Guardians at Keighley in Yorkshire to allow vaccination caused a national outcry. This was not a case of Dickens's 'vestry claiming its independent right to have as much typhus fever as pleases itself'. Objections to vaccination were raised by a thoughtful man like Alfred Russel Wallace (1823–1913), who considered *Vaccination a Delusion, its Penal Enforcement a Crime* (1898); and by a forceful one like Joseph Arch, the founder of the agricultural labourers' union, who refused to have his 'children treated as if they were cattle'.[18] Eight men were willing to pay the bail of £1,000 when the Keighley guardians were ordered to prison by the Queen's Bench Division.

Provincial hospitals, which were often established by individual effort and supported chiefly by 'congregational collections', appealed to young and ambitious doctors. Such a one was Tertius Lydgate, portrayed by George Eliot in *Middlemarch* (1871–2). To Lydgate the New Fever Hospital was a stepping stone to fame; but to the townsfolk it was a place where patients were allowed to die 'for the sake of cutting them up without saying by your leave or if you please'. It was not only the uneducated who voiced complaints. At the annual general meeting of the Dorset County Hospital questions were raised concerning the increased consumption of beef, beer and wine, of which orders were large 'enough to float a man of war'.[19]

While poor patients, allegedly, were being overfed, wealthy ones, according to Dr R. B. Grinrod, paid to be starved. At Malvern those taking the water cure bore 'on their faces the evidences of being washed out . . . as though they had parted with every particle of coloured blood in their body'.[20] A strange alliance had been made between workhouse infirmaries and expensive hydropathic institutions.

With neglect in the workhouses and experiments in provincial hospitals, it is not surprising that apothecaries maintained their popularity. The most notable of these was Henry Jephson (1798–1878), who made Leamington Spa as attractive to invalids as it was to hunting men. Trained in a chemist's shop, Jephson was 'coarse in appearance and uncouth in his manner';[21] but he was sensitive enough to perceive the malaises of his time. An over-tasked incumbent obtained a respite when Jephson paid for a curate, flagging governesses were treated free of charge, and 'sickly, jaundiced and deeply damaged orientals on their return from their baneful presidencies' were encouraged to believe that dieting and exercise might enable them to live until their retirement.[22] Dr Augustus Granville (1783–1872) considered that Jephson's residence, Beech Lawn in Leamington, would be 'pointed out in after years . . . as the habitation of one whose success as a physician had no parallel in his own time'.[23]

Even in an age of experiment the number of pilot balloons floated by the medical faculty in the nineteenth century was remarkable. The neo-romanticism of cures orientated to fresh air, plain feeding and exercise had a considerable influence on population movements in the countryside. To survive, large numbers of invalids made their way to rural retreats from which, in order to live, the inhabitants were emigrating to the cities. Two doctors, Sir James Clark (1788–1870) and Augustus Granville, both with Italian affiliations, were largely responsible for the emergence of the health resorts on the south coast. Moving southward the invalids took in their train a number of professional auxiliaries. At Torquay Granville found 'eighty-two spinsters, nineteen medicals, twelve divines, and only two attorneys'; he also discovered that the 'peculiar smell of the back water . . . [was] particularly offensive'.[24] Yet Granville had nothing but praise for the 'true, stinking' sulphur wells at Harrogate. So efficacious was one of these springs that disputes over its ownership ended 'as such cases generally terminate, in the men of law gaining everything, and the litigants nothing'.[25]

III

Though he was a much travelled man of the world, Granville viewed the law in the same light as did an English countryman. Since the subsidence of the manor courts and his exclusion from the vestry, the voice of the husbandman carried little legal weight in England. His legal horizons ended with the Bench. The justices of the peace who tried minor offences were familiar with the countryside and with their neighbours; not, at least initially, with the law. It was the justices' clerk who, even before some legal training was enforced in 1877, guided the magistrates through the limited range of misdeeds presented to them. When he came before a justice at Ipswich, Mr Pickwick was rescued by the 'pale, sharp-nosed, half-fed, shabbily clad' clerk. The offence with which justices were most familiar was poaching which, to landowners, was as threatening as were the barricades to law-abiding citizens on the continent. A long line of those infringing the Game Laws filed before the magistrates. Unless violence was used, poachers were generally let off with a fine, which was allegedly paid by the receiving City poulterers and fishmongers.

The first steps towards achieving a professional legal career were often daunting to the young. As an articled clerk, Robert Smith Surtees (1803–64) at the age of sixteen entered the office of a London conveyancer, a lawyer concerned with the transference of property. For the payment of a hundred guineas a year, he 'had the run of a dingey, carpetless room, the use of some repulsive-looking desks, and liberty to copy twenty volumes of manuscript precedences'.[26] Surtees soon left to become a celebrated sporting writer.

Articled clerks who became solicitors in the mid-nineteenth century had more varied prospects before them than those which had faced their predecessors. The aspirations of many country lawyers had centred on a jog-trotting clientele which included some solvent landowners and one or two insolvent ones who needed a legal land agent to ease them out of their difficulties. By the 1850s young solicitors had before them many profitable openings not connected with land management. Railway companies were proliferating; and round the necks of local Boards of Health had been hung the millstone of supplying sewerage and water, with all the concomitant legal complications of rights of way and of pipes smashed by those not favouring new-fangled schemes.[27] Local authorities were not always to be blamed for floundering in the sanitary shallows. As a result of conflicting advice from lawyers, surveyors and contractors, Dorchester was supplied in 1859 with an underground drain which twenty years later 'did not in any way fulfil the conditions of a sewer';[28] and a water-supply system whereby this small country borough daily consumed more water than Glasgow. The frequency of such mishaps throughout the country was due to legal uncertainties, to local fears of incurring high expenses, and to the whole sanitary question meeting 'a yawning House of Commons in the small hours of the morning'.[29] There was no yawning in the House during the railway mania of 1845, when 'the two Houses were an Eldorado to certain favoured lawyers who were alternately paid for speech and *silence* with reckless profusion'.[30] Little of this golden rain fell on country lawyers; as a Devon solicitor observed, local men did all the work while the railway company's London lawyer sat back 'with his handsome salary of £250 per annum'.[31]

Though the length and expenses of a legal training appeared to many besides the needy Tommy Traddles as 'a great pull', many made the ascent. Whether they started as an articled clerk in a solicitor's office, from the chambers of a special pleader who prepared cases for the bar, or from the university, most barristers experienced a bleak and nail-biting time waiting for briefs. The careers of successful barristers are well documented; but the aspirations and setbacks of struggling men appear only in their journals and in contemporary novels. Although the manuscript diary of W. H. Roberts covers only the years 1851–3, it gives an insight into the daily concerns of a struggling and quixotic barrister. Born in 1815, Roberts was the only son of a widowed and domineering mother who managed the small family property at Easton in Huntingdonshire. He was admitted to Lincoln's Inn from Emmanuel College, Cambridge, in 1837, and was called to the bar five years later. Though associated with eminent lawyers, like Lord Campbell, Roberts felt himself 'forsaken by all the world, at least by all who can promote my welfare';[32] but indeed the diversity of causes he supported made it hard for him to find a patron. As Roberts lived near Kettering, where much of the parish was still held in 1853 by the ancient tenure of copyhold, he realized the financial losses likely to be incurred by the enforced enfranchisement of such tenants; and on their behalf distributed copies of the *Cry of the Copyholder*. Though he dismissed accusations that he was 'mixing with the Chartists' as 'all a falsehood', Roberts continued his championship of the underdog. He made known his sympathies with the workmen who were sent to prison for 'seeking a well-settled price book rather than force a high rate of payment'.[33] When his views aroused family resentment, Roberts solaced himself by retiring to read *Swiss Family Robinson* and the novels of Surtees; and by cleaning out the drains on the family property, only pausing to admire 'the dandelions and etc. growing luxuriantly'. This combination of legal activities in London and of rural avocations was frequent among briefless barristers in the mid-nineteenth century.

As well as having a predilection for outcasts, Roberts had religious views which were unfashionably ecumenical. He attended mass at a Roman Catholic church, but only committed himself to putting one halfpenny in the charity box; he received 'two Mahomitans from Alexandria'; and read the psalms in Hebrew and other portions of the Bible in German. In this language Roberts was helped by his sister, Mary. Mary's existence, overshadowed by an exacting mother and harassed by a necessitous brother, exemplifies the urge of many women in the 1850s to seek wider spheres of action. In the following decades they stormed hospitals and local government boards; but despite the efforts of Lydia Becker (1827–90) they did not invest the Inns of Court until early in the next century.

IV

The legal reforms of the 1870s aimed at centralization under a Supreme Court of Judicature and a greater expedition of legal processes. As an earnest that law and equity were truly united, the term attorney, with its undertones of greed and shuffle, was dropped. This overhaul of a creaking machine occurred at a time when activities such as gardening, auctioneering and surveying were emerging as professions. This development was largely due to the greater diversity of subjects taught in the National Schools, and to the example of two pioneers: John Loudon (1783–1843) and George Robins (1787–1847). Loudon's story is the familiar one of a Scotsman who by his own efforts achieved a high degree of education and moved southward to utilize it. A landscape gardener by profession, Loudon considered that any work connected with the land entailed a thorough study of 'Arithmetic and Book-keeping, Geometry, Mensuration and Practical Trigonometry, Mechanics, Hydro-statics and Hydraulics, Land-Surveying, Levelling, Planning and Mapping, Architectural Drawing and Isometric Projection and Perspective'.[34] In the early nineteenth century, thanks to the efforts of men like Loudon, John Abercombie and Charles McIntosh, gardening blossomed into an art and a science. Head gardeners who had mastered surveying in order to lay out shrubberies, made popular by Mrs Siddons's taste for 'Evergreens . . . of the most sombre, sable and tragical cast';[35] hydrostatics to construct the falls of water essential to the pleasure grounds; and aestheticism to ensure the approach to the hermitage 'should be rather rough and even difficult',[36] were entitled to be both professional men and autocrats. Charles McIntosh, who could trace the pedigree of every English apple, and also of the 'magnificent Rhododendron arborea from the Nepaul Mountains', brooked no interference from his employers who included the Earl of Breadalbane, Sir Thomas Baring and Prince Leopold of Saxe-Coburg.

Mansions with lordly grounds could hardly be let or sold by the efforts of obliging neighbours or notices in shop windows, as was the usage with lesser habitations. In the 1820s the disposal of stately homes was monopolized by a man who gave a new dimension to the selling of property. Sales by auction, allegedly introduced into England by a nabob in the early eighteenth century, were transformed by George Robins (1778–1847). Under his management auction sales became not only outstandingly profitable, but also social occasions on the grand scale. Trained in the shadow of Covent Garden by his auctioneering father, Robins had an aptitude for displays and the wit to make them entertaining. He also had the stamina to conduct the 'twenty-four days' sale' of Horace Walpole's collections at Strawberry Hill,[37] and to entertain Byron at 'a splendid dinner, full of great names and high spirits'.[38] Believed to earn £12,000 a year, Robins could afford to give Lucullan banquets, resuscitate Drury Lane and Covent Garden, and support the sea-bathing institution at Margate.

The secret of Robins's success was his ability to plumb the aspirations of successful traders and manufacturers to become landowners. The new men seeking old acres turned instinctively to the 'immortal Robins', who well knew how to sell an estate by dropping 'a sly hint as to the possibility of the property influencing the representation of the neighbouring borough of Swillingford'.[39] Robins made his fortune despite the increasing government duties imposed on auction sales. These were replaced a few years before his death by a licence costing £10, a change for which Robins had asked. Soon every town had its auctioneers, whose witticisms were passed around at markets. Many descendants of such men are still auctioneering in the same districts.

Though surveyors had formed a chartered institute in 1868, they long remained the mavericks of rural society. Armed with his Gunter's chain and his cross-staff, the surveyor stood above criticism of his work and his charges. A lawyer observed, perhaps not without envy: 'Nothing has ever been done which can fix the charges of a land valuer or surveyor, and, having regard to the work done, they are more extortionate than those of any other class of professionals.'[40] Surtees's small farmer put these words more bluntly when he shouted to a surveyor: 'I'd as soon think of setting my 'ard sow to survey an estate!'

Until well into the nineteenth century the exact functions of a surveyor were not clearly understood. The Leamington councillor who considered the posts of surveyor and scavenger could be 'filled by the same individual' expressed a general belief.[41] With cholera in the county, the town councillors of Dorchester sought to expedite their sanitary plans by appointing a new surveyor. As applicants demanded salaries ranging from £50 to £250 a year, some had scavenging rather than surveying in mind. The council was not interested in such refinements, and was concerned only that the surveyor should not interest himself in 'private connections' to the main sewer.[42] That such connections had been made, and with considerable profit, by surveyors in the past explains the near collapse of the borough's sanitary system in the 1870s. A brisker attitude to public health was not immediately detectable after the establishment of county councils in 1888. Salaries for surveyors in Merionethshire were raised to £205 a year, but the 'insanitary notices' still fluttered like autumn leaves on the habitations without any form of sanitation.[43] Until the surveyor produced acceptable plans for draining and for supplying water the councillors were irrationally annoyed that the engineer sent 'his bills but not his plans' to follow schemes which were so often rejected.

Although abused locally, surveyors left lasting monuments to their industry and accuracy: the enclosure and tithe maps. These beautiful, if sometimes unwieldy, maps bear witness not only to the conformation of the fields of between 1830 and 1850 but also to the surveying activities of two brothers, the younger of whom was Alfred Russel Wallace. In 1837 Wallace became an apprentice surveyor in Bedfordshire under his brother's direction, and, on his own initiative, a close observer of the natural world and of his fellows. Surveying in Higham Gobion in Bedfordshire for the commutation of tithes, Wallace observed 'the whole parish was one large farm'; and began to ponder on the ethics of land ownership.[44] The larger parish of Hitchin gave the young surveyor scope to observe the influence of the rock formations on the flora.

297

The influence of the poet on thinking men in the mid-nineteenth century can hardly be exaggerated. Philip Gosse, the pietistic zoologist, spoke for them all when he declared that by reading Byron's *Lara* he 'acquired a new sense'.[45] This new acquisition was to many an awakened sensitivity to the conditions imposed on society by industrial expansion. Such a feeling accounts for William Budd's belief that without a common concern for the victims of dirt and disease, a common grave threatened society. The musical and poetry-loving Henry Moule subscribed whole-heartedly to this belief and took down-to-earth measures to avert disaster. Though practicalities did not come easily to William Roberts, he did not watch unmoved, or without putting his hand in his pocket, the weary march of villagers to swell disease in the cities. The imminence of danger which stirred thinking men into action in the 1840s and 1850s also accounted for the violence at meetings of vestries and local boards of health; and for the higher standards and wider scope of a professional training. The effects of these reforms were particularly noticeable in the countryside where local boards had long endeavoured to set the pace for professional men. Their emancipation from such bodies strengthened the position of parsons and doctors in rural society; while reforms in training and administration rendered the services of lawyers, engineers and surveyors more predictable and acceptable to countrymen.

Notes

1 *Peterborough Gazette*, 20 August 1864.
2 Smith, 1956, 139.
3 Idstone (Rev. T. Pearce), 1874, 7.
4 Information concerning Nonconformist ministers in Wales was kindly sent by the Rev. G. M. Roberts, president of the Calvinist Methodist Historical Society.
5 Colvin, 1963, 101.
6 *Leamington Spa Courier*, 21 April 1838.
7 *Suffolk and Essex Free Press*, 27 March 1856.
8 Moule, 1870, 9.
9 Kingsley, 1899, 148.
10 Quoted in *Once a Week*, 6 August 1859.
11 Mitford, 1848, I, 511.
12 *Western Flying Post*, 14 June 1849.
13 Budd, 1873, 10.
14 *Ibid.*, 40.
15 *Examiner*, 27 February 1867.
16 *Kingsbridge Gazette*, 22 January 1870.
17 *Dorset County Chronicle*, 15 March 1866.
18 Arch, 1898, 55.
19 *Dorset County Chronicle*, 8 January 1866.
20 *Ibid.*, 25 January 1866.

21 MS diary of Elizabeth Galton, 1833. This fascinating diary has been edited, but not yet published, by J. L. and J. A. K. Moilliet, connections of Elizabeth Anne Galton (1808–1906).

22 Granville, 1841, II, 243.

23 *Ibid.*, II, 243.

24 *Ibid.*, II, 486.

25 *Ibid.*, I, 40.

26 Surtees, 1854, 166.

27 *The Times*, 17 November 1875.

28 Report of Gotto & Beesley, Westminster, in *Dorset County Chronicle*, 9 May 1878.

29 Hope, 1875, 10.

30 Jeaffreson, 1867, I, 234–5.

31 *Kingsbridge Gazette*, 26 March 1870.

32 All quotations from MS diary of William Henry Roberts kindly shown me by the late Miss D. H. Roberts of Portsmouth.

33 *Morning Chronicle*, 25 October 1851.

34 Loudon, 1845, sub-title.

35 Hogg, 1824, 107.

36 McIntosh, 1828, II, 809.

37 Robins, 1908, 87.

38 Moore, 1830, I, 398.

39 Surtees, 1958, 233.

40 Idstone, 1874, 276.

41 *Leamington Spa Courier*, 10 March 1838.

42 *Dorset County Chronicle*, 11 August 1859.

43 *Towyn-on-Sea and Merioneth County Times*, 28 November 1895.

44 Wallace, 1905, I, 106.

45 Gosse, 1890, 25.

22   Country Tradesmen

J. A. Chartres

Until very recently the increase in the numbers of rural tradesmen was regarded as a feature of late eighteenth-century England, one which continued well into the nineteenth century. The village shop, the grocer, draper, or butcher, were uncommon before 1800; their coming was a consequence of the growing population and improved communications of the nineteenth-century countryside.[1] Recent work on the history of pre-industrial England by Willan and others has shown this view to be somewhat misleading, and by 1700 'shops' of several kinds were to be found in the substantial villages of England.[2] To treat Victorian England as the period in which the country tradesman's shop evolved is therefore to confound origin and growth. While the beginnings of rural retailing date from well before 1800, the real dissemination of these trades was a feature of the Victorian countryside.

I

As in other studies of occupations in this period, it is far from easy to define numbers and trends in employment or to assess the business structure of such trades. However, the two familiar sources of trade directories and the census reports, from 1851 especially, do offer some basic answers for the variety of trades that characterized the countryside of this period, and it is to an analysis of these materials that we turn first.

In order to place the detailed history into perspective, it is important as a preliminary to examine the general trends in employment in the wide variety of

Table 22.1 *Employment in trades, England and Wales, 1851–1901 ('000)**

Trade group	1851	1861	1871	1881	1891	1901
(a) *Food and drink*						
Milk, dairy, cheese, and provisions	30.56	32.95	38.47	46.77	56.82	66.16
Butchery and meat	68.39	68.11	75.85	81.70	98.92	112.60
Fish, poultry, and game	14.68	14.58	18.27	21.50	29.71	34.83
Bakers and confectioners	76.40	68.67	76.05	96.57	130.82	171.08
Greengrocers and fruiterers	16.55	18.05	25.82	29.61	40.96	52.63
Grocers†	86.04	93.55	111.09	129.82	181.86	201.17
Eating, coffee, boarding, and lodging houses	26.24	24.94	31.38	45.55	62.71	69.18
Inns, Hotels, and beersellers	75.72	82.03	93.41	86.69	95.62	99.92
(b) *Agricultural commodity trades*						
Corn, flour, seed, and milling	48.29	43.46	42.83	33.43	34.41	40.06
Livestock dealers and salesmen	7.77	6.24	5.84	5.75	5.35	5.36
Drovers	3.23	3.13	2.95	2.59	2.83	2.84
(c) *Other tradesmen and services*						
General shopkeepers	29.80	14.58	39.99	54.86	53.61	53.58
Costermongers and hawkers	37.85	37.58	49.78	47.11	58.94	61.34
Drapers	45.39	57.65	74.34	82.36	107.02	135.66
Tailors and milliners‡	518.72	523.11	549.40	621.91	718.21	765.76
Tobacco retail and manufacture	8.61	9.78	14.37	19.73	28.97	44.37
Ironmongers	11.29	10.78	17.37	16.12	21.44	28.21
Fuel and coal merchants	14.21	15.55	20.25	25.79	29.73	32.85
Carriers	82.40	97.33	120.06	125.34	170.26	272.96

†Includes tea and chocolate makers and dealers.
‡Sum of 1901 Census categories 303, 302, 306, 307, 308, 304, 305, and 311 male, and 303 female.
*Based on Census Reports for 1851, 1861, 1871, 1881, 1891, 1901.

trades that were found in both town and country. The census categories are far from constant, but in Table 22.1 the broad trends in total trade employment for England and Wales for 1851–1901 are presented. It is immediately clear that the growth of country trades such as these was but part of the more general explosion of retail distribution that has been termed the 'retailing revolution'.[3] If the first half of the nineteenth century was striking for the rapid growth of industrial employment, then the second half, with which we are here concerned, was remarkable principally for the growth of the trade and service sectors. With the single exception of category (b) in Table 22.1, the traditional agricultural trades which stagnated from the 1850s, employment in the trade sector grew rapidly in our period, by an average of 87 per cent between 1851 and 1901 in our sample trades.

Such figures cannot be taken quite at face value, and problems of definition confuse several categories, none more so than the 'tailors and milliners' group, under which a wide variety of trades, manufactures, and employments has been subsumed. Broadly, though, these statistics are reasonably representative of general trends in the growth of trades. Unfortunately, historians of retail distribution, such as Alexander, and specialists in applied economics, like Jefferys, have concentrated on urban shopkeeping trades rather than on those which spread, as part of the general movement, into the country towns and villages.[4] But the general tendency towards the proliferation of separate trades and fairly rapid general growth was mirrored in the countryside. It was after all a feature of the retailing revolution that the food trades grew more rapidly than total population, a result both of improved communications and rising living standards. In the towns this opened the way to the chain grocery stores, such as Lipton's, while in the villages of the Victorian countryside it marked the arrival of the specialist food retailers.[5]

The impact of these changes between the 1820s and the 1870s can best be illustrated by a detailed examination of specific villages and market towns. Therefore, a number of settlements in the North Riding of Yorkshire have been compared in Table 22.2, with a view to demonstrating the arrival at village and country town level of various tradesmen. The fifteen places have been grouped by size, but cannot be regarded as a scientific sample of the population: they are no more nor less than a number of examples of changes from a relatively remote upland rural shire.

Table 22.2 *Tradesmen in North Yorkshire, 1820 and 1879 (businesses)**

Categories and place	Grocer		Butcher		Shopkeeper		Victualler		Carrier		Draper	
	1820	1879	1820	1879	1820	1879	1820	1879	1820	1879	1820	1879
(a) *Market towns*												
Askrigg	3.5	1.5	2	2.5	0	2.5	5	3.5	2	2	0	1
Bedale	7	5	5	4	0	2.5	12	14.3	2	4	3	3
Castleton	1	2	1	3	0	2	2	4	2	3	1.5	2
Easingwold	0	1.5	6	3	5	6	18	16	2	1	5	4
Stokesley	14	7	7	6	4	8	16	12.5	2	2	8	3
(b) *Larger village* (<500 in 1871)												
Ampleforth	0	0.5	–	–	3	6·5	2	2	0	1	–	–
Great Ayton	4.5	5.1	4	5	0	6.5	4	2.5	1	3	0.5	1
Middleton Tyas	–	–	2	2	1	1	3	4.5	0	0.5	–	–
Ormesby	1	0	1	1	0	1	2	2	–	–	–	–
West Tanfield	2	0.3	2	1	0	4	3	4	–	–	–	0.3
(c) *Smaller village* (<500)												
Baldersby	–	0.5	–	–	–	–	–	–	–	–	–	0.5
Hauxwell	–	–	–	–	–	1	–	0.5	–	–	–	–
Kilburn	–	–	3	1	4	4.5	3	1.5	–	1	–	–
Skelton	–	–	–	0.5	1	–	1.5	1.5	–	–	–	–
Thornton Steward	1	–	–	1	1	1	3	1	–	–	–	–

*Based on Baines, 1823, and Kelly, 1879.

Bearing this caution in mind, the figures none the less add to the picture suggested by the general trends in employment, and indicate that the pattern of businesses was much the same as that of employment. Perhaps the first and clearest conclusion should be that the retail trades had already settled in the market towns and diffused downwards to the larger villages before 1830. Inevitably, evidence like this, drawn from directories, involves considerable problems of definition, but it is clear that the grocery trades were already well-established in such places by the 1820s. The figures also suggest that the retail butchery business reached a peak population before 1880, much as suggested by Perren's recent work. Although meat consumption *per capita* rose from around 87 lb per head in the decade 1831–40 to 110 lb in the 1870s, and 132 lb in the early 1900s, and employment in the trade grew roughly in proportion, there may have been some relative decline in small butchery businesses, much as suggested by Table 22.2. Better communications, a growth in the dead meat trade, and improved public health regulation of butchery served to increase the pressures on such small enterprises in both town and country.[6]

More striking than this evidence of the relatively early date at which two of the principal retail trades reached village level is the position of the other groups in the survey. Like the butcher and the grocer, the village innkeeper, beerseller, or publican was a long-established feature of country life, and indeed may have been the earliest of the retail trades to diffuse to that level.[7] It is apparent, therefore, in the figures of Table 22.2 that the number of such businesses may already have reached a maximum in the early years of Victoria's reign, a view supported by the relatively slow growth of employment in this area. Similarly, the trade of the draper, frequently and even normally tied with grocery, continued to permeate down the hierarchy of settlements, but in our Yorkshire examples made little progress between 1820 and 1879.

The two remaining trades, those of the carrier and the general shopkeeper, appear to have been rather different. In the first half of the century, the growth of road transport services was very rapid, but from the 1840s with the replacement of the road carrier by the railway on trunk and regional routes the business was far from finished. As Everitt has demonstrated, the wagons and carts of the carrier remained of significance in the country districts long after the railway had supplanted them on trunk routes. Indeed, far from acting as an agent of his decline, the railways, developing branch lines and extending their network into agricultural districts after 1850, provided a powerful stimulus to carting and carrying.[8] This same force may have been the source of the remarkable growth of general shopkeeping which, while visible in the figures of Table 22.1, is much more striking in Table 22.2, especially at the village level. This above all was the symbol of change in the retail trade, the aspect of the 'revolution' most striking in the rural districts.

Another way of assessing the significance of these tradesmen at village level is to identify the population thresholds at which they appeared. This is far from easy, for commercial directories are a notoriously shaky foundation, though detailed analysis has been attempted for parts of Norfolk in the 1830s and for some areas of the North

Riding of Yorkshire in the late 1870s. The results appear below in Table 22.3. In these figures the definition of these threshold populations has been taken as the midpoint between the average size of villages with such a trade and those with none, there being no overwhelming precision about either figure. Such a definition probably approximates to reality, but in one respect distorts the pattern. Most of the figures represent populations slightly lower than those at which such businesses were found, but in one case they have been distorted upwards by this approach. Alone in this sample, publicans in the North Riding showed a higher 'threshold' than the average village with a pub, and for those settlements with a public house, inn, or beerseller's shop the average population was below 220.

The consistent rank order of these trades is suggestive of their significance in village life, and it is vital to understanding this to examine in greater detail the functions they performed. Broadly speaking, the figures of Tables 22.2 and 22.3 represent whole businesses, but quite commonly tradesmen followed more than one occupation. As already indicated, grocer and draper were very commonly linked in this way, thus permitting the appearance of each trade at a rather lower threshold than would otherwise have been possible. Similar links were commonly found between blacksmiths and beersellers. For both craftsmen and tradesmen the markets attainable in the Victorian countryside were often too small to permit of total specialization: the solutions were the same as those typical of pre-industrial society, and took the form of either a duality of occupation or the adoption of a semi-itinerant style of life. Both effectively spread market areas and helped to sustain more specialized occupations.

Table 22.3 *Population thresholds at which tradesmen appeared in Norfolk and the North Riding of Yorkshire**

Norfolk (1836)		North Riding of Yorkshire (1879)	
Publican	377	Publican	296
Shopkeeper	463	Shopkeeper	309
Grocer	498	Butcher	372
		Grocer	489

*Based on White, 1836, and Kelly, 1879.

II

In part this was a period in which shops and similar settled outlets for trade grew to replace the more traditional means of retail distribution, the market and the fair. Of the two, the former was the more vital in respect of the retail trades, but it declined during our period as the growth of shops, of hawkers and costermongers, and of communications all invaded its monopoly. Alexander's study of the early nineteenth century has made it clear that there were differential effects of the coming of the

59 *above* Horncastle's ancient horse fair, a great occasion which attracted many spectators as well as well as dealers and their customers (Hallgarth Collection)

60 *below* Market Street, Gainsborough, Lincolnshire, on market day—apparently not a great cause of disturbance in this quiet country town (Hallgarth Collection)

61 Loughborough Cattle Market, about 1890. Meetings of farmers and dealers at local markets were as much a social as a business occasion (Loughborough Library Photographic Collection, Leicestershire Libraries and Information Service)

62 The Haven Flour Mill, Lincolnshire, 1892. Barges carried up the wheat and took away the flour.
Large steam-powered mills, located at ports and on rivers, were rapidly driving out the local windmills
by the later nineteenth century (Hallgarth Collection)

63 *above* Barges drying their sails on the Witham at Lincoln. Barges were widely used for carrying bulky goods like corn, flour, cattle and horse feed, fertilizers and coal, as well as the products of Lincoln's important agricultural engineering industry (Hallgarth Collection)

64 *left* Mr Maughan and wife outside their cottage tailor's shop in Tetford, Lincolnshire (Hallgarth Collection)

65 *right* The larger country towns developed a variety of plants for the processing of local produce. Here the staff, predominantly female, of a pickle factory in Lincoln pose with ingredients and equipment, late nineteenth century (Hallgarth Collection)

66 *left* A Market Harborough ironmonger displays
his wares, *c.* 1900. The stock includes rakes, pitchforks,
scythes and rolls of barbed wire, and the shop carries
an advertisement for McCormick harvesters
(Leicestershire Museums)

67 *above* The saddler's and currier's shop of W. F.
Francis, 13 Market Street, Falmouth, about 1910.
Leather goods in many forms fill the windows
(Museum of English Rural Life)

68 *above* A country-town parson, the Rev. McCarthy in the garden of Gainsborough Vicarage, with his wife and two daughters and staff of three (Hallgarth Collection)

69 *left* A group of Kesteven country doctors: a photograph taken at Bassingham (Hallgarth Collection)

70 A familiar domestic scene: servants of a country rectory at Henley, Suffolk
(Suffolk Photographic Survey)

71 *left* A rural vignette of the 1880s: a vanished corner of old Binbrook, once an important centre of country crafts near Market Rasen in the Lincolnshire wolds (Hallgarth Collection)

72 *below* A village shopkeeper poses in front of her establishment. Her windows display household goods and clothing as well as an advertisement for biscuits (Museum of English Rural Life)

73 *above* Mr Harrison, miller of South Willingham, near Gainsborough, Lincolnshire, with a cartload of flour (Hallgarth Collection)

74 *right* 'Shep' Mumby of Caistor: shepherd, veterinary expert, and pigkiller—seen here in the last of these roles (Hallgarth collection)

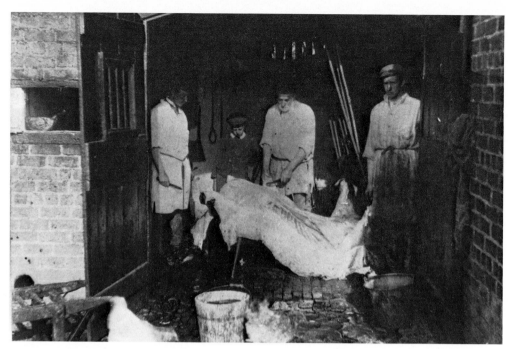

75 *above* Blackburn's butcher's shop at Swaby, Lincolnshire (Hallgarth Collection)

76 *below* John Lee, fish, fruit and game merchant of Market Rasen, on his delivery round (Hallgarth Collection)

77 *above left* An elderly milkman with yoke and pails at Nocton, a few miles south-east of Lincoln (Hallgarth Collection)

78 *above right* Matty Allwood, sweep, of Laceby, near Grimsby (Hallgarth Collection)

79 *above* Thatching was a skilled craft which sometimes occupied a whole family. Here such a family, the Grants, are seen making thatching pegs at South Ormsby, Lincolnshire (Hallgarth Collection)

80 *above right* William Dalley, of Turvey, Bedfordshire, ratcatcher, ploughwright, cooper and carpenter, drawn from life April 1830 (From John Higgins's Turvey Abbey Scrap Book)

81 *right* John Warren of Turvey, mason, drawn January 1830

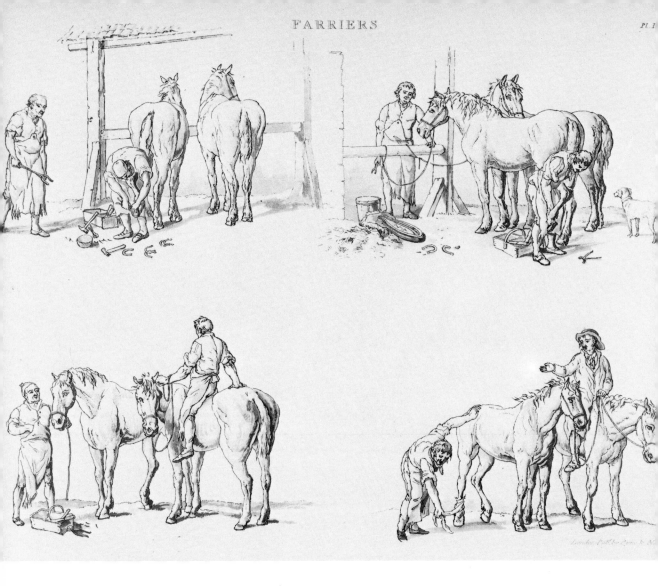

82 Farriers, illustrated by W. H. Pyne in the early 1800s, but reissued as appropriate representations of the craft up to 1845. The top two show shoeing, bottom left, farriers and horses, and bottom right, a countryman bringing a lame horse to a farrier (W. H. Pyne, *England, Scotland and Wales*, London: Ackermann, 1827)

83 Thomas Millward, of Turvey, whitesmith, with his 'machine or travelling apparatus', 1830s

84 Wheelwrights, illustrated by W. H. Pyne. Top left, making cart wheels; top right, adjusting a cart wheel; bottom, repairing mill work (W. H. Pyne, *England, Scotland and Wales*, London; Ackermann, 1827)

85 Rod stripping, stripping the bark from willow wands, using a scissor-like metal brake, occupied women and children in the osier beds along the banks of Thames, Trent and Dove. The rods were used for basketmaking or, as in this photograph, (taken near Oxford about 1900) for making eel traps and crayfish creels (Oxfordshire County Libraries)

BUYING CUT STRAW

SELLING PLAIT.

GOING TO MARKET WITH PLAIT.

A PLAITERS HOME

86 *above* The Dunstable straw-plaiting industry illustrated. Cottage women bought the cut straw, and they and their children (sometimes working in straw-plaiting schools) plaited the straw in a variety of patterns. Completed lengths of the plait were then taken to market and sold for use in the Bedfordshire straw hat trade (*The Queen*, 9 November 1861)

87 *right* A Bedfordshire straw-plaiter with her bundle of splints under her left arm (Luton Museum and Art Gallery)

88 Late nineteenth-century Bedfordshire lacemaker with her labourer husband (Luton Museum and Art Gallery)

89 Child lacemakers with their three-legged stools and pillows. A photograph taken in Buckinghamshire at the end of the nineteenth century (Buckinghamshire Country Library)

90 *above*   The industrialized village: handloom
weavers' cottages at Golcar, Yorkshire. The long
range of upper-storey windows was designed to give
ample light for working the handlooms, while the
living quarters were below (Colne Valley Museum)

91 *below*   Street, Somerset: an industrial village
which grew into a small town with the success of its
local shoe firm—C. & J. Clark—in the later nineteenth
century. Clark's, a Quaker firm with a strong interest
in its locality and workpeople, planned much of the
town and built numerous streets of solid model
cottages (such as these at Brutasche Terrace, *c.* 1900)
combining the local architectural tradition with their
own refinements (C. & J. Clark)

canal and the railway on the large and small urban centres. The country markets became increasingly less attractive to local producers, and by the 1880s had become the targets for attack by the shopkeeping community.[9] The noise, disorder, and smells consequent upon the weekly market had come to outweigh their commercial benefits. Sensitive testimony to this effect came before the Royal Commission of 1888–9 from one of the great market toll ingrossers of later Victorian England, Mr Joseph Frederick Mark, who according to the deputy commissioner 'speaks from considerable experience, but of course under a strong bias'.[10] Mark's comments were as follows:

> As a rule throughout the country the markets are going down; there may be a few exceptions in London, Birmingham, Manchester and so on, where they have a larger area to work on; but the trade is diverted into shops and from shops again to the travelling shops that are going round the country.[11]

While this probably expressed the fundamental reasons for the waning of country markets, many survived and remained to 1900 and beyond as important occasions for trade, if themselves less vital trading institutions. In 1888 a witness from Romford made just this point:

> the inhabitants and shopkeepers are perhaps rather shortsighted in running against it [the market], for this reason, that if they abolished this market, they would do themselves a very great deal of harm. It is the market that brings people in, and brings custom to the shops.[12]

It is important, therefore, not to overstate the extent of the decline of the country market, and the continuing relationship of the trips of the country carrier on the market day of the local town is strong testimony to its survival.[13] For the people of the countryside, market day remained an important local occasion even if the immediate contact with retail trades had become that with shopkeeper or hawker.

By contrast, the other traditional institute of internal trade, the fair, quickly lost its relevance to commerce, except as an occasion for commerce and as a livestock mart. The seasonal peaks of fairs, illustrated in Figure 22.1, matched the requirements of trades in animal products and livestock, and had been inherited from the expansion of the eighteenth century. While between 1792 and 1888 there seems to have been some evening out of this seasonal pattern, as more regular, monthly, fairs were held in the cattle-producing regions such as Wales, the fair as an institution was incapable of meeting the challenge of new and more regular means of supply. Smaller country fairs, while still extremely numerous, were by the second quarter of the nineteenth century often no more than the occasion for sideshows and the hawking of 'toys': as the trade core declined the peripheral activities became predominant. Golding's recent study of Essex demonstrated a significant growth of such pleasure fairs as a proportion of the county total, and by 1848 over half were of this type.[14] As the change took place so public attitudes towards them altered, and in the second half

INDEX

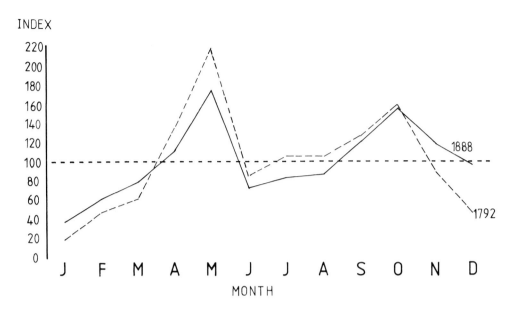

Figure 22.1   Monthly index of fairs, England and Wales, 1792 and 1888

of Victoria's reign pressures for their abolition grew. At Penzance, in 1888, the only survivor of seven annual fairs was described as a 'three day carnival', and trade interests at Taunton regarded its two remaining fairs as 'a very great nuisance'.[15] Such events did continue to benefit tradesmen, and H. P. Smith, deputy mayor of St Albans, regarded the abolition of its fairs in the early 1870s as a grave error because they had generated sufficient trade effectively to pay a man's rent for the year.[16] One form of fair, the statute fair or hiring, survived in parts of the north, in the Midlands, and in Kent, and offered a great if infrequent stimulus to the trade of grocers and drapers, shopkeepers, and, in the eyes of their opponents, publicans. Such fairs survived at Canterbury to the 1880s, and in the north to beyond 1914, and despite allegations of their immorality they found supporters who appreciated their lasting commercial value:

> I am a strong supporter of the fair, because I have benefited by it to a great extent, my trade has been a country trade, and I have realised an independency by it for my old age, and the fair is one of the greatest boons to the trade of the city [Canterbury] that we have. There is not anything that causes the same amount of money to be spent as that does. . . . The men receive their wages at Michaelmas which they spend in clothing, shoes, and drapery, and different things.[17]

Moreover, it was argued elsewhere that such seasonal events were the poor man's right, offering the opportunity to spend his savings when the rich could 'purchase more refined pleasure'.[18] While all forms of the fair declined, particularly after 1850, it did not quite disappear as a feature of the retail trade and in the hirings, at least, it created a short boom in activity for the country tradesman.

III

It was within this changing institutional framework that the fundamental country trades developed and contributed to further change. Central as a social institution in the villages, and by the 1850s distributed throughout the country more densely than any other trades, were the public houses and beershops. Such tradesmen fell into three groups: at the top were the innkeepers, the elite of the victualling trade to the 1840s, when the disappearance of the stage-coaches reduced most to the level of common public houses; the publicans, keeping legitimately licensed alehouses where beers were retailed to consumers; and the beershops, where beer could be retailed but not legitimately consumed. Despite this formal legal hierarchy, functional distinctions in the trade were often less clear-cut, and a detailed look at the village of Wortham in Suffolk through Richard Cobbold's account of 1860 helps considerably in understanding this point. Cobbold described five public houses in the village: two inns, the Queen's Head and the Magpie; two public houses, the Dolphin and the [Tumble Down] Dick; and one beershop, the Cherry Tree. Before his time the two inns and the Dolphin had all enjoyed greater status in the trade, being not only village meeting places but also the principal supports of a road-based transport industry. As this faded so they declined, as Cobbold's account of the Dolphin indicates:

> Not a single stage coach runs now along that London Road. My boys in days gone by used to go to and from the Charterhouse and get up and down at the Dolphin. All parcels from London, Bury, Norwich used to be left at the 'Dolphin'. Now all coach speculations have ceased! The Dolphin has, like all road-side public houses, even the Old Scole Inn, become a mere pothouse.[19]

This decline, in Cobbold's view, was not unassociated with the conviction of one of the Hammants, who were a publican family, for handling stolen wheat.

Like other members of their trade, Wortham's publicans were by-employed in various ways, or were the proprietors of subsidiary businesses. The Queen's Head had a dependent smithy, kept according to Cobbold to create trade:

> A blacksmith's forge is often a place of Gossip in a Village, and—the nearer to a public house—so much the more is it a place of resort for idlers. It was with an eye to business that the Landlady of the Queen's Head built a blacksmith's shop upon her premises.[20]

The previous proprietor of the Dick, John Smith, was also a mole-catcher, and 'went mole-catching in the morning and drank with his customers in the evening'.[21]

More important in village life than the subsidiary trades practised by publicans were the varied services generated from their primary activity. Publicans frequently acted as small-scale creditors, as did other tradesmen, and also played host to meetings of the early village friendly societies. It was against this double-edged sword of thrift and its enemy, drink, that more genteel well-wishers fought during the second half of the century, and helped to establish temperance village halls and clubs and independent friendly societies.[22] Despite this, the public house remained a key institution in village and hamlet, in many ways the rival as a social centre of church or chapel. It remained to 1900 what has been called 'the countryman's own club', the importance of which was demonstrated by its presence at relatively low levels of population. Its significance and character were perfectly assessed by Flora Thompson:

> Fordlow might boast of its church, its school, its annual concert, and its quarterly penny reading, but the hamlet did not envy it these amenities, for it had its own social centre, warmer, more human, and altogether preferable in the taproom of the 'Waggon and Horses'[2].
>
> There the adult male population gathered every evening, to sip its half-pints, drop by drop, to make them last, and to discuss local events, wrangle over politics or farming methods, or to sing a few songs 'to oblige'. . . .
>
> It was exclusively a men's gathering. Their wives never accompanied them; though sometimes a woman who had got her family off hand, and so had a few halfpence to spend on herself, would knock at the back door with a bottle or jug and perhaps linger a little, herself unseen, to listen to what was going on within. Children also knocked at the back door to buy candles or treacle or cheese, for the innkeeper ran a small shop at the back of his premises, and the children, too, liked to hear what was going on.[23]

IV

The union in Flora Thompson's Juniper Hill of alehouse and shop pointed clearly to the basic importance of the two trades to the village community. As we have seen, many of the specific trades, such as those of grocer and draper, had been established in market towns and the larger villages by the first quarter of the century. For much of our period it was the gradual spread of general shopkeeping which was of primary importance, and it is to the definition of this trade and its content that we now turn. More clearly than most other trades the general shopkeeper in the villages was commonly female, and for at least the first half of our period one gains the impression that it was an occupation developed by or chosen for the widow.[24] Casual entry to shopkeeping may have been important in its early growth and its spread down into

308

the countryside. A full analysis is not at present possible, but it is clear that the census figures of employment indicate a higher proportion of female activity than in most other trades. In 1851 males outnumbered females in grocery by nearly four to one; in baking and confectionery by five and a half to one; and in butchery and the meat trades by thirty-three to one. In contrast, the general shopkeeper category exhibited in both 1851 and 1901 a slight excess of females over males of around 9 per cent.[25] While this position was not constant, and some of the intervening censuses revealed a slight balance in favour of males, the contrast between this and most other trade employments, except for the keeping of boarding-houses, was both remarkable and consistent. Although the proprietorship of general shops may have differed from the pattern of employment in them, it is clear that for the number of women working in it this trade was unusual.

Given the variety of trades exhibited in Table 22.1, and more specifically located in the selected towns and villages of Table 22.2, it is something of a puzzle to meet the general shopkeeper. In what exactly did he trade? Answers are not easy to find, and trade terminology may be somewhat imprecise. Again, the Rev. Cobbold's account makes definitions easier, and although this single piece of evidence is unsatisfactory, the shopkeepers of Wortham in 1860 seem not untypical of the generality of their trade. The village had two such businesses, both in this instance run by males, one a fairly substantial place called 'the village shop', and the other a 'very small closet of a shop, into which two large persons could hardly be so accommodated as to be able to turn about therein'.[26] Both were effectively general stores, dealing in groceries, clothing, and many other goods. Thurlow's, the small shop near the village workhouse, was 'to all intents and purposes a shop for bread, cheese, butter, tobacco, snuff, sometimes a piece of meat—generally salt port—together with tea, sugar, thread, needles, pins, buttons, string, sweetments, and occasionally fruit may be purchased'.[27] Mr C. Y. Browne's rather grander village shop probably performed similar general-store functions, but it enjoyed official patronage which made it a place of considerable resort quite apart from 'all the private considerations of each person's traffic': it was both Post Office and the place of business for the parochial relieving officer.[28] Evidently the conflict between the general shopkeepers at the lesser village level and the more specialized tradesmen in the market towns was somewhat illusory: despite their coexistence in the larger centres, the two were not necessarily exclusive, and as market size increased so the specialist 'grocer', 'draper', 'greengrocer', or 'dairyman' emerged.

Such shops in the smaller villages were not by any means monopolists. Even in Flora Thompson's besieged fortress of 'Lark Rise' there were visits from itinerant tradesmen, such as Jerry Parish, the huckster who sold fish and fruit, the baker, the odd salesman, and the last of the tinkers.[29] Even in the smaller villages, there were contacts with market towns, intermittently in person and more regularly through the agency of the country carrier. Both town and country carrier offered supplies of clothing and household stores rather more cheaply, and therein lay the secret of the lasting attraction of market day in the local town. In this context the pull of the village Post Office was powerful and thus a useful commercial weapon for the village trader. Hence with more efficient and cheap posts from the 1840s and later rising literacy, village populations became more sensitive to its attraction. Commercially the village tradesman subsidized the public service and gained in his own business. Nor was this all, for the fundamental and recurrent poverty of many of his customers gave in the extension of credit a further means to tie trade. Even Thurlow's small shop at Wortham found customers among the poor for groceries, who might otherwise have purchased at the neighbouring market town, Diss.[30] Pamela Horn's researches confirm this effect, and in the last decade of the century a Devon shopkeeper took payment in barter from both labourers and smallholders, and poultry, grain, straw, and potatoes were employed in the attempt to defray debts.[31] Somewhat paradoxically, such credit facilities led others towards the co-operative movement, where there was no 'tick' but fairer trade and distributed profits. Although the countryside was less affected by the co-operative movement than the towns, it might be noted that between 1862 and 1903 the number of societies rose from 400 to 1,455, and estimated membership and sales both quadrupled between 1881 and 1905.[32] The village shopkeeper, then, served his customers and provided credit perhaps almost involuntarily as part of the cost of selling to the lower orders of village life. Certainly to Flora Thompson, writing of the 1880s, clear contrasts could be drawn between the man who, like the grocer at 'Candleford Green', sold to all and sundry, and he who, like the draper, missed the rich through fashion and the poor through the pocket.[33]

V

As we have seen, the shop, if not a new feature of rural England, did undergo a transformation in Victoria's reign. It was then that the general custom of trade through shops was established, a practice regarded as an innovation of the previous half-century by Thorold Rogers in 1889.[34] With the widening of the gap between producer and consumer, a feature particularly marked as imported foodstuffs grew in importance from the mid-1870s, the significance of wholesalers and intermediaries was increased. In the countryside the carrier was a key tradesman in the supply of village shops, the vital two-way link between producers and markets. Fortunately, this figure has already been the object of detailed modern research, and the following sketch of this last country tradesman is based largely on Everitt's study.[35]

The development of the country carriers' services probably occurred after those of the long-distance men, and in the sense of the establishment of formal networks and regular schedules their increase dated from the second half of the eighteenth century. Services from the countryside into the county town of Leicester trebled between 1815 and 1884, and the number of calls listed in directories expanded by twice that amount over the same period, while the number of carrier businesses only doubled.[36] Although this evidence cannot be regarded as conclusive, it being impossible to allow for such things as the changing comprehensiveness of the directories, it seems clear

310

that Victorian England experienced a considerable growth in the numbers of, and services from, the country carrier. Crucially, as the employment statistics of Table 22.1 suggest, this growth was not impeded by the development of the railway. Despite the proliferation of branch lines and the extension of railheads and country halts after 1850, a development which helped to extinguish the long-distance droving trades, relatively few among the villages of rural England gained such direct links with the railway. It was therefore in part as a response to the stimulus of the railway that the country carrier system developed and expanded, and reached its peak in the last years of Victoria's reign.

Apart from the obvious function suggested by this link with the railway, that of distributive and delivery agents from the railhead, country carriers performed three other important services. As suggested in Flora Thompson's account of the visitors to 'Lark Rise', the country carrier acted as shopping agent, much as the gentry had employed the London carriers in the previous century. On request, therefore, the village carrier fetched goods of all kinds from the market town, and continued to perform this service until 1914 and beyond. The carrier from Croydon-cum-Clopton, Cambridgeshire, 'took commissions all along the road—a packet of needles for Mrs This, and a new teapot for Mrs That—and delivered them all correctly on the way back'.[37] Carriers also provided passenger conveyance before the beginnings of country bus services, the earliest of which dated from the 1850s and were little different from the carrier's cart in form or schedule. It was because of these two important functions that carrier services tended to be bunched to coincide with market day in the principal town with which they communicated. In the 1880s, the country carriers entering Leicester made half their weekly calls on Saturday, the town's principal market day, and another 39 per cent on the second market day, Wednesday.[38] The phasing of their activity thus coincided with the trading peak of the week, incidentally reinforcing an earlier observation on the lasting importance of the occasion of market day.

The final function may well have been the oldest and possibly also the most important. The carrier took goods from country producers to the towns. In the area of Powerstock, Dorset, in the 1880s one of these carriers was recalled by Mrs Sanctuary, the vicar's wife:

> Owing of course to the lack of locomotion, there were 'Higglers' who went round collecting eggs, chickens, butter, and other farm produce, which they took to the Weymouth market, driving all the way in a cart. In my day Mrs Knight of Milton was a notable one, and I believe she had to start on her journey almost in the middle of the night.[39]

In a real sense this was the primary function of the carrier, though one that may have waned towards the end of our period. In Wortham, before 1860, he had certainly been the prime mover of trade with the outside world, as Cobbold's account makes clear, and coals were brought in as cheap back-carriage by higgler-farmers transporting produce to market.[40] In both directions, then, the growth of the country carriers provided the links which developed the new market structure of later Victorian England. In this they were vital factors in the successful development of shop trades at the village level.

Many carriers shared with other country tradesmen some alternate occupation, several uniting the two growth trades of carrying and shopkeeping into a single business. In Everitt's study of the Leicester region, *c.* 1880, forty-three of the 204 carriers were part-timers, and of these twelve ran village shops, six were publicans, and fourteen were graziers. In the carrying services of the lesser towns, such as Melton Mowbray, the proportion of carriers with alternate occupations rose considerably.[41] Thus George Smith of Middleton Tyas, one of the Yorkshire villages of Table 22.2, listed in Kelly's directory of 1879 as 'farmer and carter', was quite representative of his fellow carriers.[42] In this he illustrated the most salient points to be drawn from this brief survey of the country tradesmen.

It was clear that the reign of Victoria saw the growth and diversification of country trades but many of these shared common experiences. Most were very sensitive to the fluctuating fortunes of the farmers and labourers who provided their custom, and in many ways they were closer to rural craftsmen and smallholders than to their more prosperous urban counterparts.[43] Their growth was symptomatic of the gradual reduction of the isolation of the countryside through the improvement of communications. Common problems were encountered in trade credit or other sources of small debts, and the smallness of the markets in which they sought to operate led many to secondary occupations. In all these senses, then, the development of country trade businesses after 1830 was a sensitive indicator of more general change in rural society and in the economy as a whole.

Notes

1   Alexander, 1970, 231–8; Davis, 1966, 262–3.
2   Willan, 1976, 76–106.
3   Mathias, 1967.
4   Alexander, 1970; Jefferys, 1954.
5   Mathias, 1967, 16–29.
6   Perren, 1978, 154–6.
7   Everitt, 1973, 93–7.
8   Everitt, 1976, 186–7.
9   Alexander, 1970, 49–50.
10   BPP 1888 LIV 163.
11   *Ibid.*, 169.
12   *Ibid.*, 68.
13   Everitt, 1973, 226.
14   Golding, 1975, 64.
15   BPP 1888 LIV 159, 269.

16 *Ibid.*, 51–2.
17 *Ibid.*, 147, 148.
18 *Ibid.*, 153.
19 Cobbold, 1860, 149–50.
20 *Ibid.*, 106.
21 *Ibid.*, 115.
22 Horn, 1976b, 145.
23 Bonham-Carter, 1952, 214; Thompson, 1945, 57–8.
24 Davis, 1966, 256.
25 Census 1851, BPP 1852–3 LXXXVIII 222–7.
26 Cobbold, 1860, 106.
27 *Ibid.*, 106.
28 *Ibid.*, 112.
29. Flora Thompson, 1945, 120–37.
30 Cobbold, 1860, 106.
31 Horn, 1976b, 35.
32 Jefferys, 1954, 16–17, 461.
33 Flora Thompson, 1945, 523–7.
34 Jefferys, 1954, 16.
35 Everitt, 1973, 213–40; 1976, 179–202.
36 Everitt, 1976, 189.
37 *Ibid.*, 180.
38 Everitt, 1973, 226.
39 Best, 1971, 25.
40 Cobbold, 1860, 124.
41 Everitt, 1973, 230–1.
42 Kelly, 1879, 225.
43 Horn, 1976b, 10.

23 Country Craftsmen

J. A. Chartres and G. L. Turnbull

For much of Victoria's reign, the output of English agriculture continued to expand. More intensive forms of husbandry and more extensive application of machinery stimulated a rise in agricultural horsepower and created new employments for country craftsmen. The two principal crafts, those of the blacksmith and the wheelwright, retained their importance to 1900 and beyond, for even in 1914 England was still essentially a horse-drawn society. Although the years before 1900 had seen the development and application of steam ploughs, mechanical cultivators, and donkey engines, the final abandonment of the horse for both power and draught in the countryside did not come until the middle years of the present century.[1]

The horse was the basis for the most important country crafts of Victorian England. It is worth considering briefly the essential details of the horse-based society. Thompson's estimates of horse populations indicate that between 1851 and 1901 the 'commercial sector', primarily urban in orientation, more than quadrupled its employment of horses. Over the same period private ownership of riding and carriage horses, used in both town and country, more than doubled. By contrast, although an exact comparison is not possible from Thompson's statistics, agricultural horses and other horses on farms rose in number more slowly, by perhaps a third between 1811 and 1901. All types reached their peak about 1901, and thereafter horse populations and the craft employments dependent upon them declined. In both town and country, then, Victoria's reign saw the apogee of the horse world. It represented one of agriculture's principal markets in the supply of hay, corn, and straw. So, too, the support of horse traction was a great source of employment, from the smith's traverse to the knacker's yard, much of it craft- rather than factory-based.[2]

Such, therefore, was the traditional base for farming and transport which sustained the market for the many crafts that served them. But the changes of the later nineteenth century meant that increasingly the life of town and country was in contrast. While both required the services of wheelwrights, smiths, and farriers, there were very real differences between the life of the town blacksmith, who did very little but farriery work, shoeing van, tram, omnibus, and carriage horses, and that of his country counterpart, who was able to remain a creative craftsman. If the absolute decline in the craft dated only from 1901, in some senses the tide had turned by 1880. A similar contrast appeared in the leather crafts. Just as the motor car and more obviously the bicycle were of little immediate menace to the riding horse before 1900, so too the leather work supportive of horse traffic continued to enjoy an important position in the employment of labour.[3] The countryside tended to contain both the real craftsman and a dense population of poor boot, shoe, and clog makers, while much of the horse furniture industry had become concentrated on the market towns. Broad conclusions drawn on the basis of employment trends or business populations may therefore conceal real differences between town and country.

For most of our period the countryside remained a place in which traditional methods were employed and traditional crafts sustained. Iron rather than steel, together with leather, wood, straw, and osiers were the materials symbolic of rural crafts. Together with the blacksmith and the wheelwright, the Victorian countryside contained carpenters and joiners, painters, plumbers and glaziers, thatchers and masons, mostly earning a livelihood from small local markets. It is the number, the distribution, and the nature of these basic rural crafts that form the subject of the present chapter.

I

From 1851 the census provides the means to assess broad trends in employment in these crafts. The analysis, however, is not without difficulties. Occupational classifications changed from census to census, and to abstract the purely rural craft groups is difficult. The numbers employed in the principal crafts, regrouped for present purposes, for England and Wales in 1851–1901, are presented in Table 23.1. The figures include both masters and employees, and group together residents of both rural and urban districts. Where smiths and saddlers are concerned this matters relatively little, but the shoemaking groups and carpenters and joiners, lines 10 and 11, are heavily distorted by town industries.

None the less there are some important general points to be drawn from these simple figures. None of the horse-related crafts in lines 1–3 exhibited any real decline in absolute terms during Victoria's reign. The only notable fall occurred with the farrier category (line 1) largely for reasons of definition, the figures for 1891 and 1901 relating only to veterinary surgeons. Allowing for whitesmiths and other metal

Table 23.1   *Numbers employed in rural crafts, 1851–1901 ('000)**

Occupational group	1851	1861	1871	1881	1891	1901
1 Farriers and veterinary surgeons	6.10	6.80	6.65	7.51	3.19	2.94
2 Blacksmiths	94.78	108.17	112.47	112.52	140.02	137.07
3 Saddlers and whip and harness makers	16.80	19.41	23.01	28.87	27.32	30.68
4 Straw manufacture, including bonnets	46.54	48.04	48.86	30.98	18.38	16.28
5 Thatchers	5.89	5.36	4.14	3.72	3.21	N.S.R.
6 Basketmakers—all cane, rush, willow crafts	14.70	8.95	10.14	11.54	12.33	11.52
7 Coopers	15.89	17.82	19.24	18.70	17.21	15.78
8 Wheelwrights	28.02	30.07	30.31	28.73	27.95	28.92
9 Millwrights	7.61	8.22	7.54	6.94	6.11	5.29
10 Carpenters and joiners	156.61	177.97	205.83	235.23	221.01	270.71
11 Clog, shoe, boot, and patten makers	243.94	255.58	224.56	224.10	248.79	251.14

*Based on censuses, 1851–1901.

workers included in this category, lines 1 and 2 should be added together, and on this basis growth continued to 1891, part of the subsequent fall being attributable to the effect of the Boer War.[4] The horse-based metal crafts and the emergent veterinary profession remained linked sufficiently strongly in functional terms to justify treating them together.

After the iron and leather trades, the crafts employing straw, rush, cane, and willow formed a coherent group, located mainly in rural districts. Much of the straw industry was confined to southern England, and its principal component, straw-plait manufacture, is discussed elsewhere in this volume. At least a part of this craft was devoted to the needs of the horse, and straw bonnets were used in both town and country to protect horses against flies and dissuade them from bolting. This craft, with those of the hurdle, flat, and basket makers, and the thatchers, was in decline from the 1850s. All suffered from more general changes in the economy. As the slate industry grew and tile manufacture emerged, so the requirement for skilled thatchers diminished, and with skilled thatching of corn ricks also declining the thatcher found himself squeezed by lack of both domestic and agricultural customers. As will be seen, it had been a craft limited to the southern and western counties and East Anglia, all maritime areas and thus vulnerable to the penetration of rival and simpler roofing materials. For as long as fruit was grown and butter, eggs, and cheese produced, the basket trades were able to sustain themselves, and these activities, with the growth of demand from the furniture industry, confined their decline as crafts to relative and not absolute terms before 1901. Even so, they were being sucked into urban workshops in towns such as Bedford and Leighton Buzzard.[5] The agricultural demand for such products as hurdles, still lively in a corn and sheep country in 1850, had faded by 1900, and the needs of commerce for hampers and baskets increased proportionately in importance. Though these craft manufactures were in 1900 still important intermediate inputs to market gardening and fruit growing, their location was increasingly urban not rural.

The third group of crafts, those of lines 7–10, working primarily in wood, provide even more analytical problems. Coopers were frequently employees, and by the 1880s men were employed in cooperage on a vast scale at such brewing centres as Burton-on-Trent.[6] But their increase in numbers was not entirely a function of the output of the brewing industry. After 1871 the growth in the output of English beer and spirits and in the size of the domestic dairy herd far outstripped that of employed coopers. The relative decline of the craft and its absolute fall from 1871 were the consequence of the introduction of machine tools and of galvanized iron products.[7] Although his was a distinct branch of wood crafts, in the countryside the cooper did not necessarily follow his craft to the exclusion of others. William Dalley of Turvey (Bedfordshire), illustrated in Plate 80, was in the 1830s ploughwright, cooper, and carpenter, and had earlier acted as the local ratcatcher.[8] In the countryside hard distinctions between the different crafts were not necessarily meaningful. The demand for carpenters was tied to the fluctuations of the building trade, of which it was part, and in this urban demands were paramount. Even so, if the rapid increase in the numbers of carpenters between 1891 and 1901 is ignored, employment in the other three woodworking crafts peaked in the 1870s, and in this they shared a fate in common with the straw crafts. The 1870s represented the point at which machine joinery and new technology began to make serious inroads into the woodworker's market. Industrialization, having first assaulted manufactures and lesser trades, began in the middle years of Victoria's reign to invade traditional crafts.

Most of these crafts found markets in both town and country, and none was therefore completely rural, but all reached their peak in terms of employment during Victoria's reign. They were affected at different times by the arrival of machine techniques, but for all the impact was clear by 1901. The number of horses grew at double the rate of blacksmiths between 1871 and 1901, and similar gains in labour productivity were made in the saddlery and related crafts. For most of our crafts, then, adjustment to the demands of an industrial society meant, first, growth along traditional lines and, second, albeit at differing times, the consequences of labour and product substitution. Victorian England thus saw both the peak and the transformation of the craft activities of the countryside.

For a more exact assessment of the significance of these crafts it is necessary to disaggregate to county level. Some general assessment of their significance in urban and rural life can be made by analysing the crafts in the context of total employment and of contrasting enumeration regions. This is attempted in the figures of Table 23.2, in which the incidence of the crafts of Table 23.1 is expressed as a rate per thousand of occupied population. For simplicity, the crafts have been grouped into the following categories: (a) blacksmiths (lines 1–2 of Table 23.1); (b) saddlery (line 3); (c) straw,

Table 23.2 *Rate of craft employment in selected counties, 1851–1901 (numbers per '000)**

Group and county	1851	1861	1871	1881	1891	1901
1 London						
(a)	4.09	4.17	3.64	2.95	3.01	2.51
(b)	1.16	1.23	1.20	0.98	0.92	0.92
(c)	1.61	1.41	0.80	0.76	0.62	0.53
(d)	2.72	2.82	2.48	2.10	1.60	1.42
(e)	9.93	9.84	9.75	9.99	7.68	7.26
(f)	16.20	15.27	10.97	9.80	9.26	7.53
2 Sussex						
(a)	5.48	5.12	4.67	4.08	4.13	3.31
(b)	0.95	0.92	0.86	0.77	0.76	0.75
(c)	1.59	1.33	0.93	0.67	0.49	0.28
(d)	3.13	2.75	2.98	2.39	1.96	1.56
(e)	10.49	9.87	10.47	12.09	8.64	10.30
(f)	11.24	10.84	7.06	4.81	4.01	3.48
3 Devon						
(a)	6.83	6.81	6.01	5.39	5.16	4.42
(b)	0.85	0.80	0.84	0.86	0.83	0.73
(c)	3.17	2.28	1.95	1.59	1.36	0.45
(d)	2.79	2.65	2.41	2.18	1.93	1.53
(e)	12.38	12.11	11.55	11.47	10.18	10.49
(f)	15.22	14.31	10.50	8.59	6.89	4.89
4 Norfolk						
(a)	6.19	6.19	6.21	5.82	5.80	5.22
(b)	1.10	1.14	1.18	1.14	1.11	0.99
(c)	2.71	2.25	1.67	1.38	1.10	0.60
(d)	3.50	3.43	3.10	2.76	2.40	2.43
(e)	10.02	10.29	9.37	9.69	8.40	9.46
(f)	19.99	22.78	17.97	17.77	18.57	19.73
5 Hereford						
(a)	7.35	7.00	6.57	6.17	5.96	5.45
(b)	0.87	0.82	0.80	0.75	0.74	0.77
(c)	1.78	1.48	0.90	0.80	0.49	0.43
(d)	5.28	4.59	4.44	3.77	3.27	2.97
(e)	11.80	12.60	11.18	10.20	8.49	9.09
(f)	13.12	11.03	8.65	7.00	5.56	4.11
6 Warwickshire						
(a)	4.96	5.55	5.44	4.59	5.16	4.40
(b)	2.24	2.62	2.99	2.44	2.30	2.31
(c)	1.53	1.07	0.69	0.58	0.57	0.52
(d)	2.60	2.42	2.25	1.70	1.54	1.34
(e)	8.35	7.70	7.68	7.82	7.01	7.05
(f)	13.81	12.38	9.36	7.73	5.88	4.36

Group and county	1851	1861	1871	1881	1891	1901
7 *Cheshire*						
(a)	4.96	5.73	5.10	4.24	5.01	4.38
(b)	0.65	0.70	0.64	0.62	0.58	0.52
(c)	0.72	0.72	0.68	0.42	0.30	0.25
(d)	3.16	3.22	2.81	2.59	2.39	1.98
(e)	7.18	7.38	8.58	8.76	7.62	8.73
(f)	15.04	14.41	11.39	7.47	5.08	4.35
8 *Yorkshire, East Riding (including York)*						*(All Yorkshire)*
(a)	5.76	5.96	5.90	5.32	5.87	4.76
(b)	1.03	1.10	1.04	0.81	0.75	0.54
(c)	1.67	1.30	0.86	0.47	0.42	0.21
(d)	4.07	4.25	4.14	3.11	2.43	1.42
(e)	9.59	10.40	11.41	10.98	8.91	7.68
(f)	15.37	12.90	8.82	5.99	4.59	5.72
9 *Yorkshire, North Riding*						
(a)	7.37	6.91	6.48	6.21	6.46	
(b)	1.23	1.19	1.02	0.76	0.69	
(c)	0.87	0.55	0.37	0.23	0.21	
(d)	2.79	2.29	1.74	0.95	0.90	
(e)	11.02	11.37	10.57	9.32	8.01	
(f)	15.58	13.02	9.59	6.32	4.93	
10 *Yorkshire, West Riding*						
(a)	4.65	4.82	4.63	4.42	5.39	
(b)	0.56	0.54	0.53	0.46	0.49	
(c)	1.16	0.39	0.39	0.32	0.30	
(d)	2.36	2.50	2.33	1.68	1.50	
(e)	7.00	6.84	7.83	7.37	6.28	
(f)	12.21	10.28	8.18	7.19	7.04	
11 *Westmorland*						
(a)	5.91	5.71	5.71	4.52	5.16	4.61
(b)	0.75	0.75	1.00	0.87	1.10	1.40
(c)	1.46	0.69	0.72	0.44	0.23	0.25
(d)	2.07	1.80	2.50	1.94	1.93	1.85
(e)	10.76	9.96	11.65	11.23	9.14	10.85
(f)	11.63	12.29	13.00	8.82	11.96	13.24

*Based on censuses, 1851–1901.

thatch, and basket (4–6); (d) woodworkers (7–9); (e) carpenters (10); and (f) footwear (11).

These figures present a complex picture which cannot be fully explored here. There are, however, certain salient features which are worthy of comment. In general, the pattern revealed in Table 23.1 is confirmed. Employment in virtually all crafts and in most of the selected counties dropped consistently from the 1861 or the 1871 census, and in many places the incidence of country crafts per thousand of population fell from 1851. In part this was the consequence of the development of other industries and employment opportunities, but it makes the early peak of craft employment all the more clear.

Some commentary on the variations of the figures of Table 23.2 is necessary. In most counties, one of the greatest declines occurred in group (c), the straw, thatch, and basket crafts, and although these figures overstate the extent of this decline, in that in 1901 thatchers were not separately enumerated, it was sharpest in those counties such as Devon and Norfolk which had the greatest incidence in 1851. More remarkable was the relatively small degree of variation observable in these craft groups between the purely urban county of London, the mixed counties such as Warwickshire, and the various agricultural shires, from Norfolk to Devon and Westmorland. Broadly the same trends applied to employment in the smithy trades and to the saddlery crafts.

This leads to a further conclusion. The two categories of the leather crafts, (b) and (f), exhibited signs of regional concentration in terms of the relative importance of such employments. Warwickshire, with its old-established urban horse-furniture industries, retained its position throughout the period, numbers employed more than doubling between 1851 and 1901. In this it shared the experience of its neighbour, Staffordshire, a county whose leather and metalworking towns, such as Smethwick, West Bromwich, and above all Walsall, were national specialists in the manufacture of reins, spurs, and other horse furniture.[9]

The other important feature of the leather crafts, one which is demonstrated by Norfolk and Westmorland, is that it was often a rural putting-out trade or by-employment, rather than an independent craft. Besides the noted manufacturing centres for footwear in cities like Leeds and towns such as Northampton, shoemaking took place in the villages, where cheap labour represented an alternative to the emergent machine technology. A recent study of Northamptonshire has shown the craft in existence at seventy-three places between 1841 and 1861.[10] This mixture of town and country manufacture was clearly paralleled in Norfolk and Westmorland where employment, albeit on a lesser scale, actually increased between 1851 and 1901. Like the noisome tannery industry which supplied their raw material, the leather crafts retained a rural presence until the twentieth century, even if urban centres like Wellingborough, Walsall, or Northampton, were the main centres of manufacture.

II

Having assessed the general trends in such craft employments and examined some of the more striking county contrasts and similarities for the eleven selected registration groups, it becomes possible to relate the incidence of these craftsmen to the size of settlements. In so doing it is possible to assess the significance of an extensive market region to the viability of specific crafts. At what level the craft specialist was to be found is therefore of significance to the assessment of his importance to the rural community and to the evaluation of the central place functions of both the larger villages and the market towns.

There have been relatively few studies of this subject, the most notable being by John Saville on the South Hams region of Devon, which drew attention to the growth and subsequent decline of rural crafts during the nineteenth century.[11] It is impossible to provide definitive answers to the problem here, but by using some of the directory material for Norfolk in the 1830s and the North Riding of Yorkshire in the 1870s it is possible to suggest some general conclusions. The figures of Table 23.3, derived from this material, represent an attempt to define the population threshold at which each craft group appeared. There is no certainty that these two examples are representative of the country as a whole, and no great significance should be attached to the actual population figures. But the rank order of the threshold populations (defined, as in the previous chapter, as the midpoint between the average population of villages with and those without the specific crafts) is broadly consistent, and may be taken as a crude measure of the order in which such businesses could be sustained in rural England. Excluding the urban districts, assessment of census returns for Warwickshire in 1851 yielded a broadly similar ranking. Taking only figures of employment, and ranking crafts on that basis, the leading six craft groups were, in descending order: blacksmiths, saddlers, wheelwrights, straw-plait and hat makers, coopers, and basketmakers.[12]

Table 23.3 *Population thresholds at which craft businesses appeared in Norfolk and the North Riding of Yorkshire**

Norfolk (1836)		North Riding of Yorkshire (1879)	
Blacksmith	475	Tailor	330
Wheelwright	500	Blacksmith	340
Saddler	550	Wheelwright	350
		Mason	400
		Saddler	530

*Based on White, 1836, and Kelly, 1879.

These two measures demonstrated a broad consistency between the incidence of craft businesses and employment. Evidently the blacksmith and the wheelwright and carpenter were craftsmen to be found at the level of each village. They were the two fundamental crafts of the Victorian countryside. In Yorkshire the tailor, too, was to be found at roughly the same levels, though this was probably in part an urban putting-out trade like footwear, rather than a craft dependent on purely local markets. No tailors appeared at this level in the Norfolk villages of the 1830s, but they were no doubt there. In neighbouring Suffolk, in about 1860, the village of Wortham had two blacksmiths, a carpenter and a wheelwright, and two tailors, and thus matched the Yorkshire pattern.[13]

At the opposite end of the distribution the figures suggest the relative dominance of the towns in other crafts. It was typically in the market towns of Norfolk and Yorkshire that the greatest populations of saddlery businesses were to be found. Like the more specialized of the country tradesmen—bakers and confectioners for example—such crafts were concentrated at the market centre and not distributed to village level. Carpentry and joinery for vehicles or houses and furniture, small building work, blacksmithery, farriery and general ironwork, and some tailoring were required and provided where they were needed, at village level.

Finally, it is important to analyse the services provided by these craftsmen, since, as has been suggested, this was not self-evident from occupational titles. Over time many of the census categories changed, as did the content of specific 'crafts'. The occupational nature of Victorian England is therefore far from easy to assess. In addition, as casual examination of commercial directories shows, craftsmen were not always specialists to the exclusion of other interests. Blacksmiths and others hedged with a refreshing by-employment as beersellers and, more naturally, acted as coal or lime merchants, or as mechanics. The mixture of crafts and trades characterized most of our period. The case of the 'farrier' illustrates the second basic point, that of the changing content of crafts. This craft, strictly that of a man who shod horses, and disappeared from the census occupations by 1891. The bridge it had formed between the ironworking specialists, the smiths, and the developing skills of animal care, those of the veterinary surgeon, had been broken by the latter's professionalization. Bearing in mind these issues, the final sections examine the two principal craft groups, assessing their changing contribution to rural life, and the impact on their work made by broader economic changes.

III

The blacksmith and the farrier were related and commonly united crafts, distinguished by the latter's specialism in shoeing work. From the anatomical expertise required of the farrier stemmed his high status and his more general work, illustrated in the last sketch of Plate 82, as a horse doctor. At the extremities of this craft farriers were the toolmakers and veterinary surgeons of early Victorian England, and thus were required and found at the level of the middling village community. At the beginning of our period they had another function which led to a string of smithies being located in the hamlets of Wales and Scotland at the beginnings of the great overland drove routes. In north Carmarthenshire alone, cattle-shoeing compounds existed at Llanybydder, Farmers, Waun rhyd yr ychain, Rhydcymerau, Cwm y gof, Caeo, Blaendyffryn, Llansawel, and Crugybar, all within a corridor of no more than sixty-five square miles.[14] This last aspect of the craft was as hazardous and specialized as any, as the account from Hugh Evans's *The Gorse Glen* indicates:

> The cattle feller and his assistant tied a rope to the horns of the steer. The feller then took the animal by the horns while his assistant lifted one of the steer's fore-feet from the ground, bending the leg at the knee. The feller would then give the horns a twist and down went the beast, being kept down by the feller while the assistant made it secure with the rope that had been attached to the horns. An iron rod, about a yard long, pointed at one end and forked at the other, was driven into the ground and the rope with which the beast's feet were bound was passed through the fork. The animal was then ready to be shod.[15]

By contrast, work with horses, illustrated in the top two parts of Plate 82, was more straightforward and more enduring. The shoeing forges of the droving trades faded quickly from the 1850s and 1860s as the growth of the railway and the steam coaster enabled the producers at last to enter the more profitable marketing of fatstock.[16] More than compensating for the decline of such peripheral centres of the craft was the rapid growth of urban demand which at once generated employment and led to the differentiation of the creative craft of the countryside and the more limited services of the town.

Although it is difficult to define the exact nature of the country craft within this range, its essence was its creativity. This was captured in a beautiful nostalgic account of the work done by Charles Cooper of Ashdon, near Saffron Walden, in the early years of the century:

> Farm workers came with problems, for most of the labourers had to find their own tools. They asked for left-handed scythes, wider or narrower hoe blades to chop out weeds from wide or narrow drillings; men with big arms would demand longer scythe blades, and gamekeepers and poachers asked for long bladed curved spades to dig out rabbits and ferrets. He sharpened bill-hooks, scythes, sickles, axes, and every type of edged tool, often replacing the broken or split staves and stales. He made pitchforks and four-tined forks, plough spuds, coulters, shears, drills and harrows; sometimes renewing the entire set of teeth on worn out harrows.[17]

Such skilled toolmaking could make real savings in a day's work, and according to George Ewart Evans 'blacksmith made' represented the highest praise that could be accorded to a hand tool.[18] But our period saw the growth of mechanization of many farm activities and this gradually added to the range of tasks demanded of the village smith. Welding was involved in one of the smith's basic tasks, the retyring of wooden wheels, and fire-welded repairs to farm machines became an increasing element in his work.[19] By the end of the century repairs and the fabrication of new parts and alterations to machines were, with bicycle and mechanical work, the growth areas of the traditional craft.[20] Close examination of the collections in many of our agricultural museums reveals just how widespread were the smith's toolmaking functions.

Although these smithies remained generally small in scale, commonly, like Dorcas Lane's at 'Candleford Green', of two to four men, this did not completely differentiate them from some urban forges doing similar work.[21] Certainly on the evidence of Arthur Welton, scale was achieved simply by the multiplication of forges. Welton left a village smithy at Benhall in Suffolk in 1903 and entered Ransome's plough shop in Ipswich, but although he was working in a large shop he did so, as at Benhall, at his own forge.[22] Village forge work, though threatened by factory-made tools and even shoes, was distinct in its skills, and it was probably with shoeing that the clearest differences emerged. The skilled farrier could correct, with proper shoes, faulty stances in horses, and Clifford Rose's account of his work early in the present century makes it clear that this was one of many knacks used by farriers in shoeing.[23] Young shoeing smiths were confined to the less prestigious work, such as that with donkeys. The real skill lay in fitting the shoes, and although quiet times in the forge were spent in making stocks of shoes, or in sharpening mill bills (used in dressing mill stones), none the less the art was still that of the bespoke. After adjusting shoes for a mare, Matthew, foreman at the 'Candleford Green' smithy, said to his charge, 'You'll be able to run ten miles without stopping with them shoes on your feet.'[24] Shoes had to be 'roughed' for icy conditions which were particularly severe on country horses entering tarred town streets. A sharp frost could generate a great deal of pressure in the smithy, and Clifford Rose recalled a day at Needham Market when between 6.30 a.m. and 6 p.m. 107 horses were thus served.[25] In both shoeing and toolmaking, then, work was skilled and hard, but small in scale and creative in approach.

Like many country craftsmen, smiths faced markets for their services that remained too small to sustain them fully. The response, typically, was to adopt an itinerant approach or, more commonly, to diversify by adopting another trade. With their forge work, blacksmiths were little able to adopt the former approach, but one related end of the trade, that of the tinsmiths and braziers—the whitesmiths—commonly did so. The settled blacksmith can be contrasted with Thomas Millward of Turvey (Bedfordshire) who in the 1830s set up 'a machine or travelling apparatus' for his work, and who described himself thus on the side of his caravan, illustrated in Plate 83: 'Thomas Millward Turvey Beds. Brazier and Tinplate worker, whitesmith, keys to all kind of locks neatly fitted here. Smoke-jacks cleaned and repaired, kitchin furniture neatly t'ind. Chimneys sweep etc.'[26] Village smiths did some tinning, but only incidentally, and the selling of beer, coal, and coke were more common subsidiary employments. Until the waning of the agricultural use of lime, many smiths in Yorkshire acted as agents for the commercial limeburners.[27] Others were drawn at times into general dealing since craftsmen, no less than country tradesmen, faced the problem of liquidity in addition to that of limited markets. The barter economy which agriculture often forced on to those who served it affected smiths no less than grocers. In the 1840s Robert Phillips of Pen-pont was paid in scrap iron, wheat, barley, and swedes by the farmer whose plough he mended and whose horses he shod and doctored.[28] This experience was typical of the trade mechanisms of the countryside and of the market served by country smiths throughout our period.

IV

The second case study, of the wheelwright, was of a trade very closely related to that of the smith, since in the pursuit of the basic craft a smith's services were required. The final but essential part of building a wheel, tyring, was smithy work, and for this reason perhaps some businesses, like Mrs Lane's at 'Candleford Green', united the two trades.[29] Typically, though, the wheelwright acted also as village carpenter and sometimes as cooper or millwright. Pyne's early-nineteenth-century sketches of the craft, reproduced in Plate 84, certainly linked the two basic functions of wheel-wrighting and millwrighting; two sketches illustrate the construction and fitting of a cart wheel, and the other two the repair of mill work. As the classic account of the woodworking crafts by Walter Rose made clear, these were the two principal aspects of the services performed by the village wheelwright and carpenter.[30] There were others which, if less central, were still important to the village community. General carpentry involved repair work for houses and agricultural buildings, and what was disparagingly known as 'hedge-carpentry', repairs to field gates, posts, and fences. Despite the invasion of cast iron, wooden pumps, normally of elm, continued to be employed on farms to the end of the century, and the village woodworker supplied new borings to accompany the old ironwork. The countryman sat, no doubt, on chairs and at tables repaired by the carpenter, and enjoyed also a final service from him. The wheelwright and carpenter acted as village undertaker, a junction of functions which has survived to the present day.

There is some evidence of technical improvement in wheelwrighting in our period, although the basic changes were also the consequence of parallel improvements in metalworking. As J. G. Jenkins has shown, hooped tyres spread from the later eighteenth century, and had become fairly general by 1850, representing a measure of the improvement of the craft and its design skills. Greater skill was required in the manufacture of a wheel for a hooped tyre, particularly in achieving the correct coning, but the end result was correspondingly stronger. But in parts of mid-Wales the straked tyre survived to the end of the century, and did so also in the Cotswolds, south Shropshire, and the Sussex downs. This did not necessarily represent technological backwardness, since there were some advantages to straking. It was cheaper in terms of skilled labour—both from wheelwright and smith—as it was in fuel; and, perhaps crucially, it made repairs by the unskilled farmer possible. Straked tyres slipped less in traversing hills and were thus particularly suited to the uplands.[31] But areas of greater agricultural poverty probably sustained less craft skill from both smith and wheelwright, and thus influenced the final product.

Like the blacksmith, the wheelwright remained a creative craftsman throughout the period, but it is far from clear to what extent he was the manufacturer of carts and wagons. As George Sturt showed, the true wheelwright had sufficient skill to be also a wainwright and to build wagons without much troubling a smith, but this work seems to have been undertaken by specialists, even in the 1830s when most vehicles were still craft-built.[32] By the end of the century the position had changed. Although the regional wagon and cart types which had evolved by the early years of the century were retained, increasingly the craft market was invaded by factory-built vehicles. From 1847 Crosskills of Beverley were factory-building carts, and from the 1850s wagons. By 1900 such products probably outnumbered the craft-built in Yorkshire and, by example, influenced wheelwrights. Crosskill wagons, with such elements as iron hubs and what Sturt called 'steam wheels', penetrated widely through England, as did the products of Woods & Company of Stowmarket, a firm with branch agencies at Bury St Edmunds, Newmarket, Norwich, Ipswich, and Sudbury.[33] This gradually eroded the craftsman's position as vehicle builder or, as George Sturt recalled, opened up a previous local monopoly, not merely to the factory wagons but also to those craftsmen of neighbouring shires able to produce more cheaply.[34] The distinctive regional types began to face standardized competition.

Other changes, too, affected the country woodworker. In the second half of the nineteenth century, and with greater speed from the 1880s, windmills and watermills were passing out of use. By the 1850s Wortham's new miller, Youngman, had 'added a steamer to his mill, so that when the winds cease to blow still the mill-wheels may go and the corn be ground'.[35] With the parallel decline of the horse gin the millwright's trade faded, and with it another element in the complex craft of the rural woodworker. More than any other area of the craft group, it had remained entirely traditional in its techniques.[36] Mills belonged essentially to the age of wood and leather, and ancient methods were those appropriate to their repair.

A further skill of the craft lay in the securing of proper supplies of wood. Depending on use, a variety of English local timbers were the staples of the craft, some of which gradually fell into disuse during our period. A sound cart wheel, for example, employed elm for the nave or hub, spokes of heart-of-oak, and ash felloes. All were purchased, sawn, and seasoned by the wheelwright or the carpenter, large and small timbers suiting their different purposes, small elm too bent for the carpenter being usable as felloes. The wych was the toughest of the three common elms, the best wood for the shafts of wagons, and even the soft horse-chestnut, no longer a commercial timber by 1900, was once the preferred wood for hand-coopered dairy buckets.[37] Some idea of the risk and care involved in this cutting and seasoning of timber may be attained from the preparation of a wheel hub. The cross-cut timbers were bored and seasoned in the bark for up to six years for a twelve-inch hub, being brushed and inspected regularly for rot.[38] The management of a timber stack, its cutting, and selection, were therefore key elements in the craft skill, and represented fairly hefty capital stocks. Both Rose and Sturt make it clear that even in the 1880s and 1890s these investments rarely found their way into prices. A final common feature of the country crafts was their very rudimentary costings: tradition endured not only in materials and methods but also in prices.[39]

In many ways these country craftsmen shared common experiences in Victoria's reign, and the history of rural wood crafts paralleled that of the smiths. Most diversified from the primary occupation of wheelwright or cooper into more general carpentry or joinery as their craft was squeezed by competition from the machines and factories of the towns. As mills fell out of use, millwrights combined their calling with work as wheelwrights, smiths, ironfounders, carpenters, joiners, and mill-builders.[40] These common traits suggest perhaps how the development of the Victorian economy first stimulated growth in these crafts and then the gradual replacement of the traditional methods by new materials and modes of production. Galvanized iron had destroyed the rural cooper's market by 1900, and better communications and the new methods of marketing which favoured standardized products had become serious threats to other country crafts. Walter Rose took the view, shared by other commentators, that by 1900 these changed circumstances had devalued the status of the craftsman's skills. Country crafts for long delayed the consequences of the industrialization and urbanization of England, but by 1900 were in general decline. Further changes, particularly the consequences of the 1914–18 war, accelerated that decline, and by the late 1930s many of the traditional crafts were on the verge of disappearance.[41]

Notes

1 F. M. L. Thompson, 1976, 63; Ministry of Agriculture, 1968, 54–5, 61.
2 F. M. L. Thompson, 1976, 78–9.
3 Woods, 1975, 82; Evans, 1967, 206–12.
4 Census 1901, BPP 1904 CVIII, I, 93.
5 Bagshawe, 1972, 164.
6 Kilby, 1971, 163.
7 *Ibid.*, 152.
8 Higgins, 1830, 71, 75.
9 *Victoria County History: Staffordshire XVII*, 1976, 202–4.
10 Hatley and Rajczonek, 1972, 26–30.
11 Saville, 1957, 172–247.
12 Census 1851, BPP. 1852–3 LXXXVIII pt I, II, 474–9.
13 Cobbold, 1860, 103–12.
14 Colyer, 1976, 137.
15 Colyer, 1973, 992.
16 Colyer, 1976, 78–86.
17 Ketteridge and Mays, 1972, 41–2.
18 Evans, 1969, 134.
19 Woods, 1975, 32–3.
20 Flora Thompson, 1945, 419.
21 *Ibid.*, 413.
22 Evans, 1969, 140.
23 Evans, 1967, 199.

24 Flora Thompson, 1945, 419.
25 Evans, 1967, 197.
26 Higgins, 1830, 199.
27 Information kindly supplied by Mr M. B. Hutt.
28 Jenkins, 1970, 9–10.
29 Flora Thompson, 1945, 407–8.
30 Rose, 1937; Sturt, 1923.
31 Jenkins, 1962, 73.
32 Sturt, 1923, 67.
33 Vince, 1975, 128–34.
34 Sturt, 1923, 199.
35 Cobbold, 1860, 105.
36 Rose, 1937, 113; Freese, 1957, 131–48.
37 Rose, 1937, 29–33.
38 Jenkins, 1962, 63–4.
39 Sturt, 1923, 197–203.
40 Freese, 1957, 131.
41 Woods, 1975, 250–1.

24 Country Outworkers: The Men's Trades

Jennifer Tann

I

Although by the time Victoria came to the throne Britain's industrial revolution had been under way for well over fifty years, the transfer to the factory system was by no means complete in even the leading sectors of British industry, whilst it had hardly begun in others. Urban domestic craftsmen and outworkers and their rural counterparts were at least as numerous, and probably more so, than factory operatives. Manufacturing industry employed almost a third of the occupied population in 1881, and contained three main groups of people: factory masters, managers and operatives; independent craftsmen such as wheelwrights and blacksmiths; and the largest group—outworkers.

Outworkers were skilled and semi-skilled craftsmen working in their own homes, or in workshops or mines belonging to their 'employers'. Men, women and children all engaged in this system of production, but the greatest number were men. Although the processes involved in the manufacture of different articles were, to some extent, responsible for differences in organization between trades in which outwork was usual, the central feature distinguishing outwork from other forms of craft production was the fact that whilst in some branches of industry outworkers could, to some extent, organize their own working week, they were only nominally independent, and the vast majority could not be regarded as independent at all.

The lead miners of the northern Pennines were amongst the more independent outworkers in the mining industries, which between them employed four per cent of the workforce. From four to eight miners would contract with the mine owners to work a stretch of ground for a certain term, bargaining pay by the piece—so many shillings for so much ore raised. Miners shared the bad fortune with the mine owners but did not share the good to the same extent, for the richer the vein the less they were paid for the ore. If lead prices fell disastrously the poorer veins were abandoned and the miners dismissed. Whereas in the eighteenth century miners had been free to work irregular hours, there was a considerable tightening of the mine agents' control by the mid-Victorian period and miners were forced to work regular shifts of approximately six hours per day whilst many of the traditional holidays and celebrations disappeared.[1]

By comparison, the Black Country coal miner had little independence, for here the sub-contracting system dominated mining organization. The miners were hired servants, not of the mine owner, but of a contractor or butty. Like the northern lead miner the butty engaged with the owner to deliver coal at so much per ton, though unlike the lead miner he did not mine himself but engaged miners who worked for either piece or day rates. Wages were not, however, decided by the sub-contractor but by the mine owners in accordance with the 'market price of coal or demand for labour'. For his part, the butty responded to the profit stimulus and, having been recruited from the ranks of the miners, brought with him a 'knowledge of the business' combined with an 'acquaintance with the habits of men'.[2]

In the manufacturing industries the 'putting-out' system allowed a nominally greater freedom, for the craftsmen generally worked in their own homes or in adjacent workshops, receiving or collecting their materials from the employer or his agent. Their workday was, therefore, more flexible than that of the miners or quarrymen. By the mid-nineteenth century even this was illusory amongst, for example, the handloom weavers and stockingers, for their numbers had increased and real wages had fallen to the point where, when work was available, the outworker was forced to work a full day.[3] Nail and chain makers, too, found themselves in a similar position in mid-Victorian times.

Lancashire cotton weavers, Yorkshire clothiers and west of England woollen weavers, coal and lead miners, nail, chain and other small metal workers, basket and hurdle makers, all generally owned their looms and tools, whereas the midland framework knitter usually did not. This meant that, in principle, these outworkers could change more easily from one employer to another. But the fact that the majority of these outworkers, the Yorkshire clothiers apart, did not own the materials or the more expensive pieces of equipment such as reeds for the loom, and did not engage in marketing their products, meant that while they possessed a certain freedom the majority were, in effect, wage-earners, employed by capitalist manufacturers. A further limitation on even this modest freedom was imposed in the more remote country districts where there might be only one manufacturer or his agent from whom it was possible to obtain materials. Furthermore, the outworker might have obtained a loom from, or mortgaged his equipment to, a certain employer, and might have rented a cottage from him, all of which impeded changing employer.

Finally, the very nature of the employment, its flexibility and potential irregularity, combined with the scattered nature of the industries and the numerous body of outworkers, further weakened any effective freedom and meant that concerted industrial action was extremely difficult to organize.

An important feature of much of the men's outwork in rural areas was that it was not engaged in on a full-time basis but was a dual occupation, usually practised in conjunction with agriculture. Recognizable dual economies had emerged in several regions of Britain before the industrial revolution where some form of outwork had been undertaken to augment a meagre living gained from the soil.[4] The hand knitting/farming region of the Yorkshire dales (the outwork being performed, in this case, by women), the pottery/farming region of Staffordshire, the hosiery/farming region of the east Midlands, the small metal-working/farming regions of the west Midlands and south Yorkshire and the handloom-weaving/farming areas of Lancashire and Yorkshire are well-known examples. It has been suggested that a necessary precondition for a flourishing dual economy was a populous community of small farmers—mainly freeholders—who pursued a pastoral economy on soils that were generally poor.[5] But though soils were poor in some parts of the Yorkshire dales, eastern Staffordshire and the Black Country, they were not universally so. Moreover, it has been observed that the eighteenth-century metalworker/farmers of the south Yorkshire Pennines were on the whole better off than the arable farmers on richer soils where agriculture was the sole means of support.[6]

By the mid-nineteenth century urban growth in the Sheffield region, the Black Country and the Potteries had led to a sharp decline in the practice of combining outwork with agriculture, but it did still occur in the rural fringes of these regions. The spectacular growth of the Lancashire cotton towns, similarly, led to its cessation in and near these towns, but the ranks of the handloom weavers were augmented in rural areas in the early part of the century and here the practice of a dual economy continued. It is estimated that nearly two-fifths of the entire population of north-east Lancashire were weavers in the 1820s and in 1833 30,000 weavers were thought to live in the remotest part of the hundred of Blackburn and in the adjacent part of Yorkshire.[7] These farmer-weavers were largely unskilled, weaving plain, coarse cloths, unlike the better-paid urban weavers of fine and fancy cloths. But it should not be imagined that the combined occupations of weaving and farming in rural Lancashire were activities of the older inhabitants only. 'Younger men are rarely persons having no other resources than the loom', wrote a parliamentary commissioner. 'They calculate upon field-work in harvest-time; upon the produce of their potato settings; in some districts upon fishing; and upon occasional employment in various capacities.'[8] In the west of England textile region, on the other hand, few weavers had enough land on which to grow vegetables by the late 1830s. As early as 1806 one witness to a parliamentary inquiry had remarked: 'There is not one family in twenty who have as much land as this room.'[9]

Many northern lead miners had smallholdings: approximately 3 acres of meadow and 3–4 acres of pasture, together with room for two cows. A survey of two estates owned by the largest mine owners, made in 1861, shows that almost 60 per cent of the miners had smallholdings.[10] The shorter working day, together with a customary holiday at hay harvest, enabled dual occupations to continue in the region. Indeed it was to the landlord's advantage, for much of the smallholding land was marginal and might have remained un-let otherwise. The agent to the Blackett-Beaumont estates commented in 1866: 'If by raising rents and being chary of repairs the revenue of the land is increased, yet I much fear that in a still greater degree are the permanent mining emoluments endangered.' The land should be viewed as 'a useful adjunct to the mines. I think the smallholdings of cottages and grass for a cow or even a small garden have had an important influence in making the people attracted to the place.'[11] But these smallholdings were too small and too poor to be viable as a sole alternative to mining when the lead trade depression set in during the 1870s.

Dual occupation—the practice of industrial outwork together with farming, more rarely with shopkeeping or innkeeping—was, in the mid-nineteenth-century context, a survival of a pre-industrial occupational pattern and, moreover, a system of production that has few modern counterparts.

II

It is notoriously difficult to construct wage series for factory operatives, but wage series for outworkers pose an even greater problem. Firstly, it is frequently unclear whether the wages quoted in parliamentary papers, newspapers and law writs are the average earnings of a person engaged full-time in the production of a particular article, or whether they are, for instance, average weekly earnings of a man with two occupations. Sometimes family income figures are confused with those for a male wage-earner. Moreover, since wages of outworkers were paid at piece rates, one man's output might vary considerably from that of another, so that 'average' earnings can hardly be said to have existed. Such series as have been published are frequently the rates paid per piece rather than actual individual earnings, whilst cost of living indices are often based on wholesale, not retail, prices. Piece rates were subject to frequent short-term fluctuations corresponding with periods of prosperity and depression. In 1815 the average piece rate for a north Lancashire calico weaver had been 4s. 2¼d., but by 1835 it had fallen to 1s. 9d. and it fell still further to 1s. 2d. in 1837, rising by 1d. over the subsequent three years and falling to 1s 1d in 1841. There was an improvement in 1843–4 when a 30 per cent increase took place, but as far as the cotton handloom weaver was concerned 1826 had marked a turning-point, and after the slump of that year piece rates never recovered to anything like their former levels.[12]

Weavers in the west of England earned less than any other category of male worker in the wool textile industry in 1838. Whilst even in 1805 they were not amongst the most highly paid textile workers—their weekly earnings had averaged 16s.—thirty-three years later the average earnings had fallen to 10s.[13]

The northern lead miner, too, was paid at a piece rate, but the total sum due to him was generally calculated only at the end of the year, a subsistence allowance being paid monthly during the intervening period. In the early 1840s lead miners' annual earnings were in the region of £31 to £39. They remained at around £39 until the 1860s, when figures ranging from £39 to £50 are mentioned. By the early 1870s a lead miner is estimated to have earned on average £55 per year. Subsistence payments of over 50s. per month were made to its miners by the London Lead Company in the 1870s, by far the greater part of the miners' earnings, therefore, taking the form of a regular monthly wage.[14] For most of the nineteenth century, however, lead miners' wages were lower than those of coal miners.

III

Outworkers, such as chain, nail and file makers, whose occupations required separate working premises, lived in small cottages or terraced housing with a forge hearth in the garden, and no particular functional adaptations seem to have been made to the dwellings.[15] Framework knitters and handloom weavers, on the other hand, employed a room of their house for the frame or loom and frequently used attic space for storage. Many of these textile workers' dwellings were purpose-built. In villages to the east of Nottingham, framework knitters' houses were generally two storeys high with 'top shops' lit by long windows, whilst those to the west were three storeys high. Up to six knitting frames were housed in the workshops, providing employment for all the family and possibly a journeyman or two.[16] Long windows, divided by stone mullions, are a characteristic feature of woollen weavers' cottages in the villages around Halifax and Rochdale and cotton weavers' cottages in south-east Lancashire.[17] They are not, however, a feature of the west of England woollen weavers' cottages. In the Cotswolds loom shops were generally lit by two or three small lights, and weavers' cottages are indistinguishable from others from the outside. The west of England was a broadcloth area and loom shops were, therefore, rather larger there than elsewhere. When handloom weaving declined there in the 1830s much cottage property was found to be too large for occupation by agricultural labourers.[18]

Black Country coal miners lived in the old settlements on the coalfield, but in the east Midlands, south Yorkshire and the north-east a number of new settlements were built by the colliery owners in the mid-nineteenth century as new pits were opened.

> Within the last ten years collieries have been opened in very many places between the Wear and the Tees; and wherever a colliery has been opened a large village or town has been instantly built close to it, with a population almost exclusively of the colliery people, beershop people and small shopkeepers.

Coxhoe (Durham), for example, was a newly built, straggling settlement extending for about a mile along both sides of the main road, with streets leading off to right and left every ten houses or so. The cottages, built of lime-plastered stone, had no yards to back or front and comprised two rooms and a semi-attic bedroom. Each cottage cost £52 to build and was let for £5 a year, bringing an annual return to the colliery proprietor of 9.6 per cent.[19] In the east Midlands, colliery housing generally consisted of a 'colliery row' rather than any attempt on the part of the owner to create a village. As tenants of their employers, the miners were prevented from having dual occupations—mining and framework knitting, for example—for it had been the custom to choose between these occupations according to the state of either trade at any one time.

One of the largest coal owners of Nottinghamshire in the middle of the nineteenth century was Thomas North who, taking advantage of the extension of the railways, was operating four large collieries by 1861. Cinderhill, a few miles to the west of Nottingham, was the centre of his operations, and here he built two squares of cottages, the larger one containing fifty-four two-storey dwellings. There were two main rooms on each floor, a living room and kitchen/pantry on the ground floor, and two bedrooms above. These, too, were merely groups of dwellings, though planned with some recognition of the social needs of the occupants, but there were no shops, school, church or chapel. Later in the century, as mining extended into the concealed part of the coalfield, new settlements consisting of monotonous rows of terraced houses were built. Usually there was almost no garden ground attached to the dwellings, but New Annesley was an exception with a 500-foot area between the backs of the terraces, intended to be used for allotments.[20]

The northern Pennine lead miners more generally lived in scattered cottages than in villages. A traveller to the area in 1859 wrote: 'Allenheads is to be regarded rather as the nucleus, containing a few shops and an inn, of the houses scattered over this part of the dale, than as a village.' But there was considerable pressure on housing by the 1840s and 1850s, and Thomas Sopwith, a mining agent, noted that one of his frequent problems was that of finding houses for his employees, 'for in these Mountain wilds inhabited only by Miners and those dependent on Mines, population presses closely on habitations'.[21]

The isolated dwellings occupied by many lead miners consisted of 'longhouses' of eighteenth-century or earlier date. These were two-storeyed buildings having a large kitchen/living room at one end and a cattle shed at the other, with one or two bedrooms and a hay loft above. But in the nineteenth century purpose-built company housing was provided by the London Lead Company, and this compared favourably with most of the housing occupied by agricultural labourers, model estate cottages excepted, and also with much colliery housing. After visiting 227 rural houses in the north east in 1864, Hunt concluded: 'The majority of Northumbrian and Durham peasants, whether rich or poor, hind or collier, live in but one room day and night, with all the family.' He added:

> The lodging which is obtained by the pitman ... is perhaps on the whole the

worst and dearest of which any large specimens can be found in England . . .
[because of] the high number of men found in one room, in the smallness of
the ground plot on which a great number of houses are thrust, the want of
water, the absence of privies, and the frequent placing of one house on top
of another.[22]

But elsewhere it appears from other evidence, colliery housing was then adequate.

When mines and pits became exhausted and new ones were opened the miners and
colliers did not always move house to follow their employment. In these cases they
found lodgings during the week, returning home at weekends. Many preferred to
lodge in private houses or boarding houses, but some lodged in 'shops' provided by the
mining companies. In 1864 the usual price for a working week's lodging was 9*d.* to 1*s.*
in the lead-mining district, two men sharing a bed, making their own crowdie in the
morning and having their potatoes boiled for them in the evenings; for most miners
brought their week's provisions with them from home. Lodging shops built by the
companies invoked strong criticism in both the 1842 Chadwick Report and the 1864
Hunter report; although by 1861 the London Lead Company, whose shops had been as
bad as any in 1842, had added 'a library and reading room at each mine-shop, and it is
one of the rules that a portion of Scripture be read and papers opened at the most
convenient hour every evening'.[23]

Such information as is available on the furnishing of working-class housing of the
period, and it is most inadequate, suggests great contrasts between the interiors of
dwellings occupied by outworkers in the different trades. One observer commented
on the contrasts to be observed between the exteriors of the northern pitmen's
dwellings and their contents. He found that the cottages contained relatively costly
furniture: an eight-day clock, a good chest of drawers with brass handles, a
mahogany four-poster bed with printed calico coverlet and dess-beds (similar to
chiffoniers in appearance) for the rest of the family.[24] But whereas many handloom
weavers and framework knitters had been able to live in some comfort at the end of
the previous century, their condition had changed by the mid-Victorian period. By 1840
many woollen weavers' cottages had been mortgaged for twenty years or more.

> the only furniture in many being an old stool, a broken table and a few
> cracked and broken cups and pans. In one or two cases I found them sitting
> on the stair steps, having no chair or stool. In others a log of wood is a
> substitute.

One auctioneer in Gloucestershire commented that a weaver's belongings, if
auctioned, rarely produced more than £2.[25]

IV

In some industrial regions the nature of the employment or the particular methods employed in one or other of the processes, led to an especially low life expectancy for large numbers of employees. Factory work had its own dangers—accidents due to exhaustion, unfenced machinery or fire—that were less frequently met with in certain kinds of outwork, but the accident rate in coal mines was highest of all. It has been estimated that the annual accident rate in coal mines was between 4.5 and 5 per 1,000 employed around 1850. There was noticeable variation in the incidence of accidents between coalfields. In the Black Country it was approximately 7 per 1,000 employed, while in the north east the rate was 3.5. Between 1838 and 1842, 562 miners of fifteen years of age and over were killed in Black Country mines. Roof falls accounted for a large proportion of these deaths, though the most frequent cause of death amongst children was falling down the shaft, which, in the Black Country at least, was usually unfenced.[26] From 1850 onwards mines were regularly inspected by government officials. This was necessary

> not only to force the owners to do what had not obviously been in their economic interest to do but also to induce them to do what, without state and legislative backing, they would most likely never have been able to do: discipline a traditionally unruly labour force in strict, tedious and often wage-reducing cautionary procedures.[27]

The lives of all miners, and of other workers engaged in jobs which produced large amounts of dust, were shortened by pneumoconiosis. A survey carried out in 1858 compared mortality rates in two lead-mining parishes, an agricultural parish and the city of Liverpool. The report noted:

> The men of Alston and Reeth die in a much larger proportion than the men of Liverpool. Thus a district remote from city influences, situated in the midst of a most salubrious district . . . loses a larger annual proportion of its adult male inhabitants from diseases of the chest than the unhealthiest city in the kingdom. . . . It is the injurious character of the male occupation which causes Alston, the most exclusively lead mining district in England, to be the place where there is a larger proportion of widows than in any other place in the kingdom.[28]

Although it was recognized that miners were dying from some form of respiratory disease, medical practitioners knew neither its cause nor its precise nature. A number of witnesses to the 1864 commission observed that miners were hesitant to admit that they were suffering from lung disease, and there was a reluctance on the part of the companies to admit that the disease was caused by mining. Nevertheless, the largest companies in the north east initiated a medical service for miners and their families. Deformity, rather than disease, afflicted the handloom weaver and stockinger who suffered from curvature of the spine after several years' stooping over the loom or frame, particularly if he had been set to the machine for long periods when young.[29]

V

The form and extent of leisure activities amongst male outworkers was closely related to the state of their particular trade, wages, attitude of employers and education. Where a dual economy was practised, particularly where one of the occupations was agriculture, the working day was long and leisure activities revolved around Sunday and the occasional fair or feast day. Outworkers in declining trades such as handloom weaving and framework knitting were required to work long hours to make a living, and there was no incentive and still fewer opportunities for leisure activity beyond the beerhouses which sprang up in great number in these areas.

Leisure activities such as pigeon racing and cock fighting were generated by the small metal workers and Black Country miners, whereas the larger coal- and lead-mining companies played a paternalistic role, making provision for leisure activities of an 'improving' kind. Agricultural and horticultural shows took the place of the feasts that had accompanied the annual wages settlement and hirings. Cricket, brass bands and volunteer corps replaced cock and dog fighting, although hare coursing lasted until the 1870s.

Contemporary observers were quicker to comment favourably on the lead miners than on the coal miners. Lead miners needed a knowledge of geology for their activities to be profitable; they needed, moreover, to be skilled at calculating and making a bargain. In 1861 nearly every lead miner's house was said to contain books, and by that date schools had been established by the two major companies as well as by the established church. Libraries were provided by one mine agent, Thomas Sopwith, with the intention that they should be both instructional and recreational. And when in 1861 the reading and writing abilities of parents in the north-east coalfield were compared with those of parents in the lead-mining region, it was discovered that while 22 per cent of fathers and 28 per cent of mothers in the coal region were illiterate, in the lead-mining region only 4.3 per cent and 10 per cent respectively could not read and write.[30] Other kinds of outworkers were less fortunate in their educational facilities. Though some of the larger cotton manufacturers employed several thousand handloom weavers, none of them provided any form of schooling for the children, or other educational and recreational activities for the weavers. Similarly, nothing was provided by the employers of framework knitters and woollen weavers, and those of the chain and nail makers.

VI

As the nineteenth century progressed many of the outwork trades declined, the majority in the face of mechanized, factory-based competition. But the time scale varied from industry to industry. The textile outworkers were the first to succumb. Ribbon weaving declined in the villages around Coventry in the 1830s and 1840s, although it survived longer in Coventry itself where a last-ditch stand against the factory system was taken by some weavers who built 'cottage factories' using a shared steam engine to drive the Jacquard looms in their homes.[31] The market for knitted goods was heavily overstocked by the 1840s. The number of frames had increased from an estimated 25,000 in 1812 to 48,500 in 1844, of which 43,900 were estimated to be in the east Midlands.[32] By this date many knitters were in abject poverty, and although power was not successfully applied to the frame until later in the nineteenth century the number of frames began to fall from that time onwards. The Yorkshire wool combers, their position having deteriorated ever since the failure of their strike in 1825, were in dire poverty by 1845 and were finished by Lister's combing machine introduced shortly afterwards. More than 10,000 hand combers in the villages around Bradford were 'unable to pay the rent for a comfortable dwelling, a large number [of them] huddled together in one apartment. . . . That their physical well-being was neglected the emaciated appearance of [them] most plainly betokened.' By 1851 there were only 5,600 hand combers left in the Bradford district and six years later 'they were almost extinct as an industrial class'.[33]

The number of handloom weavers began to decline from the mid-1820s. It is estimated that there were approximately 360,000 cotton weavers in Britain in 1820, but by 1830 the number had fallen to between 200,000 and 250,000.[34] By 1820 power-loom weaving was established as the best technique in practice and handloom weavers were rapidly displaced in the plain cotton lines. Many handloom weavers therefore transferred to the production of more specialized fabrics, swelling the number of men competing for work, which in many cases was hit by falling demand. The adoption of the power loom by the cotton industry was slow and spasmodic for both technical and commercial reasons. Moreover, power looms, once introduced, were established on the whole in the spinning towns, outside the major cotton handloom weaving areas, and were generally operated by women. These factors combined to make it difficult for adult male weavers to abandon their cottage industry, particularly in remoter areas where no alternative sources of employment could be found. But by 1850 the cotton handloom weaver was a rarity. 'Thus passed away', wrote Marsden,[35] who could have been speaking for all outwork, 'a type of industry picturesque far beyond its successor. . . . Though it has only just disappeared, it has hardly left as many footprints behind it as have the Roman legions that . . . tramped over the Country in which it was carried on.'

The handloom weavers in the west of England were 'undoubtedly in deep and severe distress' by the late 1830s. The governor of Horsley prison (Gloucestershire) noted that weavers left with regret, and the number of pauper cases relieved both in the workhouse and outdoors increased in nearly all the cloth-making parishes. Bisley, with a population in 1841 of 5,339 persons, had 3,501 cases relieved in 1838.[36] In this region the employers were suffering too. Demand for high quality broadcloth was stagnating and increased mechanization led to many firms being squeezed out of the market in a period of intense competition.

Copper mining was on the wane in Cornwall from the 1860s,[37] and lead mining did not recover from the disastrous fall in prices which occurred in the early 1870s. The demand for Cornish china clay, on the other hand, grew steadily towards the close of the nineteenth century as other markets besides the pottery industry were found.[38] But the coal industry was by far the largest extractive industry. The nature and organization of outwork varied from coalfield to coalfield, but the demand for coal continued to grow throughout the later years of the century and Cobbett's statement that 'their work is terrible to be sure . . . but at any rate they live well' was as true at the century's end as in the 1840s. Standards of housing and social amenities had improved greatly and unionism—weak, if it existed at all, in other branches of outwork—was militant from the middle of the century and politically active by the end of the Victorian era.

Some outworkers, such as quarrymen, woodland craftsmen,[39] boot and shoe makers,[40] nail, chain and other workers of small metal goods, continued to find a demand for their labour until the close of the century, either because they produced goods that could not, easily or well, be produced in factories, or because they were catering for the upper end of the market, where mass-production techniques were uneconomic. Nails, for example, could be cast by machinery before 1820, but the best horse-shoe nails had to be hand forged and the large horse population kept many Black Country outworkers in business throughout the century.

Rural factories and workshops began to compete in the traditional outwork trades from the middle of the century but they did not necessarily lead to the immediate death of outwork. The distinction between workshop and factory was a fine one in trades which required no power. Chain shops containing up to a dozen hearths could be found in the Black Country by 1850, besides frame-work knitting shops with ten or more frames in the east Midlands, shoe-making workshops in Stafford and Northampton, and coopers' workshops in the Lake District. By mid-century small portable steam engines could be cheaply purchased and these proved an economical source of power for rural factories where water power was insufficient. Tanneries, bobbin factories, agricultural machinery works, saw mills, iron foundries and corn mills were expanded or newly built in villages and country market towns, providing alternative employment for some outworkers from declining trades.

Where no large-scale alternative employment to outwork was available, a rural area could become temporarily over-populated. Smallholdings were insufficient to provide a family living and migration or emigration were often seen as the only alternatives. Nearly 400 people emigrated from Gloucestershire between 1835 and 1840, and a few others found work in Yorkshire, but 'unfortunately for the weavers they are not a class of persons in request'.[41] Yorkshire wool combers found equal difficulty in obtaining alternative employment elsewhere. The protracted decline and eventual death of outwork in manufacturing industry, and the movement of outworkers away from the countryside, had a profound social impact. 'Locally it might be beneficial,' observed an employer of handloom weavers,[42] 'but as a general principle it is like bleeding a person, only a temporary expedient.'

Notes

1   Hunt, 1970, 37–9.
2   Taylor, 1960, 216–18.
3   Bythell, 1969, 38; Felkin, 1867, 459.
4   Rowlands, 1975, 3–13; Hey, 1972, 18–31.
5   Thirsk, 1961, 70–88.
6   Hey, 1972, 18–31.
7   Bythell, 1969, 56.
8   Quoted *ibid.*, 58.
9   BPP 1806 III 336.
10 Hunt, 1970, 145–52.
11 Thomas Sopwith, quoted *ibid.*, 148.
12 Bythell, 1969, 95–106.
13 BPP 1840 XXIV 394.
14 Hunt, 1970, 61–76.
15 Moseley, Chainmakers, 1970/71, 58; Davies and Hyde, 1970, 44–51.
16 Smith, 1965, 34–48; Chapman, 1967, 26–7.
17 Chapman, 1971, 249–73.
18 BPP 1840 XXIV 453.
19 Atkinson, 1966, 42.
20 Smith, 1965, 130–7.
21 Hunt, 1970, 139–40.
22 *Ibid.*, 142–3.
23 *Ibid.*, 165.
24 BPP 1842 XV 751; Atkinson, 1966, 42.
25 BPP 1840 XXIV 429, 433.
26 Hair, 1968, 559.
27 *Ibid.*, 560.
28 General Board of Health, Annual Report, 1858, 63–4, quoted in Hunt, 1970, 209.
29 Birmingham Reference Library, Poor Law Guardians Minutes, Vol. II.
30 BPP 1861 II 332–3.
31 Prest, 1960, 96–112.
32 Smith, 1965, 31.
33 Sigsworth, 1958, 41–3.
34 Bythell, 1969, 54.
35 Marsden, 1895, 232.
36 BPP 1840 XXIV 429, 433, 444; Tann, 1967, 60–1.
37 Barton, 1966, 59–71.
38 Hudson, n.d., 24.
39 Davies-Shiel and Marshall, 1969, 161–79; Hart, 1971, 322–35.
40 Church, 1966b, 148–9; Hopkins, 1976, 30–3.
41 BPP 1840 XXIV 546–7.
42 *Ibid.*, 549.

25 Women's Cottage Industries

Pamela Horn

I

Although domestic service remained the major employer of women's labour throughout the nineteenth century, there were certain areas of the country to which this did not apply. Sometimes the reason lay in competing employment opportunities in local factories or, especially in the mid-Victorian years, in the survival of a cottage industry. This latter was particularly true of the rural Midlands and south where, unlike the situation in the north of England, not only was there little factory employment available but male agricultural wage rates were low. A wife's earnings were, therefore, all the more necessary to help support the household. In Lancashire and Yorkshire, on the other hand, industrialization had already undermined traditional domestic clothmaking, and the greater earnings of the men reduced the pressure on their wives to work. Nevertheless in the coastal districts of Lancashire women and children did take part in shrimping and cockling, this last being carried on extensively in the Morecambe Bay area. The cockles were sent to supply the manufacturing towns of Lancashire in what was a highly lucrative business.[1]

In the southern and midland counties the wives and daughters of agricultural labourers and village craftsmen were engaged in a whole range of different activities. Pillow lacemaking in the south Midlands and Devon; straw plaiting for the hat and bonnet trade round Luton and Dunstable; glovemaking in Somerset, Devon, Dorset, Worcestershire and Herefordshire; buttonmaking in east Dorset; hosiery work in the east Midlands; and netmaking or 'braiding' on the East Anglian, Dorset and Cornish

341

coasts, were but a few of the many tasks involved. Sometimes, as in the Blything area of Suffolk, these jobs were taken on as an alternative to agricultural employment. In Blything in the early 1840s eight domestic tasks were listed as carried out by women, in addition to farm work. They comprised plaiting, knitting, tailoring, braiding herring nets, shoe-binding, making labourers' gloves, 'washing for families' and dressmaking.[2] The women themselves maintained that they preferred indoor work 'because of the wear and tear of clothes in the fields, and the opportunity which indoor employment [gave] to attend to the domestic duties'.

In pastoral areas, however, cottage industries might provide employment for the whole family. This was the case in the Yorkshire dales, where the countryside was described in 1843 as 'one large grazing and breeding farm'. With the exception of a few men who were engaged on drainage work, there was no demand for day labourers, the house servants of each farm 'being sufficient to accomplish all that is requisite'. This had driven the people to support themselves by hand knitting stockings, jackets, sailors' caps and similar items. At the small town of Hawes, one factory owner delivered wool to villagers who lived up to ten miles distant: 'they work it up at home, and bring back the articles when finished to the mill. A clever knitter might perhaps earn 3s. in any given week by incessant toil . . .; a child, according to its age and proficiency earns 6d., 9d., up to 1s. 3d. in the same time.' Yet although the earnings were so small this was 'in some degree compensated by the cheapness of provisions and the low rent of their cottages'.[3]

Despite the growing competition of the northern factories, domestic clothmaking also survived in some areas. George Edwards of Marsham in Norfolk, later a prominent agricultural trade union leader, recalled that in the 1840s and 1850s his mother worked as a handloom weaver for a Norwich firm, along with a number of her fellow villagers. One man from the parish was deputed to visit Norwich each week to fetch the raw material from the factory and to return the finished work. The weaving was paid for by the piece, with 'a certain sum deducted to pay the man for the time spent in carrying the work backward and forward'. But as George bitterly noted:

> If there was any defect in the weaving, . . . another sum was deducted from
> the price which should have been paid, and the employers never lost an
> opportunity of doing this. Poor sweated workers were robbed at every turn.
> I have known my mother to be at the loom sixteen hours out of the twenty-
> four, and for these long hours she would not average more than 4s. a week,
> and very often less than that.[4]

Her experience was sadly characteristic of that of most other outworkers, and yet the contribution which a mother and her children could make in this way provided a much-needed supplement to family income. In Bedfordshire and Buckinghamshire, in the early 1860s, extra earnings from straw plaiting could equal the weekly wages of the head of the household if he were an agricultural labourer on a basic rate of 11s. or 12s.;[5] Whilst in George Edwards's home, without his mother's earnings from weaving 'the family would have been absolutely starved'.

Apart from economic factors, however, some of the younger unmarried women preferred the freedom which cottage industries bestowed to the restrictions of domestic service. As one critic noted disapprovingly of the West Country lacemaking and glovemaking districts in the early 1840s: 'many . . ., quite fit to "go to service" and "stir about," said they preferred the trifling remuneration they obtained and their liberty'. In his view the feeling was very general, 'for the two "trades" seemed glutted and impoverished, and I heard many complaints of the unfitness of the young persons who followed them for household service and housewifery'.[6] Likewise, in the plaiting areas of Buckinghamshire, Bedfordshire and Hertfordshire a 'native servant [was] scarcely to be had'. Girls preferred outwork even when trade was depressed 'to the restraints of service; and having an extreme fondness for dress they no doubt often resort to prostitution as a means of adding to their scanty earnings; and this they could not readily pursue in service'.[7] Allegations of immorality were frequently—and not always justifiably—levelled at both lacemakers and plaiters. Nevertheless, in the mid-1860s the percentage of illegitimate births in Bedfordshire, at 7.8, was well above the national average; and in areas such as the Luton and Biggleswade poor law unions, where plaiting was of particular importance, the rates of illegitimacy were still higher, at 9.3 per cent and 8.3 per cent of total births respectively.[8] There were also claims that family ties were weakened by the early financial independence of the youngsters. According to the vicar of Ivinghoe, an important Buckinghamshire plait centre, in 1854 the willingness of children to leave home in order to assert their independence made 'parents afraid of offending [them]', and so they became 'hardened and intractable'. His colleague at Fenny Stratford agreed: 'When they begin to earn money the parents in great measure lose influence over them, they cease attending the Sunday School and do not willingly come to Church.'[9] Clearly the 'generation gap' is no modern phenomenon.

II

Workers in cottage industries began to learn their trade at an extremely early age. In the case of lace, experts considered that a child must make a start at five or six years old, for only so, it was believed, could they acquire the dexterity essential for the execution of the best work in later life. And it is worth noting that at the 1851 census around one fifth of the lacemakers in Buckinghamshire and Bedfordshire were under the age of fifteen, while in Essex, where lacemaking was of comparatively minor significance, about one in three of those recorded were under fifteen.[10]

For straw plaiting, which was particularly concentrated in Buckinghamshire, Bedfordshire, Hertfordshire and Essex, where the most suitable straw was grown, a still earlier start might be made. Cases are quoted of infants of two or three years old engaged in clipping off the loose ends of straw from the plait, 'with their scissors tied to their bodies'. At four they would begin to make plait.[11] Likewise in glovemaking and hosiery, youngsters of five or six were regularly recruited; in the case of hosiery, the first stage was for trainees to become seamers and winders. Promotion to the knitting frames was delayed to the age of ten or eleven.

Initial instruction in these various crafts might be given at home by a mother to her own children or, especially in the case of lacemaking, plaiting and gloving, the youngsters would be sent to a special craft 'school' conducted in a nearby cottage. For the youngest 'pupils' these schools also offered a child-minding service—thereby permitting mothers to get on with their own work free from the care of their offspring. Few opportunities were given to the children to pursue their ordinary education since a 'mistress's' only justification for running her school was normally her skill in her trade and perhaps her iron discipline in extracting the maximum output from her charges. Working conditions were uncomfortable, with youngsters crammed into small, poorly ventilated and badly lit cottage rooms. As late as 1871 one of the factory inspectors complained that young plaiters had to work

> in any numbers, from 5 or 10 to 50 of them, sitting on little benches or stools, or anywhere where they can find a seat, in rows generally one behind the other; the master or mistress presides over them often with cane in hand to remind the idler of its duty . . . I . . . have been told that one of the reasons why parents send their children to the plaiting school instead of allowing them to plait at home is because the master or mistress 'gets more work out of them' than they could venture to attempt themselves.[12]

The children would also plait as they walked to and from school, in order to complete their regulation stint. Indeed, according to one visitor to Essex in about 1840, it was rare to meet

> a woman, or child over five years old, whose fingers were not busily plaiting—the bristling roll of finished plait under one arm: the bunch of split straws under the other; and frequently a selection from these [was] carried in the mouth, where most of them were moistened before they found their way into the piece.[13]

He noted, too, that within the cottages themselves a bowl or pail of water was kept in which the newly purchased straw strips were steeped to make them more pliable for use in the plait. The 'smell of the straw (to which a dash of brimstone also was added) pervaded all the humble dwelling'.

In the pillow lace trade working conditions were far more uncomfortable than those for plait, since the fabric was made up on a hard, round cushion, stuffed with straw, which the worker had to support upon her knees, or partly upon her knees and partly upon a pillow-horse or bench. There was little freedom of movement as she bent over the pillow, learning to manipulate her bobbins and pins at speed and to follow the intricate pattern of the lace. But perhaps most harmful of all was the practice adopted by some of wearing a 'strong wooden busk in their stays to support them

344

when stooping over their ... lace; this being worn when young, while the bones [were] yet soft, [acted] very injuriously to the sternum and ribs causing great contraction of the chest', and permanent damage to the health of the children concerned.[14] Eye-strain, too, was common where the women and girls worked on into the evening, struggling to follow their complicated designs by the shared light of a candle.

In the craft 'schools' disease spread rapidly from one youngster to another, while the sedentary nature of the employment caused pulmonary and digestive disorders, with tuberculosis particularly prevalent among the lacemakers. Doctors also condemned the practice of plaiters and lacemakers in keeping a pot of lighted charcoal or ashes under the hem of their skirts to keep their feet warm. Not only did the acrid fumes emitted add to the foetid atmosphere and irritate the workers' throats and lungs, but many of them suffered from 'chilblains and swelled ankles'.[15] Similarly, in glovemaking during the cold winter months the children's hands were 'rendered incapable of working from time to time by contact with the brasswork of the gloving machines', which were used to keep the stitching even. Skin diseases were a serious problem, too, with scabies particularly common. In the mid-1870s one witness from south Somerset claimed to have seen 'the hands of these glovers (in one instance nine in a cottage) covered with scabies while making the best kind of kid gloves'. And as he pointed out, the disease could easily be transmitted to the eventual purchasers, since the children repeatedly put their fingers inside the gloves whilst they were working.[16]

III

In an attempt to protect these youngsters from exploitation and to increase their educational opportunities the Workshops Regulation Act was passed in 1867, following disturbing disclosures about their conditions of employment by a Royal Commission earlier in the decade. The Act laid down that no child was to be employed in any handicraft under the age of eight, while between eight and thirteen he or she must attend an approved elementary school for at least ten hours per week, on the half-time system, and must obtain a certificate from the teacher stating that this had been done. Unfortunately, even when supplemented by the general education legislation of the 1870s, the restrictions proved difficult to implement. Initially the police and local sanitary authorities were given the task of enforcement, but this proved unsatisfactory, and so in 1871 the factory inspectors assumed responsibility. Nevertheless, as one writer has said of the plait schools, the 'children would slip out through the back door when anyone in authority called ..., while the number plaiting at home was too great to be dealt with by the factory inspectorate or the police'.[17] But the situation here was complicated by the fact that initially not even the Home Office itself could decide whether plait schools were covered by the 1867 legislation. For the children in them were 'employed' by their parents rather than by the teachers, with the former providing the raw materials used and disposing of the finished product. In 1871, therefore, one of the factory inspectors was ordered by the Home Office to institute proceedings in a test case against a plait school proprietor to obtain a court decision as to 'whether or no, these . . . schools were . . . within the Workshop's Act'.[18] In the event the courts decided that they were—but despite that, infringements of the regulations continued. Only with the decline of the cottage industries in the final years of the nineteenth century were such problems finally resolved. As late as 7 October 1892, however, the head of Yetminster school, Dorset, was noting sadly: 'Attendance small on Wednesday & Friday owing to the girls being employed in carrying their mother's work to the gloving master.' Earlier she had recorded: 'many of the elder girls were absent, being kept at home to assist their mothers with the gloving'.[19]

In the 1870s and 1880s, nevertheless, complaints by teachers about the poor attendances of the 'half-timers' and their unsatisfactory academic work had been a great deal more common. On 17 June 1874 the head of Buckingham Girls' School, in a lacemaking area, recorded despondently: 'I never felt so disheartened since I have been in the school as to-day. What with so many who pretend to come as half-timers and the ignorance of Standard I the past year has been one of very hard work.' And at the plaiting village of Ivinghoe in the same county—where the master had noted in January 1875 that the greater number of the attendances were by 'half-timers'—there were repeated comments on their unsatisfactory academic record. One problem was that they refused to work more than the minimum of ten hours per week needed to fulfil their legal obligation. This meant that they arrived in the mornings at 9.45 instead of at 9, as the other children did. But the head's efforts to persuade them to change their ways were for long unsuccessful. As he wrote on 17 November 1876: 'in one or two cases [I] have received insolent messages from the parents . . . the half-timers coming in at 9.45 greatly disturbs the working of the school'.[20] About four months later he was again bewailing his

> great difficulty in getting the half-timers to attend regularly. . . In fact many
> of the parents would not send their children to school if they could help [it],
> hence they keep them as much as they can. This is the great drawback to
> the progress of the children.

Even visits by the factory inspectors did little good. Only with the decline of the plait trade itself at the end of the decade did the problem at last disappear.

IV

For adult workers, the need to remain constantly employed in order to maximize output—and thereby income—meant that home life was sadly disrupted and domestic duties often neglected. Sarah Moore, a Nottinghamshire framework knitter, was a typical example. Each morning she began work at 5.30 and continued until 9 p.m., taking only two hours off for meals and one hour for household chores. On Fridays she might work on until 11 p.m. or later in order to complete her stint of fully-fashioned cotton stockings. Then, on Saturday afternoon she would walk to Nottingham, which was about six miles distant, to dispose of her wares. For these she obtained an average of 7s. per week, but had to pay 1s. 1d. for the rent of her frame, $2\frac{1}{2}d$. for needles, 1s. for seaming and, in the winter months, 7d. a week for lamp oil, so that despite her formidable exertions she only cleared about 4s. 1d. a week.[21] Inevitably, given such long working hours—which were characteristic of all the domestic trades—critics pointed to the 'dirty home, the slatternly habits, and the neglected children' which resulted, and which drove 'the husband to the public house'. In the hosiery districts, indeed, the living rooms were crowded with 'frames, furniture, and inmates, and noisy with the rattle of the frames'. In these cramped surroundings meals had to be cooked and eaten, 'infants nursed or put to sleep, and the other home work done, of which . . . cleaning seems to form but a rare part'.[22] However, some critics attributed male beer drinking habits not so much to an unsatisfactory home environment as to the fact that where the wives and families earned enough to support themselves, the men took 'no care about them', and felt free to spend all their own spare cash on alcohol.[23]

In disposing of their finished products, the women—and their children—were very much at the mercy of the middlemen with whom they dealt. Although in the case of straw plait outlets might be found at one of the regular plait markets, such as those at Luton, St Albans and Tring, in most instances the goods would be sold to local shopkeepers or merchants. Here a system of barter or 'truck' was the order of the day, even though as early as 1779 a bill had been passed specifically forbidding truck abuses in the lace industry. In return for purchasing the lace, plait, gloves or other items, the dealer would often compel or persuade the workers to take articles which they did not want or which were of a more expensive quality than they desired. On the rare occasions when cash payments were made, it was common for lace merchants to deduct discount at the rate of about 1d. in the 1s. The lacemakers would also have to buy their raw materials from the dealers—on the dealers' own terms, which provided another fertile source of exploitation.

The Oxfordshire glove trade, centred about Woodstock, was likewise subject to these practices. As one gloveress complained bitterly in the late 1860s: 'If I want 1s. 6d. they make me spend 1s. 3d. in the shop, or they would "sack" me. . . . They sell sugar at $5\frac{1}{2}d$. a pound when we could get it at $4\frac{1}{2}d$. if we had ready money. Candles they charge $6\frac{1}{2}d$. instead of 6d.'[24] Yet despite their resentment, there was little the women could do to rectify the position, poorly educated as they were, and living in isolated communities with few opportunities for making contact with the outside world.

V

The cottage-based clothmaking industries were the first to fall victim to the new era of mechanization and mass production which characterized the industrial revolution. But from the middle of the nineteenth century most of the other domestic trades suffered a similar fate. Dorset 'buttony', for example, was hit by the production of machine-made buttons. At one time the making of wire buttons had employed hundreds of women and children in east Dorset, with those youngsters who attended the ordinary elementary school kept 'pretty constantly busied in buttonmaking between their lessons'. Farmers complained that it was almost impossible to obtain children to scare birds away, so involved were they with 'buttony'. Then in 1851 came Ashton's buttonmaking machine, and within a few years the industry was virtually dead. So great was the poverty and distress that resulted that a number of the workers were helped to emigrate, about 350 people leaving Shaftesbury alone.[25]

Lacemaking, by contrast, was hit not only by the greater production of machine-made lace but also by changes in fashion, so that the number of workers employed upon it began to fall sharply from the later 1850s. In one of the major centres—Buckinghamshire—the total of female lacemakers had dropped from 10,487 in 1851 to less than 4,500 thirty years later, and to a mere 789 by 1901. In nearby Bedfordshire the total of 5,734 shown as employed in 1851 had also fallen, albeit less dramatically, to 1,144 by 1901.[26] Despite the efforts of such philanthropic organizations as the Midlands Lace Association, founded in 1891, and the North Bucks Lace Association, established six years later, the industry's collapse proved to be irreversible. Nevertheless, these organizations did seek to improve the quality of the fabric produced and to provide workers with a guaranteed market for their finished product. Or, as the North Bucks Association put it, they sought

> to discourage and stamp out as far as possible vulgar and degenerate forms of lace, to ensure the use of proper materials, and last, not least, to facilitate the sale of the lace direct from the worker to the purchaser, thus securing to the worker an adequate return for skilled labour, and saving the large profits made in all trades by the middleman.[27]

By the early twentieth century the association had established classes for children and young girls in various centres and was employing 'some three hundred lace makers'. But such achievements were a far cry from the scale of operation of the industry in the middle of the nineteenth century.

In the case of straw plait the decline was longer delayed, and in the main centre of Bedfordshire the number of workers actually doubled between 1851 and 1871, as some former lacemakers switched over to what was still a prosperous trade. Among girls aged ten to fifteen about one in three worked as a plaiter at the later date. Then, with the growing importation of cheap Chinese and Japanese plaits in the final quarter of the nineteenth century, the industry collapsed rapidly, its decline being reinforced by fashion changes in favour of small hats and those made from other fabrics. By 1901 Bedfordshire had only 485 female plaiters—compared with 20,701 in 1871—and their wages had been reduced to the starvation level of 1s. or 2s. a week, 'whereas formerly as much as 10s. a week could be earned easily by a fairly good hand'.[28]

348

Glovemaking suffered from the effects of mechanization and foreign imports, too, though here the process of change was more gradual. Even in 1896 Messrs Dent of Worcester were said to be employing several thousand outworkers.[29] Nevertheless, as J. L. Green noted of the Rous Lench area of Worcestershire in the mid-1890s, whereas in earlier years 'many a cottage . . . had its little toothed machine (called a "donkey" machine) at which the women worked away with incredible diligence', by the end of the century, thanks to factory competition, numbers had slumped until 'now but one [gloveress] works . . . in Rous Lench'.

Similarly in the Askrigg area of Yorkshire, where hand knitting of coarse woollen stockings, vests, drawers and other items for the use of sailors engaged in the Greenland fishery industry had once been a thriving home industry, as a result of 'the introduction of machinery . . . [it was] . . . all but extinct'.[30]

In some districts, though, as one industry declined another took its place. In late-Victorian Buckinghamshire and Bedfordshire some women found fresh employment in tambour work, sewing glass beads on to silk to provide ornaments for ladies' dresses, mantles and other fashion goods. And in the villages around the chairmaking centre of High Wycombe, chair caning provided an alternative. L. J. Mayes suggests that in High Wycombe itself as the plait trade died out and machinery killed pillow lace, 'more and more women turned to chair seating, caning at first, rushing later'.[31] Caning was a comparatively simple process and the equipment needed to carry it out was also inexpensive—just a few small steel pegs in wooden handles for clearing holes in the chair seats or frames, an old knife for cutting the cane and a little wooden mallet to drive home the tiny wooden wedges which held the cane in place. A woman from Beaconsfield Old Town remembers walking each day to a local chair factory to collect the chair seats or frames and the canes and wood for pegging that her mother needed for the work. Then, whilst the children were at school, the mother would complete her task ready for the finished products to be returned to the factory and fresh materials collected. But the rate of pay for the work was poor, at about 2*d.* a chair.[32]

A number of women turned to the more highly remunerated rush-seated chairs, though the 'matting' process which that involved was harder. Until about 1880 this work had been the prerogative of the men, but then, as in many other domestic trades, with a fall in the rate of pay it no longer became worthwhile for males to carry it out, and the women took over. It was an uncomfortable occupation since before the rushes could be used they had to be soaked in water to make them malleable. Then whilst carrying out their work the women had to sit on the floor, or on very low stools, 'among the draughts . . . and the dust and the damp'. The main skill lay in deciding how many rushes should be twisted together, how tightly they should be rolled, and how and when to tie in extra rushes so as to give the finished chair a pleasing appearance.

The comfort and lasting quality of a rush seat depended to a large extent on the tightness with which the inside was stuffed, and this stuffing with odd or broken reeds was another hard job. As well as being dirty the rushes had an unpleasant smell, and 'you could smell a matter a mile off' was the way one woman put it.[33]

In the Cottenham district of Cambridgeshire, women worked in the market gardens during the summer months and in the profitable swansdown industry during the winter. According to J. L. Green, for the latter they purchased one pound of swansdown for 3s., and the calico on which to work it for 9d. a yard. From this outlay, when the down was completed, they would get 7s. 6d., 'the waste being preserved and taken back, for which 2½d. an ounce is obtained'.[34]

Sometimes old-established trades were still flourishing even at the end of the Victorian era. This applied to the Dorset net braiding industry around Bridport, where in the early years of the present century women were employed in considerable numbers. The twine which they used was given out from one of the local mills, and was brought by carrier's cart to the villages in which they lived. There was a good deal of geographical specialization—so that some communities would specialize in small-meshed nets, others in large-meshed ones, or perhaps in nets for a particular trade. The records of the firm of Thos Tucker & Company for the 1870s and early 1880s show that women at the hamlet of Eype were regularly engaged in producing trawl nets.[35] Children learned to braid by helping their mothers, though there were complaints that school regulations prevented them 'from learning to work as well or as fast as the previous generation'. But perhaps that was just part of the common philosophy that things are always better in the past![36] During the 1890s, too, in villages around Colchester about 3,000 women and girls were engaged in domestic sewing for tailoring firms in Colchester, Ipswich and London. In the view of one of the factory inspectors this involved 'considerable "sweating"', with which he was 'powerless to deal'.[37]

VI

Yet, despite such ventures, by 1900 cottage industries had ceased to be significant contributors to the income of labouring families in the way they had once been. And in view of the history of exploitation which attached to most of them, their disappearance was not a matter for real regret—even if it did reduce total household income. Indeed, thanks to a fall in food prices in the final quarter of the nineteenth century and the slightly higher cash earnings of agricultural labourers in the 1890s compared with the position thirty years earlier, a fall in real income was not necessarily the experience.

Of course, domestic employment always had its brighter side. The lacemakers enjoyed their traditional feast days on 25 November (St Catherine's Day) and 30 November (St Andrew's Day), when special cakes were made and gifts were exchanged. And in most of the trades the women spent at least part of their day working in groups, where they could enjoy some of the pleasures of companionship and local gossip as they completed their daily tasks. None the less, when all this has been taken into consideration, the evidence of Elizabeth Emerson of Newport Pagnell, Buckinghamshire, one of many witnesses to the 1863 Children's Employment Commission, sounds an authentically sombre note on what had been, in most respects, an unhappy phase of Victorian country life:

> My little girl Charlotte, aged 6, has been at Mrs Harris's lace school three months and has made lace at home for two years. When she first began I set her two hours a day, and after a month two hours twice a day. She goes to the lace school now at 8 or 9 o'clock in the morning and gives over at 4 or 5 in the afternoon. She makes 4d. a week and pays 2d. out of it for schooling. . . . Besides the schooling there is the silk to pay for, which takes 4d. in the 1s., and cotton 1d. in the 1s. The buyers make you take these when you sell your lace and take them out of your lace [money].
>
> That is where they get their profit, and therefore they will not let you buy it elsewhere.[38]

Both Charlotte and an elder sister, who was also a lacemaker, suffered 'very much from the headache'.

Clearly, against this background the demise of cottage industries could only be seen as in the long-term interests of both the women workers and their children. As such it was welcomed by most contemporary social observers.[39]

Notes

1 BPP 1868–9 XIII 559.
2 BPP 1843 XII 229.
3 *Ibid.*, 295–6.
4 Edwards, 1922, 18.
5 Horn, 1974b, 795.
6 BPP 1843 XIV D.6.
7 *Ibid.*, A.10.
8 BPP 1867–8 XVII 522.
9 Bodleian Library, Oxford: for Ivinghoe, MS. Oxf. Dioc. Pp. d. 701; for Fenny Stratford, MS. Oxf. Dioc. Pp. d.179.
10 Horn, 1974b, 112.
11 Horn, 1974b, 790.
12 BPP 1871 XIV 55.
13 *Victoria County History: Essex II*, 1907, 376.
14 Horn, 1974b, 99.
15 BPP 1843 XIV A.13.
16 BPP 1876 XXIX Appendix D (19a), 150.
17 Dony, 1942, 84.

18   PRO HO 87/5, letters 19 January, 4 February and 6 February 1871, 247, 260–1, 262:
     Dony, 1942, 82–3.
19   Dorset RO: S. 89/2/1.
20   Bucks. RO: for Ivinghoe, E/LB/116/1; for Buckingham, E/LB/29/5.
21   BPP 1843 XIV, Evidence, f.93.
22   BPP 1863 XVIII 265; Horn, 1976b, 103.
23   Pinchbeck, 1930, 238.
24   BPP 1868–9 XIII Evidence, 344.
25   Acland, 1914, 73; BPP 1843 XII 16 and 86–7.
26   Horn, 1974b, 796.
27   Bucks. RO: *The North Bucks Lace Association*, 1907, 5.
28   Green, n.d., 57.
29   PRO: HO 45/9859/B. 12601.
30   Green, n.d., 129.
31   Mayes, 1960, 18; Horn, 1976b, 106–8.
32   Buckinghamshire Federation of Women's Institutes, 1975, 94, 99.
33   Mayes, 1960, 20.
34   Green, n.d., 63–4.
35   Dorset RO: D203/A64.
36   *Victoria County History: Dorset II*, 1908, 351–3.
37   PRO: HO 45/9859/B. 12601.
38   BPP 1863 XVIII, Evidence, 259.
39   Woods, 1921, 139, 162.

26 Industrialized Villages

David Hey

I

Industrialized villages were already an old feature of the countryside when Queen Victoria came to the throne. In some parts of England and Wales rural crafts had formed a distinctive and important part of the economy since medieval times, providing work for an increasing number of landless people and extra income for families chiefly or partly occupied in other tasks. By the seventeenth century industry was at least as important as agriculture in certain regions, and by the beginning of the Hanoverian era a number of rural communities, such as the metalworking villages and hamlets of south Staffordshire, already had a pronounced industrial character.[1] During the reign of Victoria many of these old craft centres declined in the face of mechanization, and some hand trades disappeared completely, but at the same time the coming of the railways, the sinking of deep coal mines and the development of large quarries meant that the total number of industrialized villages nevertheless rose significantly. The new Victorian villages dominated by a single workplace, where not only the means of livelihood but also the houses and public buildings were owned by a company of absentee capitalists, had few antecedents in an earlier age, and in several important ways were different from contemporary industrial settlements of the traditional kind. They made a distinctive contribution to the industrial revolution and played a vital role in the growth of the national economy.

Industrialized villages were not confined to those parts of England and Wales that lay near to the great urban industrial centres, though naturally they were most prominent and numerous there. Even in the south, villages occasionally had a semi-industrial character. Country folk in the Oxfordshire redlands around Banbury specialized in making the fine plush for liveries, upholstery and furnishings, Kentish villages along the Thames and the Medway had paper mills, brickyards and cementworks, and elsewhere quarries, brickworks and small potteries were scattered around the countryside.[2] Moreover, in many parts of the south Midlands women and girls earned extra money for the family by plaiting straw or making lace or gloves. In the predominantly agricultural regions such industries gained a foothold in those open villages and hamlets where the property was divided amongst many small freeholders. Populous and rambling, free of supervision by a squire, and attractive to poor immigrants, these open communities were often untidy, ill-disciplined and radical in politics and religion. The greatly increased national population, and the lack of agricultural employment on land converted to pasture upon parliamentary enclosure, meant that many villagers had to turn to industry for at least a major part, if not all, of their income. This process was especially marked in those midland villages that adopted framework knitting, but it can be observed on a smaller scale in many other places. For example, Middle Barton originated as a hamlet or no-man's-land settlement on the parish boundaries of older Oxfordshire villages. It was typically open in character, and its inhabitants supported themselves by farming, milling, and by work in the claypits, brick and tile works, and lime kilns. In 1869 the Poor Law Commissioners criticized the place as badly congested, with 150 or so cottages owned by some forty different owners; a one-up, one-down cottage could be occupied by as many as nine people. And lying, as it did, well away from the parish church at Steeple Barton, it became a stronghold of dissent with chapels erected by the Wesleyans and the Primitive Methodists.[3]

Victorian Northamptonshire is generally thought of as a rural backwater characterized by estate villages; two out of every three of its villages were owned by a squire or a small group of large proprietors. Nevertheless, many of the more open settlements had long since acquired an industrial tinge with a variety of local crafts and small industries. The manufacture of boots and shoes, in particular, had spread from Northampton into the smaller towns and the countryside during the eighteenth century, and by the beginning of Victoria's reign many villages near Northampton, Wellingborough and Raunds contained a great many shoemakers. Their number almost doubled during the next twenty years, and in the late-Victorian period expansion was even more rapid. Earls Barton typifies the way that an open agricultural village developed into a considerable footwear centre. The industry seems to have been introduced here during the third quarter of the eighteenth century, and by 1841, when 1,079 people resided in the village, 107 men and boys and three females worked at the trade. Twenty years later the population had risen to 1,557, but the proportion of the workforce employed in footwear had increased even more dramatically, for now not only were 301 men and boys working at the trade, but 241 women and girls also.[4] For most people the manufacture of footwear remained a cottage industry, and factories never dominated the Northamptonshire villages. The population was not entirely dependent on the boot and shoe trade, nor was it entirely working-class in character. Such places were very different from the pit villages and quarry settlements, but different also from villages where families earned their living only from farming or from trades intimately associated with agriculture. They do not fit easily into any neat category and have been largely neglected by historians, but a very large number of Victorian people lived in semi-industrial communities and such settlements were profoundly characteristic of the age.

A little further north, the craft of framework knitting took such a hold on both the rural and urban parts of Nottinghamshire, Leicestershire and south Derbyshire that the fortunes of many villages were controlled not, as in the past, by the weather and the state of the harvest, but by the fluctuating commercial prospects of the hosiery trade. The baptism register of the Leicestershire village of Countesthorpe is typical of many others in showing that 70 per cent of the fathers of baptized children during the five years beginning 1 January 1813 were framework knitters.[5] The conversion of arable land to pasture after enclosure and the enormous increase in the population had transformed a craft which had once been happily combined with farming into a miserable cottage industry, wholly dependent upon the towns and upon middlemen known as bag-hosiers. Its geographical spread had been largely determined as early as the second decade of the eighteenth century,[6] but the numbers employed in the trade soared when knitting became the only alternative to unemployment. Whereas many villages had previously had only one or two knitters, by the nineteenth century these humble craftsmen formed the majority of the local population. At Thurmaston, just north of Leicester, sixty of the ninety-one fathers who baptized a child between 1813 and 1817 (inclusive) were framework knitters. Thurmaston people specialized in children's socks, work which women and the older children could share in. The village had 400 frames in 1844, and nine years later the 1851 census returns reveal that of the 237 heads of households, 143 (60 per cent) were framework knitters, 38 were farm labourers and 56 had other occupations. The number of women and juniors who were also engaged in knitting emphasizes how necessary was this trade to the well-being of the local community. Workshops with up to a dozen frames had appeared in Leicestershire by the 1830s, but knitting was essentially a cottage industry until late in the reign of Victoria.[7]

While many midland villages had an occupation structure similar to that of Thurmaston and Countesthorpe, others bore more resemblance to Earls Barton in their variety of employment opportunities. Of the 120 fathers who baptized a child in Thurmaston's neighbouring parish of Syston between 1863 and 1867 (inclusive), only thirty were framework knitters, two were framesmiths and twenty-one were farm labourers; a further nine worked on the railways; one was a coal merchant, one a gas house keeper and another a gas fitter; the other craftsmen comprised four bricklayers and a brickmaker, three blacksmiths, two tailors, two shoemakers, two potters, two carpenters, a wheelwright, a cooper, a plumber and glazier, and a painter; the rest included two gentlemen, a clerk in holy orders, a surgeon, three farmers, two general

355

dealers, two grocers, a draper, two cattle dealers, seven butchers, one tripe dresser, a pig jobber, a fellmonger, two gardeners, two grooms, a coachman and two commercial travellers.[8] Clearly, Syston was a semi-industrialized village with a healthy variety of occupation; only one man in four worked at a frame, and the continued importance of farming is even more evident when the smallholdings of some of the craftsmen and tradesmen are taken into account. Another village which supported a Victorian middle class and a variety of trades and crafts in addition to its framework knitters was Wigston Magna, which over the centuries had always been the largest village in Leicestershire and a classic example of an open community free of the influence of a resident lord. As Professor Hoskins has written, 'It was an industrialised village that not only gave some sort of alternative employment to its own dispossessed peasantry but attracted those of the purely farming villages for miles around.' Wigston was still a country village in the middle of Victoria's reign, with its 'principal inhabitants' at the Hall, the Cedars, the Elms and the Grange, and with its National and British schools, its Independent, Wesleyan, Primitive Methodist and General Baptist chapels, its Mechanics' Institute, Working Men's Club, Industrial Co-operative Society and several benefit clubs; but from 1870 onwards it was transformed into an industrialized, wage-earning township. And whereas South Wigston consisted merely of a few scattered houses until the Midland Railway Company built railway sheds there in 1883, within the next seven years it acquired 600 identical brick cottages and a population of 2,400, who found jobs not only with the railway but in three footwear factories, an iron foundry, a large timber yard, a biscuit factory and a brick and tile works. The Victorian transformation was completed in 1894 when Wigston was made an Urban District.[9]

II

Amongst the other textile regions the West Riding stands out as having been very different from the hosiery centres of the midland plain. In this hilly region scattered hamlets and isolated farmsteads were as common as villages, and here the traditional economy of the weaver-farmer, whose workplace was his home, flourished well into the Victorian period. In this region town and country people alike took part in the expansion of the woollen and worsted industries during the eighteenth and nineteenth centuries; all the villages and hamlets were industrialized to a large extent, some overwhelmingly so. In the river valleys scribbling and spinning mills attracted new housing and the old settlements around the fulling and corn mills were transformed, but the weavers stayed in the hills and their craft long remained at the domestic stage. The first edition six-inch Ordnance Survey maps of the early 1850s mark hundreds of tenters in the crofts behind rural houses all over the region. Villages and hamlets were full of small manufacturers (with a warehouse but not a mill until the middle of the nineteenth century) and a rapidly growing wage-earning class, whose hand looms were normally kept in the stone-built cottages rented from the manufacturers. When weaving finally came to be done by power the mills were built in the upland villages and hamlets, near the homes of the manufacturers and their workmen. Most of these places retain their character to the present day, the houses clustered in folds or facing the street, their upper windows divided by mullions and extending all along the front so as to catch the light; when the demand for weavers arose to match the output of yarn from the spinning mills, an extra storey was simply added to a cottage to hold more looms.

Some hamlets, such as that of Wilshaw, four miles south of Huddersfield, were dominated by a single manufacturer. Wilshaw was the home of Joseph Hirst, who rose from being a humble cowman, carter and higgler to become a manufacturer. In 1849 he built a large warehouse, a weaving room with eighteen broad looms, a counting house, a row of workers' houses and Ash Cottage for his manager. He won medals at the 1851 Great Exhibition for his first-class fancy woollens, and later built a dye-house and developed the warehouse into a mill. Only after his death in 1874 were power looms and engines installed, but then the business declined rapidly. Other villages had several warehouses and mills, and so were not controlled by a single manufacturer whose power was little different from that of a squire in a purely agricultural village. Kirkburton, for instance, had at least seven of the warehouse type of woollen mill, famed in their day for their woven stays. Some of these tried to move with the times and brought in power looms, but none managed to expand. Three miles away Skelmanthorpe was another upland village with a number of clothiers' warehouses, whereas the scribbling and spinning mills were down in the river valley at Scissett and Denby Dale. Many other villages were coupled in this way, the one preparing the yarn, the other weaving it.[10]

The manufacture of iron was anciently a rural industry, and though many of the new ironworks were established in an urban setting or had attracted a settlement too large still to be called a village by the Victorian period, smaller works flourished in the countryside and some of the old hand crafts survived into the twentieth century. The great nineteenth-century expansion in the metal trades took place in the rural as well as the urban parts of the major industrial regions. Village specialization in particular products, such as scythes, forks or scissors, was an ancient feature still in evidence during the reign of Victoria; the countryside continued to fulfil a vital role in the regional economy. Furthermore, its river valleys provided sites and water power for rolling mills and forges. The farming side of the traditional dual occupation of the metalworker was vestigial or non-existent by the middle of the nineteenth century (and in some cases long before), and some of the old hand crafts such as nailing had already succumbed to new machines and had become as poverty-stricken as framework knitting. But in most cases decline was protracted and villages and hamlets were sometimes able to turn to other crafts or to coalmining. Ecclesfield, some five miles north of Sheffield, had been the ancient centre of the south Yorkshire nailmaking industry, but by 1851 only fourteen of its families still made nails, whereas seventy households chipped files, nineteen made forks, nine different branches of the Ridge family made brace-bits and gimlets, eight households made screws and bolts and two made cutlery. File-cutting was a trade to which nailers could turn easily, and though the villagers now became increasingly dependent upon Sheffield factors it was late in the reign of Victoria before most of them had to seek work in the city. In the meantime, many nailing smithies were converted into file shops and women turned their kitchens into workshops for a few hours a day. In an earlier age women had not been allowed to work in the south Yorkshire smithies.

Like other communities of this type, Ecclesfield had a reputation as a rough-and-ready sort of place, much given to drunkenness and cruel sports. The Rev Alfred Gatty ruefully told a story against himself of his arrival in the parish in 1839. Remonstrating with a metalworker who had not touched his cap upon greeting his vicar, he received the reply, 'Go to hell!' Gatty was the incumbent at Ecclesfield almost as long as Victoria was on the throne, and he came to feel in later life that the church and the three chapels had exerted a sobering influence on the place. Ecclesfield was a clannish community, and Gatty spoke of his shame when twenty villagers had sworn to an obviously false alibi for a neighbour caught poaching and a J.P. asked in exasperation who was the vicar of such a dishonest parish. But the villagers also had milder pastimes; the band, for instance, was a flourishing institution, and Gatty was struck by the musical abilities and traditions. They also had their code of moral conduct, and on the night of 19 June 1850 as many as 300 people took part in a 'riding the stang' ceremony to express their disapproval of a couple's adultery and the ill-treatment of the woman's husband.[11]

III

The ancient and almost entirely rural lead industry had passed its peak by Victorian times, but small partnerships as well as large companies continued in the manner of previous generations. In 1856 twenty-six small mines in Cromford were worked by an average of five men each, and as late as 1872 nearly two hundred separate concerns were still mining the Derbyshire lead field. The Poor Law Commissioners reported in 1834 that nearly all the miners in the long and straggling village of Middleton by Wirksworth owned their cottages and had a few acres of grazing land attached. Many leadminers were landless, but several Victorian commentators noted the survival of the farming side of the traditional dual occupation in the Yorkshire dales, and family incomes were supplemented by the women's earnings in the various textile trades. Leadminers normally lived in old-established villages close to where the earliest veins had been discovered. Greenhow Hill was somewhat exceptional in having started life as a seventeenth-century hamlet on the 1,300-feet-high ridge between Nidderdale and Wharfedale; by 1851 it had grown into a village of eighty houses, nearly all occupied by leadminers. In Derbyshire, villages like Winster, which lay near the deep mines of the large companies, contained some fine middle-class houses and preserved a reasonably ordered appearance in contrast to the usual straggling arrangement of small groups of terraced cottages in other villages. Bradwell was much more typical in that its growth was haphazard, with cottages of all shapes and sizes occupying any available piece of land in the valley bottom and alongside the tracks leading up into the mining grounds. Bonsall, too, was open in character, and like many another industrialized village up and down the country had once been a small market centre. Many of its houses were small farms with a few acres for grazing cattle, while some of the cottages were involved in domestic work for the mills further down the valley at Cromford. The coexistence of industry and agriculture, whether in combination or not, was still normal in the Peak District during the reign of Victoria. In the Hope Valley, for instance, settlement consisted of nucleated villages of farmers, miners and craftsmen, industrial hamlets of textile workers near the mills by the rivers, and isolated farmsteads dotted about the hillsides.[12]

The colliers of the Forest of Dean enjoyed ancient privileges similar to those of the Derbyshire leadminers and they too combined their trade with the keeping of a few pigs and sheep. Geographical isolation and the hereditary nature of their occupation made them inward-looking and distinctive as a group long before colliers in most other parts of the country. Elsewhere, collier-farmers had been integrated into the rural communities, of which they formed only a small part until the canals and the railways opened up new markets and transformed the industry. Many of the colliery settlements of the generation before the accession of Victoria were associated with major ironworks which consumed great quantities of fuel. The best way to attract the necessary labour force to places which were frequently distant from established centres of population was to provide housing of a quality far superior to that in the agricultural villages. On the other hand, the standard of accommodation at places such as Elsecar and Moira could also reflect an owner's philanthropy.[13] At Ketley in the Shropshire coalfield the Gowers gradually took over the 'wretched huts [which] have been erected from time to time on the waste' and replaced them with better cottages, thus gradually turning an open settlement into a closed village which they ruled with paternalistic concern. In neighbouring parts development was much more haphazard. As Barrie Trinder has written, 'The Shropshire coalfield had no recognisable commercial centre, but was rather a grouping of scattered settlements, many of them with no ancient origins.' The main focus of social life was the village or hamlet, communities that were far from uniform. Coalbrookdale's ironworkers, colliers and other industrial craftsmen had a tradition of skilled work and of intellectual self-help, and the Darby family of ironmasters had provided an unusual range of communal facilities. Coalport, a new settlement of the 1790s, lacked strong community institutions but shared an interest in religious dissent, politics, Chartism and teetotalism. More typical, however, were the villages that were simply blocks of overcrowded company houses, raw 'frontier' settlements hostile to strangers, limited in their range of occupations, and very different in character from Coalport and Coalbrookdale. Moreover, their superficial similarity masked important internal differences; Hinkshay, for example, had a pub but no chapel, whereas its neighbour, Dark Lane, which at first sight was one of the crudest of the new settlements, had no pub, and its Primitive Methodists were exceptionally strong.[14]

In Cannock Chase the names of such mining settlements as Cheslyn Hay, Great Wyrley, Heath Hayes and Norton Canes betray their origins as rural villages and hamlets that were swallowed up in the mining expansion, whereas Chasetown was a completely new Victorian settlement.[15] In the western parts of south Yorkshire, where mining was an ancient activity, many old settlements grew out of all recognition into Victorian pit villages. Silkstone, the focal point of a large medieval parish, had given its name to a famous seam of coal, but in 1806 only eleven of its seventy-one men aged between 18 and 45 were colliers; by 1841, however, coalmining was the principal occupation of the village and the place was notorious for the number of girls employed in the pits. The principal coalmaster had become the village squire, with a secluded hall and park at one end of the village, and during the 1850s his widow was to rebuild the chancel of the church and fill it with family monuments. The coalmaster also owned many of the houses and did not hesitate to evict the families of those who went on strike in 1844. Elsewhere in the parish, the hamlet of Dodworth was transformed into a pit village and a new mining community settled on Silkstone Common.[16] More dramatic developments came later in the century in the central and eastern parts of the county where there were no indigenous miners. Few immigrants had come to south Yorkshire before the 1860s or 1870s, but then thousands of men from Staffordshire, Lancashire, Cheshire, other parts of Yorkshire and many other places came to work in the new, deep pits and to live in rows of small terraced houses erected near their place of work.[17] The squires of the old villages nearby benefited from royalties, but made sure that the miners were housed in separate communities out of sight of their halls. Thus Hickleton remains to this day an attractive and neat estate village, with neither pub nor chapel, its houses all of the same period, solidly built of magnesian limestone and roofed with pantiles, and tastefully assembled by the gates of the hall and park; but the colliers who worked at Hickleton Main lived beyond the village boundaries at Goldthorpe or Thurnscoe, two former hamlets turned into pit villages as large as towns but lacking their amenities.

The company pit village was a new kind of settlement imposed on the countryside, and nowhere more dramatically than on the fields, woods and moors of the Rhondda valley. Such places consisted of monotonous rows of compact terraced houses, their number governed purely by the size of the workforce required at the pit. Unimaginative in design and cheaply built, they provide a poor contrast to the model villages built for colliers in the early twentieth century, and at worst they look ridiculous; Arkwright Town, built by the Staveley Company in north Derbyshire, is simply a few parallel rows of terraces put down in the countryside miles from anywhere. In south Yorkshire, a group of colliery owners from further north sunk a pit near the old hamlet of Denaby, at what was then the eastern extremity of the coalfield, and founded the new village of Denaby Main. The company provided the parish church, the village schools, the hotel, the original store and nearly all the houses. These two-up, two-down cottages, with no bath and only an outside water closet, were tied to the job, and on four occasions between 1869 and 1903 the families of strikers were evicted from their homes. Denaby Main quickly developed a reputation for militancy in the face of owners who consistently took a hard line over industrial disputes. The newness of this settlement was emphasized by the need to attract immigrant labour; the 1871 census returns, taken three years after the opening of the pit, reveal that only ten of the 166 coalminers were born in Yorkshire. The shared experience of working in the mine, however, soon welded these immigrants into a closely-knit community.[18] But not all company-owned villages had such a history of conflict and strife. In the Deerness valley in County Durham, Pease & Partners offered housing of a high contemporary standard. Until the 1860s sufficient miners walked from the local hamlets to work in drift mines, but with the coming of the railways deep mining became profitable and the company built 151 houses at Waterhouses by 1874; the new village acquired its final physical shape by 1890. The colliers took part in a wide range of leisure activities involving sport, music, lectures and informal social occasions, and the binding social force of Methodism inhibited the growth of class-consciousness and trade unions and prevented major trouble.[19]

The Welsh slate quarries also witnessed bitter and persistent industrial battles, exacerbated by the contrast between the English-speaking, Tory and Church of England owners and the Welsh-speaking, Liberal and passionately Nonconformist workers. Away from the quarry, however, the villagers practised the ideals of industry, thrift and respectability. The Penrhyn slate quarries employed 3,000 men and boys and were the largest in the world, but small concerns were much more typical; at the beginning of Victoria's reign on the Isle of Portland, 56 different quarries were worked by a regular labour force of only 240 men.[20] Headington Quarry near Oxford may well represent a common type of industrialized village. Originally a squatters' settlement, it retained its common rights on a wide tract of moorland and still afforded opportunities for men to erect a cottage or extend a garden on ownerless pieces of land. In summer time the stone-getters and brickmakers earned high wages, but in winter there was little to do by way of regular work. As Raphael Samuel has written, 'No two families made their livelihood in precisely the same way.... Earnings were built up higgeldy-piggeldy rather than by reliance upon a single weekly wage.' Women took in washing from the Oxford colleges and hotels, pigs and poultry were kept in the gardens, vegetables grown in allotments and rabbits poached from neighbouring land. The village had a very bad name locally as a rough, undisciplined place, lacking resident gentry and without a church until 1849; the *Oxford Times* of 1894 described it as 'a hotbed of the most rampant, reasonless Radicalism'. In Samuel's words, 'For centuries it had enjoyed what was virtually an extra-parochial existence, a kind of anarchy, in which the villagers were responsible to nobody but themselves.'[21]

IV

Nineteenth-century industrial activity produced communities that were markedly different from their older neighbours. Contrasting types could be found not only within the same region but within the same parish or township. A single example, that of the south Yorkshire township of Worsbrough, containing 3,778 acres, illustrates how the settlement pattern could be changed out of all recognition within two or three decades. At the top of the hill stood the 'pleasant country village of Worsbrough' with its hall, church and ancient grammar school, and though the dominion of the Edmunds family did not extend to the freeholders in the outlying parts of the parish, their role as village squires was unchallenged. Then in 1804 the opening of a canal along the picturesque Worsbrough Dale led to the creation of an entirely new settlement. By 1838 White's *Directory* could report that here were 'extensive iron, coal, lime, chemical, and flint glass works, with wharfs, boat-yards, a paper mill, and a large assemblage of houses, presenting a scene of bustle not often excelled in market towns'. Stone quarries, a glue manufactory and a gunpowder works soon completed this strange assortment of industries. The Wesleyans, the Wesleyan Reform movement and the Primitive Methodists each built a chapel, the choice of denominations reflecting the basic differences of outlook between the inhabitants of this lively industrial community and those who resided in the old estate village at the top of the hill. The enclosure of the commons between 1817 and 1826 freed land for further building at the extremities of the parish. Two pit villages were founded at Birdwell and at Blacker and a colony of linen weavers was established on the Barnsley boundary. A survey and valuation of 1840 records 199 houses in this new settlement of Worsbrough Common. Most houses had two, three or four looms, and a few had as many as six. In all, 518 looms in 162 houses provided domestic employment.[22] The character of this settlement was very different not only from that of the old estate village but from those of any of the other new communities within the township. During the reign of Victoria the rural communities of England and Wales were more diverse in type than ever before.

Notes

1 Rowlands, 1975, 131–4.
2 Emery, 1974, 177–8; Mingay, 1976b, 107.
3 Emery, 1974, 176.
4 Hatley and Rajczonek, 1972; Everitt, 1972, 52.
5 Leics. RO: Countesthorpe parish registers.
6 Public RO: I.R. 1/41/1 to 3.
7 Leics. RO: Thurmaston parish registers; *Victoria County History Leicestershire III*, 1955, 2–23.
8 Leics. RO: Syston parish registers.
9 Hoskins 1957, 261–82.
10 Crump and Ghorbal, 1935, 82–9.
11 Hey, 1968, 58–60, 69–74, 123–4; Hey, 1972, 5–7, 59–60; Gatty, 1884.

12   Samuel, 1977, 64–6; Raistrick and Jennings, 1965, 310; Millward and Robinson, 1975, 194–204; Fletcher, 1971, 181.

13   Mee, 1975, 140; Griffin, 1977, 276–82.

14   Trinder, 1973, 319–33.

15   Palliser, 1976, 118.

16   Prince, 1922, 12, 54–5; Sheffield Central Library: Clarke records; Wakefield RO: J. F. Goodchild collection.

17   MacFarlane, 1976, 92–3.

18   *Ibid.*

19   Moore, 1974.

20   D. Jones, 1977, 130; Samuel, 1977, 17.

21   Samuel, 1975a, 139–245.

22   Wakefield RO: J. F. Goodchild collection.